# RELIGION, TRUTH, AND SOCIAL TRANSFORMATION

# Religion, Truth, and Social Transformation

## Essays in Reformational Philosophy

LAMBERT ZUIDERVAART

McGill-Queen's University Press
Montreal & Kingston • London • Chicago

ISBN 978-0-7735-4708-7 (cloth)
ISBN 978-0-7735-4709-4 (paper)
ISBN 978-0-7735-9891-1 (ePDF)
ISBN 978-0-7735-9892-8 (ePUB)

Legal deposit first quarter 2016
Bibliothèque nationale du Québec

Printed in Canada on acid-free paper that is 100% ancient forest free (100% post-consumer recycled), processed chlorine free

The publication of this book is supported by generous grants from the Centre for Philosophy, Religion and Social Ethics at the Institute for Christian Studies and from the Priscilla and Stanford Reid Trust.

McGill-Queen's University Press acknowledges the support of the Canada Council for the Arts for our publishing program. We also acknowledge the financial support of the Government of Canada through the Canada Book Fund for our publishing activities.

---

**Library and Archives Canada Cataloguing in Publication**

Zuidervaart, Lambert, author
Religion, truth, and social transformation : essays in reformational philosophy / Lambert Zuidervaart.

Includes bibliographical references and index.
Issued in print and electronic formats.
ISBN 978-0-7735-4708-7 (cloth). – ISBN 978-0-7735-4709-4 (paper). – ISBN 978-0-7735-9891-1 (PDF). – ISBN 978-0-7735-9892-8 (ePUB)

1. Christianity – Philosophy. 2. Reformation. I. Title.

BR100.Z84 2016 190 C2015-907016-3
C2015-907017-1

---

This book was typeset by Interscript inc. in 10.5/13 Sabon.

*For John VanderStelt and John Van Dyk,*
*my first teachers in reformational philosophy*

# Contents

# Preface

This is the first of two volumes that collect my essays in and about reformational philosophy. The essays in this volume span several decades of academic writing, and they range across social philosophy, ontology, epistemology, and philosophy of religion. The essays in the second volume, while spanning the same years, will address a wider public on topics in the arts, culture, and education.

I was introduced to the reformational tradition as an undergraduate philosophy major at Dordt College in Sioux Center, Iowa and then pursued graduate studies with reformational scholars at the Institute for Christian Studies (ICS) in Toronto and the VU University Amsterdam. Although better known for my work on Theodor W. Adorno and Critical Theory, I am also well versed in reformational philosophy. I have addressed its issues and questions throughout my career, and central insights in reformational philosophy have guided all of my work.

This book brings together many of my essays on such topics for the first time. It has several goals. First, it is intended to make my writings on reformational philosophy more readily available to others in this tradition, inviting them to test the validity and relevance of my ideas and offer their responses. As will become clear when you read the book, many chapters emerge from debates within the tradition, and they call for continuing conversation. Second, the book aims to introduce a wider academic audience to central insights and claims within reformational philosophy. Because it has roots in the Netherlands and has not entered the canon of contemporary Western philosophy, reformational philosophy has not received the attention and scrutiny it deserves. I hope this book helps change that. Third, I also wish to present my own reformationally informed conceptions of rationality, religion, science, truth, and social critique. This book fills in the epistemological and ontological background to my better-known writings. It also provides alternative views on topics that have recently gained a higher profile in academic work, such as the ontological turn in recent philosophy and interdisciplinary debates about globalization and a postsecular society.

Just over half of the essays collected here have been published before. Chapters 3, 5, 6, and 14 originally appeared in *Philosophia Reformata*, the journal of record for reformational scholarship since 1935, and they are republished here with permission from an editorial team headed by Gerrit Glas and from the publisher Brill. Chapter 1, first published by *Faith and Philosophy*, the journal of the Society of Christian Philosophers, and chapter 12, first published by the online *University of Toronto Journal for Jewish Thought*, also appear here with permission. Three other chapters stem from books of collected essays and are used by permission from the editors and publishers: chapter 7, from a book edited by Ron Kuipers and Janet Wesselius and published by University Press of America, an imprint of The Rowman & Littlefield Publishing Group; chapter 11, from a book edited by Jamie Smith and Jim Olthuis and published by Baker Academic, a division of Baker Publishing Group; and chapter 13, from a book edited by Gerrit Glas, Jeroen de Ridder, Govert Buijs, and Annette Mosher and published by Springer. Complete details about the original sources appear in "Publication Information" at the end of this volume. I wish to thank all of the editors and publishers mentioned for letting me gather these essays into a new publication. I also acknowledge with gratitude the generous grants this book has received from ICS's Centre for Philosophy, Religion and Social Ethics, directed by Ronald Kuipers, and from the Priscilla and Stanford Reid Trust.

Teaching at the Institute for Christian Studies has provided an inspiring context for revisiting the reformational tradition and working out my own philosophical conceptions. One of my first tasks as Hendrik Hart's successor in systematic philosophy was to revise the annual seminar in reformational philosophy that is central to ICS's graduate curriculum. I first offered this revised seminar in the fall of 2002, under the new course title "Religion, Life, and Society: Reformational Philosophy." Leading this seminar every year gave me fresh insights into the strengths and weaknesses of the reformational tradition, as each new cohort of graduate students discussed classic texts by Dooyeweerd and Vollenhoven along with writings by their successors and by leading thinkers in analytic and continental philosophy. I am thankful for the enthusiastic support my ICS colleagues showed for this course and for the probing, honest, and generative dialogue ICS's graduate students provided. I have learned much from all of you; you have shaped my own appropriation of reformational philosophy.

I also have benefited from the help of several graduate research assistants at ICS. In 2006 and 2007, Michael DeMoor and Tricia Van Dyk revised the materials of the Reformational Philosophy seminar so it could be offered off campus. Working with them on this project gave me new clarity about issues in the reformational tradition. Tricia then went on to offer the course in distance mode, demonstrating that a new audience exists for work in this tradition. Around the same time Matthew Klaassen, who had assisted me on other book projects, suggested that I publish my essays in reformational philosophy as a collection. Although several years would pass before I could begin this work, I took his good suggestion to heart. Once I was ready to start, I hired master's student Sarah Hyland to help edit the essays for stylistic consistency, bibliographic completeness, and collective coherence. Her eye for detail and her astute comments have been very useful. So have the final editing provided by PhD candidate Benjamin Shank and the indexing accomplished by PhD candidate Joe Kirby. It has been a delight and a constant encouragement to work with such dedicated and gifted research assistants.

Tricia Van Dyk, who is completing a doctoral dissertation under my supervision, is the daughter of my first instructor in philosophy. I began Dordt College in the fall of 1968 as an English major and Greek minor, intending eventually to enter church ministry. One year later I took my first philosophy course, with Professor John Van Dyk, and that set me on an exciting new path. Discovering a love for philosophical inquiry, I also found a true calling: to be a life-affirming scholar and teacher in the reformational tradition. By confirming my gifts and interests, Professor Van Dyk awakened me to this calling. Soon I switched to a double major in philosophy and music, with a minor in history. I have never looked back.

The next semester I took my first course with Professor John VanderStelt – interestingly enough, a theology course, not a philosophy course, on the history and content of Calvinism. Professor VanderStelt, too, took a direct interest in my life and work. Both in his philosophy courses and in many extended conversations, he imparted a passion for reformational thought that has sustained me ever since. He also arranged for me to meet Calvin Seerveld, who would become my graduate mentor, and pointed me toward ICS, still in its infancy, as the right place at the right time for my graduate studies.

Professors Van Dyk and VanderStelt retired many years ago, but their inspiration and influence continue in the students whose lives they touched. I have always hoped to embody their generous spirit and life-changing instruction. With deep respect and enduring gratitude, I dedicate this book to them, my first teachers in reformational philosophy.

# Note about Citations and Revisions

All citations of Herman Dooyeweerd's *A New Critique of Theoretical Thought* come from the four-volume edition translated by David H. Freeman et al. (Philadelphia: Presbyterian and Reformed Publishing, 1953–58). This work is both a revision and a translation of the three-volume Dutch magnum opus *De Wijsbegeerte der Wetsidee* (Amsterdam: H.J. Paris, 1935–36). Where the English version translates an equivalent passage in the Dutch version, I sometimes use square brackets to indicate nuances in Dutch not caught in the English translation. I also silently modify the translation in other ways, usually to render it in more idiomatic English. Citations use the abbreviations NC and (where appropriate) WW, followed by the volume and page number, like this: NC 1: 8, WW 1: 10.

The date under the title of each chapter in this book indicates either the date when it was first published, or, in the case of essays not previously published, when I presented it as a lecture or conference paper. More details appear under "Publication Information" near the end of this book (the publications listed there are not included in the book's bibliography). I have updated the endnotes in various chapters to indicate where the essays cited may be found in this volume, and I have made other minor silent revisions to essays that have been published before: namely, chapters 1, 3, 5, 6, 7, 11, 12, 13, and 14. Where significant new material has been added to a chapter, it appears either in a preface or postscript that carries its own date or in a clearly marked *addendum*.

# RELIGION, TRUTH, AND SOCIAL TRANSFORMATION

# Introduction: Transforming Philosophy

The only philosophy which can be responsibly practised in face of despair is the attempt to contemplate all things as they would present themselves from the standpoint of redemption.

Theodor W. Adorno[1]

Reformational philosophy tries to consider all of created existence from the standpoint of redemption. The effort arises, in the first instance, not out of despair, however, but out of hope: hope that, in the end, societal evil will not win out, that the voices of the oppressed and Earth's lament finally will be heard. To introduce what impels this effort and what it comes to, let me quickly sketch its historical background, explain some generative themes of reformational philosophy, and say how my own work incorporates these themes to address contemporary concerns. I shall conclude with a brief summary of the essays in this book.

## 1. KUYPERIAN ROOTS

Reformational philosophy has roots in the Reformed tradition of Protestant Christianity. "Reformed" refers to a worldwide movement that stems from the Calvinist Reformation in sixteenth-century Europe. Ecclesiastically it includes Presbyterians of various persuasions, Reformed churches in or from continental Europe, and more recent ecumenical formations such as the United Church of Canada and the World Communion of Reformed Churches, the third largest body of Christians in the world, after the Roman Catholic Church and the Eastern Orthodox Church. The term "reformational" indicates an intellectual and social current within Reformed Christianity whose main impetus comes from the nineteenth-century Dutch theologian, educator, and politician Abraham Kuyper (1837–1920).[2] Kuyper's vision of life and society received a full-fledged philosophical articulation in the early part of the twentieth century, and that philosophy in turn has inspired later generations of scholars and public intellectuals around the world.

As I indicate elsewhere, three Kuyperian emphases sustain the reformational tradition.[3] One is a theological narrative that always returns to everything having been created good, and that ever looks forward to a culminating renewal of all creation. A second, stemming from this narrative, is the conviction that members of religious communities and their organizations are called to be agents of renewal in culture and society, including scholarship and education. Third, although such renewal has a personal side to it, it is not simply about changing persons. It is equally about criticizing and changing cultural practices, social institutions, and the very structure of society where these impede the interconnected flourishing of all Earth's inhabitants. Hence reformational scholarship tends toward a comprehensiveness of social vision and a depth of cultural engagement that do not harmonize easily with either individualism or political liberalism. It also has a directness of approach, a freedom from ecclesiastical supervision or mediation, that runs counter to either sacramentalism or religious fundamentalism.

Perhaps this directness of approach helps explain why philosophy, not theology, has been the preferred discipline for reformational scholars. The central figures of the tradition in the generation after Kuyper are the legal theorist Herman Dooyeweerd (1894–1977) and the systematic philosopher Dirk Vollenhoven (1892–1978). Brothers-in-law and close conversation partners, Dooyeweerd and Vollenhoven together transformed the central insights and commitments of the Kuyperian tradition into an ambitious and expansive philosophy – a Dutch Reformed parallel, in some ways, to the work of Franz Rosenzweig and Martin Buber in Jewish thought and to the neo-Thomism of Etienne Gilson, Jacques Maritain, and Bernard Lonergan in the Catholic intellectual tradition.[4]

This religiously inspired philosophy came to North America by way of H. Evan Runner (1916–2002). Runner was a Harvard-trained Presbyterian who studied with Vollenhoven in Amsterdam before taking up a philosophy position in 1951 at Calvin College, the denominational liberal arts school of the Dutch-immigrant Christian Reformed Church, itself the most noticeably Kuyperian church in North America. Runner sent many of his best students to study at the Vrije Universiteit (VU) in Amsterdam, the school founded by Kuyper in 1880 that now goes by the name VU University Amsterdam. When they returned to the United States and Canada, they took up key positions in religious, political, and academic organizations – notably at the Institute for Christian Studies (ICS) in Toronto.

The 1950s were heady times for the development of Protestant Christian philosophy in North America. Not one but two schools of Kuyperian philosophy began to take shape at Calvin College: both reformational philosophy and Reformed epistemology, as it later came to be called. Alvin Plantinga and Nicholas Wolterstorff (both born in 1932), the best-known Reformed epistemologists, studied philosophy at Calvin in the 1950s, as did prominent reformational philosophers such as Calvin G. Seerveld (born 1930) and Hendrik Hart (born 1935). Despite their common heritage and interpersonal connections over many decades, however, the leading figures in these two schools of thought developed their ideas in different directions. This is due in part to the philosophical discussion partners that helped shape their articulations of Kuyperian themes. Reformational philosophy arose primarily from the Kantian and phenomenological traditions in continental Europe,[5] and it has not shared Reformed epistemology's appreciation for Scottish Common Sense Realism (e.g., Thomas Reid) and for the Aristotelian and Platonic elements of medieval thought.[6] Nevertheless, it is remarkable that both schools of thought gestated at Calvin College in the 1950s, fed by the Kuyperian vision of a good creation, cultural renewal, and social critique. Equally remarkable is the part both Reformed epistemology and reformational philosophy have played in the blossoming of Christian philosophy among Protestants in North America and beyond.[7] One sees this, for example, in the founding of the Society of Christian Philosophy in 1978 with its highly respected journal *Faith and Philosophy*, where Reformed epistemologists have had a prominent role, and in the establishment of ICS in 1967 as a free-standing graduate school for interdisciplinary philosophy in the reformational tradition.[8] It is to the central themes of this tradition that we now turn.

## 2. GENERATIVE THEMES

As Theodor Adorno once claimed, philosophy resists being summarized. The fact that Dooyeweerd and Vollenhoven disagreed on fundamental points and had different technical vocabularies simply increases the difficulty of summarizing reformational philosophy. Anyone who presents their work as a common project runs the risk of both whitewashing their differences and misrepresenting their individual conceptions. Perhaps, however, one can use their disagreements as a clue to what they centrally embraced and thereby sketch the main lines of reformational philosophy in its first generation. Let me pursue this approach with reference to three *Leitmotiven* or generative themes: namely, created existence, social normativity, and religious direction. Dooyeweerd and Vollenhoven disagree about how precisely to account for these matters, while agreeing on how important they are. Later I shall show how these themes inform the essays collected in this volume and indicate how my appropriation of reformational philosophy responds to contemporary concerns.

### 2.1 *Created Existence*

Inspired by the Kuyperian vision of a good, broken, and yet redeemable creation, both Dooyeweerd and Vollenhoven insist on an ontological distinction between God and creation, and they affirm that creation exists only by virtue of its relation to God. Moreover, they understand creation in a very broad sense to include human beings and their culture and society. They characterize the relation of creation to God in differing ways, however. Dooyeweerd does this in terms of "meaning": all of created existence is temporal, he asserts, and it has meaning – or, better, *is* meaning – with reference to its creator: it refers beyond itself to God as its transcendent Origin. As he succinctly states at the outset of his opus magnum, "*Meaning* [*zin*] is the *being* [*zijn*] of all *creaturely beings [creatuurlijk zijnde*], the mode-of-being [*zijnswijze*] of our selfhood too – religious in root, and divine in origin."[9] Vollenhoven describes the same relationship in terms of created existence "being subject," in the sense that it completely depends on its Creator and is entirely subject to God's law(s). As Vollenhoven says near the beginning of the syllabus for the mandatory core course in systematic philosophy that he taught every year, "That which is created is completely dependent on the Creator, that is to say, wholly subject to [God's] sovereign law, Word revelation, and guidance."[10] So both Dooyeweerd and Vollenhoven regard the relation to God as definitive for creaturely existence, although they disagree about whether this relation is referential.

#### ONTOLOGICAL FRAMEWORKS

This shared emphasis on creation's relation to God thoroughly informs the overarching "categories" of reformational philosophy in its first generation, even as the difference in how to characterize this relation flows into these "categories."[11] Like Kuyper, both Vollenhoven and Dooyeweerd think that structural diversity is intrinsic to the goodness of creation. They also elaborate the Kuyperian notion of sphere sovereignty – the notion that distinct social institutions (e.g., church and state) and cultural sectors (e.g., art and science) receive their own norms, authority, and tasks from God and not from any other sphere – into two sorts of structural diversity. Accordingly they distinguish and relate two ontological frameworks that apply to all creatures: a modal or aspectual framework, and a framework of individuality and typicality.[12] The modal framework pertains to the different levels or dimensions in which creatures have features or are active – physical, biological, psychological, etc. The framework of individuality and typicality has to do with what distinguishes one individual creature from another (e.g., this coffee mug and that coffee mug), one class of creatures from another class (e.g., plants and animals), and one type of social institution from another (e.g., church and state).

Within the modal framework, both Dooyeweerd and Vollenhoven distinguish among fourteen (later fifteen) "modalities." They discuss the order and interrelations among these modalities in terms of the "moments" or "analogies" within each modality whereby it refers to the other modalities, both those that precede it (via analogies called "retrocipations") and those that succeed it (via analogies called "anticipations"). The physical modality of created existence, for example, is preceded in the intermodal order by the spatial modality and the numerical or arithmetic modality, and it is succeeded by the biotic or organic modality and the psychic modality as well as many more.[13]

Within the second ontological framework, that of individuality and typicality, both Dooyeweerd and Vollenhoven draw the most fundamental distinctions in terms of the modal levels at which one finds the most characteristic properties or functions of a class of creaturely existents (or "subject units" in Vollenhoven's vocabulary). For example, whereas the worship community (church, synagogue, mosque, etc.) is characterized by the leading role played by faith and worship – it has a "pistic" qualifying function (Dooyeweerd) or prevailing function (Vollenhoven) – the state is characterized primarily by the pursuit of public justice – it has a juridical qualifying or prevailing function. All the other activities, tasks, and operations of either church or state need to be understood in light of its modal qualification. On this basis, then, one can give a rigorous philosophical articulation and defence to Kuyper's more diffuse insistence on sphere sovereignty as a key to institutional diversity in modern society.

## DIVINE LAW

Despite these large areas of agreement, however, a very important divergence emerges in the ontologies of Dooyeweerd and Vollenhoven. As Vollenhoven notes in a confidential report from 1953, they had different approaches in how they understood divine law. Referring to himself in the third person, Vollenhoven writes:

> Dooyeweerd placed both law and subject in the cosmos, using the term "cosmos" to refer to the part of that which is created that finds its centrum in [humankind]. That is why he distinguished … law-side and subject-side, which he takes to be related as that which is universal to that which is individual. In contrast, Vollenhoven spoke of the triad God-law-cosmos, in the sense that God exists independent of law and cosmos and is not their correlate, but sets the law for the cosmos [God] created such that law and cosmos (cosmos taken as a *whole*) are each other's correlate. That is why he could not talk about the "law-side" and "subject-side" of the cosmos. He understood the law to always stand above the cosmos, such that what was subject to this law was identical to the cosmos, not one of its sides.[14]

In other words, divine law is a side of creaturely existence for Dooyeweerd, and it is a line or limit (*grens*) between God and creaturely existence for Vollenhoven.

As both a result and a manifestation of this divergence, Dooyeweerd finds a plethora of laws in creation – modal laws, typical laws, and even laws of individuality – but Vollenhoven does not. Vollenhoven tends to talk only of modal laws and the central "law" of love. Further, whereas Dooyeweerd speaks of anticipations and retrocipations on both the law-side and the subject-side of the various modalities, Vollenhoven limits his analysis of anticipations and retrocipations to the functions that creaturely beings have – to "subject functions" in his vocabulary, which Dooyeweerd would analyze as the "subject-side" to various modalities. There are advantages and disadvantages to both approaches: Dooyeweerd, unlike Vollenhoven on a certain reading, avoids the problem of postulating law as a "third thing" between God and creation, and Vollenhoven, unlike Dooyeweerd on a certain reading, avoids the problem of turning creaturely patterns and regularities into divine laws. The struggle over how to conceptualize divine law characterizes much of reformational philosophy in the next generations, including my own work.

## 2.2 *Social Normativity*

Answers to the question of how created existence relates to God, and the place of divine law in this relationship, directly shape the theme of social normativity. The Kuyperian emphasis on sociocultural renewal gives urgency to this second theme. For if religious adherents are called to be agents of renewal, then it is crucial for them to understand what makes for better or worse cultural practices and social institutions, and not simply to react to current trends or revert to outmoded patterns. In their accounts of social normativity, Dooyeweerd and Vollenhoven inherit an emphasis on creational ordinances from Kuyper and his followers. As Kuyper explains in his *Lectures on Calvinism*, all created life "bears in itself a law for its existence," and God institutes this law. More precisely, there are ordinances of God for everything God has created, including our bodies, our thoughts, our imagination, and our morality, ordinances "urged upon us as the constant will of ... God, who at every instant is determining the course of life, ordaining its laws and continually binding us by [God's] divine authority."[15] This implies that nothing in human culture and society, not even logic or aesthetic experience, lies outside the scope of divine law.

### NORMS AND PRINCIPLES

Dooyeweerd and Vollenhoven tend to agree with Kuyper on this point, although they do not take over Kuyper's speculative construction of such ordinances as the eternal thoughts of God.[16] Yet they draw different implications for social normativity. Dooyeweerd, with his emphasis on the cosmos as meaning and as comprising both law-side and subject-side, tends to stress continuity across the entire array of modal laws, such that modal laws pertaining primarily to human functioning – laws pertaining to social solidarity, economic resourcefulness, and political justice, for example[17] – are not that different from what other philosophers would call natural laws. Nevertheless, Dooyeweerd insists such modal laws must be "positivized" by human beings within their practices and institutions; in that sense they are what he calls "norms" and not natural laws. Beginning with the logical modality, the order of creation gives human beings modal laws only in principle, he says; we can violate them (e.g., we can think illogically), and we must work out what they mean. As Dooyeweerd states in *Roots of Western Culture*, "Norms are given in the creation order as *principles* for human behavior," and these principles "require *formation* by competent human authorities."[18]

Although Vollenhoven employs a similar distinction between modal laws and modal norms (or laws that have norming character, as he puts it), he sees principles as the fallible and changeable results of human attempts to formulate laws that have norming character. The so-called laws of logic are, he says, "nothing other than the very law for that which is logical, to the extent that human thinking was successful in putting these laws into words." In other words, the so-called laws of logic are humanly formulated principles, and a principle at best "includes no more than what someone has grasped of God's law. That is why principles can sometimes be altogether false and, even when they appear to be sound, are never unchanging, as are God's laws, but must be revised repeatedly."[19]

## THE CALL TO LOVE

Whereas Dooyeweerd's emphasis on norms being *creationally given in principle* makes human "positivizations" seem less fallible and changeable, Vollenhoven's emphasis on the *human giving of principles* makes the norming character of modal laws seem less natural and law-like. Indeed, this points to another divergence between Dooyeweerd and Vollenhoven concerning what one could call the rationality of norms. Vollenhoven's 1953 report suggests, as he says elsewhere, that, when it comes to human beings, the law of God is simply the command to love God above all and our neighbour as ourselves, and, again when it comes to human beings, all the diverse modal laws are simply differentiations of that summation of God's law for the modal diversity of functioning within human life. In other words (not Vollenhoven's exact words, however), the call to love God, neighbour, and self comes to human beings as a call to show (social) solidarity, practice (economic) resourcefulness, and pursue (political) justice, among other modally delimited callings.[20]

This suggests, on the one hand, that the so-called laws investigated and formulated in the natural and social sciences are not really laws. Instead they are patterns of regularity displayed by creatures in the cosmos. For example, statistical patterns concerning homicides and birthrates are neither laws nor norms in Vollenhoven's sense. One can always ask whether the practices reflected in statistical trends are in line with the call to love God and neighbour and with modal specifications of that call. As Vollenhoven puts it in his typically cryptic fashion, "the rules or, if one prefers, laws in the cosmos have to do with the regularity both of what does and of what does not line up with the law in the sense of norm."[21]

On the other hand, Vollenhoven's approach to social normativity also suggests that one cannot map the difference between normative and non-normative laws directly onto the difference between higher and lower modalities, as Dooyeweerd does (and as Vollenhoven appears to have done in earlier writings). Whereas Dooyeweerd denies that the call to love is a norm and explicitly ties normativity to the modal levels at which human beings function – specifically to logical and postlogical modalities[22] – Vollenhoven regards the call to love as the central norm that pertains also, for example, to the psychological well-being and organic health of human beings: "health stands over against sickness also in psychic and biotic modalities as the correlate of conforming to the norm or not," he writes, and these levels of functioning are definitely pre-logical for Vollenhoven, as they are for Dooyeweerd.

### NORMATIVE AUTHORITY

The upshot to all this is that Vollenhoven relaxes the linkage between social normativity and rational understanding, without denying it altogether, and he relativizes the role of science in helping us discern what makes for human flourishing, without denying the important insights that the sciences yield. This in turn complements another divergence from Dooyeweerd, barely touched on in the 1953 report, concerning the relation between societal structures and social normativity. Both Dooyeweerd and Vollenhoven assign the task of humanly "positivizing" modal laws primarily to those who hold positions of authority within social institutions – "competent human authorities" in Dooyeweerd's formulation or "office bearers" in Vollenhoven's terminology.[23] In Vollenhoven's words, "those in authority in each institution have to positivize the laws holding for that [institution] in consultation with those who pay respect."[24] Following Kuyper's notion of sphere sovereignty, both Dooyeweerd and Vollenhoven also think that the shape of authority is distinctive for each (type of) social institution; as Vollenhoven puts it, "the task of the office bearers in each [institution] is unique."[25] Moreover, those who carry authority (the office bearers) are themselves "subject to the norm in the various societal connections."[26]

So far as I can tell, only Dooyeweerd attempts to specify such positions of normative authority – i.e., the authority to say what divine law requires – in terms of the "structural principle" of each distinctive type of social institution, such as families, marriages, states, and worship communities. Because societal structural principles belong to the "law-side" of created existence, this quickly lands Dooyeweerd in the problem of ratifying as abidingly normative what is only a temporary social form of organization, something that becomes more apparent, of course, in historical hindsight. Hence, for example, Dooyeweerd specifies that "the societal relation of authority and subordination" is intrinsic to all social institutions (his term for social institutions is "communities" – *samenlevingsverbanden*). He also argues that, according to the structural principle of "the family," parents have moral authority to which children are subordinate, and, "according to the divine order of creation," husbands have marital authority over their wives.[27]

This close alignment of normative authority with specific forms of social organization raises all sorts of issues for contemporary reformational thinkers who embrace more democratic modes of parenting and reject patriarchal patterns in marriage. It seems Dooyeweerd would have to reject such approaches to marriage and family life as double violations of divine law, both because they do not uphold the patterns of normative authority secured by "the" structural principles of "the" family and marriage, and because they seem not to follow the modal laws, as specified by Dooyeweerd, that govern the "qualifying functions" of such institutions. Even if Vollenhoven shared Dooyeweerd's particular understanding of what makes for good families and good marriages, as he most likely did, his reticence about populating society with law-like structural principles, together with his overriding focus on the call to love as the norm from which all modal laws flow, allows for greater flexibility in one's approach to questions of social normativity.

## 2.3 *Religious Direction*

The third shared theme over which Dooyeweerd and Vollenhoven disagree concerns what they would call "religious direction." This theme, like their disagreement about it, receives extensive commentary in the secondary literature, and it returns in several chapters within this volume.[28] So my treatment here can be brief.

### MATTERS OF THE HEART

The two founders of reformational philosophy have a radical view of religion. For them, religion (what I would call "spirituality"), as distinct from faith, is not some part of life or some level of functioning or some type of social organization. Rather it is the very root (*radix*) of human existence in all its parts, levels, practices, and institutions. It is the fundamental direction in which life is lived and the most basic orientation for our cultural practices and social institutions. In short, it is the very core of how human beings are related to God as Creator, the very summation of how we respond to the call to love.

This radical understanding of religion relies on a philosophical anthropology that breaks dramatically with much of the Western tradition in philosophy and theology. Against all forms of monism and dualism that distinguish body and soul as different substances or different functional complexes and then try to relate them, Dooyeweerd and Vollenhoven insist that human beings exist bodily in all their functions, whether physical or emotional or logical or ethical, etc. All of these corporeal functions flow from and to the human heart in its relation to God or to what one takes to be God. All of them have a religious root.

Precisely here, however, their agreement ends. Dooyeweerd throughout his career insisted that the heart is "supra-temporal," unlike any of the diverse corporeal functions, which are temporal. Further, only because of the heart's supra-temporality can humans be related to God, who is eternal. Vollenhoven denied this, both because the notion of supra-temporality opens the door to problematic monisms and dualisms and because nothing about human existence is beyond time.[29] Accordingly, Vollenhoven always spoke of the heart as "prefunctional" rather than "supra-temporal." Moreover, although, like Dooyeweerd, he saw faith as the highest function in "the cloak of functions,"[30] he did not talk about faith as "lying at the boundary of time and eternity" or as "the window facing eternity."[31] As Vollenhoven phrases this in a lecture to Catholic students about faith, "faith is not identical with heart, but is determined by the heart in its direction towards good or evil, i.e., in obedience to the law of love or not. In other words, the whole [human being] is religious, and [human] life is a walk before the face of God in obedience or disobedience."[32]

## HOLISTIC AND NORMATIVE PLURALISM

This divergence over how to understand religious direction is particularly important for a Kuyperian emphasis on social transformation. If contributing to sociocultural renewal requires the critique and revision of cultural practices, social institutions, and even the structure of society as a whole, then it matters whether the direction for such transformation comes via a supra-temporal heart finding the fulfillment of meaning in that which transcends time or whether the direction comes via a prefunctional heart responding to the call to love. The first approach – Dooyeweerd's – suggests that the fundamental problems in society are ones of differentiation and integration. The second approach – Vollenhoven's – suggests that the fundamental problems in society are ones of good and evil, understood here as the pursuit or the rejection of the call to love. The two approaches are not mutually exclusive. Both are versions of a radically holistic and normative pluralism, according to which the legitimate social differentiation of distinct tasks and organizations anchors itself in a fundamental unity of purpose. Yet Dooyeweerd and Vollenhoven give this holistic pluralism two significantly different inflections, and these inflections reinforce their divergences over created existence and social normativity.

One sees, then, that reformational philosophy in its founding generation systematically articulates Kuyperian emphases on creational goodness and redemption, sociocultural renewal, and societal transformation by accounting for created existence, social normativity, and religious direction. The generative challenges of reformational philosophy, even today, arise in and through the divergences between Dooyeweerd and Vollenhoven over how exactly to provide such articulation and how to give such accounts. Certainly this is so of my own efforts, as I hope to show now in a preliminary way.

## 3. CONTEMPORARY CONCERNS

The holistic and normative pluralism of reformational philosophy in its founding generation both distinguishes it from other schools of philosophy and connects it with them. It also sets the stage for the concerns of the current generation of reformational philosophers. Let me demonstrate this in three areas where the reformational tradition can make significant contributions to contemporary philosophy: ontology, social philosophy, and epistemology.

### *3.1 Ontology*

Although sharply critical of the metaphysical tradition that stems from Plato and Aristotle, Dooyeweerd, Vollenhoven, and their successors emphasize the priority of ontology over epistemology. They do not start with the question of what we can know, but with the question of what it means to exist. Dooyeweerd begins his *New Critique of Theoretical Thought* by asking what first strikes him about "reality" as it is given in ordinary experience and then is confronted with a theoretical scientific analysis (*uiteen-stelling*). He immediately replies, an "intermodal cosmic coherence" that points beyond itself to "a deeper totality."[33] Vollenhoven opens his introductory lectures on philosophy by asking about "the place of philosophy in the cosmos," and he quickly establishes that philosophical knowing (like all knowing) "is a component of being."[34] The priority given to ontology displaces a modern emphasis on the division between a subject who knows and an object that can be known. In fact, both Dooyeweerd and Vollenhoven challenge the modern epistemological subject/object paradigm and give a much wider and more ontological account of relations between subjects and objects. In these ways, classical reformational philosophy resembles Martin Heidegger's *Being and Time*, wherein the meaning of being is the primary question for philosophy and for human existence, and the modern subject/object paradigm gives way to our "being-in-the-world." Like Heidegger, Dooyeweerd and Vollenhoven challenge an epistemological focus among both neo-Kantians and logical positivists in the 1920s and 1930s.

When postwar philosophy in these traditions challenged its own epistemological emphasis and took linguistic and interpretive turns, as it did in ordinary language philosophy (e.g., J.L. Austin) and philosophical hermeneutics (e.g., Hans-Georg Gadamer), classical reformational ontology began to appear outdated. Dooyeweerd seems to have had little awareness of the linguistic mediation of either "naïve pre-theoretical experience," as he called it, or "theoretical scientific analysis." Vollenhoven seemed not to worry about the hermeneutical character of human "being subject." Such a lack of linguistic and hermeneutical concern shows up in their modal ontology, where the "logical" or "analytic" way of functioning depends directly upon sensory experience. It also shows up in how they present this ontology, paying little attention to how ordinary language and the interpretation of "given" phenomena work. Accordingly, one concern for reformational philosophers today is to reformulate reformational ontology after the linguistic and interpretive turns.

As the essays in this volume indicate, I have tried to do this in at least two ways. First, following the lead of Calvin Seerveld and Hendrik Hart, I have postulated a considerably revised intermodal order. Whereas Dooyeweerd and Vollenhoven say our abilities to think logically, to make distinctions, and to understand connections directly depend on our abilities to sense and feel, I suggest they equally depend on our abilities to make and shape things, to engage in imaginative practices that include creative interpretation, and to communicate in language. This intermodal reordering leads to a more hermeneutical and linguistic understanding of rationality and science. It also lets one give proper weight to the importance of art talk and faith talk in the social institutions of art and religion.[35]

Second, I have begun to work out a social ontology in which intersubjective interactions, cultural practices, and social institutions – rather than intentional actions, individual agents, and societal connections (Vollenhoven) or structural principles (Dooyeweerd) – are the primary categories. This shift from the personal and structural to the intersubjective and historical both incorporates and fosters greater attention to how linguistic communication and the interpretation of needs help constitute social life. It also promotes a stronger emphasis on civil society and the public sphere than one finds in classical reformational philosophy.[36]

### *3.2 Social Philosophy*

A distinctive trait of the reformational tradition is the comprehensive social philosophy it offers: not an ethics or moral philosophy, as became common after Kant, and not merely a political philosophy, although Dooyeweerd offers that as well. What Vollenhoven sketches, and what Dooyeweerd paints in great detail, is a social philosophy whose task, for Dooyeweerd, in Jonathan Chaplin's words, is "the critical, systematic elucidation of the invariant normative structural principles undergirding the actually existing institutions populating modern society."[37] Whatever one thinks of Dooyeweerd's achievements in this area, his ambitions are both grand and unique. Outside the traditions of neo-Thomism (e.g., Jacques Maritain) and Western Marxism (e.g., the Frankfurt School), few Western philosophers in the first half of the twentieth century saw the need for such a comprehensive and systematic account of society as a whole, and even fewer attempted one.

For many years after the Second World War, the entire project of a comprehensive social philosophy seemed to have collapsed. Then John Rawls published his groundbreaking *A Theory of Justice* in 1971 and Jürgen Habermas published his two-volume *Theory of Communicative Action* in the early 1980s, and the prospects for a comprehensive social philosophy gradually brightened. Yet, unlike classical reformational philosophy, the newer contributions to social philosophy do not employ a robust social ontology, nor do they offer a strong account of social normativity. Indeed, in the wake of ordinary language philosophy and under the impact of feminist, poststructural, and neopragmatist critiques of both ontology and moral universalization, many philosophers today would harshly criticize classical reformational accounts of societal structures and modal norms. Perhaps the clearest example in this regard is the radical contextualism of Richard Rorty. So Dooyeweerd and Vollenhoven's successors now face the challenge of rearticulating reformational social philosophy both to address contemporary contexualism and to help make sense of the world in which we live.

Reformational thinkers have attempted this in various ways. They have explored relationships between universal norms and particular contexts.[38] They have distinguished more clearly than Dooyeweerd and Vollenhoven did among what Sander Griffioen calls contextual, structural, and directional pluralities or pluralisms.[39] They have debated the paradigmatic Kuyperian notions of creation order and creational ordinances.[40] And they have given up Dooyeweerd's insistence on the invariance of social structural principles by arguing that "the normative design of social structures emerges out of a *normative conception of the human person*."[41]

In my own work, I have tried to address issues surrounding social normativity by developing the ideas of societal principles and interconnected flourishing.[42] Taking a cue from Vollenhoven's approach to norms and principles and his emphasis on the central call to love, I have located the key to social normativity in human fidelity to societal principles. Although one can delimit these societal principles in a modal fashion, they are not given in the structure or order of creation. Instead they are historically unfolded and unfolding summations of what makes for human flourishing and, insofar as human beings are in relationship to other creatures, what makes for the flourishing of all creation. Societal principles issue from and give content to the call to love God and neighbour. But they do so only within the dynamic unfolding of culture and society, amid struggles over what makes for interconnected flourishing.

Contra Dooyeweerd, then, it is not social institutions or their structural principles that are normative, but societal principles as fundamental and historical love-callings to solidarity, resourcefulness, justice, and the like, always in light of the potential flourishing of all Earth's inhabitants. Which specific forms of institutional organization these callings urge upon us is continually open for exploration, discussion, and historical judgment. Moreover, the task of discerning and enacting what the callings require is not restricted to specific "office bearers" or "competent authorities." Rather, it is distributed among all who to some degree are responsible and responsive to the call to love. Such distribution allows one to see "contextual pluralism" not as an obstacle or threat to normative discernment, but as intrinsic to and historically necessary for human fidelity to societal principles. Such fidelity includes our diversely articulating and rearticulating what justice and solidarity and the like come to, and thereby our continually struggling to shape societal principles. In this way, the linguistic and hermeneutical turns can also inform one's view of social normativity.

I have not abandoned Dooyeweerd and Vollenhoven's concerns about differentiated social institutions and appropriate societal structures, however. Rather, I see their nuanced accounts of institutional diversity as among their most distinctive and valuable contributions to social philosophy. Yet I have tried to recast these accounts to deal with the contemporary array of institutions as well as patterns that seem most oppressive and trends that seem most destructive to interconnected flourishing – what I have labelled "societal evil." This has led to my theorizing three societal macrostructures – for-profit economy, administrative state, and civil society – and proposing a critique of both their normative deficiencies and their structural interrelations. Following Kuyper's usage, I call this an "architectonic critique" whose long-term practical aim is what I call a "differential transformation" of contemporary society.[43] I believe this approach enables one to take up the most sustained contemporary criticisms of anti-democratic politics, ecological destruction, and economic injustice without ignoring the normative resources that reside in the ethical traditions of cultural and religious communities around the world.[44]

### *3.3 Epistemology*

In tandem with such revisions in ontology and social philosophy, I have also begun work on an ontologically framed epistemology in which knowledge is not only holistic and multidimensional, as Dooyeweerd and Vollenhoven suggest, but also wholly hermeneutical and linguistically mediated. The clearest evidence of this transformation in epistemology occurs in the essays where I examine Dooyeweerd's conception of truth and propose an alternative.[45] When worked out in detail, this alternative will make good on the promissory note in both Dooyeweerd and Vollenhoven that knowledge and truth occur in many distinct and interrelated ways – something Hegel was one of the few philosophers to understand.[46] Moreover, these ways are linked to distinct social institutions that have their own legitimacy and normative tasks, as Dooyeweerd and Vollenhoven always claimed.[47] Because their primary accounts of knowledge and truth did not have room to accommodate interpretation and linguistic communication and did not connect very well with their social philosophies, Dooyeweerd and Vollenhoven did not or could not fully develop the holistic and pluralistic epistemology their ontology suggested.

Holism and pluralism have not been the watchwords of mainstream epistemology over the past hundred years. Despite a distinction between knowledge by acquaintance and knowledge by description, the influential logical atomism of Bertrand Russell and of Ludwig Wittgenstein's *Tractatus Logico-Philosophicus* held little room for interconnected modes of knowing; the logical positivist push for a unified science by Rudolf Carnap and others challenged any claim that the various academic disciplines have legitimately diverse methods and fields; and more recent semantic and deflationary approaches to truth, associated with names such as Alfred Tarski and Willard Quine, have undermined the thought that "truth" might be a substantial and complex idea.

There are exceptions to this story, of course. The pragmatism of John Dewey and others linked knowledge and truth with practical engagements; Heideggerian philosophy emphasized the interconnectedness of human modes of being; and Critical Theory highlighted the social embeddedness of human cognition. More recently, feminism and social epistemology have called attention to the politics of knowledge,[48] and a kind of pluralism has emerged in truth theory, although it is a pluralism with respect to propositional truth, not with respect to truth that may be nonpropositional.[49] Yet there have been few attempts to give a systematic account of knowledge as a whole, to show how various cultural practices and social institutions make specific contributions to the acquisition and testing of knowledge, and to propose a comprehensive idea of truth that does justice to the entire scope of knowledge practices and institutions while making sense of the roles that propositional knowledge and scientific inquiry play in contemporary society. In fact, for many specialists in epistemology, such an attempt would not count as epistemology at all.

All of this poses a formidable challenge for someone who wishes to develop the holism and pluralism of reformational epistemology in a contemporary setting. The key to meeting this challenge, it seems to me, lies in retaining but reshaping the radicality of reformational philosophy as a whole. As I suggest in chapters 3 and 14, this implies a thorough reexamination of Dooyeweerd's conception of theoretical truth and a dialogical critique of the leading truth theorists and truth theories from the past hundred or so years. It also implies that the ontological and social-philosophical revisions already described will inform a reformulated and reformational conception of truth.

The radical character of this project rests in the claim, stemming from both Dooyeweerd and Vollenhoven, that human beings, in all of their practices and institutions, are deeply spiritual creatures, centrally oriented and directed to respond to the call to love. If, as Dooyeweerd and Vollenhoven thought,[50] the search for truth is fundamentally spiritual, fundamentally a matter of overall orientation, direction, and responsibility, then we need a conception of truth that is sufficiently radical to acknowledge this spirituality of truth, yet sufficiently complex and nuanced to account for both modal and social-institutional differences and interrelations in how truth and the search for truth occur.[51] In such a conception, propositional knowledge – the focus of most epistemologies and truth theories – will be truth-seeking, but not all truth will be propositional. Similarly, all social institutions – not simply science or, more broadly, the academic enterprise – will be knowledge-seeking, but not all of human knowledge will occur within social institutions.

Such an epistemology requires a philosophy that is interdisciplinary in the best sense, one that not only takes up the latest findings and debates within its own discipline but also interacts with the philosophically central issues in other disciplines, across the spectrum of mathematics, natural sciences, social sciences, and the humanities. This epistemology also calls for a critical and dialogical approach to other philosophies, one that neither fears to talk about matters of the heart nor hesitates to learn from other approaches. And it invites a philosophical engagement with the burning social questions of our day and with underlying patterns and trends that either foster or destroy the interconnected flourishing of all Earth's inhabitants. This is what reformational philosophers have offered in the past, and it is what they can continue to strive for today: an interdisciplinary, spiritually open, and socially engaged philosophy that seeks sociocultural renewal and the transformation of society.

## 4. THREE GENERATIONS

Let me conclude by briefly surveying the essays in this book. The book contains fifteen chapters, organized into three parts, and followed by an epilogue that says what motivates my work as a scholar. Each part begins with its own introduction summarizing the five chapters to follow and placing them in a wider context. The first ten chapters address both the first generation of reformational philosophy – primarily Dooyeweerd and Vollenhoven, and the focus of Part I (Critical Retrieval) – and the second generation – primarily my own former graduate instructors at ICS, and the focus of Part II (Reforming Reason). In Part III (Social Transformation) I use the results of my engagement with the previous two generations to put reformational insights into dialogue with other philosophers and to present my own third-generational thoughts on religion, truth, and social transformation.

My approach to the tradition of reformational philosophy is one of critical retrieval, as I explain and exemplify in Part I. A critical retrieval examines the philosophy of an earlier generation by raising or responding to legitimate objections and proposing viable alternatives. While indebted to the contributions of an earlier generation, a critical retrieval aims to offer a redemptive critique of these contributions, with a view to contemporary concerns. The chapters in Part I attempt to do this with respect to Dooyeweerd's transcendental critique of theoretical thought, his conception of truth, his ontology of the modes of existence, and his social philosophy.

This does not mean, however, that I simply repeat the objections and revisions provided by the second-generation reformational philosophers with whom I studied at ICS, in particular Hart and Seerveld. Their work, too, deserves the attentiveness of a redemptive critique. The first three chapters in Part II address issues in Hart's ontology and epistemology, with an emphasis on his account of the relation between faith and reason. The fourth responds to Seerveld's appropriation of Vollenhoven's approach to the history of philosophy, and the fifth explores the implications of Hart's work for understanding what it means to be human, a central issue in philosophical anthropology.

Although the essays collected in Part III continue to refer to earlier generations, they have a more fully constructive intent. They aim to articulate my own reformational understandings of modernity, social critique, truth, and science, in dialogue with such thinkers as John Milbank, G.W.F. Hegel, Jürgen Habermas, Martin Heidegger, and Joseph Rouse. Nevertheless, the issues I emphasize, and how I approach them, are embedded in a critical retrieval of the reformational tradition.

The epilogue, titled "Earth's Lament," is the inaugural address given in 2003 when I took up my position as Professor of Systematic Philosophy at ICS. It appears here with only minor revisions. Some readers may want to begin with this epilogue. I originally presented it to a mixed audience of ICS supporters, faculty, staff, and students as well as academics from many other fields and schools. My eighty-nine-year-old mother, who had only nine years of schooling, was in the audience; I tried to speak to her just as much as to my academic colleagues. "Earth's Lament" voices the concerns and passions that motivate my work. It calls for a philosophy that does not ignore the suffering of God's creatures, a philosophy that seeks comprehensive wisdom in order to critique societal evil. In issuing this call, I also suggest how the philosophy I envision arises from my reworking of reformational philosophy, as articulated in this book. Like Dooyeweerd and Vollenhoven, and like Hart and Seerveld, too, I pursue the inner reformation of philosophy for the sake of a transformed world.

# PART ONE

# Critical Retrieval

Herman Dooyeweerd (1894–1977) and Dirk Vollenhoven (1892–1978) are the most important members of the first generation of reformational philosophy: Dooyeweerd, as the author of the seminal three-volume *De Wijsbegeerte der Wetsidee [The Philosophy of the Law-Idea]* (1935–36) and the founding editor of *Philosophia Reformata*, the movement's academic journal of record; and Vollenhoven, as the head of the philosophy department at the Vrije Universiteit in Amsterdam who trained an entire generation of reformational thinkers and became the first chairperson of the Association for Calvinistic Philosophy (later, the Association for Reformational Philosophy), and the publisher of *Philosophia Reformata*. I consider both figures to be equally important, and they receive equal billing in the annual graduate seminar on reformational philosophy at the Institute for Christian Studies (ICS).

Nevertheless, midway through the aughts of the current century a debate broke out in *Philosophia Reformata* about whether Dooyeweerd or Vollenhoven represented the authentic version of reformational philosophy. The question struck me as a non-starter. So I was happy when the late Theodore (Ted) Plantinga organized a symposium on this topic at Redeemer University College in 2006. The symposium featured a panel that included John Kok, a former student of Vollenhoven who has edited, translated, and interpreted his writings; Daniël (Danie) F.M. Strauss, the general editor of Dooyeweerd's collected works in English translation; and ICS philosophical theologian James Olthuis, who is perhaps best known for his work on Jacques Derrida and John Caputo. Chapter 2 below, titled "Reformational Philosophy after Dooyeweerd and Vollenhoven," is the lightly revised text of my contribution to this panel. The chapter presents critical retrieval as the appropriate way to take up the generative sources to one's own intellectual tradition. It also indicates that this approach is itself both indebted to Dooyeweerd and Vollenhoven and critical of their own preferred modes of critique. By "critical retrieval" I mean the project of acknowledging valid objections to their philosophies and, in light of such objections, providing a redemptive critique. I argue that reformational philosophers today should take up criticisms of the first generation's work, show where these are valid or invalid, and then offer alternatives that, while inspired by the first generation of reformational philosophy, also avoid its problems.

Dooyeweerd's preferred mode – a transcendental critique of theoretical thought – is the topic of chapter 1. There I explain, defend, and question his attempt to root philosophy in religion. Titled "The Great Turning Point," this essay was written at the invitation of Bill Hasker, then editor of the Society of Christian Philosophers' journal *Faith and Philosophy*, and in response to an essay on Dooyeweerd by Hugo Meynell, a Canadian Catholic philosopher. Although I do not similarly devote an entire essay to Vollenhoven's "(anti-)thetical critique," as I describe it in chapter 2, I take up Vollenhoven's historiography in the chapter on "Metacritique" in Part II below.

The other three chapters in Part I address interrelated areas in Dooyeweerd's work: his epistemology, his philosophy of science, and his social ontology. Biographically, these essays lie quite far apart. Chapter 3, titled "Dooyeweerd's Conception of Truth," arises from my current work on the idea of truth; it first appeared in *Philosophia Reformata* in 2008. Chapter 4, titled "Dooyeweerd's Modal Theory," is the stylistically revised version of a research paper I wrote in 1973 for Hendrik Hart's yearlong graduate seminar on *A New Critique of Theoretical Thought*. It reflects my keen interest, as a first-year graduate student at ICS, in Calvin Seerveld's work on a "modal aesthetic theory." Chapter 5, titled "Fantastic Things," stems from the early stages of work on a two-volume philosophy of the arts, eventually published as *Artistic Truth* (2004) and *Art in Public* (2011). I first presented "Fantastic Things" at a 1994 conference in the Netherlands marking the centennial of Dooyeweerd's birth, and then published it one year later in *Philosophia Reformata*.

Despite the many years these essays span, several strands of continuity stand out. One is a deep appreciation for the holism, normativity, and radical character of reformational philosophy. Another is a growing dissatisfaction with Dooyeweerd's tendency to treat societal structures as immutable laws and to substitute theoretical intuition for intersubjective argumentation. A third link is the effort to uncover both Dooyeweerd's contributions and their limitations through a close reading of his work. In that sense, all three essays are exercises in critical retrieval, even though I did not become clear about what critical retrieval involves until I began to teach the reformational philosophy seminar at ICS in 2002, gave my ICS inaugural lecture in 2003, and published *Artistic Truth* in 2004. The chapters in Part I aim to illuminate specific strengths and weaknesses of reformational philosophy in its founding generation. They also provide preliminary sketches for the trajectory of my own work in epistemology, aesthetics, and social philosophy.

# 1

# The Great Turning Point: Religion and Rationality in Dooyeweerd's Transcendental Critique

## (2004)

> The great turning point in my thought was … the discovery of the religious root of thought itself. This shed a new light on the [continual] failure of all attempts, including my own, to bring about an inner synthesis between the Christian faith and a philosophy rooted in faith in the self-sufficiency of human reason.
>
> Herman Dooyeweerd[1]

Faith and philosophy, two central themes for the Society of Christian Philosophers, drove the life work of Herman Dooyeweerd. Writing from Amsterdam in 1935, Dooyeweerd announces that his massive reconceptualization of Western philosophy has not come without intense spiritual struggle. "Originally," he says, "I was strongly under the influence first of the Neo-Kantian philosophy, later on of Husserl's phenomenology" (NC 1: v, WW 1: v).[2] Then a great intellectual conversion occurred.

The passage surrounding the epigraph above suggests that both continuity and discontinuity characterize the turn Dooyeweerd's thought took. On the one hand, Dooyeweerd continues the search for transcendental conditions that make thought itself possible. He claims to have radicalized this search in a way that neither Kant nor Husserl could have allowed. Yet the search itself is a fundamentally Kantian enterprise. On the other hand, Dooyeweerd breaks with the commitment to rational autonomy that sustains transcendental philosophy from Kant through Husserl. He has discovered, he says, that thought itself has a "religious root," that human reason lacks "self-sufficiency," and that philosophical claims to the contrary sprout from a type of "faith" to which Christian faith cannot be successfully grafted. The source of his discovery is a new appreciation of "the central significance of the 'heart,' repeatedly proclaimed by Holy Scripture to be the religious root of human existence" (NC 1: v, WW 1: v–vi).

Many of the issues raised by Dooyeweerd's critics go back to his innovative and complex articulations of this discovery. Early on, the most vocal critics were Dutch theologians who perceived a threat to traditional Calvinism. They faulted Dooyeweerd and his close colleague D.H.Th. Vollenhoven for employing either insufficient or unorthodox theology in their philosophy. They especially objected to a philosophical anthropology whose emphasis on the heart radically recast the distinction between body and soul.[3] When Dooyeweerd's writings began to circulate in the English-speaking world,[4] the dynamics of these criticisms, although not the precise details, recurred among fundamentalist Presbyterians[5] and intellectualist Kuyperians[6] at American colleges and seminaries.

Catholic scholars in Europe also raised penetrating questions. The first of these was H. Robbers S.J., a Thomist professor of philosophy at the Catholic University of Nijmegen who reviewed all three volumes of *De Wijsbegeerte der Wetsidee*.[7] Dooyeweerd responded in detail, and an extended discussion ensued over thirty years. The relations between nature and grace, between reason and revelation, and between Creator and creature were the central topics in their debates. In the 1950s M.F.J. Marlet S.J., a younger Thomist philosopher, began his own dialogue, with a dissertation published in German for which Dooyeweerd wrote an enthusiastic foreword.[8] Marlet demonstrates much greater affinity with Dooyeweerd's thought than does Robbers, and he tries to rescue Thomas Aquinas from Dooyeweerd's criticisms by giving Aquinas a more personalist interpretation. While seeking to accommodate Dooyeweerd's emphasis on the religious roots of philosophy and the fundamental dependence of creation on God, Marlet retains the classic Thomist formulation of nature and grace and the notion of "being" as encompassing both Creator and creature. In response, Dooyeweerd questions the accuracy of Marlet's reading of Aquinas. Dooyeweerd also rejects any metaphysical concept of being that includes both God and creatures, as well as any Aristotelian concept of substance that disguises creatures' dependence on God.[9]

The most thorough discussions of Dooyeweerd's "discovery," and its implications for philosophy and culture, have come from other reformational philosophers.[10] These range from debates between Dooyeweerd and Vollenhoven concerning the nature of the human heart to criticisms from Dooyeweerd's younger colleagues and students directed at his accounts of transcendental criticism, theoretical thought, and the relation between faith and religion.[11] Indeed, the first dissertations written in English about Dooyeweerd regard faith-oriented transcendental critique as both the generative core of his project and a crucial source of unresolved problems.[12]

It is not surprising, then, that similar themes surface in Hugo Meynell's "transcendental Thomist appraisal" of Dooyeweerd's philosophy. Because so much has already been written on these themes, however, and because many readers may be unfamiliar with Dooyeweerd's own writings, it is not obvious how a reformational philosopher should respond to Meynell's appraisal. Also, in answering a wide range of different critics, Dooyeweerd significantly changed his approach to transcendental critique. So one has ample potential for communicative disaster. Perhaps I should begin with the contours of and changes to Dooyeweerd's own conception. Then I shall defend Dooyeweerd from several of Professor Meynell's criticisms. Since his criticisms also call attention to problems in Dooyeweerd's conception, however, I shall conclude by identifying these problems and indicating how they should be addressed.

## 1. TWO CONCEPTIONS

Most Dooyeweerd scholars agree that he had more than one conception of what he calls "the transcendental critique of theoretical thought." They disagree, however, about the number, content, and significance of those conceptions. They also face a peculiar complication: Dooyeweerd's *New Critique* adds significant new material to the already lengthy "Prolegomena" that began the first volume of *De Wijsbegeerte der Wetsidee*. Moreover, the English version recasts the material in the Dutch original and neither clearly distinguishes nor smoothly joins the new material and the old. A first-time reader lacking access to the Dutch original or to the relevant secondary literature would not easily detect that Dooyeweerd had changed his mind about the scope and motivation of his own project. Exacerbating the problem is the fact that the two popularized versions of Dooyeweerd's philosophy in English draw on different phases in his project.[13] Whereas J.M. Spier's *Introduction*, which Meynell cites, stems from a book published in 1938 and based on *De Wijsbegeerte der Wetsidee* (1935–36),[14] L. Kalsbeek's *Contours*, which Meynell does not cite, derives from a book published in 1970 and based on *A New Critique of Theoretical Thought* (1953–58) and other of Dooyeweerd's later writings.[15]

John Kraay suggests that Dooyeweerd had three different conceptions of the relation between faith and philosophy, and *New Critique* contains two of them.[16] The first of the three, dating from around 1926, gives primacy to the "life-and-world view" of the philosopher's religious community. In this conception, the idea of God's universal law is both the core and the "organon" of a Calvinist worldview, to which Dooyeweerd's own philosophy would give expression. The second conception, most prominent in WW and other writings from the 1930s, gives primacy to the transcendent "Archimedean point" that every philosopher must find. The Archimedean point is the "fixed point" that enables a philosopher to form "the idea of the totality of meaning [*zin-totaliteit*]" (NC 1: 8, WW 1: 10). On this point depends every philosophy's "law-idea" or "cosmonomic idea" (*wetsidee*), which is always a "transcendental ground-idea" (*wijsgeerige grondidee*). The Archimedean point chosen by Dooyeweerd's own philosophy resides in "the root, reborn in Christ, of the human race, in which we participate via [the religious, time-transcending root of our individual personality,] our reborn selfhood" (NC 1: 99, WW 1: 64).[17] Dooyeweerd worked out his third conception in the 1940s. He consolidated it, interestingly enough, in *Transcendental Problems of Philosophic Thought* (1948), his first book in English. Here primacy goes to "ground motives" as the dynamic spiritual forces that drive not only philosophy but culture as a whole. "Worldview" and "Archimedean point" no longer play a central role in Dooyeweerd's mature conception of the relation between faith and philosophy. He argues instead that every philosophy must employ three "transcendental ideas" – ideas about origin, unity, and coherence – whose direction is set by the dominant religious ground motive in a culture or subculture. According to Kraay, it is only with this third conception that Dooyeweerd formulates a "transcendental critique" in the proper sense. Now transcendental critique replaces the "law-idea" or "cosmonomic idea" as the key to Dooyeweerd's philosophy.[18]

Whatever the precise historical details, it is clear that Dooyeweerd has more than one conception of the relation between faith and philosophy. Indeed, the "Prolegomena" to *New Critique* (NC 1: 1–165; cf. WW 1: 3–135) presents two different ways in which to carry out a transcendental critique.[19] The first way hinges on Dooyeweerd's Archimedean point conception.[20] It argues – from ontological claims about creation, epistemological claims about the nature of everyday experience and theoretical thought, and metaphilosophical claims about philosophy itself – that every philosophy requires an "Archimedean point" whose origin cannot itself be solely theoretical or philosophical. Rather, every philosophy's Archimedean point presupposes a "choice of position" with respect to the "Archè," the origin of everything, including philosophy and philosophers themselves (NC I: 11–12, WW I: 13–15). This choice can only be made by the entire human being in his or her heart. As such, the choice, like the Archè, is religious, not merely theoretical or philosophical. In this fundamental sense religion makes philosophy possible, regardless of the details of a particular philosopher's work.[21]

Fully worked out, however, an argument along these lines seems to presuppose what it wishes to conclude. In addition, it neither explains nor promotes the possibility of philosophical dialogue across religious boundaries. Strictly speaking, it is more a transcendent critique than a transcendental one. Although Dooyeweerd had responses to such criticisms, dissatisfaction with his argument led him to develop what the *New Critique* labels a "second way." From here on I shall understand this second way as "Dooyeweerd's transcendental critique."[22] Certainly it is most in keeping with his own description of a transcendental critique of theoretical thought as "a critical inquiry (respecting no single so-called theoretical axiom) into the *universally valid conditions which alone make theoretical thought possible, and which are required by the immanent structure of this thought itself*" (NC I: 37).[23]

## 2. DOOYEWEERD'S TRANSCENDENTAL CRITIQUE

What are the universally valid conditions that make theoretical thought possible? Essentially, says Dooyeweerd, there are three. They can be indicated by asking three transcendental questions. First, what makes it possible for theorists to engage in abstraction from ordinary experience and from the structures of creation, which people ordinarily experience in a holistic fashion?[24] Dooyeweerd's answer lies in the notion of a "Gegenstand relation" that is peculiar to theoretical thought and is distinct from an ordinary subject/object relation.[25] His answer goes roughly like this: The only way for scientists and philosophers to proceed is to develop careful, logical definitions and explanations of what they study. To do this, they must exclude many sorts of phenomena from their field of investigation, even though the phenomena themselves resist such exclusion. When theorists carry out the theoretical process properly, the result is an intentional abstraction that neither directly "corresponds" to "reality as such" nor arbitrarily imposes a mental construct on the subject matter.[26] In Dooyeweerd's own vocabulary, it is unavoidable that, in the act of theorizing, the logical and nonlogical aspects of thought (and of creation) stand in opposition, even though people ordinarily experience no such opposition outside theoretical endeavours.

This gives rise to a second transcendental question: What makes it possible for theorists to achieve a synthesis between those aspects of experience and of creation that must stand in opposition when theorizing occurs?[27] Dooyeweerd's answer to this "problem of intermodal synthesis" has two parts.[28] First, he argues that the required synthesis cannot be achieved starting from either side of the unavoidable opposition, either from the logical or from the nonlogical side. Such an approach would simply transpose the original opposition into yet another opposition; the theoretical antithesis would not be transcended. Second, he suggests that the only possibility for such a synthesis lies in the fact that the theorist is more than a theorist. The act of theorizing is itself carried out by a unitary agent in whom the various aspects of experience and of creation always already cohere. This agent cannot be a Cartesian or Kantian *cogito*: to be able to think, the "I" that thinks must be more than its thinking. Kant was right to posit the necessity of critical self-reflection for solving the problem of theoretical synthesis. But Kant failed to see that the underlying unity provided by the human self is "a *central and radical unity*," and it "*transcends*" all the aspects of experience and creation that theorists can distinguish and understand, including the logical aspect (NC I: 51).[29] Theoretical synthesis necessarily presupposes "a supra-theoretical starting-point which must transcend theoretical diversity" (NC I: 46).

Now a third transcendental question arises: What makes it possible for theorists to engage in such theory-transcending and critical self-reflection?[30] Again Dooyeweerd's answer has two parts. First, the act of theorizing cannot itself make such self-reflection possible, since the antithetical structure of theoretical thought excludes the underlying and rich unity needed. Second, what alone can make such self-reflection possible is the radical unity of the self itself. Only such a radically unified self can give theoretical thought a "concentric direction" pointing theoretical thought beyond itself. Once theoretical thought takes this concentric direction, it finds that the self, too, despite its radical unity, is nothing in itself. Rather, the self is highly dependent on something (or, better, someone) other than itself. To put it more explicitly, the self who, among other activities, engages in theoretical thought, depends for its own existence on the human community to which it belongs and on the "absolute Origin" of everything that exists. Since Dooyeweerd considers this relation of dependence to be the core of religion, he can say that the critical self-reflection structurally necessary for engaging in theoretical thought is itself made possible by the religious nature of being human. By "religion" he means "the innate impulse of human selfhood to direct itself toward the *true* or toward a *pretended* absolute Origin of all temporal diversity of meaning, which [diversity] it [human selfhood] finds focused concentrically in itself" (NC I: 57). As the Dutch text makes clear, religion is a matter of the heart and its direction.[31] On the heart's direction depends everything human beings are and do, including their scientific and philosophical activities. Hence the "central significance of the 'heart'" for Dooyeweerd's all-important "discovery of the religious root of thought itself" (NC I: v, WW I: v–vi).

So Dooyeweerd's transcendental critique of theoretical thought argues that every philosophy has a religious root, regardless of its specific stance on issues of faith, theology, and traditional topics in philosophy of religion. This is so, not because every philosopher has consciously and carefully decided for or against the God revealed in scripture, creation, and Jesus Christ, but because philosophical thought could not even get started if theoretical abstraction, theoretical synthesis, and their supratheoretical transcendence were not possible. In the end, what makes all of this possible is the integrity of the human self in relation to its true or supposed origin.

Were this the end of Dooyeweerd's account, we might think that he has not really explained the relation between faith and philosophy. And in one very obvious sense Dooyeweerd would agree, for he does not equate faith and religion.[32] Whereas religion encompasses and connects all of human existence with its origin, faith is simply one aspect of human existence alongside others.[33] Religion sets the direction of faith just as much as it sets the direction of thought or politics. But faith is no more optional to human existence than is thought or politics. To trace the relations between faith and philosophy, a follower of Dooyeweerd would need to do at least three things: show how, as modes of human existence, both faith and thought stem from religion; show how the activities of faith relate to the activities of theoretical thought; and show how, in a specific sociohistorical setting, the content of a particular tradition of faith intersects the content of a particular school of philosophy. In recent years, it seems to me, most Christian philosophers addressing the relation between faith and philosophy have started with the third of these and have only sporadically considered the first and second. Dooyeweerd could provide a valuable correction in this respect.

Here is where Dooyeweerd's much-disputed discussion of "ground motives" plays a crucial role. Having made the argument that philosophy would not be possible without religion in Dooyeweerd's sense, he proposes a detailed account of how religion actually informs philosophical thought.[34] In brief, he argues that all human communities are driven by spiritual dynamic forces working through what he calls "religious ground motives."[35] Philosophy is no more immune to these spiritual forces than is faith or politics. They take shape within philosophy itself by virtue of three "transcendental ideas." Not surprisingly, these ideas concern the (1) coherence, (2) totality or radical unity, and (3) origin of "all meaning" (NC 1: 69) – i.e., of all creation. Taken together, they constitute the "cosmonomic idea" (*wetsidee*) or "transcendental ground-idea" inherent to any philosophy. By calling such ideas "transcendental" Dooyeweerd indicates both that philosophy (indeed, all of theoretical thought) cannot avoid having such ideas and that the ideas concern whatever sets the conditions for theoretical thought yet exceeds its complete grasp. According to his fundamental intellectual-historical hypothesis, a significant correlation obtains between the actual content of these ideas in philosophy at a certain time and the religious ground motives that drive the communities from which particular philosophies arise and to which these philosophies contribute.

Implicitly following Abraham Kuyper,[36] Dooyeweerd says four ground motives have been dominant in Western philosophy and culture. The first, an outworking of the Holy Spirit, is the motive, central to the Bible, of "*creation, fall, and redemption by Jesus Christ in the communion of the Holy Ghost*" (NC 1: 61). Two other ground motives are outworkings of "the spirit of apostasy from the true God." They occur as the dialectic of form and matter ("form-matter motive") that dominates classical Greek culture and philosophy and as the dialectic of nature and freedom ("nature-freedom motive") that dominates modern humanist culture and philosophy (NC 1: 61–2). Dooyeweerd describes the fourth ground motive as follows: "The scholastic ground motive of nature and supernatural grace originates from the attempt to accommodate the Greek form-matter motive and the radical biblical ground motive to each other. In the scholastic theology of Thomism it gains its hold on Christian thought; it permeates Roman Catholic church doctrine, theology, philosophy and sociology. Reformed Protestant thought also, by and large, continues to be open to the religious influence of the scholastic ground motive – as a result it soon loses its reforming impulse."[37] Even without Dooyeweerd's detailed attempts to document the "nature-grace" ground motive, his implicitly linking it with apostasy and his explicit rejection of such a synthesis would be enough to set Thomist teeth on edge, not to mention traditionalist Calvinists and intellectualist Kuyperians. If his intellectual-historical intuitions were approximately right, however, this would call for a massive reconstruction of Christian philosophy and theology.

It is only against this backdrop that Dooyeweerd's concern for the "inner reformation" of philosophy and all the sciences begins to make sense. As Geertsema explains,

> One of the ground motives determines the content of the cosmonomic idea ... of any given thinker. In this way the religious ground motive controls the direction of thought via the transcendental ground-idea. The transcendental ground-idea forms the inner point of contact between [religion] and science. Inner reformation, then, is guided by the biblical ground motive, which is expressed in the transcendental ground-idea of divine Origin, unity in Christ ... and coherence and diversity within time. In the first place this inner reformation applies to philosophy, but because the various disciplines ... necessarily imply a view of diversity in reality and so of unity and origin, it also relates to the sciences in general.[38]

Hence the transcendental critique of theoretical thought provides a way to explore the impact of religion on the unavoidable "boundary concepts" of philosophy and science, past and present. It simultaneously serves to remind Christian scholars of their spiritual direction on the issues that matter most. And it does all of this without burying philosophy and science in the details of a particular tradition of faith or theology. In that sense, Dooyeweerd's transcendental critique accomplishes for scholarship what Kuyper accomplished for social policy: to be both unreservedly modern and unashamedly Christian. Not surprisingly, the strongest objections have come from those who would rather have modernity without Christianity or Christianity without modernity.

## 3. RELIGION, RATIONALITY, AND RADICAL DEPENDENCE

"Transcendental Thomists" such as Bernard Lonergan share Dooyeweerd's general sense of the challenges facing Christian scholars. They, too, want their philosophy to be genuine philosophy, not crypto-theology, even as it raises the transcendental questions that hard-bitten secularists might dismiss or avoid. So I find it a bit surprising that Hugo Meynell's objections draw so heavily on traditional Thomism. In part these objections stem from misreadings of Dooyeweerd, encouraged, perhaps, by relying too heavily on the simplistic and combative prose of the popularizing pastor J.M. Spier, whose book lacks the subtleties of Dooyeweerd's transcendental critique. But in part they stem from those intellectual commitments to rational autonomy and self-subsistent existence that Dooyeweerd attacks in Greek, medieval, and modern philosophy. Rather than give an extensive response to each of Meynell's objections, I shall group them under the headings of religion, rationality, and radical dependence.

### *3.1 Religion and Fideism*

Meynell's essay suggests in various places that Dooyeweerd is a fideist for whom no common basis can exist for dialogue and debate across "ground motives" and especially between fully Christian and "apostate" philosophy. The flip side to this suggestion is a worry that Dooyeweerd would require Christians to avoid the methods and practices of established academic disciplines such as differential calculus or standard behavioural research on the Norway rat. These concerns are misplaced. They can easily be alleviated within Dooyeweerd's own conception. Let me explain.

Dooyeweerd, like Kuyper, has a strong notion of "common grace." Thanks to God's providential care, much good occurs in society and culture (including philosophy) regardless of the life-direction ("religion" in Dooyeweerd's very broad sense) from which a particular product, practice, institution, or social pattern arises. It occurs despite the fall, "original sin," "total depravity," and all the other obstacles identified in traditional Calvinist theology. Accordingly, Dooyeweerd's ground motive analysis gives only part of his assessment of Western philosophy and philosophies. He also tries to show that the fundamental structures of God's creation make possible philosophy and all other human endeavours and accomplishments. These structures the participants both acknowledge and (mis)interpret. A Christian faith commitment gives one no special advantage in that regard, both because all humans are finite and fallible and because the antithesis between good and evil cuts right through humanity and through each human heart. Dooyeweerd cannot credit whatever good occurs, whether in philosophy or elsewhere, either to the faith commitment of the practitioner or to some shared "rationality," but only to God's common grace, as sustained and carried out through God's laws for creation ("creation" in a broad sense that includes human beings, culture, and society). He *can* say forthrightly and from the outset, however, that his criticisms of "immanence-philosophy" are cases of "self-criticism" (NC 1: viii, WW 1: x).[39]

Now I admit Dooyeweerd has a more fideist side, especially in his writings prior to the 1940s, a side stressed by J.M. Spier. But it conflicts with the "common grace" side, which allows a more generous understanding of culture and welcomes dialogue, debate, and learning across philosophical and religious divides. The fideist side alone cannot explain Dooyeweerd's battles with the radical fideists in his own theological tradition, both Dutch Calvinists and American Presbyterians such as the "presuppositionalist" Cornelius Van Til. In any case, Meynell neglects the tension between fideist and nonfideist tendencies in Dooyeweerd's own conception. This tension has generated considerable creative effort among reformational philosophers, especially at the VU University Amsterdam and the Institute for Christian Studies in Toronto.

Yet there is one crucial respect in which Dooyeweerd simply cannot be a fideist. He does not think that faith, whether as a human capacity or as the content of a particular tradition, sets the direction for philosophy and science. Religion does, and religion is ontologically and epistemologically prior to both faith and scholarship. In this sense, whether or not one makes "explicit reference to God or Christ" is beside the point of whether a certain ground motive is at work in the transcendental ideas informing one's philosophy. Similarly, if Dooyeweerd wishes Christians who philosophize to be "Christian all the way down," this cannot mean that he wants them to substitute faith talk for philosophy proper. Moreover, he opposes all "immanence philosophy" not, first of all, because it "is built up ... independently of God and God's revealed Word"[40] but because it misunderstands the nature of philosophy, denies the dependence of theoretical thought on something beyond itself, and finds the locus and origin of meaning in creation.

For such reasons I think it is fundamentally mistaken to say that "for Dooyeweerd, as for Barth, belief cannot argue with unbelief, but only preach to it." Dooyeweerd's crucial insight is not that human thought lacks satisfactory foundations or that "no satisfactory foundations for human thought can be set out."[41] Rather it is his claim that most attempts to spell out such foundations miss the actual "foundation" of human thought in the human heart and thereby in either the true origin of existence or some substitute. Dooyeweerd can affirm with Lonergan the importance of "attentiveness," "intelligence," and "reasonableness." But Dooyeweerd would deny that these provide the sort of foundation that, say, Descartes vainly sought. He would also deny that they supersede the dependence of even the most attentive, intelligent, and reasonable thought on that which transcends thought and makes it possible.

### *3.2 Rationality and Scientism*

All of this has relevance for questions concerning rationality in Meynell's essay. At one place, for example, he says: "Apparently Dooyeweerd would deny ... that some people can teach others the principles of good reasoning, and [the] scientific method in particular, while prescinding from the question of whether the Christian faith is true."[42] On my own reading, Dooyeweerd would not deny that such "faith-neutral" or "faith-detached" teaching and learning can occur. The fundamental antithesis does not lie between faiths, for faith itself is only one aspect of human life among many. It lies instead between comprehensive life-directions – toward God or toward some part of creation. Presumably a Christian could be just as torn between these two directions as anyone else. Hence the Christian should, in all due humility, learn and be ready to learn from others, whatever their faith.

Dooyeweerd would not point to "rational principles" as the basis or enabling conditions for such learning, however, but rather to the laws of God's creation and the Holy Spirit's ongoing presence in history, culture, society, and human life. Dooyeweerd would also ask why philosophers, whatever their faith or purported lack of faith, put so much stock in "rational principles." And he would ask whether the account he gives of "rationality" might not do two things better than other accounts: (1) explain the importance of culturally bound "positivizations" of God's laws in this area (e.g., the rules of first-order logic) and (2) explain the inherent limitations, fallibility, and cultural variability of such "positivizations."[43] For Dooyeweerd, "rationality" is a limited but important aspect of human life as God has created this. Like all such aspects, rationality is made possible by God's laws and sustained by God's Spirit. When exercised by human beings in community, rationality is no less susceptible to evil and no less open to redemption than any other aspect of human life. The key to such renewal, however, does not lie in rationality itself but in how God's Spirit works in the hearts of humanity.

For Dooyeweerd, as for many other non- or anti-foundationalists, two questions must arise whenever someone appeals to "rational principles" as the basis for dialogue and debate: (1) What counts as rationality? (2) Why does such rationality count for so much? Dooyeweerd is by no means an irrationalist, of course. He seeks a better basis for rationality, properly understood, than that founded by the great celebrants of reason such as Kant, the obvious chief target of *A New Critique of Theoretical Thought*. Still, Dooyeweerd is not primarily interested in grounding Christian apologetics or explaining the intrinsic "rationality" of a "Christian position." Rather he aims to work out the philosophical implications of a creation-oriented life-direction that takes seriously both radical evil and God's great sovereignty and love. In some ways, his is a very Augustinian project of philosophical construction. As Alvin Plantinga suggests, such a constructive approach remains "the most difficult" and "in some ways the most important" task facing Christian philosophy today.[44]

Why, then, would rationality be important in Dooyeweerd's account? Because the capacity to analyze, argue, and reach conclusions yields logical insight into God's laws and their human outworkings that would otherwise be unavailable. Yet logical insight is not the only kind of insight human beings need, and it is itself subject to divine laws, as are all other aspects of human existence. Does this mean that science, where specialized searches for logical insight occur, can be properly pursued only on the basis of extra-logical and faith-oriented insights, as Meynell interprets Dooyeweerd to be saying? Does Dooyeweerd hold that "all scientific work is really committed to a philosophical, and so indirectly to a religious stance"?[45] Yes and no. Yes, insofar as no academic discipline can avoid boundary questions concerning the relationship of its subject matter, methods, and results to those of other fields. To that extent, no academic discipline can do without transcendental ideas concerning origin, unity, and coherence of the sort that arise in philosophy and that express religious ground motives (NC 1: 545–66, WW 1: 508–30). Yet this does not imply that all scientific work is "really committed" to philosophical and religious stances in the sense that scientists themselves must hold specific philosophical theorems or beliefs of faith, either surreptitiously or properly, or must let these control the course of investigation.[46] Like Geertsema, I doubt that Dooyeweerd's talk about the inner reformation of the sciences "really meant that the Christian starting-point would change the disciplines in the same way that it changed philosophy ... In any case the fruitfulness of Dooyeweerd's philosophy ... seems to lie not so much in an alternative way of doing science, with its own theories and results, as in indicating the limits of science's pretensions and presenting a framework in which scientific theories and results can be interpreted. This applies both to specific sciences and to science as such."[47] In other words, Dooyeweerd exposes scientism and rejects ontological and methodological reductionism, but he does not make the sciences subservient to either faith or philosophy. In this, too, he wishes to be both modern and Christian.

Perhaps the confusion in Meynell's reading here arises from his assuming that "the human subject" is the individual human being rather than a transcendental subject. This assumption is suggested by Meynell's talking about how "a person's Christian commitment should affect her work as a scientist," his asking rhetorically what part "Paul's Christian faith had in his tent-making business," and his wanting to say that there can be "the honest seeker" who is not just an "apostate."[48] When Meynell says that a transcendental Thomist "would strongly agree with Dooyeweerd that the human subject is at the base of all philosophy or scientific theory,"[49] it is not clear that Meynell and Dooyeweerd have the same "subject" in mind. Dooyeweerd's "ego" or "heart" or "religious root of human existence" is not the existing individual as such. Neither is it a Kantian transcendental subject, in the strict sense. It is the central, dynamic, and directed relationship that all human beings sustain, in their entirety, both individually and corporately, toward God, toward fellow humans, and toward the rest of creation.[50] Dooyeweerd's transcendental critique tries to show that the very possibility of theoretical thought, and hence of science and philosophy, depends upon thought's being subject to God's laws and being oriented either toward the very source of those laws or toward some substitute. Accordingly his fundamental questions lie at an altogether different level from the question of what difference an individual's faith-commitment makes for their practice of philosophy and science or for the results of such practice. Meynell's essay overlooks this difference in level.

### *3.3 Radical Dependence*

Dooyeweerd held that his transcendental critique of theoretical thought would doubly enhance "the mutual exchange of ideas between the different schools of philosophy." First, schools that oppose each other but share the same ground motive could "meet with better mutual understanding" once they understood how their opposition stemmed from "the same central ground motive." Second, schools that proceed from different ground motives could learn to evaluate their own starting points and begin to understand "that fruitful philosophical dialogue can only begin when the transcendental problems of philosophical thought *as such* are critically accounted for." The dialogue between his philosophy and neo-Thomism, carried out on this basis, "has led to increasing mutual depth of insight," he says. He invites "every school of thought" to be a "partner in this critical discussion, which replaces dogmatic defensiveness with mutual critical self-reflection, and replaces the *hubris* of exclusivism with philosophical modesty born of insight into the *relativity* of all philosophical totality views." He welcomes them all to the table, not because he is a philosophical relativist, but because he recognizes how everything, including philosophy, is relative to its origin: "*Meaning is the being of all that has been created; it is religiously rooted and is of divine Origin.*"[51]

This idea of creation's radical dependence on the Creator marks both the continuity and the discontinuity between reformational philosophy and transcendental Thomism. Both schools affirm that "reality" is God's creation, but they disagree about the implications of their affirmation for philosophical categories. Professor Meynell frequently suggests that traditional categories inherited from Aristotle's metaphysics will do just fine, and that even Dooyeweerd implicitly employs such categories. Dooyeweerd, by contrast, goes out of his way to show why categories such as "being" and "substance" are religiously loaded and philosophically problematic. Yet, as Meynell notes, even some of Dooyeweerd's followers suggest that his philosophy is more Aristotelian than he admits.

A key question here, it seems to me, is not whether Dooyeweerd resembles Aristotle, since it is hard to find any major philosopher after Aristotle whose thought does not resemble Aristotle's in some respect. One wants to know instead whether Dooyeweerd breaks with Aristotle on central questions of ontology, epistemology, and ethics. I think the answer has to be yes, he clearly does. Dooyeweerd's "modal order" implies no hierarchy of levels. His "structures of individuality" are functional rather than substantial. His emphasis on creational law and the radical distinction between Creator and creature resists any metaphysics of being. And his critique of theoretical thought rejects any privileging of theory, even in the form of philosophy or theology.

The other key question is why Dooyeweerd so adamantly opposes ideas such as "being" and "substance." Contra Meynell, it is not simply because they are "infected by the form-matter religious ground motive."

It is certainly not because Dooyeweerd fails to recognize that his discussion of the "individuality structures" of "things" addresses what "traditional philosophy" has dealt with "under the rubric of 'substance.'"[52] Dooyeweerd opposes the idea of "substance" because he finds the notion of permanent self-subsistence both untrue to ordinary experience and internally antinomous.[53] In addition, of course, Dooyeweerd regards this category as incompatible with the radical dependence of creation on the Creator. Given such charges, it will not do simply to cite Aristotle or Thomas as authorities or to claim without adequate backing that on balance they got things mostly right. Dooyeweerd argues that when it comes to understanding plants, animals, human beings, cultural products, and social institutions, the substance theories of Aristotle and Thomas get things significantly wrong. He also proposes an elaborate alternative theory of the "structures of individuality,"[54] and he shows how his theory is compatible with the functional concepts of modern science. In that respect, too, I find he has more in common with Lonergan than Meynell's essay highlights.

## 4. SECOND THOUGHTS

I have tried to show why Dooyeweerd is not a simple fideist, why he considers rationality important, and why he rejects Aristotelian metaphysics. Yet I do not want to leave the impression that Meynell's objections lack all merit or that Dooyeweerd's philosophy does not warrant criticism. Let me mention some problems in Dooyeweerd's conception of transcendental critique, in order to suggest how one could address them without abandoning his project. The problems pertain to the flawed structure of his argument and perplexities surrounding his notion of religion.

### 4.1 *Logical Slippage*

Reduced to its barest outline, Dooyeweerd's transcendental critique of theoretical thought goes like this: (1) No one could engage in theoretical thought were it not for universally valid conditions that make such thought possible. (2) Any philosophy can identify these conditions by analyzing the structure of theoretical thought itself. (3) Such an analysis shows that three universally valid conditions make theoretical thought possible: (a) the "Gegenstand relation" between logical and nonlogical aspects, (b) the supra-theoretical unity of aspects found in the theorizing agent, and (c) the agent's radical dependence on something other than itself that makes this agent possible. (4) This dependence can only be either on the "absolute Origin" of everything that exists or on some substitute that is itself dependent on the "absolute Origin." (5) No system of theoretical thought[55] can avoid employing all-pervasive ideas about the ontological status of the universally valid conditions that make theoretical thought possible: ideas about the coherence, unity, and origin of everything. (6) The most crucial and unavoidable sources for the content of such ideas are supra-theoretical and religious ground motives that grip human beings in their hearts and direct them either toward the "absolute Origin" or some substitute. (7) A biblical ground motive is the crucial and unavoidable source for the transcendental ideas guiding this account of how theoretical thought is possible and how it is necessarily religious in root. (8) The transcendental ideas guiding this account concern (a) the temporal and intermodal coherence of meaning, (b) the "deeper identity" of the modal aspects of meaning "in a religious unity" (NC 1: 79), and (c) the divine origin of meaning in its coherence and unity.

For the sake of argument, let me ignore complications from the *New Critique*'s combining two "ways" of transcendental critique, overlook infelicities in Dooyeweerd's actual formulations, and assume the soundness of each premise. Even with all those concessions in place, I think two sorts of logical slippage beset his transcendental critique. In the first place, it seems self-referentially incoherent. That is to say, his critique does precisely what it declares impossible: it provides a theoretical account of that which surpasses the limits of theoretical thought. Given Dooyeweerd's account of theoretical thought, his philosophical identification of the supra-theoretical unity of aspects and the agent's radical dependence would need to set certain aspects of this unity and dependence over against the logical aspects of thought itself. But if that were done, the unity and dependence could not be grasped as supra-theoretical unity and radical dependence. On the other hand, if the grasping of unity and dependence were not achieved by Dooyeweerd's own theoretical thought but in some supra-theoretical fashion, then this would bode ill for any philosophy that theoretically attempts to identify the universally valid conditions for theoretical thought. So Dooyeweerd's account of the universally valid conditions for theoretical thought seems to subvert the very attempt to give such an account. He tries to get around this by saying that "critical self-reflection in the concentric direction of theoretical thought to the ego necessarily appeals to self-knowledge (which goes beyond the limits of the theoretical [G]egenstand relation)" (NC I: 59). But he fails to see that philosophical reflection *on* such critical self-reflection – philosophical reflection such as his transcendental critique provides – is not in itself the same as critical self-reflection. The question remains whether, on Dooyeweerd's account of theoretical thought, such philosophical reflection can be theoretical. If it cannot be theoretical, then it cannot be philosophical either.

The second sort of logical slippage concerns circularity in Dooyeweerd's argument. If premises 5–8 are right, then they cannot help but be presupposed in premises 1–4. There are specific cases of this. It seems impossible, for example, to formulate the notion of the "Gegenstand relation" (3a) without presupposing a temporal and intermodal coherence of meaning (8a). It also seems impossible to conclude that the agent's radical dependence can only be on the "absolute Origin" or a substitute (4) without presupposing the divine origin of meaning (8c). In some places Dooyeweerd even acknowledges such circularity and embraces it. He says, for example, that his philosophy's "posing of the transcendental problem is controlled from the start by those supra-theoretical presuppositions which are not exposed until the final stage of the transcendental critique."[56] Better to have one's theory controlled by supra-theoretical presuppositions that "free theoretical thought from dogmatic 'axioms' standing in the way of a veritable critical attitude" and to acknowledge this up front, he says, than to have one's theory enslaved to unacknowledged supra-theoretical presuppositions while pretending that it is, and that all theory should be, free from such presuppositions (NC I: 56). But this rejoinder would be somewhat beside the point I am making. To move from premises 1–4 to premises 5–8, it seems to me, Dooyeweerd must presuppose the *content* of his idea of the divine origin of meaning (8c) and import it into his *formal* claims about the agent's radical dependence (3c) and (4). Otherwise one could grant that the agent's radical dependence is required for theoretical thought to be possible and still not suppose that the "other" on which it depends is either the "absolute Origin" or some "substitute." Since Dooyeweerd's transcendental critique intends to convince other philosophers of the validity of that critique, such circularity, while not "vicious," is certainly troublesome for Dooyeweerd's own project.

I do not have the space here to provide adequate repairs to Dooyeweerd's argument. It would not suffice to introduce a more "transformational" and less "antithetical" picture of how Christian philosophy relates to other schools of thought, although that would help.[57] Nor would the problems disappear if one took Dooyeweerd's transcendental critique in "hermeneutical" directions, although that would help as well.[58] Both the problem of self-referential incoherence and the problem of circularity stem from his (neo-Kantian) understanding of the limits to theoretical thought. What he formulates as "transcendental conditions" are intended to show that theoretical thought is not self-sufficient, that it unavoidably depends on that which is not itself theoretical. But one can construe this notion of "that which is not itself theoretical" in more than one way. It can refer to human activities and experiences that are not theoretical, or to topics and objects that are not theorized, or to processes and structures that make theoretical thought possible. It can also refer to whatever in principle exceeds the grasp of theoretical thought. Dooyeweerd combines some of these meanings, so that the processes and structures that make theoretical thought possible cannot in principle be theoretically grasped, although they can be indicated by way of "transcendental ideas." Since his transcendental critique is itself a theoretical enterprise, however, made possible by the same "supra-theoretical" matters, he finds himself in the awkward position of doing in theory what his theory of theory says cannot be done. Not even importing "supra-theoretical" religious content by way of a presupposed "transcendental idea" can extricate him from what Hegel would call the dialectic of the limit. The only way to salvage some version of Dooyeweerd's transcendental critique, it seems to me, is to redescribe the structure of theoretical thought, recognizing that every theoretical attempt to declare something beyond the limits of theory has already surpassed those limits.

## 4.2 *"Religion"*

An inescapable corollary to such redescription would be thoroughly recasting Dooyeweerd's notion of religion. I do not intend to propose an alternative notion here, but simply to indicate why I think one is needed to salvage Dooyeweerd's transcendental critique. As I understand Dooyeweerd, his notion of religion tries to accommodate three sets of competing considerations. Consequently it embodies tensions between unity and diversity, between universality and particularity, and between transcendence and historicity.

The first tension arises from the necessity of distinguishing religion from that which is not religion while holding that religion is all-encompassing. On the one hand, Dooyeweerd sees religion as an inescapable and all-embracing condition of being human. It is not simply a part of human existence, and it is not something added to the rest of human existence. Rather, it is all of human existence in its deepest unity and in relationship to the (pseudo-)origin of all existence. On the other hand, he cannot avoid using language and categories that distinguish religion from that which is not religion – philosophy, for example, or science, or art, or politics. Such distinctions can make it sound as if religion has sufficient independence to "express" itself in philosophy or science or art and to "give direction" in these affairs. Add to this the complication that Dooyeweerd does not identify religion with faith, and one begins to wonder what content his notion of religion holds. These matters are crucial for Dooyeweerd's transcendental critique: his entire argument turns on the claim that theoretical thought would not be possible if it did not have a "religious root." Indeed, Dooyeweerd's own intellectual conversion occurred with "the discovery of the religious root of thought itself" (NC I: v, WW I: v).

With respect to the second tension, it is clear that, although Dooyeweerd understands religion as an inescapable condition of being human, he does not want to leave it at that formal level of universality. He sees religion as a matter of life and death, as that on which an individual's or a community's destiny hinges. So religion also needs to be something each of us experiences – or, better, each of us is and enacts – in the depths of our particular selves. The tension between transcendence and historicity arises for similar reasons. On the one hand, Dooyeweerd understands religion as the directed connection between human beings and God or some substitute for God, and he understands God as transcending all of creation. On the other hand, he wants to say that such a connection occurs within human history. It develops, it takes new turns, it involves a world-historical battle between good and evil. Otherwise there would be little point to identifying "religious ground motives" and tracing their historical manifestations in philosophy and culture.

When push comes to shove, however, Dooyeweerd's notion of religion privileges unity, universality, and transcendence over diversity, particularity, and historical phenomena. And this unitary, universal, and transcendent thrust results in a type of mysticism that reinforces the logical slippage I have already identified.[59] The reinforcement comes when Dooyeweerd describes the human heart, the religious root of human existence, as "supra-temporal." This makes religion "supra-theoretical," even though religion is at the core of human existence. Consequently, what is most central to being human, and what unifies all we are and do, cannot be grasped philosophically, theologically, sociologically, or in any other theoretical way. But Dooyeweerd's transcendental argument cannot afford to declare religion off-limits for theoretical inquiry. Nor does his own practice of identifying and tracing religious ground motives support such a view of religion, even though he assigns minimal content to these dynamic spiritual forces as such. Dooyeweerd leaves us with a perplexing, internally conflicted notion of religion that nevertheless serves as the pivot to his transcendental critique.

Any attempt to salvage Dooyeweerd's project must address both the logical slippage in his transcendental argument and the conceptual confusion in his account of religion. A brief comparison of two books that do much to rearticulate Dooyeweerd's philosophy for a North American audience will bear this out. In *Understanding Our World*, Hendrik Hart reserves discussion of the issues raised by Dooyeweerd's transcendental critique for what he titles "Appendix: A Concluding Prescientific Postscript."[60] There, Hart avoids the problems in Dooyeweerd's argument by abandoning the idea that either the transcendental relation between theory and religion or the specific version of that relation in a Christian philosophy can be successfully argued. In this way Dooyeweerd's theoretical prolegomenon to reformational philosophy threatens to become a personal faith-professing postlude, as I have shown elsewhere.[61] Hart retains Dooyeweerd's transcendental impetus without the critique.

Roy Clouser's *The Myth of Religious Neutrality*, by contrast, begins with the claim that everyone has "religious beliefs" in something that has "the status of not depending on anything else" or of being "self-existent."[62] From there Clouser needs only a few steps to conclude that every comprehensive theory, whether philosophical or scientific, is controlled by the contents of the religious beliefs it presupposes. And because of the abstractive character of theorizing, any theorist who takes something other than the God revealed in Scripture to be the self-existent being on which everything else depends must make claims that are "self-performatively incoherent."[63] So it seems Clouser skirts the problems in Dooyeweerd's argument by turning it into what Dooyeweerd would call a "theologically transcendent critique," one that "subjects the different results of philosophical thought to the test of Holy Scripture or of a church dogma that is thought to be infallible."[64] Clouser retains Dooyeweerd's critical impetus without the transcendental argument.[65]

The difference between Hart's and Clouser's appropriation of Dooyeweerd's transcendental critique – personal confession on the one hand, transcendent criticism on the other – strikingly illustrates two ways to avoid addressing the problems in Dooyeweerd's argument.[66]

Neither way addresses the dialectic of the limits to theoretical thought. Moreover, Hart and Clouser's fundamentally opposed accounts of religion, which emphasize different sides to the notion of religion in *New Critique*, do not provide convincing alternatives to Dooyeweerd's own account. Although Professor Meynell does not discuss either Clouser or Hart, he has identified puzzles in Dooyeweerd's bold project that neither adequately addresses. These puzzles merit the attention of anyone who thinks seriously about the relation between faith and philosophy. They remain generative challenges for the tradition of reformational philosophy that Dooyeweerd helped create.[67]

# 2

# Reformational Philosophy after Dooyeweerd and Vollenhoven

## (2006)

Let me begin by quoting from an essay that prompts the discussion at hand. J. Glenn Friesen concludes his article "Dooyeweerd versus Vollenhoven" as follows: "Reformational philosophy may choose to follow Dooyeweerd. Or it may follow Vollenhoven. But it cannot purport to follow both philosophers. It may of course decide to reject both and to strike out in some entirely new direction."[1] I want to propose that these are bad options. Reformational philosophy should not follow Dooyeweerd. It also should not follow Vollenhoven. And if it were to "reject both" and "strike out in some entirely new direction," it could no longer pretend to be reformational.

### 1. LIVING TRADITION

I have two reasons to say "following" and "rejecting" are bad options. One has to do with the character of an intellectual tradition. The other has to do with the meaning of philosophical critique. On the first topic, I submit that living and lively intellectual traditions do not thrive on discipleship, nor on repeating the master's words, nor on keeping the tradition pure from contamination. If "following" Dooyeweerd and Vollenhoven only means accepting and spreading their doctrines, or restating their positions in more contemporary language, or defending their ideas from corruption, then following them, paradoxically, will kill their contributions. Jürgen Habermas's comment about ethnic cultures applies to intellectual traditions as well: "Cultures survive only if they draw the strength to transform themselves from criticism and secession."[2] Yet to transform through criticism is not to reject the founding figures and texts of a tradition and to head in an "entirely new direction" either. Rather it requires coming to terms with the generative challenges of one's own tradition.

My second reason to refuse the choice between "following" and "rejecting" concerns the meaning of philosophical critique. Now there *is* a style of doing philosophy that simply repeats what the masters have said. Some critics of continental philosophy might accuse its worst practitioners of doing exactly this. Let me call it the sycophantic style. This style turns the "big figures" into sacred gurus and the covey of commentators into uncritical acolytes. Others might accuse the worst practitioners of analytic philosophy of just the opposite tendency: always being on the attack, seldom accepting what other philosophers have said as truly worthwhile, and never letting on how much one has learned from those whom one attacks. Let me call this the idiopathic idiom. It turns every potential contribution into grist for the critic's own logic-chopping mill. Like Dooyeweerd and Vollenhoven, I believe that both the sycophantic style and the idiopathic idiom are incompatible with genuine philosophical critique, and genuine philosophical critique is central in coming to terms with one's own philosophical tradition. Hence neither uncritical acolytes nor logic-chopping millers are likely to address the generative challenges of reformational philosophy as they are found in Dooyeweerd and Vollenhoven.

Instead I recommend what I call a "critical retrieval" of Dooyeweerd and Vollenhoven. This is the project of acknowledging valid objections and, in light of such objections, providing a redemptive critique of their philosophies. It is not enough, in my view, simply to defend Dooyeweerd or Vollenhoven against misinterpretations, to reject inadequate criticisms, and to promote the concerns and claims their critics neglect. One also needs to address legitimate criticisms of Dooyeweerd and Vollenhoven and to suggest viable alternatives. Otherwise the retrieval of their projects will not be a fully critical retrieval. Accordingly, reformational philosophy today should take up such criticisms. It should show where these are valid or invalid, and then offer alternatives that, while inspired by the first generation of reformational philosophy, also avoid its problems. Through such critical retrieval, we can propose new directions for reformational philosophy *after* Dooyeweerd and Vollenhoven. This philosophy will be "after" them in a triple sense: being indebted to them, it will "come after" them, but only by "going after" their loyal critics.

We are fortunate that Dooyeweerd and Vollenhoven were their own best critics: best, not in the sense that they sparred successfully and frequently in public, but rather that their differences mattered and they knew that they mattered. Dooyeweerd and Vollenhoven knew very well the contours of the land they surveyed and the significance of variations between the maps they drew. But they never lost sight of the fact that they were philosophical pioneers from a shared confessional tradition who could accomplish more in concert than in conflict. Because of this, one can find in their differences, as articulated in their own reticent words, the generative challenges of reformational philosophy as an intellectual tradition. Let me discuss one such challenge by considering how they themselves attempt a genuine philosophical critique.

## 2. MODES OF CRITIQUE

The project of Dooyeweerd and Vollenhoven is breathtaking in its scope. They attempted nothing less than to reexamine the entire tradition of Western philosophy and to develop a comprehensive alternative that resonates with the Good News of Jesus Christ. A central question for both of them is, "How should Christian scholarship position itself with respect to Western philosophical traditions?" They have somewhat different answers. In the early work of Dooyeweerd and Vollenhoven from the 1920s and 1930s, one finds an emphasis on antithetical critique. Later, especially in Dooyeweerd's writings from the 1940s and 1950s, one finds this antithetical emphasis incorporated into a more dialogical model, in the form of a transcendental critique. Whereas antithetical critique positions Christian scholarship as distinct from, and significantly opposed to, much of Western philosophy, transcendental critique positions Christian scholarship as calling everyone's attention to that which makes any scholarship possible.

Actually Vollenhoven's approach can better be called (anti-)thetical critique, to highlight the fact that he wished to begin with certain theses, to be "thetical." The most important theses derive from a Calvinist understanding of central themes in scripture. Hence Vollenhoven called for a "scriptural philosophy," for a philosophy that is in line with scripture. Such a philosophy will work out the philosophical implications of the most fundamental insights that come from God's "word revelation" and are mediated by a specific (Calvinist) faith tradition.[3] At the same time, however, scriptural philosophy must always distinguish itself from traditions of thought in which such insights are lacking. Such distinguishing can be called "(anti-)thetical." It is still *thetical*, since its own fundamental insights or theses shape its interaction with other traditions, but it is also *anti*-thetical, because the primary concern motivating such interaction is to distinguish one's own position and tradition from other positions in other traditions.

It is not hard to see how the spectre of relativism could haunt (anti-) thetical critique. Correlatively, however, such critique has unusual strengths as a mode of articulating the philosophical implications of a specific tradition, whether it be a faith tradition or some other cultural or social tradition. Moreover, for Vollenhoven the point of establishing differences between the basic themes of "scriptural" and "unscriptural" philosophy is so that Calvinism can *contribute* to the *reformation* of philosophy itself.

Before turning to Dooyeweerd's approach, let me highlight one other thing. Vollenhoven locates the key to a philosophy's being unscriptural in its "basic themes" – i.e., in what it actually says as a philosophy, not in its motivation, or the philosopher's life, or what effects the philosophy may have. Examples of such "basic themes" in Vollenhoven's historiography are subjectivism and objectivism or nominalism and realism. In other words, Vollenhoven does not confuse the question of content with the question of intent. Nor does he reduce questions of validity to questions of genesis and effects. So too, his objections to synthesis aim at the basic themes of a philosopher's work, not simply at the philosopher's presuppositions or intellectual tradition or associations with others.

Where Vollenhoven emphasizes "basic themes," Dooyeweerd emphasizes "ground motives." A ground motive is a spiritual dynamic that pervades a society and culture and comes to philosophical expression in certain "ground ideas" or "transcendental ideas." A central point of Dooyeweerd's transcendental critique is that every philosophy is unavoidably in the grip of one ground motive or another. Moreover, only philosophy in the grip of the "biblical ground motive" can be radically Christian.

By a "transcendental critique of theoretical thought" Dooyeweerd means "a genuinely critical ... inquiry into the universally valid conditions which make the theoretical attitude possible and which *are demanded by the intrinsic structure of the latter.*"[4] Dooyeweerd distinguishes a transcendental critique from either a philosophically "immanent" or a theologically "transcendent" critique. An immanent critique would stay within someone else's philosophical position and ask whether this position is consistent with its own claims. A theologically transcendent critique would evaluate someone else's philosophical position from outside, asking how that position measures up to what the Bible or church teaching says. By contrast, a transcendental critique examines those "universally valid conditions" that make possible any and every philosophical position, including one's own position. Without a transcendental critique, a transcendent critique would be "dogmatic … and … of no value to philosophy," Dooyeweerd says.[5] It is not clear to me whether he would regard Vollenhoven's notion of "scriptural philosophy" as tending toward transcendent critique and perhaps in danger of becoming "dogmatic."

In any case, Dooyeweerd's leading question is whether autonomy is required in order for philosophy to be genuine. His answer is no: autonomy is not required. In fact, autonomy is impossible, and when attempted, it undermines genuine philosophy. That is why he talks about the "pretended autonomy" of theoretical thought. But what does "pretended autonomy" mean? *In the Twilight of Western Thought* formulates this in various ways: as the claim that genuine philosophy and science must be independent of "all religious presuppositions"; or that "the ultimate starting-point of philosophy should be found in this thought itself"; or that genuine philosophy "lacks any presupposition of a supra-rational character"; or that autonomy "is a necessary condition of any true philosophy."[6] What the claim comes to depends somewhat on which philosophical position is making the claim. To call the claimed autonomy "pretended" means that, although independence from any religious or supra-rational presuppositions may be avowed, such independence is not genuine, and the claim made for such independence is not supported by truly critical argumentation.

Elsewhere I have called attention to problems in Dooyeweerd's transcendental critique.[7] Yet it is important to see the genius in Dooyeweerd's approach. His attempt to position the reformational contribution to Western philosophy does not appeal to the content of a certain confessional tradition. Rather it appeals to the structural conditions that make possible any philosophy. Although he is not entirely consistent in how he makes this appeal, and although some of his own successors have challenged it, one has to admire his playing the game the way other philosophers play it, and his challenging them to play at a higher level than they have heretofore.

## 3. IMMANENT CRITICISM

What is missing from Dooyeweerd's approach, however, and not sufficiently emphasized in Vollenhoven's notion of scriptural philosophy either, is a proper appreciation of the role of immanent criticism.[8] Immanent criticism holds another philosopher's position to its own internal standards and criteria, thereby taking seriously the claims this position raises. Without immanent criticism, it becomes too easy to dismiss another philosopher's position without really understanding the issues at stake or the philosopher's actual contribution. That is why, in my own work, I have emphasized immanent criticism "with metacritical intent."[9]

So we return to where this brief discussion began. I claimed earlier that neither following nor rejecting Dooyeweerd or Vollenhoven is a good option. Now I can say that, given their own differences about modes of critique, and the underlying unity of their commitment to an inner reformation of Western philosophy, the best way to continue what Dooyeweerd and Vollenhoven began is to engage in a critical retrieval of their own philosophies, and of the philosophies they would criticize. Neither an (anti-)thetical nor a transcendental stance will suffice. Immanent criticism is important for anyone within the reformational tradition who comes after their philosophies; it is a hallmark of critical retrieval.

# 3

# Dooyeweerd's Conception of Truth: Exposition and Critique

## (2008)

[T]he decisive blow against the idea of religiously neutral philosophy must be delivered on the field of the problem of truth ... The postulate of neutrality always stands and falls with an idea of truth that takes theoretical truth to be self-sufficient.

Herman Dooyeweerd[1]

A transformed idea of truth is central to the project of reformational philosophy. If, as Dooyeweerd claims, the postulate of religiously neutral philosophy depends upon the purported self-sufficiency of theoretical truth, then reformational attempts to free scholarship from "immanence philosophy," without returning to "Christian synthesis thinking," will stand or fall with an idea of truth that does *not* take theoretical truth to be self-sufficient. Surprisingly little progress has occurred on this idea beyond Dooyeweerd's own efforts and Vollenhoven's insistence on "the necessity of a Christian logic."[2] Yet considerable headway has been made on the postulate of religious neutrality and the structure of theoretical thought. Now reformational philosophers need to rearticulate the insights into "truth" formulated by Dooyeweerd, Vollenhoven, and their generation, while building on subsequent contributions about religious neutrality and theoretical thought.

That is why "truth" has become my primary research project. Inspired over the years by Hendrik Hart's work on epistemology,[3] and by the genial insights of my *Doktorväter* Calvin Seerveld and Johan van der Hoeven, I have decided to reexamine the philosophical idea of truth. The project has two stages. The first stage, already published, concerns the contentious concept of "artistic truth."[4] The second stage is to present a comprehensive idea of truth, for which the concept of artistic truth provides one articulation. As I hope to show, this project takes seriously Dooyeweerd's conception of truth. The current essay summarizes his reflections on "truth" in *A New Critique of Theoretical Thought* and explains where I agree and disagree. A subsequent essay indicates how my preliminary account of truth addresses problems in Dooyeweerd's reflections.[5]

## 1. HORIZONAL TRUTH

Opposing any attempt to isolate "theoretical truth" from the "religious fullness of meaning," Dooyeweerd insists on the "perspectival structure of truth." This means that any particular truth claim, and any type of truth, will derive its truth character from its location within layered and interlinked horizons of human experience and vis-à-vis "transcendent Truth."[6] After Nietzsche, however, subjectivistic connotations often accrue to the terms "perspective" and "perspectival." So I prefer the term "horizonal" and often substitute it for Dooyeweerd's "perspectival" (*perspectivisch*).

### 1.1 *Synthesis and Intuition*

The notion of truth's horizonal character responds to what Dooyeweerd identifies as the central problem of theoretical knowledge: namely, to explain how the "intermodal synthesis of meaning" is possible.[7] His solution has two parts. First, he distinguishes and relates three types of epistemic coherence. Second, he claims that all three types are made possible by and informed by a radical unity that exceeds all three.

The three types of epistemic coherence are "meaning-systasis" (*zin-systase*), "logical synthesis" (*logische synthesis*), and "intermodal meaning-synthesis" (*inter-modale zin-synthesis*). *Meaning-systasis* is not a type of synthesis, strictly speaking. Rather it is the pre-synthetic coherence that makes possible the integral and full-bodied experience people ordinarily have when they are not engaged in theoretical inquiry. Dooyeweerd insists that ordinary meaning-systasis has "cosmological priority" over theoretical intermodal synthesis. In fact, anyone who ignores this priority "cannot even properly pose the [problem of knowledge]" (NC 2: 429, WW 2: 359). *Logical synthesis*, the second type of epistemic coherence, occurs within both ordinary experience and theoretical inquiry. It has to do with the logical unity we achieve among distinct concepts and judgments, always in relation to a logical object-side.

Unlike meaning-systasis and logical synthesis, *intermodal synthesis* occurs only in theoretical contexts. Although it is made possible by both meaning-systasis and logical synthesis, it is made necessary by the peculiar structure of theoretical thought. For in theoretical inquiry we must abstract the various aspects of experience and reality from their systatic coherence and make explicit distinctions among them, such that the logical aspect virtually opposes nonlogical aspects. In Dooyeweerd's terms, theoretical thought is uniquely characterized by this "Gegenstand relation" between logical and nonlogical aspects and by the problem of intermodal synthesis.

The cosmological priority of ordinary meaning-systasis and the operation of logical synthesis in all thought do not solve the central problem of theoretical knowledge. To secure intermodal synthesis requires deeper transmodal connections. Dooyeweerd finds these deeper connections in two locations: theoretical intuition and cosmological self-consciousness.

"Theoretical intuition" gives Dooyeweerd a way to connect theoretical abstraction with that from which abstraction is made. Theoretical thought typically abstracts from the continuity of cosmic time that pervades and sustains all experience. Yet the act of theoretical abstraction cannot itself occur abstractly. Rather, our thought's logical function, which we oppose to nonlogical functions, remains "embedded in cosmic time itself." This embedding occurs through intuition. Intuition is the "temporal bottom layer" (*tijdelijke dieptelaag*) whereby logical thought remains "in continuous temporal contact with all the other modal functions [that] our selfhood can claim in time *as its own*" (NC 2: 473, WW 2: 408). Insofar as this connecting of logical and nonlogical functions specifically supports our achieving intermodal synthesis, it can be called "theoretical intuition." Theoretical intuition is the meaning-connecting and meaning-distinguishing insight at work in theoretical thought (NC 2: 479, WW 2: 414). As a precondition whose "continual temporal character" exceeds the grasp of theoretical thought, theoretical intuition "cannot be theoretically isolated" (NC 2: 473, WW 2: 408). Theorists cannot grasp it in a concept or category. They can only approximate it in a transcendental idea, through which theoretical thought, led by faith, rediscovers itself in cosmic time.

Theoretical intuition does not rest with making transmodal connections, however. It pushes toward cosmological self-consciousness and, in "intuitive reflection [*bezinning*]" (NC 2: 479, WW 2: 414), refers beyond itself to the "religious root" of all knowing: "In the transcendental temporal direction of theoretical intuition, our selfhood becomes *cosmologically conscious of itself* in the temporal coherence and diversity of all its modal functions." The selfhood thereby becomes aware of itself as "the religious root" of all knowing, a root that "transcends" all of the self's "temporal acts and modal functions" (NC 2: 473, WW 2: 408).

### 1.2 *The Horizon of Experience*

This capacity for intuitive, reflective, and cosmological self-consciousness is crucial for freeing epistemology from the postulate of religious neutrality. Nevertheless, Dooyeweerd believes there is something right about Kant's epistemological notion of "the *a priori*," about its predecessor in Aristotle's metaphysical notion of "'the universal' as the ... 'ground of being' of individual things," and about Husserl and Scheler's phenomenological notion of essential possibilities. What such notions indicate, but misconstrue, is the multilayered "horizon of human experience" (NC 2: 543–7, WW 2: 475–8).

To account for this horizon, Dooyeweerd initially distinguishes between a "structural" and a "subjective" a priori complex, or, more simply, between "the *structural* and the *subjective a priori*" (NC 2: 548, WW 2: 478). The structural a priori is a multilayered horizon of human experience that "has the character of a *law*." Cosmological rather than epistemological, it amounts to "the *a priori meaning-structure of our cosmos itself*" that "is given in the Divine order of ... creation [*goddelijke scheppingsorde*]" (NC 2: 548, WW 2: 478–9). The subjective a priori, by contrast, is epistemological rather than cosmological. It is "*the subjective a priori insight*" into the structural horizon of human experience. Necessarily "enclosed within" this structural horizon and "determined and delimited" by it, such insight, unlike the structural horizon itself, "can be *true* or *false* in an epistemological sense." Contra Kant and Husserl, however, subjective a priori insight "can never be the self-sufficient foundation [*grond*] of truth" (NC 2: 548, WW 2: 478).

When Dooyeweerd describes the various components to the horizon of human experience, he begins with the transcendent and necessary religious horizon as both a structural and a subjective a priori. It is *structural* in the sense that God's central law – to love God above all and our neighbour as ourselves[8] – holds for all human experience and makes it possible. The religious a priori is *subjective* in the sense that, being "at bottom religiously determined," all human experience proceeds in one of two directions: either toward God, or away from God and toward some creaturely substitute (NC 2: 552, WW 2: 482).

The other four components are the cosmic temporal, modal, synthetic, and plastic horizons. In their ontological scope, they can be depicted as successively smaller concentric circles, all of them encompassed by the transcendent religious horizon (NC 2: 560, WW 2: 491–2). But in their accessibility to ordinary experience, they could be portrayed in reverse sequence as a narrowing funnel, from the largest and plastic horizon, which lies near the surface of ordinary experience, to the religious horizon, which "belongs implicitly to human experience" and "is only made explicit in ... transcendental and in ... radical religious self-reflection" (NC 2: 550).

Whereas the religious horizon is *transcendent*, cosmic time is the *transcendental* horizon of human experience. All of human experience, like the cosmos to which it belongs, is held together in a "temporal meaning-coherence," in accordance with God's "order" for creation (*scheppings-ordinantie*) (NC 2: 552, WW 2: 482). Such temporality becomes manifest in the other three horizons. The modal horizon is the coherence and diversity of modal aspects that provide an a priori structure for all human experience, both theoretical and pre-theoretical (NC 2: 553–4, WW 2: 483–4). The next horizon is specific to "theoretical experience." It is the intermodal meaning-synthesis whose structure governs all theoretical knowledge. Correlated with this structural a priori is theoretical insight into it. Properly acquired only via transcendental self-reflection, such insight is "the *subjective-fallible a priori* of all epistemology" (NC 2: 554, WW 2: 484–5). Finally there is the a priori plastic horizon of human experience – the entire latticework of "structural principles" that govern different types of entities, events, and societal relationships. The plastic horizon is a priori in the sense that "it *determines* the experience of the variable individuality of things and alone *makes it possible*" (NC 2: 559, WW 2: 490). It is with reference to this account of horizonal components that Dooyeweerd distinguishes between religious and theoretical truth.

### *1.3 Religious Truth*

Dooyeweerd's account of experiential horizons implies that "religious" or "transcendent" or "absolute" Truth has priority over all other expressions of truth. It has priority, not as one *type* of truth that has greater importance than other types of truth, but rather as the very *fullness* of

Truth without which no true knowledge of any sort would be possible. Well aware of the potential objection that his approach makes "epistemology end in a Christian sermon or in a dogmatic [assertion]," Dooyeweerd forthrightly embraces the scandal of the cross. We "cannot attain ... true self-knowledge [*waarachtige zelf-kennis*]," or true knowledge of the created world either, he says, "without true knowledge of God, which cannot be gained outside of the divine revelation in Christ" (NC 2: 562, WW 2: 494). Both scripture and John Calvin provide this insight, and both "synthesis philosophy" and "immanence philosophy" have lost sight of it. The inclusion and dependence of all true knowledge, including theoretical truth, vis-à-vis the true knowledge of God "is the only purely Biblical view [of knowledge] and the alpha and omega of any truly Christian epistemology" (NC 2: 561, WW 2: 492).

This means that Dooyeweerd's own conception of truth relies very heavily on his account of religious Truth and of its relation to theoretical and pre-theoretical truth. His initial account (NC 2: 560–5, WW 2: 491–7) goes like this. The religious horizon encompasses all the others and radiates (*heen-straalt*) through all of human experience. Yet this horizon – the religious root of human existence – is not self-sufficient. Rather, it exists only in relation to its divine origin (NC 2: 560, WW 2: 492). All of human knowing (*kennisactiviteit*) is directed either toward "the absolute Truth" or toward "the spirit of falsehood," thanks to "the transcendent religious subjective *a priori* of ... cosmic self-consciousness." We know (*weten*) temporal reality in its relationship to the structure of human selfhood as a religious community (*religieuze verbands-structuur*), in which individuals participate (NC 2: 562, WW 2: 494).

Not only is such knowledge structurally possible but also, in knowledge about God (*in de kennis omtrent God*) from God's revelation, we actually and worshipfully (*aanbiddend*) understand "the absolute Truth," albeit in mortal weakness and limitation. Such knowledge is primarily "enstatic" rather than synthetic, pre-theoretical rather than theoretical, and thus in a strict sense not theological either. "[T]rue knowledge of God and of ourselves" concerns "the *horizon* of human experience." It rests upon a childlike and trusting acceptance, "with our full personality and with all our heart," of divine revelation in the "indissoluble unity" of both its "transcendent-religious" and its "cosmic-immanent" meaning. In order for such knowledge to occur, the entire person must be turned around (*omkeering*) in a life-giving (*levend-making*) restoration of the horizon of our experience. This restoration makes it possible again to understand reality "in the light of Truth" (NC 2: 562–3, WW 2: 494–5).

Dooyeweerd gives two reasons why a lengthy discussion of *religious* truth is important for his account of *theoretical* truth. On the one hand, it helps him address the failure of modern immanence philosophers, when opposing relativism and skepticism, to provide a sufficiently robust conception of truth. On the other hand, his idea of religious truth helps fill a gap in Christian philosophy: namely, the lack of its own "*Christian idea of truth*" – i.e., an idea "really ... fed by its Christian religious root" and not simply borrowed from either Greek metaphysics or modern immanence philosophy (NC 2: 565–6, WW 2: 498). Dooyeweerd, by contrast, calls for an "inner penetration" of Christian philosophy by Christian religion.

### *1.4 Standing in the Truth*

Although Dooyeweerd does not abandon Kant and Husserl's search for "the *a priori* structure [*zin-structuur*] of truth," he accords truth the same horizonal or perspectival character as the horizon of experience. Hence the only proper approach to truth will take its departure not from the "absolutized ... theoretical-synthetical horizon" but from the "transcendent, religious fullness of Truth." This point of departure "does not concern an abstract theoretical function of thought. It [concerns] our full *selfhood* ... the *heart* of the whole of human existence, consequently also the [heart] of our theoretical thought" (NC 2: 571, WW 2: 504).

So the fullness of Truth is not first of all something to be understood but something to stand within. It is to be lived and experienced by "standing in the Truth." For Dooyeweerd, to stand in the Truth is to participate (*deelhebben*) "in the fullness of meaning [*zin-volheid*] of the cosmos in Christ." To stand in the Truth is to take hold of (*aangrijpen*) God's revelation with all of one's heart, and thereby to break free from "the prejudices of immanence philosophy" concerning the horizon of human experience and to no longer overestimate the roles of theory and science in human life (NC 2: 564, WW 2: 496–7).

The "hearted" character of Truth, if I may call it that, is so crucial that Dooyeweerd devotes several paragraphs to showing how this emphasis both accords with scripture and aims to transform scientific inquiry from top to bottom. The primary link with scripture lies in the notion of "standing in the Truth." Derived from biblical interpretation, the phrase suggests the dependability, certainty, and trustworthiness that "truth" means in the Bible. The selfhood's standing in the Truth, by wholeheartedly accepting God's revelation, is the primary prerequisite for thought's having a "truthful *a priori* attitude [*apriorische ware instelling*]." Such acceptance occurs through faith, as a complete confidence or trust (*vertrouwen*) in the dependability (*vastheid*) of God's word. This does not rule out either the noetic effects of sin or the discovery of relatively true insights by non-Christian thinkers. Yet it does suggest that all "relative truths" can be *true* "only … in the *fullness* of [Truth], revealed by God in Christ." They become untrue when "absolutized into a 'truth in itself.'" The challenge for Christian scholarship is to let this radical and holistic idea of truth "permeate scientific thought from root to crown," rather than resting content with "an edifying confession of faith" that does not disturb "the immanent course of scientific investigation" (NC 2: 572, WW 2: 504–5).

## *1.5 Theoretical Truth*

Only after insisting on our whole-heartedly "standing in the Truth" does Dooyeweerd present two general ideas of theoretical truth and two more specific criteria. The two ideas correlate, more or less, with the temporal and the synthetic horizons of experience, and the two criteria with the modal and plastic horizons. All involve an accordance (*overeenstemming*) between the subject-side and the law-side of such horizons.[9] Dooyeweerd labels the two general ideas "transcendental truth" and "transcendental theoretical truth" (NC 2: 573, WW 2: 506). The more specific criteria pertain to transcendental theoretical truth (NC 2: 579–80, WW 2: 513–15).

In implied opposition to Aquinas, Dooyeweerd says that transcendental truth cannot be an "*adequatio intellectus et rei.*" Rather, we should define it as an accordance between "subjective *a priori* knowledge" and "a priori structural laws of human experience." This knowledge is "enclosed [*omsloten*] by the temporal horizon" and is "expressed in a priori judgments." So too, the laws of experience occur "within this temporal horizon," in openness (*ontslotenheid*), on both law-side and subject-side, to "the light of the transcendent Truth in Christ" (NC 2: 573, WW 2: 506).[10] To arrive at transcendental truth, our subjective knowing (*kennisactiviteit*) must be in a "normative relation" with the "*a priori* structural laws" that obtain for it. Even this relation "is *not self-sufficient*," however. It must be open to transcendent Truth. The philosopher's heart must be gripped by divine Truth, which discloses (*ontsluiten*) and liberates the transcendental horizon of our experience (NC 2: 573–4, WW 2: 507–8).

Whereas accordance between a priori knowledge and a priori structural laws defines transcendental truth in general, the accordance peculiar to "transcendental theoretical truth" occurs between "the subjective *a priori* meaning-synthesis" and "the modal structure [*zin-structuur*]" of the intended Gegenstand. The subjective synthesis becomes actual (*actueel*) in a priori "theoretical insight" and receives expression in a priori "theoretical judgments." Moreover, the Gegenstand occurs within a universal (*alzijdig*) and temporal "intermodal coherence" that depends on Truth's "transcendent fullness of meaning [*zin-volheid*]" (NC 2: 575, WW 2: 509).[11] This definition provides the criterion of transcendental theoretical truth at work in Dooyeweerd's general modal theory. Each academic discipline must strive for an accordance between its meaning-synthesis and the relevant modal structures, he says, within the temporal coherence of experience, and "in relation to the religious fullness of Truth" (NC 2: 576–7, WW 2: 510–11). Nor does transcendental ignorance provide an excuse: every theoretical insight, whether a posteriori or a priori, must justify (*rechtvaardigen*) its claim to relative truth before "the forum of the Divine world-order" – even though one cannot have true philosophical insight into this order if one does not stand "in the full religious Truth of Divine Word-Revelation" (NC 2: 577, WW 2: 511).

Next Dooyeweerd takes up the possible objection that his account makes "the structure of theoretical truth" dependent on subjective insight into it. He replies that although subjective insight does not determine or govern the structure of theoretical truth, such insight is necessary in order to discover this structure. Then he indirectly repeats a suggestion made before: that his own account is not only in accord with the divine order of creation but also made possible by his own "religious standing in the Truth" (NC 2: 578, WW 2: 512).

Dooyeweerd offers two criteria that "*a priori* theoretical insight" must meet to be in accord with the divine world-order.[12] The first criterion pertains primarily to the modal horizon. It is the principle of excluding antinomies, to which Dooyeweerd always refers with the Latin phrase *principium exclusae antinomiae*. Antinomies arise, he says, when theoretical thought violates modal sphere sovereignty and intermodal coherence. The *logical* principle of noncontradiction is simply a dependent aspect of this "*cosmological* criterion" (NC 2: 579, WW 2: 513). To be justified, theories must avoid antinomies.[13] The second criterion pertains primarily to the plastic horizon. Dooyeweerd does not give this criterion a title. Perhaps we can call it "the principle of respecting individuality": theoretical thought should account for, and neither misconstrue nor ignore, the structures of individuality as these are "*given* in naïve experience" (NC 2: 579, WW 2: 514).[14]

Not even the findings of empirical scientific research are exempt from these two principles, nor from the general requirements of transcendental theoretical truth. For transcendental truth encompasses and makes possible factual truths. Ultimately, it is only because of the divine world-order, which obtains for both theoretical and pre-theoretical experience, that science can theoretically disclose (*ontsluiten*) reality and thereby "discover [*onthullen*] relative theoretical truths" (NC 2: 582, WW 2: 517–18).

To summarize: Dooyeweerd holds that religious Truth, which can be attained only by personally standing in the Truth, encompasses and makes possible all theoretical truth. So too, theoretical truth, which involves an accordance between subjective knowledge and the structural horizon of experience, encompasses and makes possible all so-called empirical truth in the academic disciplines. The two criteria according to which purported theoretical insights must be justified are the avoiding of antinomies and the respecting of individuality. In other words, religious Truth and its attainment are the *sine qua non* for theoretical truth. This raises the questions of whether Dooyeweerd's account puts authentically Christian scholarship in a privileged position, and whether it devalues the insights of scholarship that is not Christianly faith-oriented. Dooyeweerd readily acknowledges that other philosophers will likely find his account of truth scandalous. Whether the reason for this is the "scandal of the cross" remains to be seen.

## 2. CRITICAL RETRIEVAL

The question of whether Dooyeweerd privileges Christian scholarship arises from the centre of his project – namely, to deliver a "decisive blow against the idea of religiously neutral philosophy" (NC 2: 565, WW 2: 498). As we have noted, his entire account of theoretical truth relies very heavily on his account of religious truth. Moreover, Dooyeweerd's way of connecting religious and theoretical truth elicited many of the objections and reservations he met, not only from the neo-Kantians and phenomenologists of his day but also from reformational colleagues and successors.

That is why Dooyeweerd's conception of truth deserves and requires a critical retrieval. By this I mean the project of either raising or acknowledging valid objections and, in light of such objections, providing a redemptive critique of his contribution. To begin a critical retrieval of

Dooyeweerd's conception of truth, let me first identify the claims through which he has made an important contribution to philosophical truth theory. There are at least nine such claims:

1 That truth is "perspectival" or "horizonal" in character.
2 That the distinct horizons of truth are interlinked and point beyond themselves to the "fullness of truth."
3 That an adequate philosophical account of truth must distinguish and relate a "subject-side" and a "law-side."
4 That disclosure and truth, although not identical, are intimately connected.
5 That theoretical truth has an important place in human life but is not decisive in our meeting the requirements of truth.
6 That traditional notions of "*adequatio*" and modern notions of "correspondence" are inadequate ways to characterize both truth in its fullness and theoretical truth.
7 That propositional truth requires logical "objectivity," or, in my own terms, predicative availability and predicative self-disclosure.
8 That "standing in the truth" is crucial for acquiring insight into the "nature" of truth (although, I would argue, it is not a guarantee).
9 That a reformational theory of truth must take seriously scriptural notions of truth, including Jesus's description of himself as "the way, and the truth, and the life."[15]

My own proposals concerning truth and artistic truth incorporate all of these claims. Yet I think the way in which Dooyeweerd presents them is internally problematic, with the result that he does not offer an adequate and convincing conception.

Dooyeweerd's conception of truth suffers from two sorts of problems. On the one hand, he exaggerates the role of religious truth and misconceives its relation to theoretical truth. On the other hand, in exaggerating that role, he overlooks central questions of epistemology and truth theory. Let me demonstrate these problems by returning to five topics from my previous exposition – religious truth, horizon of experience, theoretical intuition, theoretical truth, and standing in the truth – and addressing them in that order.

### 2.1 *Structuralized Religion*

Dooyeweerd's conception of truth stands or falls with his account of religious truth. As section 1.3 showed, he treats religion as the transcendent horizon of experience. This treatment does not mesh with Dooyeweerd's own preferred understanding of religion.[16] Whereas in general structural horizons of experience are ontological *conditions* that make human life possible, religion for Dooyeweerd is the all-pervasive *direction* in which human life is oriented or the all-pervasive *spirit* in which it is lived. Although he speaks of religion as a fundamental relationship between human beings and (what they take to be) the origin of creation, this "relationship" differs dramatically from the relationships that make up the temporal, modal, and plastic horizons. In those horizons it makes sense to posit ontological relationships between structures that universally obtain and variable manners of creaturely existence, between a "law-side" and a "subject-side." But the "relationship" that characterizes religion is of a different order. It is one of divine invitation and human acceptance or rejection, of divine instruction and human learning, of divine guidance and human discovery.[17]

Dooyeweerd suggests this when he says divine truth must grip us (NC 2: 574, WW 2: 507), and we, in response, must take hold of God's revelation with all of our hearts (NC 2: 564, WW 2: 496). At bottom, as Dooyeweerd himself understands, religion is a relation of call and response. In this relation our response becomes a call to the God who calls, and the God who calls responds to our response. In other words, the relationship that characterizes religion is dynamic and dialogical, and it is not of a sort that can be captured in an ontological picture of structure and existence.[18]

Yet this ontological picture is precisely what Dooyeweerd paints when he writes about religion as the transcendent horizon of experience. He describes religion as the root of self-consciousness in which human experience transcends time (NC 2: 540, WW 2: 472–3). He talks about religion as a necessary structural and subjective a priori, a relationship in which God's central law determines, limits, and makes possible all human experience (NC 2: 552, WW 2: 482). He also says that the religious horizon encompasses all the other horizons. In each of these ways Dooyeweerd suggests that religion involves an ontological relationship between structure and existence, just as the other horizons of experience do.

Recognizing, however, that religion is of a different order, he tries to distinguish it from the other horizons by calling it "transcendent." So he ends up with a transcendent and supra-temporal horizon that nevertheless encompasses and makes possible all the other horizons, which are immanent and temporal through and through. Dooyeweerd never fully explains how that which is transcendent and supra-temporal can encompass and determine that which is immanent and temporal, an omission noted by several of Dooyeweerd's reformational colleagues, including Popma and Vollenhoven. This puzzle is the result, I think, of his compressing into a permanent structure the dynamic and dialogical relationship of divine call and human response, a structuralizing of religion with respect to both its directionality and its genetic unfolding in time. In effect, religion becomes the supra-temporal structure that makes all temporal structures possible.[19]

Dooyeweerd's structuralizing of religion has two undesirable consequences for his idea of religious truth: ontologically, religious truth must be both transcendent and immanent but cannot really be either; epistemologically, it must be unique and all-pervasive but cannot be both. As a result, theoretical truth loses its distinctive character and can truly be true only as a manifestation of religious truth. Let me explain.

We have seen that Dooyeweerd gives religious truth priority over all other expressions of truth. It is the very fullness of truth that makes any true knowledge possible. But what does it mean to say that religious truth makes all other truth possible? Two responses are available within Dooyeweerd's conception, one of them ontological and the other epistemological. Ontologically, religious truth is the condition of truth's possibility. Without it all the other horizons, and indeed experience itself, could not exist. Now there is a sense in which this is so: if human beings could not hear God's call and respond, then their lives would lack ultimate direction. Yet that is quite different from describing the structures that make human life possible as *dependent for their possibility* on religious truth. For in the latter formulation, God's call to love and human responses thereto turn into a permanent superstructure that lacks both processual and dialogical character. Religious truth becomes both absolute – always already trumping all other expressions of truth – and arbitrary – never changing in the context of the human responses it permeates. Yet it cannot really be absolute, since Dooyeweerd says it depends in turn on God as "Origin." Nor can it be arbitrary, for then it would not be true. So religious truth must be both transcendent and immanent but cannot be either.

Epistemologically, Dooyeweerd describes religious truth as the very fullness of meaning that serves as the "principle and foundation of all true knowledge" (NC 2: 562, WW 2: 494). The law-side to this fullness consists of God's revelation. The subject-side consists of our worshipful insight into God's revelation and our acceptance of it. Because law-side and subject-side together make up the horizon of religious truth, our ability to experience and understand God's revelation governs the extent to which the fullness of meaning can determine and enable all true knowledge. This may be the deeper reason why Dooyeweerd felt compelled to argue that his account does not make the structure of theoretical truth depend on subjective insight into it (NC 2: 577–8, WW 2: 512–13).

My worry in this context is different but not unrelated. Whereas in all other horizons the correlation between law and subject is primarily ontological, in the religious horizon this is not possible. For, as a good Calvinist, Dooyeweerd recognizes how the fall affects all responses to God's call or, in Dooyeweerd's vocabulary, all abilities to understand and accept the light of God's revelation. Moreover he inflects this recognition antithetically, setting up an unbridgeable epistemic divide between those who, having been turned toward God's revelation, can again understand reality "in the light of Truth"(NC 2: 563, WW 2: 495), and those who, having turned away from God's revelation, can at most come up with "relative truths" that are never, on their own, truly true.

This antithetical construal has two implications, both of them contrary to Dooyeweerd's own stated intentions. First, it puts a select group of people in a privileged position toward all truth, including religious truth, such that they cannot really learn from others. Second, it undermines his own repeated appeals for dialogue with other philosophers: according to his own account, they do not have access to the true religious knowledge that would make them capable of truly understanding the insights he offers. Both implications become apparent in the passage, quoted earlier, where Dooyeweerd suggests that one cannot have true philosophical insight into the divine world-order if one does not stand "in the full religious Truth of Divine Word-Revelation" (NC 2: 577, WW 2: 511).

Unfortunately this suggestion poses a catch-22 for immanence philosophers, who by definition do not stand in the Truth (see NC 2: 578, WW 2: 512). They are damned if they do seek accordance with the divine world-order and damned if they don't: so long as they are immanence philosophers, they will never stand where they should. The upshot is that, although religious truth must pervade all knowledge, it does not reach the vast majority of people, let alone the philosophers among them. Alternatively, if it were to pervade all knowledge, then religious truth would lose its distinctive character as an accordance between worshipful insight and divine revelation. Contrary to Dooyeweerd's intention, religious truth on an antithetical construal cannot be both unique and all-pervasive. This amplifies weaknesses in his conception of theoretical truth, as I shall demonstrate later.

One way to avoid such ontological and epistemological dilemmas would be to abandon Dooyeweerd's construal of religion as a transcendent horizon of experience. That would let one do justice to the categorical difference between the all-pervasive and direction-setting character of religion and the all-encompassing and condition-establishing character of ontological horizons. The religious dynamic of call and response does not set structural conditions for what is possible in human existence. Rather it sets us on, and sustains us along, the open pathways of our lives. Moreover, if religious truth is the "fullness of meaning," it is not the fullness of creational unity and coherence. Rather, it is the fullness of humanly responding, ever anew, to God's invitation, instruction, and guidance. This central insight of the reformational tradition needs to fully inform one's conception of truth.

## 2.2 *Limited Experience*

To this point I have simply accepted Dooyeweerd's account, summarized in section 1.2 above, concerning the other horizons of experience and their interconnections. Yet this account, too, is internally problematic, and it reinforces the tensions in his accounts of religious and theoretical truth. On the one hand, Dooyeweerd does not really show how the "structural a priori" in various horizons makes human experience possible. On the other hand, he builds fallibility into the very character of the subjective a priori within each horizon, raising questions about exactly what sort of a priori this is.

The first problem stems in part from Dooyeweerd's portraying the horizons as structural conditions that make other horizons possible. This portrayal distorts the subject-side within each horizon, and it makes some horizons subject to other horizons. What he should have said, it seems to me, is that there is one horizon, the temporal horizon, and this horizon makes all human experience possible. The modal and plastic "horizons" are simply different ways in which the temporal horizon obtains. They are not "encompassed"or "determined" by the temporal horizon. Rather they simply *are* that temporal horizon as it obtains both for how creatures, including human beings, exist and for what distinguishes them from one another in their existence.

Be that as it may, it is problematic to regard as "a priori" the structures that make up the temporal horizon in its modal and individual obtaining. They are not "a priori" in an epistemological sense. They may make *existence* possible, but that by itself tells us little about how *experience* and *knowledge* are possible. One notes here that Dooyeweerd actually says very little about how the structures of the modally and individually inflected temporal horizon make experience and knowledge possible. Instead, he builds a "subjective a priori complex" into the horizons of human experience. And he immediately adds that the subjective a priori is fallible. Epistemologically, however, this move raises new issues. If that which, subjectively, makes human experience possible is fallible, then it would equally, at least in certain respects, seem to make it impossible. To establish whether and when a fallible a priori does make experience possible, a transcendental philosopher would need to appeal to a superior a priori that is *not* fallible.

This, it appears, is the role Dooyeweerd assigns to the religious a priori, but only as it operates among those who have understood and accepted divine revelation. That brings back the problems already noted concerning religious truth, but with even greater impact. For now it emerges that no subjective a priori in any horizon can genuinely make experience possible if the subject of experience does not respond properly to divine revelation. Because Dooyeweerd construes religious responses in an antithetical manner, the absurd consequence follows that only Christians, or perhaps even only authentic Christians, would be subjectively capable of experience. In other words, religion would trump experience rather than direct and sustain it. We would not have an epistemology but rather a denial of epistemology. The "problem of knowledge" would be "solved" by taking it off the table. This solution would be philosophically scandalous, I admit, but hardly the "scandal of the cross." Nor do I think it is the result that Dooyeweerd actually had in view.

## 2.3 *Self-Referential Incoherence*

If, for the reasons already given, one abandons Dooyeweerd's claim that religious truth makes all other truth possible, one might regard his idea of theoretical intuition as an alternative account of what makes theoretical truth possible. For Dooyeweerd clearly regards theoretical intuition as a key to solving the central problem of theoretical knowledge, as we saw in section 1.1 above. Theoretical intuition makes possible the "intermodal synthesis of meaning." Without such a synthesis, in turn, there could be no accordance either between theoretical knowledge and structural laws in general or between a subjective "meaning-synthesis" and the Gegenstand's modal structure in particular. So theoretical intuition makes possible the intermodal synthesis that makes theoretical truth possible.

Despite the initial attractions of such a move, there are two reasons why it will not work. First, Dooyeweerd has no way, other than an appeal to religious self-consciousness, to establish the truth of theoretical intuition. In fact, he plainly states that theoretical intuition cannot be grasped theoretically. It cannot be turned into a modally delimited Gegenstand, nor does it have the abstractive and disjunctive character of theoretical thought. If the truth of theoretical intuition cannot be established theoretically, then it cannot serve as a transcendental condition of theoretical truth. If one did treat it as such a condition, one would land in a vicious circle.

The second reason is that Dooyeweerd's idea of theoretical intuition does not actually solve the problem of intermodal synthesis. The problem, we recall, is to explain how it is possible to achieve a synthesis between modal aspects that must stand in opposition when theorizing occurs. According to Dooyeweerd, theoretical intuition keeps our logical and nonlogical functions in continuous temporal contact, and, in its transcendental direction, propels us toward religious self-consciousness. But the idea of theoretical intuition does not explain how intermodal synthesis can be *achieved*. At most it explains why intermodal synthesis is *not impossible*. It indicates that a prior connection across our functions and across modal aspects is always already in effect when the act of theorizing begins. But this does not explain how a *reconnection* can actually occur once theorists have singled out the relevant Gegenstand. Dooyeweerd's "theoretical intuition" provides a source of discovery, not a source of confirmation. It helps us *discover* modal structures in their intermodal coherence. It cannot serve to *confirm or disconfirm* such discoveries once they have been worked out in theory.

In fact, Dooyeweerd's idea of theoretical intuition names a problem rather than offering a solution. It names a problem in his transcendental critique of theoretical thought. As I have explained elsewhere, the problem is one of self-referential incoherence.[20] Dooyeweerd tries to account theoretically for what he says lies beyond the capacity of theoretical thought to grasp. This is not an incidental problem, but one that lies at the heart of his transcendental critique. To account for the structure to theoretical thought, Dooyeweerd must theorize about that structure. But what is decisive in his account is the unity of modal aspects and the theorizer's radical dependence on an origin, both of which Dooyeweerd says lie beyond any theoretical conceptual grasp. Yet he himself provides a theoretical account of such purportedly supra-theoretical unity and dependence. To circumvent the dilemma of his giving a theoretical account of the supra-theoretical, Dooyeweerd introduces the notion of "critical self-reflection in the concentric direction of theoretical thought to the ego" (NC 1: 59). But this notion does not really help. For now the question arises whether his account of such critical self-reflection is itself theoretical, and thus whether he is still doing what he says cannot be done.

The idea of theoretical intuition reinforces this self-referential incoherence. For Dooyeweerd *must* say something theoretically about theoretical intuition, and one of the things he must say theoretically is that it cannot be grasped in theoretical concepts but can only be approximated in an idea. On what basis does he say this? Whence comes his insight into the nature of theoretical intuition? How can his insight be defended in the forum of philosophical debate? It is hard to see how Dooyeweerd could address these legitimate questions without employing theoretical concepts, and not simply theoretical ideas.

I have claimed that Dooyeweerd "must" say theoretical intuition cannot be grasped in theoretical concepts. He must say this because his idea of theoretical intuition provides a bridge across the systematic gap between his insisting on the fullness of religious truth and his acknowledging the distinctive character of theoretical truth. Unless he can bridge this gap, his radical claim for the religious rootedness of theoretical thought, including philosophy, would turn into a mere assertion: his epistemology would "end in a Christian sermon" (NC 2: 562, WW 2: 494). The philosopher in Dooyeweerd does not want this to happen. But I do not think his idea of theoretical intuition actually prevents this. That has consequences for his account of theoretical truth, to which we turn next.

## 2.4 *Tautologous Truth*

Dooyeweerd's general conception defines truth as a relationship between human knowledge and divine laws: between worshipful insight and God's revelation (religious truth), between human knowledge and the divine world-order (transcendental truth), and between subjective meaning-synthesis and the Gegenstand's modal structure within intermodal coherence (transcendental theoretical truth). Although one might think that he has proposed a correspondence theory of truth, Dooyeweerd does not locate the truth-defining relationship between intellect and thing (Aquinas) or between propositional truth bearers and factual states of affairs (modern correspondence theories). Rather, the relationship occurs between multidimensional knowledge and God's laws for reality and human life. Moreover, this relationship is not a correspondence but an accordance (*overeenstemming*). To be true, human knowledge must be in accord with God's laws – with the religious central law, with the structure of theoretical thought, with modal structures, and with structures of individuality. If anything, Dooyeweerd's conception is a type of coherence theory, for he emphasizes the truth-making coherence of all claims and insights within the religious fullness of truth.

The strengths of Dooyeweerd's conception, compared with many alternatives, lie in its holistic and normative character and in its radical refusal to divorce questions of direction from questions of structure. For Dooyeweerd truth is not a neutral topic of technical philosophy. It is a matter of life and death, and philosophy must do justice to this when offering a theoretical definition. Yet these strengths accompany notable weaknesses in the account of theoretical truth presented in section 1.5 above. Let me mention three.

In the first place, Dooyeweerd nowhere elaborates on "accordance." The notion points to an alignment or concurrence or concordance of the subject-side with the law-side. In what does this accordance consist? Accordance cannot simply mean the subject-side's *existing* in alignment, concurrence, or concordance with the law-side. Rather it must mean something like "having proper insight into" the law-side. What does having proper insight come to? It seems equivalent to having true insight. What distinguishes true insight from false? Dooyeweerd's answer seems to be that true insight is marked by its accordance with the law-side. Unfortunately that leaves us with an unhelpful tautology: accordance is accordance.

Dooyeweerd's two specific criteria aim to provide more content for the notion of theoretical accordance. The principle of avoiding antinomies does not really provide new content, however, since a negative principle leaves open many positive possibilities. And the positive principle of respecting individuality is so broad that any number of conflicting theories could legitimately claim to be doing just that. Yet Dooyeweerd would not say that all of these conflicting theories are true.

Second, in construing truth as an accordance between subject-side and law-side, Dooyeweerd ignores entirely the question of objectivity. This omission is striking, given both his own account of logical objectivity and prominent worries about objectivity in modern truth theories. Let me get at this issue by calling upon Vollenhoven's lecture notes on epistemology.[21] Vollenhoven introduces a tripartite distinction among the activity of coming to know (*het leren kennen*), that which can be known (*het kenbare*), and the content of the knowledge that results (*het resultaat*). All three occur in connection "with the entire cosmos" and "under the law of God."[22] We can have knowledge only if we come to know what is knowable and arrive at some content. With respect to the "cognitive interrelation" in the "analytic [i.e., logical] law-sphere,"[23] this implies that we come to know by distinguishing and relating what is knowable and arriving at concepts and judgments.

Clearly much of Vollenhoven's epistemology is compatible with Dooyeweerd's. Yet Vollenhoven's tripartite distinction is either absent or deeply submerged in Dooyeweerd's account of theoretical truth. Whereas Dooyeweerd defines such truth as an accordance between subject-side and law-side, Vollenhoven points to a crucial relationship *on the subject-side*: namely, the interconnections among knowing, the knowable, and the known. Truth in this complex could not simply be an accordance, say, between our activity of knowing and God's knowable law, nor between our concepts or judgments and God's law. It must involve a unique relationship within human knowledge among the epistemic subject's activity, the object toward which this activity is directed, and the results of such activity. Truth pertains not only to our knowing but also to what is knowable and what is known.

A third weakness in Dooyeweerd's account of theoretical truth concerns the character of human knowing. Although he recognizes the general importance of subject/subject relations and mentions the societal embeddedness of human knowledge (NC 2: 594, WW 2: 529), he does not account for the intersubjective character of theoretical knowing. Nor does he emphasize the importance of learning from others in the pursuit of theoretical truth. That, in turn, affects his general conception of truth, which lacks any notion of intersubjective validity. For Dooyeweerd, the validity of our insights and judgments is conferred by divine laws' being in effect and by the epistemic subject's having a proper stance toward these laws. It seems to make no difference how, experientially, one has come to have these insights and judgments, nor does it seem to matter whether others recognize, accept, or reject them. Indeed, theoretical insights, he says, must be justified before "the forum of the Divine world-order" (NC 2: 577, WW 2: 511) – not, strikingly enough, in response to other theorists and with respect to their concerns.

This idiosyncratic notion of justification – as justification in the court of divine law – simply ignores the intersubjective character of human knowing. It also reinforces a dogmatic potential in Dooyeweerd's account of religious truth. Because this point is controversial, let me be clear that I do not think Dooyeweerd wanted his account to be dogmatic: as a person and scholar he was admirably open to other people's perspectives. Nor would dogmatism be consistent with his self-understanding of transcendental critique as "a critical inquiry (respecting no single so-called theoretical axiom) into the *universally valid conditions which alone make theoretical thought possible*" (NC 1: 37). Yet the way in which he construes religious truth, theoretical truth, and their interrelation lends support to a dogmatic potential.

## 2.5 *Privileged Access*

In response to my concerns, Dooyeweerd might well reply that what is finally decisive for a conception of truth is whether the one proposing it "stands in the Truth," a formulation elaborated in section 1.4 above. At one level I can agree with this reply. For if truth is as comprehensive and crucial as both he and I think it to be, then no theorist can step outside it, and how one lives within it matters a great deal for the conception of truth one proposes. Yet Dooyeweerd vitiates his own conception of truth by restricting how and by whom such standing takes place.

With respect to "how," I note that the image of "standing" is partial at best, and inadequate on its own. It suggests that one has arrived and, having arrived, can stay in a fixed position. Yet the biblical passages to which Dooyeweerd appeals speak not only of *standing* in the truth but also of *walking* in the truth, of *abiding* in Christ's teaching, and of having the truth *abide in us*.[24] It would seem from scripture itself that truth is not such that one can simply grasp it once and for all. It is to be lived and enacted. To live and enact truth, one needs to learn from and with others, ever anew, what truth requires. This is implied, I think, when Jesus says to his disciples that he is "the way, and the truth, and the life" (John 14:6, NRSV).

Who are the others from whom one must learn? Are they only those with whom one lives in confessional community – fellow Christians, for example, or fellow humanists? I do not think that sort of restriction is in keeping with truth. For Jesus's teachings address everyone, not only his disciples, and many have lived out these teachings in ways that put self-identified Christians to shame. Further, if the "light of truth" shines from God's revelation for humankind, then there is no corner or community that does not live in this light. Or, to use the metaphor I prefer, if God's invitation, instruction, and guidance address all of humanity – if wisdom calls out "to all that live" (Prov. 8:4, NRSV) – then everyone will respond, in better and worse ways, to this divine call. To consider one's own response, or that of one's community, to be intrinsically superior to other responses, without question, is to try to restrict the reach of God's call. It is to say, a priori, that God's truth abides in us but not in them, and to presume that we and not others abide in the truth.

Problematic restrictions on both "how" and "who" plague Dooyeweerd's conception of truth. Yet his insistence on the "hearted" character of truth contains a genial insight. He understands that truth is to be lived, not simply claimed, and that living the truth involves all of what human beings are and do. Nevertheless, our response to God's call is not itself "the truth." At best, our "walking" and "abiding" in the truth, when they occur, bear witness to what truth requires. Rather than suggest, as Dooyeweerd does, that such a "stance" – better, such a way of living – gives someone privileged access to the truth, we should acknowledge that it gives testimony, in partial and flawed ways, to God's invitation, instruction, and guidance. Intrinsic to this way of living, it seems to me, is to welcome the testimony of others. In the theoretical arena this means, among other things, that one tries to learn from others, whatever their religious convictions, and to justify one's claims before the forum of fellow theorists. This is not to say that theorizing is religiously neutral. Rather, theorizing is so religiously freighted that complacency towards one's own religious convictions cannot be tolerated. When religiously laden theorizing is also oriented by a faith tradition, then, along with that tradition, it should offer its insights in a self-critical fashion. For what is needed today, as Ron Kuipers has argued, is not simply faith, but a critical faith.[25]

## 3. CONCLUSION

I have suggested that Dooyeweerd's conception of truth exaggerates the role of religious truth by turning religion into a permanent transcendent structure. When combined with an antithetical construal of religious insight, his account of religious truth makes moot any dialogue with others. More dramatically still, when combined with the notion of a fallible subjective a priori, his account renders most humans incapable of experience. His notion of theoretical intuition cannot rectify this absurd consequence because it reinforces the self-referential incoherence in his transcendental critique of theoretical thought. So too, by ignoring questions of objectivity and intersubjectivity, Dooyeweerd's general conception of truth as an accordance between knowledge and law ends up being tautologous. Nor is this conception rescued by his insistence on "standing in the Truth." Dooyeweerd's description of this stance displays the same structuralizing tendency and dogmatic potential that beset his account of religious truth. It also reveals the same lack of objectivity and intersubjectivity that weaken his account of theoretical truth.

Thus a serious challenge faces reformational philosophers who would critically retrieve Dooyeweerd's conception of truth. We need to find ways to think about truth that retain the holism, normativity, and radicalness of his conception, but wrest these free from incoherence, structuralism, and potential dogmatism. We need to affirm Dooyeweerd's genuine insights but rearticulate them in critical dialogue with other philosophers. I shall begin to take up this challenge in a subsequent essay.[26]

# 4

# Dooyeweerd's Modal Theory: Questions in the Ontology of Science

## (1973)

### PREFACE (2015)

Since its earliest formulations in the 1920s, reformational philosophy has been ontological in emphasis and interdisciplinary in scope. Both Dooyeweerd and Vollenhoven had professional experience and academic training that went beyond the discipline of philosophy – Dooyeweerd as a policy researcher trained in law and jurisprudence, and Vollenhoven as an ordained pastor trained in both theology and mathematics. Viewing the central philosophical issues in academic work as ontological rather than simply methodological, they abandoned the epistemological emphasis of most modern philosophy in favour of an ontological understanding of reality and human experience. In this way they took issue with the dominant neo-Kantian and logical positivist thinkers of their day, as did Martin Heidegger in his seminal *Being and Time* (1927), as well as leading figures in the Frankfurt School such as Theodor Adorno, Max Horkheimer, and Herbert Marcuse. Unlike Heidegger and the Critical Theorists, however, Dooyeweerd and Vollenhoven begin with a forthright religious affirmation: reality, including human beings and their culture and society, is God's creation, and creation exists in relation to God. Their challenge is to articulate an ontology in line with this affirmation.

As was discussed in the introduction to this book, Dooyeweerd and Vollenhoven do this in terms of two ontological frameworks, one of them modal and the other individual and typical. The modal framework pertains to the different levels at which creatures have features or are active – physical, organic, sentient, etc. Dooyeweerd discusses this framework in terms of fourteen or fifteen (modal) law-spheres, (meaning-)modalities, and (modal or meaning-)aspects,[1] and Vollenhoven approaches it in terms of law-spheres (*wetskringen*), modalities (*modaliteiten*) – both subject modalities (*subjectsmodaliteiten*) and law modalities (*wetsmodaliteiten*) – and subject functions (*subjectsfuncties*).[2] In the essay that follows, I simplify their vocabularies by speaking simply of "modes" (occasionally "modal spheres") and "functions" (occasionally "functioning").

Even with such simplification, however, it might not be immediately apparent what a modal framework aims to explain. Indeed, this has become a contentious issue within contemporary reformational philosophy. Whereas René van Woudenberg dismisses Dooyeweerd's concept of "modal aspects" and explains Vollenhoven's concept of "subject functions" as a combination of intrinsic and relational properties, Henk Geertsema objects that this attempt to translate modal concepts "into those of mainstream analytical philosophy" not only fails as an argument but also fundamentally misinterprets reformational ontology.[3] Twenty years earlier, however, Hendrik Hart had already specified the concept of function in sufficiently broad terms to include properties, calling it "a common denominator for properties, actions, states, qualities, and so on. Whenever … a relatively independent unit of action such as an atom, a planet, a plant, an animal, a human being does something, has a property, or is in a state, I will refer to that as a function of that entity." Correlatively, Hart describes a mode as "an irreducible kind of functioning."[4] So too, in 1991 Roy Clouser presented Dooyeweerd's notion of modalities as the concept of "aspects" and defined aspects as "kinds of properties and laws."[5]

The underlying modal intuition, shared by Dooyeweerd and Vollenhoven, is that different sorts of creatures (e.g., rocks, plants, animals, and human beings) display or can display the same kinds of features and operate or can operate in the same kinds of ways. This, of course, is a commonplace of Western philosophy and science: rocks, plants, animals, and human beings, for example, all display physical features and operate in physical ways. Dooyeweerd and Vollenhoven argue, however, that there are many more distinct levels of shared features and operations than most philosophers have recognized and that each level, each mode, is equiprimordial, to use Heideggerian language. Hence, for example, the fact that rocks, plants, animals, and human beings all are physical is no reason to say that they are *only* physical, for all of these creatures function in many other distinct modes. A philosophical ontology should give conceptual articulation to these modes of functioning and explain not only how they are distinct but also how they are mutually interrelated.

Dooyeweerd and Vollenhoven approach this task with feet firmly planted in everyday experience and eyes keenly focused on the academic enterprise. Everyday experience tells us, to paraphrase Shakespeare's Hamlet, that there is more variety to ordinary things than is dreamt of in professional philosophy.[6] And the academic enterprise, as it elaborates disciplinary concepts for different fields of investigation – concepts of physics, biology, psychology, and economics, for example – calls attention to the ontologically diverse ways in which creatures function. Moreover, by construing the fundamental concepts of different academic disciplines as primarily concepts of function – as understandings of how entities operate within networks of relationships – rather than as concepts of substance – as classifications of property-bearing things – Vollenhoven and Dooyeweerd update epistemology with respect to twentieth-century mathematics and physics just as their older contemporary Ernst Cassirer had envisioned.[7]

All of this leads to a strongly non-reductionist philosophy of science.[8] Such non-reductionism gives classical reformational philosophy continuing relevance today, when debates about reductionism and anti-reductionism rage just as furiously as they did in the 1930s: debates about emergence and downward causation in evolutionary biology, philosophy of mind, and cognitive science, for example, and about the relation of molecular biology to developmental biology, functional anatomy, and ecology. As developed by Dooyeweerd and Vollenhoven, modal ontology demonstrates in principle why the theories and explanations offered by distinct kinds of disciplines, such as physics, biology, and psychology, cannot and should not be reduced to a single kind of theory or explanation. Modal ontology also supports the extension of such principled pluralism to the subdisciplines within a science such as biology.

Although reformational philosophy allows one to distinguish methodological and epistemic reduction from ontological reduction, it aims to uncover the ontological underpinnings of methodological and epistemic reduction, in order to provide ontological arguments against any reduction that does not properly account for the distinct and interrelated ways in which creatures function. Thus, for example, physicalism, as the prevailing ontological, methodological, and epistemic framework for the biological sciences, meets immediate resistance from reformational scholars. Why? Because physicalism fails to distinguish sufficiently between physical and organic functions, privileges molecular and biochemical methodologies that overlook higher-order biological features, and does not really regard biology as having its own legitimate domain of scientific knowledge.

In this way classical reformational philosophy is right in step with the latest challenges to physicalist reductionism in biology – to what Philip Kitcher calls "the hegemony of molecular biology."[9] It is attuned to what Ingo Brigandt and Alan Love describe as the contemporary "proliferation and flourishing of diverse biological subdisciplines," the emergence of "inter-field theory," and the continuing salience of interdisciplinary research.[10] One could make similar observations about many other academic fields where the logical positivist push for a "unified science" has long since run out of steam and where the explosion of new subfields and new interdisciplinary projects reminds scholars that there is more to the domains they investigate, and to the methods of investigation, than older reductionist approaches dreamt of.

In other words, questions about the limits and the fruitfulness of reduction in science remain very much alive, and classical reformational philosophy provides valuable resources for addressing such questions. This, at least, is the underlying assumption of the essay that follows. Originally written in 1973, it explores the details of Dooyeweerd's modal ontology and raises technical questions about how one can use it in academic work. These are the sorts of questions anyone who wishes to employ modal ontology in a non-reductionist philosophy of science will need to address.

## 1. THE MODAL HERMENEUTIC PROBLEM

### *1.1 Central Ideas of Cosmonomic Philosophy*

Three basic ideas for Herman Dooyeweerd's philosophy of the cosmonomic idea, as elaborated in *A New Critique of Theoretical Thought*,[11] are the following: (1) Being bound by divine law, all creation is a law-side/subject-side correlation. (2) The law-bound creation is a coherent diversity. (3) All law-bound, coherent diversity refers beyond itself through the totality of its religious root to its origin. In NC these three ideas are fundamental to the criticism of other philosophies, to the general theory of the modal law-spheres, and to the discussion of the structures of individuality.

Anyone who uses the philosophical framework presented in NC must note the theory of the modal law-spheres and address the problems this theory raises. One such problem is the hermeneutical question, by what criteria are the modes of functioning to be distinguished and compared? Or, what principles must one follow when theorizing about the number and the nature of the modes one can distinguish and about the particular order one thinks the modes display? Or, to expose the connection between the hermeneutical question and its foundation in Dooyeweerd's three basic ideas, according to which criteria does one distinguish one mode of functioning from all other modes in such a way that their real, law-bound, referential coherence is maintained?

### *1.2 Debates in Aesthetic Theory*

Stated in skeletal form, the problem of the hermeneutics of modal theory may seem unduly scholastic. Yet current attempts to orient academic work towards cosmonomic philosophy struggle with the question of modal hermeneutics as a real problem. The presence of this problem in aesthetic theory demonstrates how real it is.

In NC, Dooyeweerd distinguishes an aesthetic mode. He also maintains that a special science corresponds to each mode of creation: a mode marks out the field of functional coherence that one "special science" investigates. If there is an aesthetic mode, then aesthetics should be the special science that investigates this field of functional coherence. But is this in fact the case? In light of the Western scientific tradition, the answer must be negative. Traditionally, aesthetics has not been and is not now a special science; rather, it generally constitutes a part of philosophy. Dooyeweerd, however, never advances any detailed defence for his unique position, even though, in a footnote, he boldly rejects the opinion that aesthetics (along with ethics and logic) is a part of philosophy (NC 2: 545–6n1).

NC was never intended as a detailed treatment of the special sciences as such, nor of the modes that delimit the various fields of scientific research. To that extent, one cannot severely fault Dooyeweerd for failing to argue for the special scientific character of aesthetics and for the necessity of distinguishing an aesthetic mode. Nevertheless, one cannot avoid the consequences of his position. This position has formed a basic hypothesis in the study of aesthetics at the Institute for Christian Studies in Toronto. Assuming with Dooyeweerd that aesthetics is (or should be) a special science studying the aesthetic mode, aesthetic theorists at the Institute have tried to further define the character of aesthetics and of the aesthetic mode. But what gives anyone the right to say that there actually is an aesthetic mode or that aesthetics should be a special science? In other words, what criteria must one meet in arguing for the existence or the non-existence of an aesthetic mode and of an aesthetic science?

Although Calvin Seerveld proceeds from Dooyeweerd's position with regard to the existence of an aesthetic mode and science, his aesthetic theory disagrees with Dooyeweerd's location of the aesthetic within the order of the modes. A schematic listing of the modes indicates that Dooyeweerd locates the aesthetic mode much "later" than Seerveld.[12] This difference in modal order has immediate implications, not only for aesthetic theory, but also for all the special sciences investigating functional coherence within the limits of the various other modes. According to Dooyeweerd's ordering, only scholars in jurisprudence, ethics, and theology would always expect to find an aesthetic analogue during their investigations (even when their investigations are directed towards undisclosed states of affairs). According to Seerveld's ordering, not only these scholars but also scholars in economics, sociology, logic, and linguistics would always find an aesthetic analogue. This difference of ordering would affect much of the scientific enterprise. A hermeneutic problem has arisen: what are the principles that should guide one's proposal of any particular modal order?

After many aesthetico-logical investigations, one might eventually find sufficient reasons to defend either Dooyeweerd's or Seerveld's arrangement of the modes as being more acceptable for aesthetic theory. Except for a complication: one would have to work with two crucial variables. Besides dealing with the variable order of the modes as it comes to intramodal and intermodal expression, one would always need to take into account the variable definition of the aesthetic mode itself. Dooyeweerd describes the nucleus of the aesthetic mode as "harmony"; Seerveld, as "allusion" or "suggestion." This difference immediately affects the kind of analogies one would attempt to discover, analogies by which one determines the order of the modes. A modal hermeneutic problem appears once again: what are the criteria for the description of the nucleus of a mode?

### *1.3 Reformulation*

As an outworking of the idea of a law-bound, coherent, and referential creation, modal theory forms an integral unit. The various particular problems arising from one's use of modal theory are all connected. Solution of one problem demands solution of another. Even though the discussion of modal hermeneutics can pose several problems, one must treat these as different sides of the same hermeneutic problem.

The present discussion intends to work towards a solution of that hermeneutic problem: what are the criteria that must be met during any analysis of the modes of a coherent, referential, and law-bound creation? The different sides to this problem (which any attempted solution will affect) are the following:

- What are the criteria for describing the irreducible nuclei of modes?
- What are the criteria for distinguishing a mode not previously distinguished?
- What are the criteria for eliminating an incorrectly distinguished mode?
- What are the criteria for proposing a certain irreversible order of the modes?

## 2. DOOYEWEERD'S CRITERIA FOR MODAL THEORY

To find answers to questions of modal hermeneutics, one should first examine Dooyeweerd's articulation of the general theory of the modes in volume 2 of NC. There Dooyeweerd seems to use three criteria rather consistently. Only after uncovering these criteria will the present discussion ask whether they are adequate solutions to the hermeneutic problem(s).

Dooyeweerd examines the theoretical criterion of a mode at the very outset of volume 2. This criterion, by which any particular mode can be distinguished as an irreducible and distinct aspect of creation, is the general concept of function. The basic ideas of cosmonomic philosophy, however, require that this theoretical criterion cannot serve in isolation. It can serve as a criterion only if it is seen as being grounded in the cosmic temporal order. For only the cosmic temporal order guarantees both the irreducible identity of the mode and one's theoretical isolation of such irreducible identity.

Accordingly, a fuller understanding of Dooyeweerd's explanation of the theoretical modal criterion requires a digression concerning his conception of cosmic time. The digression will connect the examination of Dooyeweerd's modal hermeneutical principles to the fundamental ideas of cosmonomic philosophy. This digression will then guide the subsequent survey of Dooyeweerd's criteria for modal theory.

### 2.1 *Modal Theory and Cosmic Time*

Dooyeweerd brings his three fundamental ideas together in the idea of cosmic time. In his own words, "The idea of cosmic time constitutes the basis of the philosophical theory of reality in this book" (NC 1: 28). Toward the end of volume 1 he writes that the problem of time "is the transcendental background of all our further inquiries" (NC 1: 542). How exactly do the three fundamental ideas come together in the conception of cosmic time? (1) The law-bound subject character of the creation comes to expression in the view that cosmic time comprises two correlated sides that cannot be dissociated: a cosmonomic (law-)side of temporal order and a factual (subject-)side of temporal duration. (2) The coherence of creation's diversity requires that the temporal order, to which all duration is subject, be understood as an indissolubly coherent, continuous order. (3) The referential character of the creation comes out in the explanation that cosmic time, as a coherent diversity of "duration determined by the order of succession or simultaneity" (NC 1: 33), has no unity or totality in itself. Rather it finds its radical unity and totality in its religious root as that root relates cosmic time to its origin.

I noted earlier that the three fundamental ideas, brought together in the idea of cosmic time, form the pervasive foundation of Dooyeweerd's modal theory. The modes themselves are modes belonging to cosmic time: "In each of its modal aspects, [cosmic time] expresses itself in a specific modality of meaning with respect to temporal order as well as duration" (NC 1: 29). Thus the three fundamental ideas appear in modal theory similarly to the way they appear in the idea of cosmic time:[13] (1) Every mode is a law-side/subject-side correlation. On the subject-side are the subject/object relations within that mode. (2) While each mode is sovereignly irreducible to any other mode, the diverse modes are fitted into an indissoluble intermodal coherence by cosmic time: "The same cosmic time-order which guarantees … modal sphere-sovereignty does in fact also guarantee the intermodal coherence of meaning between the modal aspects and their spheres of laws" (NC 1: 105). This intermodal coherence finds its expression within each mode by means of the intramodal coherence of the analogies as they give expression to the nucleus of that mode. (3) No mode is absolute. Every mode is relative to all other modes, to the unity-totality, and to the origin. The intramodal coherence within each mode refers beyond the limits of that mode to all the other modes in their intermodal coherence. The intermodal coherence of the modes – a coherent diversity bound by cosmic time in an irreversible order of before and after – refers beyond itself to a central unity-totality.[14] The referential and irreversible intermodal order finds expression within each mode in the network of analogies, in the opening-process, in subject/object relations, and in the types of modal individuality.

To summarize, every mode (consisting of a law-side/subject-side correlation) is an intramodal coherent diversity referring beyond its own limits to all the other modes as they exist in intermodal, referential, and coherent diversity. In other words, Dooyeweerd's conception of cosmic time not only embodies his fundamental ideas but also permeates his modal theory. This fact gives direction to the survey of Dooyeweerd's modal criteria to follow.

## 2.2 *Functional Coherence*

As I established earlier, although Dooyeweerd identifies the theoretical criterion of a mode as the general concept of function, he insists that this criterion is not the arbitrary construction of theoretical thought. Rather it is founded in the cosmic temporal order that makes theoretical thought possible and that maintains the irreducible identity of each mode within the intermodal order.

For Dooyeweerd, it is the nature of theory to set things apart. In order to recognize a particular mode theoretically as an irreducible and distinct mode of the creation, one must isolate that mode from all the other modes by means of a functional concept. But the modes do not actually exist in isolation. Cosmic time keeps the modes in ordered coherence. One can theoretically isolate a mode in a concept. But one cannot conceptually isolate cosmic time and the intermodal orderly coherence it maintains. The cosmic temporal order makes possible and sets limits for all concepts: "All theoretical isolation presupposes the intermodal continuity of cosmic time" (NC 3: 65). In theory, one can only approximate the cosmic temporal order in a transcendental idea of coherent intermodal order. Such an idea encompasses the fact that the modes exist in a continuous and coherent intermodal order, even while it conceives of this order as being refracted into theoretically isolatable modes. Only on the basis of such an idea can any mode be truly isolated in a functional concept: "For while the theoretical *concept* of a modal aspect is directed to the modal *diversity* of meaning and *separates* the aspect concerned from the others, the transcendental *Idea* is directed to the *coherence*, the *totality* and the *origin* of all meaning, respectively" (NC 1: 69).

The theoretical criterion of any irreducible mode is the theoretically isolated general meaning of that mode. It is a concept capturing the unique functional coherence that the individual functions of things, events, acts, processes, or social relationships display within that mode. It is the concept of a unique general way in which creation functions, in distinction from other unique general ways. This theoretical criterion, this concept, presupposes that each way of functioning is coherently related to every other way of functioning. In other words, the theoretical criterion of a mode by which one isolates an irreducible mode presupposes the cosmic temporal order (intermodal order) reflecting itself in the same manner within each mode. The cosmic temporal order, then, is the basic common denominator of the modes by which they can be contrasted and related (cf. NC 2: 8).

## 2.3 *The Principle of Excluded Antinomy*

Dooyeweerd's description of the theoretical criterion of a mode flows into his presentation of the principle of excluded antinomy (*principium exclusae antinomiae*) in chapter 1 of volume 2. Both the sovereignty of each mode (guaranteed by the cosmic temporal order) and the isolating character of theory demand that each general concept capturing a unique way of functional coherence be univocal. One can include more than one way of functional coherence within one concept only at the expense of ignoring the cosmic temporal order and contradicting oneself. Theoretical antinomies result from all such self-contradictory attempts to include more than one way of functional coherence within one concept.

On the basis of the three fundamental ideas contained in Dooyeweerd's conception of cosmic time, antinomies must be excluded in principle. In fact, accordance with the principle of excluded antinomy is the primary cosmological criterion of transcendental theoretical truth (cf. NC 2: 579). Subjective theorizing can of course form antinomies. But it can do so only by turning away from the cosmic temporal order that guarantees both the sovereignty of each mode and intermodal coherence. In forming theoretical antinomies, one subjectively violates the cosmic temporal order (the law-side of cosmic time); one misconceives coherent diversity by reducing actual diversity to a pseudo-coherence; and one eliminates the referential character of creation by ignoring one or more of the referential modes. As a *cosmological* principle, the *principium exclusae antinomiae* points one's theorizing (subject to the logical principle of non-contradiction) to the cosmic temporal order that guarantees the sovereignty of the modes in their intermodal coherence. The same cosmic temporal order that constitutes the basic denominator by which one theoretically contrasts and relates the modes also determines the limits of modal theory, limits that lead the theorist into antinomous self-contradiction when he or she tries to exceed these limits and to isolate the modes incorrectly.

The logical criterion of a mode and the cosmological principle of excluded antinomy are two of the criteria that Dooyeweerd uses in his modal theorizing. One other criterion – the irreversible order of the modes – awaits exposure prior to my illustrating how Dooyeweerd follows these hermeneutic principles in his general theory of the modes.

## 2.4 *The Irreversible Order of Succession*

After five paragraphs dealing with the criterion of a mode and the *principium exclusae antinomiae*, chapter 1 of volume 2 concludes with a section on "The Cosmic Temporal Order in the Succession of the Law-Spheres" (NC 2: 49–54). This section contains no defence of the idea of irreversible intermodal succession. It merely sets forth the following hypothesis: the idea of the coherent referential intermodal order of cosmic time requires that this order be an irreversible succession of prior and posterior. To discover this succession, as it shows up in the irreversible foundation of posterior modes upon prior modes, requires careful examination of the functional structures of the modes themselves. Moreover, one can trace this irreversible succession order in two coherence-approximating and correlated directions: the foundational direction, from posterior to prior; and the transcendental direction, from prior to posterior.

In chapter 2 ("The Modal Structures of Meaning"), Dooyeweerd gives these hypotheses more content. There he points out that the irreversible cosmic temporal order of succession of the modes cannot be grasped in a concept. The only way to discover this order of succession is by analyzing the modal structure of the theoretically isolated modes.[15] Since the intramodal structure of every mode expresses the entire intermodal coherence, the order of succession must also be expressed in the structure of each mode.

Three essential components of modal hermeneutics have now received attention: the logical criterion of a mode as a concept of function; the principle of excluded antinomy; and the hypothesis of the irreversible order of succession of the modes. These components seem to serve as the three criteria Dooyeweerd tries to meet when he develops his modal theory as a philosophical account of the facts that the sciences uncover.[16] To illustrate how Dooyeweerd allows these criteria to guide his analyses, let me now summarize Dooyeweerd's examination of the functional structures of the spatial mode and the juridical mode. Both modes receive repeated attention throughout part 1 of volume 2.

## 3. MODAL ANALYSES

### *3.1 The Spatial Mode*

Before examining the structure of the various modes, Dooyeweerd gives some examples of scientific expressions denoting concepts that have original significance in one special science and analogical significance in the other special sciences (NC 2: 55–72). One of these scientific expressions is "space." "Space" denotes no real thing, but only a mode, a way of functional coherence manifesting itself in modal relations of extension. The only branch of science that can use "space" as a scientific term with non-analogical significance is pure (but non-formalized) geometry. Adjectives used in geometry such as "n-dimensional," "Euclidean," "topological," "projective," and "metrical" are all spatial adjectives, referring to the very same mode that delimits the field of pure geometry. They do not qualify the significance of "space." Rather, they derive their significance *from* "space" as it is used in geometry. Other sciences such as physics, jurisprudence, and economics can only use the term "space" analogically. These sciences must qualify "space" with adjectives such as "physical," "legal," and "economical" in order to use that term to signify concepts arising from scientific investigations delimited by physical, juridical, and economical modes of functional coherence.

Analogical scientific uses of "space" signify analogical concepts of space that fundamentally refer to the original geometrical concept of space – pure extension – but that are qualified in non-spatial ways. These analogical scientific uses of "space" would be merely metaphorical if they could be replaced by terms having no spatial signification. But they cannot be replaced in this way. No psychologist, for example, can eliminate terms signifying the psychological concept of sensory space. No legal theorist can avoid a term standing for juridical space (e.g., "territory"). The coherence between the different analogical scientific uses of "space" receives terminological expression either in the adjectival qualifications of space denoting a non-spatial modal qualification (e.g., "physical space") or in specific nouns denoting space in a non-spatially-qualified sense (e.g., "territory").

Analogical and original concepts receive a more precise examination after Dooyeweerd outlines the structure of every mode required by the hypothesis of cosmic time: (1) a nucleus (guaranteeing sphere sovereignty), (2) surrounded by retrocipations and anticipations qualified by that nucleus but referring to the nuclei of earlier and later modes (maintaining intermodal coherence and the referential character of creation), (3) with a law-side/subject-side correlation manifesting itself in the nucleus, retrocipations, and anticipations. Dooyeweerd then engages in a preliminary analysis of some of the modes, attempting to isolate their structures in such a way that the analogical concepts developed by the various sciences can acquire univocal accuracy. A "confusing unqualified notion" such as "empirical space" can then be seen to be scientifically useless (NC 2: 79).

In analyzing the spatial mode as the way of functional coherence investigated by geometry, Dooyeweerd seeks to establish that there is indeed an irreducible spatial mode that presupposes only the numerical mode. The argument in summary proceeds as follows (cf. NC 2: 83–93):

- The nucleus of the spatial mode must be conceived as *continuous extension* in simultaneity within the spatial order of time.
- The modern formal mathematical theory of more-dimensional sets eliminates the spatial mode and thereby prematurely eliminates the fundamental problem of the inner nature of pure space.
- The relation between pure space and the analogical concepts of space used in all other (non-geometrical) sciences does not allow one to identify the spatial nucleus with the objective sensory space of perception. The spatial nucleus cannot be qualified by sensory qualities, even though this nucleus cannot be grasped apart from the analogies that it qualifies.
- One can grasp the spatial mode only as *dimensional* continuous extension because the spatial mode refers back to the numerical mode in the moment of dimensionality. Spatial dimensionality (as a law-side order of spatial extension) cannot exist without cohering with the numerical mode: spatiality can be two-, three-, or more-dimensional and thus always refers in its dimensionality to the numerical mode as its substratum. The spatial magnitude of spatial figures is a retrocipatory numerical analogy referring the subject-side of the spatial mode back to its numerical substratum.

- The spatial mode cannot be reduced to the numerical mode: every attempt to transfer original spatial continuity into the numerical aspect causes the inevitable antinomy of accepting the completed infinity of an infinite numerical series. The functions of number that form infinite series are numerical anticipatory approximations of the spatial, kinematic, and analytic modes. More specifically, the irrational functions of number approximate the spatial mode, but they never reach spatial continuity. They are always functions of (relations among) numbers but can never be considered actual numbers. To interpret numerical functions (such as irrational functions) that form infinite series as if they are actual numbers is to (a) disregard *discrete quantity* as the nucleus of the numerical mode, (b) reduce actual spatial continuity to a numerical function, (c) identify the laws holding for infinite series of numbers (such as the law of arithmetical progression) with the subjective series themselves, and (d) produce the antinomy either of the completed infinity of a series or of the actual continuity of a numerical series.

Dooyeweerd's subsequent analysis of the post-spatial modes seeks to establish (among other things) that all of these modes actually refer back to the irreducible spatial mode as a presupposed, foundational, substratum mode, and that the spatial mode refers ahead to them. Consider the following examples:

- A1. Kinematic/Spatial, referring back: The kinematic nucleus – continuous flowing in succession – can only be conceived in connection with flowing extension. Flowing extension is a spatial analogy qualified by the kinematic nucleus but referring back to the original spatial extension in which this analogy is founded. Flowing extension itself implies an analogy of spatial dimensionality – multiple directions of movement in flowing extension (cf. NC 2: 98).
- A2. Spatial/Kinematic, referring ahead: Although spatial positions cannot actually flow into one another, by the movement of thought one can form an idea of the total series of a spatial figure's discrete positions as being subject to continuous transformation. By forming such an idea, projective geometry theoretically opens up "imaginary" positional functions, subject to the anticipatory principle of progression. These imaginary functions approximate continuous flowing. But it is impossible to form a concept of continuous flowing by means of these approximative spatial functions. The attempt to find actual

continuity in the series of transformations of the spatial positions results in antinomies. The actual continuity of positional changes can be discovered only within the kinematic mode of succession, not within the spatial mode of simultaneity (cf. NC 2: 102–6).

- B 1. Physical/Spatial, referring back: The properties of physical space (energy-space) depend on (are qualified by) energy, the nucleus of the physical mode; yet physical space refers back to the original extension in which it is founded (cf. NC 2: 101–2).
- B 2. Spatial/Physical, referring ahead: The general theory of relativity conceives of physical space geometrically by means of the spatial anticipatory approximation of energy: by means of the Gaussian coordinates, i.e., the four-dimensional system of coordinates with curves varying from point to point (cf. NC 2: 101).
- C. Biotic/Spatial, referring back: The modal structure of the biotic mode requires the spatial mode as a substratum. The biotic nucleus – life – expresses itself in various retrocipations. Among these retrocipations is biotic space, the objective field of biotic action and reaction (the bio-milieu) without which no instance of life can exist. Biotic space is ultimately founded in original extension, but it is itself biotic (qualified by life), not spatial (qualified by continuous extension) (cf. NC 2: 109).

It is evident from the analysis of the spatial mode and analogies summarized above that Dooyeweerd tries to meet three modal criteria. The geometrical concept "space" is a functional concept. It is a concept of the spatial way of functional coherence. It cannot be a typical concept of any actual entity. The functional concept of space is an original geometrical concept; it is superfluous for geometry to speak of geometrical space. This fact indicates that an irreducible spatial mode delimits the field of geometrical investigations. The unavoidable, irreplaceable, and analogical concepts of space used by non-geometrical sciences also indicate that there is a spatial way of functional coherence to which these sciences refer but that remains outside the fields of their investigations. The antinomies resulting from all attempts to reduce the spatial mode to other ways of functional coherence (such as to the numerical or to the kinematic) confirm the contention that the spatial mode is an irreducible, distinguishable mode.

Thus Dooyeweerd has met two criteria for isolating a mode. He has discovered a functional concept – space. And he has shown that, to reduce the spatial way of functional coherence to another mode, one would have to violate the principle of excluded antinomy. Apparently, however, meeting these two criteria is insufficient. Much of Dooyeweerd's argument aims to meet the third criterion: the hypothesis of the irreversible order of succession of the modes. On Dooyeweerd's terms, he would not be justified in distinguishing a spatial mode if he could not show the place of this mode in the order of succession.[17]

His analysis of "the original modal meaning of space and its coherence with the meaning of number" (NC 2: 83–93) meets this third criterion by arguing that the structure of the spatial mode demonstrates how the spatial mode presupposes the numerical mode as its substratum. The crucial point in the argument is the identification of dimensionality and of magnitude as retrocipations qualified by continuous extension but referring to the numerical mode of discrete quantity. Dooyeweerd says that one can grasp space conceptually only as dimensional continuous extension. Yet dimensionality as such cannot exist in isolated continuous extension. Rather, dimensionality necessarily refers to the numerical mode of discrete quantity. Space may have two, three, or more dimensions, and thus always refers to the numerical mode as its substratum. So too, the quantifiable subjective magnitude of any spatial figure refers to the numerical mode. Since no spatial figure can exist without having spatial magnitude, spatial magnitude is a *retrocipatory* analogy. A retrocipatory analogy always refers back to an earlier substratum mode. Thus the spatial mode has been shown to presuppose the numerical mode, to which both dimensionality and magnitude refer.

Having argued that the structure of the spatial mode demonstrates how the spatial mode presupposes the numerical mode, Dooyeweerd goes on to state that the numerical mode approximates the spatial and kinematic modes in the infinite numerical series, formed by the irrational and differential functions of number. He backs up this statement by pointing out that the total discrete numerical values functioning in the infinite series can never be actually given. The irrational and differential functions of number are not actual numbers; they are only complicated numerical relations subject to the laws of number. These functions deepen and open the meaning of the natural numerical values. By this observation Dooyeweerd seeks to show how the structure of the numerical mode, because it refers ahead to the spatial mode in the irrational functions of number, also indicates that the spatial mode must follow the numerical mode in the order of succession. He seeks to prove that the foundational relation between the spatial and numerical modes is an irreversible relation of posterior to prior.

Dooyeweerd's analysis of the kinematic mode (NC 2: 93–106) uncovers spatial retrocipations: multiple directions of movement in flowing extension. These retrocipations indicate that the spatial mode is earlier in the order of succession than the kinematic mode. The discovery of the anticipations within the spatial mode referring ahead to the kinematic mode (the principle of progression and the imaginary positional functions) confirms this spatial/kinematic order. Since no mode has been discovered that refers ahead to the kinematic while referring back to the spatial mode – and since no mode has been uncovered that refers ahead to the spatial mode while referring back to the numerical mode – the place of the spatial mode in the order of modal succession has been found. The spatial mode comes just after the numerical mode and just before the kinematic mode. In other words, the spatial mode cannot exist without the numerical mode as its foundational substratum, and the kinematic and post-kinematic modes cannot exist without the spatial mode as one of their foundational substratum modes. The third criterion has been met: Dooyeweerd has located the spatial mode in the irreversible order of the modes.

## 3.2 *The Juridical Mode*

The discussion of the juridical mode provides a second illustration of how Dooyeweerd lets the above three criteria guide his modal theory. Being a philosopher of jurisprudence and a legal theorist, Dooyeweerd treats the juridical mode more extensively than many of the other modes. Like the discussion of the spatial mode, the analysis of the juridical mode occurs at various places within volume 2 of NC.[18]

The introduction to chapter 2 (NC 2: 55–74) presents some expressions denoting analogical concepts in jurisprudence: juridical unity and multiplicity; the legal space of validity for legal norms; territory; competency and legal power; juridical economy and proportion. These and other analogies in the structure of the juridical mode receive a more exact interpretation within chapter 2, section 4 (NC 2: 129–40), as one example of the structural analysis of the post-physical modes intended to give an insight into the order of succession of the modes.

Dooyeweerd begins his analysis of the juridical mode by circumscribing its nucleus with the term "retribution," a term intended to evoke "an immediate intuition" of the irreducible nucleus of the juridical mode in its general structure (NC 2: 130–1).[19] All other terms such as "equality," "proportion," and "compulsory order of communal life" denote unqualified analogical concepts that can have juridical significance only by being qualified retributively. Every truly juridical relation displays a retributive nucleus. By describing the nucleus guaranteeing the irreducible sovereignty of the juridical mode as retribution, Dooyeweerd has met the logical criterion. He has found an original concept of a distinct way of functional coherence.

Yet one can grasp a nucleus conceptually only in the context of retrocipations to substratum spheres, retrocipations that the nucleus qualifies and that give expression to the nucleus. On its law-side, retribution always entails (1) "a well-balanced harmony of a multiplicity of interests" (2) warding off any excessive enforcement of special claims detrimental to other claims (NC 2: 135–6, italics removed). The multiplicity of interests that must be harmoniously balanced include both communal interests and the interests of inter-individual relationships, interests that are strictly correlated in juridical intercourse. Similarly, the special claims can be either special communal or special inter-individual claims. Juridical harmony is an analogy referring to the aesthetic mode. Juridical non-excessiveness (frugality) is an analogy referring to the economic mode. The juridical intercourse of communal interests and of inter-individual interests is an analogy referring to the social mode. Since retribution always entails these analogies, they must be part of the retrocipatory structure of the juridical mode. Thus the juridical mode must be later than, and must presuppose, the aesthetic, economic, and social modes to which these analogies refer.

Rather than trying to determine the exact order of the modes to which the aesthetic, economic, and social analogies refer, Dooyeweerd assumes that his previous analysis of the pre-juridical modes has already indicated this order. This assumption becomes apparent in his discussion of the lingual analogy in the structure of the juridical mode (NC 2: 137–8). Dooyeweerd simply states that the aesthetic, economic, and social retrocipations "necessarily appeal to a lingual analogy" (NC 2: 137). He does not demonstrate how or why they *necessarily* appeal to this lingual analogy. He simply points out how juridical signification, which is present in all juridical relations, comes out in the binding juridical interpretation of juridical norms and facts given by competent legal organs. And he states that this juridical signification refers back to the lingual mode and remains retributively qualified.

On the basis of his previous analyses of the pre-juridical modes, Dooyeweerd has partially met the criterion of irreversible succession:

his analysis of the structure of the juridical mode has shown that the juridical mode must presuppose the aesthetic, economic, social, and lingual modes as its foundational substrata. Unlike his treatment of the spatial mode, his discussion of the retrocipatory structure of the juridical mode is not backed up by an analysis of the anticipations within these substratum modes to the juridical mode, except in the case of the lingual mode (cf. NC 2: 139–40). Later, Dooyeweerd indicates that the juridical mode anticipates the moral and pistic modes in such figures as "juridical guilt," "good faith," "good morals," and "equity." He also argues that the moral and pistic modes necessarily refer back to the juridical mode as a substratum that is foundational to their existence. Dooyeweerd has now located the juridical mode as coming just after the aesthetic mode and just before the moral or ethical mode in the irreversible order of modal succession. Since it can be so located, the juridical mode must exist as an irreducible way of functional coherence. He has met the criterion of the irreversible foundational intermodal relationship.

The principle of excluded antinomy does not play a prominent role in Dooyeweerd's preliminary analysis of the juridical mode. He does point out the internal antinomy that arises from theoretically ignoring the boundaries of juridical retribution and of ethical love (cf. NC 2: 159, 162). And, prior to chapter 2, he mentions that he has used the method of antinomy heuristically to discover the synthetical criterion of the juridical mode (NC 2: 48–9): first he attempted to reduce the fundamental juridical concepts of causality, volition, power, interpretation, etc. to the concepts of other sciences whose modal fields of research had already been defined. Since insoluble antinomies resulted, Dooyeweerd concluded on the basis of the *principium exclusae antinomiae* that his attempted reductions were theoretical violations of modal boundaries and that these fundamental concepts must be irreducible modal juridical concepts. Then he searched out the juridical nucleus (retribution) that could guarantee the modal juridical sense of these concepts, in contrast to their meaning for non-juridical sciences.

## *3.3 Reformulation*

Drawing from modal accounts such as the analyses of the spatial and juridical modes, one can reformulate the three criteria that guide Dooyeweerd's modal theorizing:

- The correct theoretical isolation of any mode within the intermodal order requires the formation of a non-analogical concept of this way of functional coherence.
- The correct theoretical isolation of any mode within the intermodal order requires the elimination or avoidance of all antinomies.
- The correct theoretical isolation of any mode within the intermodal order requires the location of that mode within the irreversible intermodal succession by means of an analysis of its modal structure.

Dooyeweerd seems to regard these three criteria as the absolutely essential principles one must follow in order to analyze the modes in a way that fully accounts for their law-bound, referential, and coherent diversity.

## 4. INSUFFICIENCY AND INTUITION

Now that we have uncovered three criteria, the following questions arise. Are the criteria Dooyeweerd uses as principles of modal hermeneutics sufficient to settle debates about the number of modes that should be distinguished, about the order of the modes, and about the nuclear meaning of any mode? Are the criteria Dooyeweerd uses adequate guidelines for modal theorizing, ones whose orientation allows modal theoretical debates to be fruitful? It seems impossible to simply answer yes or no. The answer can only emerge from the debates themselves. Yet one important characteristic of Dooyeweerd's epistemology would suggest a negative answer.[20]

### *4.1 Derivation of the Modal Nucleus*

In NC, the analyses of the spatial, juridical, and other modes begin with a description of the nuclei of those modes. This procedure is not accidental. Dooyeweerd maintains that only by first abstracting the nucleus can one discover the definitive modal qualification of the fundamental analogical concepts developed by the science investigating that mode: "The special theory of the modal law-spheres must start with a scrupulously accurate analysis of the modal nuclei of meaning and should point out the non-original character of the modal analogies" (NC 2: 77). The entire mode depends on its nucleus, and the entire scientific investigation of a mode depends on one's theoretical grasp of its nucleus. The logical criterion of a mode is a functional concept: i.e., a concept capturing the original uniqueness of a certain way of functional coherence. To be able to distinguish a mode, one must be able to grasp its original uniqueness in a functional concept: one must be able to conceive the nucleus qualifying the entire structure of a certain way of functional coherence. From a procedural viewpoint, it would seem that even one's avoidance of antinomies and one's locating a mode within the order of succession must depend upon and must follow from one's forming a non-analogical and original functional concept of the modal nucleus. How can one avoid antinomies unless one can properly distinguish the confused modes by means of functional concepts? And how can one locate modes within the order of succession unless one has a theoretical grasp of the identity of the modes? If one's account of the nature and place of a certain way of functional coherence ultimately hinges on one's conceptual grasp of the modal nucleus, however, what happens when one person's description of the nucleus differs significantly from that of another? How can this difference be fruitfully debated?

Take, for example, Dooyeweerd's description of the spatial nucleus as continuous extension. How did he arrive at this description? Certainly not by following the lead of formal mathematics. Rather, on the basis of continuous extension as the spatial nucleus, Dooyeweerd contends that formal mathematics has eliminated the spatial mode as such and has reduced pure geometry to either pure arithmetic or pure logic (cf. NC 2: 85). Yet he never argues for the correctness of his description of the spatial nucleus, despite continual appeals to it in his arguments with formalist, empiricist, and intuitionist mathematicians. What theoretical justification is there for developing a theory of the spatial mode that conflicts with three major trends in modern mathematics? What confirms the correctness of Dooyeweerd's conceptual grasp of the spatial nucleus?

Dooyeweerd is not unaware of the general problem involved here. Yet he does not actually deal with it until the epistemological considerations in part 2 of volume 2 in NC. There he addresses the problem by means of the idea of intuition, an idea that surfaces occasionally in his discussion of the modes.

## 4.2 *Intuitive Insight*

In part 2 Dooyeweerd tries to answer two fundamental questions of epistemology: "What do we abstract from the real datum of experience in the fundamental antithetical relation of theoretical thought which gives rise to the problem of the 'Gegenstand'? And … how can the theoretical antithesis between the logical function of knowledge and its non-logical 'Gegenstand' be reconciled by an intermodal theoretical meaning-synthesis?" (NC 2: 434). In answer to the first question, Dooyeweerd replies that we abstract from the continuity of cosmic time, giving rise to the problem of the Gegenstand: we theoretically disjoin the cosmic temporal meaning-systasis; we theoretically refrain from the temporal continuity of the cosmic coherence of meaning (cf. NC 2: 466–9). He answers the second question via the idea of intuition as "a cosmic intuition of time" that immediately grasps "the continuous meaning-coherence in the temporal refraction of meaning." Intuition is the "temporal bottom layer of actual analysis" through which one's "analytical function of thought is embedded in cosmic time" and "is in continuous temporal contact with all the other modal functions which our selfhood can claim in time *as its own*" (NC 2: 473).

Dooyeweerd summarizes his explanation of how intuition reconciles the theoretical antithesis as follows:

> The intermodal synthesis of meaning appears thus to be possible only through the theoretical intuition. The latter is necessarily related to the transcendent *selfhood*. I cannot grasp the modal meaning of a law-sphere in a theoretical concept, if I lack temporal theoretical insight into the aspect opposed to the analysis. My intuition moves to and fro between my deepened analysis and its "Gegenstand" to bring them into actual contact in the intermodal synthesis of meaning … Theoretical intuition is operative in deepened analysis itself, and only by its intermediary is theoretical thought able to analyze the "Gegenstand" in the intermodal synthesis of meaning. In this intuition I implicitly relate the intermodal meaning-synthesis to the transcendent identity of the modal functions I experience in the religious root of my existence …
>
> In its subjective subordination to the cosmic order of time, theoretical intuition is an absolutely transcendental condition of the cognitive meaning-synthesis. (NC 2: 478–9)

Dooyeweerd also states that "intuitive insight into the 'Gegenstand'" is "an indispensable condition of *scientific* knowledge," whether that Gegenstand be the functional basic structure of the mode, an entire mode, particular Gegenstände within an abstracted mode, or the structure of a thing, event, or societal relationship (NC 2: 469, 475).

How does the idea of intuition relate to the problem of deriving an original functional concept of a modal nucleus? According to Dooyeweerd, his idea of intuition implies certain limits to the formation of concepts and definitions about the structure of a mode. Once the nucleus, retrocipations, and anticipations of a mode "have been encompassed in the process of a correct theoretical synthesis of meaning, there is no longer any sense in asking a closer analysis of the nucleus of the [mode] analysed in this process" (NC 2: 485). This last sentence apparently expresses the reason why Dooyeweerd does not argue for the correctness of his concept of the spatial nucleus. Theoretical thought must encompass in concepts (deepened into ideas) the original modal nuclei as well as the expression of these nuclei in their surrounding analogies. In the process of theoretically grasping a mode, one's formation of a functional concept (by which one isolates that mode from the continuity of cosmic time) and one's formation of a concept-deepening functional idea (by which one approaches the limits of that mode as it points to the referential continuity of cosmic time) both rest on one's theoretically deepened intuitive insight into the mode one is analyzing (cf. NC 2: 187–8, 485–6).

Dooyeweerd sees theoretical intuition as the final court of appeal for one's conceptual grasp of a modal nucleus. This comes out in his discussion of the modes in two ways. First, he never extensively argues for his particular descriptions of the nuclei of the modes. Second, he sometimes states that one's grasp of a modal nucleus depends on one's intuitive insight, as, for example, in these sentences from the explanation of the juridical mode:

> It is the very nature of the modal nucleus that it cannot be defined, because every circumscription of its meaning must appeal to this central moment of the aspect-structure concerned. The modal meaning-kernel itself can be grasped only in an immediate intuition and never apart from its structural context of analogies.
>
> But the term by which this meaning-kernel is designated must be able immediately to evoke this intuition of the ultimate irreducible nucleus of the modal aspect of experience concerned. (NC 2: 129)

> [The genus/species method of analysis replaced] the intuitive insight into this modal meaning-kernel ... by analogical concepts detached from the inner meaning-coherence within the modal structure of the legal aspect. (NC 2: 132)

## 4.3 *Guiding Principles*

But what guarantees the correctness of one's theoretical intuition? And how does one know that one has formed a correct concept of the nucleus and of the primary structure of a mode? For Dooyeweerd, there is no guarantee that one's subjective theoretical intuition is correct, nor can one ever know beyond a shadow of a doubt that one's conceptual grasp of a mode is correct. He maintains that the structure of the intermodal meaning-synthesis and the structure of the modes themselves do condition intuition and analysis. But one's intuition and analysis are always subjective and fallible (cf. NC 2: 552–7). This fact allows Dooyeweerd to acknowledge that "the system of the law-spheres designed by us can never lay claim to material completion. A more penetrating examination may at any time bring new modal aspects ... to the light ... And the discovery of new law-spheres will always require a revision and further development of our modal analyses. Theoretical thought has never finished its task" (NC 2: 556). Dooyeweerd could also have said that a more penetrating examination may uncover *incorrect* insight into and conceptualization of any mode.[21]

If intuition and analysis are subjective and fallible, then it seems we need principles to guide the process of conceptually grasping a modal nucleus on the basis of theoretical intuition. Dooyeweerd nowhere lists these guiding principles as such. Yet one can glean them from the way in which he argues, as well as from generally recognized standards for scientific analysis. Here are several:

- The principle of respecting non-theoretical givens. One's description of a modal nucleus should make good sense. One should be able to demonstrate that this description helps to account for ordinary phenomena (cf. "The second criterion of transcendental theoretical truth," NC 2: 579–80).
- The principle of adequacy. One should show that one's description of a modal nucleus solves the major problems uncovered in isolating a certain way of functional coherence. Further, one should indicate how other possible descriptions are inadequate solutions for these problems.
- The principle of univocality. One should strive for a conceptually clear identification of a modal nucleus.
- The principle of scientific continuity. One should be able to show how one's grasp of a modal nucleus ties into current and previous scientific investigations.

- The principle of the economy of thought. One's descriptions of modal nuclei should account for the modes of functional coherence in the most parsimonious way.
- The principle of sufficient evidence. One should be able to produce sufficient evidence to justify a certain description of a modal nucleus.

Since all accounts of the nature and place of the modes hinge on subjective and fallible insight into and analysis of the nucleus of a mode, differences in descriptions of the modal nuclei and of entire modes are to be expected. Naked appeals to intuition, however, will not contribute to debate over such differences. In fact, such appeals serve only to cut off debate and to encourage a kind of skepticism. It would appear that once the debate reaches the point of an appeal to intuition, any such appeal must come clothed in a principial fabric. In other words, one should be able to show that one's intuitively based conceptual grasp of a modal nucleus meets the requirements of the principles already noted. Only then will the debate have room to develop in such a way that eventually a decision can be reached on which of the different intuitive and conceptual descriptions of a modal nucleus is more acceptable, because of how it meets these principial requirements.

The original question raised in this section was whether the three criteria uncovered earlier are sufficient to settle such debates. Their insufficiency is due to the fact that, for Dooyeweerd, the criteria can be met only on the basis of subjective and fallible intuitive insight as it shapes the conceptual grasp of a mode in its nucleus, and subjective and fallible intuitive insight implies unavoidable differences in conceptual grasps of the modes. This is why I have suggested that, in order for debates to reach provisional settlement, basic appeals to intuitive insight must strive to demonstrate that intuitive-conceptual descriptions of modal nuclei accord with such principles as respecting non-theoretical givens, adequacy, univocality, scientific continuity, economy of thought, and sufficient evidence.

## 5. VERIFICATION

In addition to the three criteria and intuitive insight, other elements of the general modal theory deserve hermeneutic consideration: the functional structure of the opening-process, the structure of the subject/object relation, and modal types of individuality. As the order of the chapters in volume 2, part 1 indicates, these other elements unavoidably depend on the functional structure of the modes already explained. Epistemologically, the explanation of these elements in the context of examining a mode presupposes intuitive insight into that mode and the satisfaction of the three criteria for distinguishing a mode.

This being the case, it makes little sense to describe these elements as additional criteria to be met in the process of modal theorizing. Rather, they serve to confirm or disconfirm the (in)correctness of modal theorizing that tries to meet the three criteria and the requirements of intuitive insight. To regard them as criteria on the same level as the three criteria already mentioned would lead one into obviously circular arguments with little hermeneutic value. For example, one can interpret a functional relationship as a modal subject/object relation only on the basis of one's understanding of the nature, number, and order of the modes. That understanding has to measure up to the three criteria. To say that discovery of such a modal subject/object relation is also a criterion for understanding the nature, number, and order of the modes would be equivalent to saying that discovery of this relation provides a standard by which to judge the understanding of the nature, number, and order of the modes that makes this discovery possible. One would be proving what the proof presupposes, or making into a criterion for modal theory an element whose very interpretation depends upon that modal theory. Saying that the opening-process, subject/object relations, and modal types of individuality serve to verify modal theory seems preferable to calling them modal criteria.

## *5.1 The Opening-Process*

In Dooyeweerd's explanation (cf. chapter 3, NC 2: 181ff), the opening-process of the modes has temporal duration, and it displays and follows the intermodal order of cosmic time (cf. NC 1: 29). When a mode is opened, the development of its anticipations deepens the primary structure of that mode (the coherence of nucleus and retrocipations). The development of a mode's anticipations can only occur under the guidance of the anticipated modes.

The indissoluble correlation between the retrocipatory (foundational) and anticipatory (transcendental) directions of time implies that no particular mode can begin to open up without the opening of its substratum modes. Nor can any particular mode be opened unless the superstratum modes guiding its opening are themselves opened. The only apparent exceptions are the pistic and historical modes. The pistic or faith mode is the only mode that has no anticipations or superstratum modes, and yet it can guide the entire opening-process or can keep the modes in a closed condition. The historical mode (as the "*nodal point* of the entire process of disclosure in the normative anticipatory spheres of the other aspects" – NC 2: 191) is the only mode whose opening does not require the opening of its substratum modes but does make possible the opening of its superstratum modes.

If Dooyeweerd's analysis of the functional structure of the opening-process is correct, then the opening-process can help verify one's provisional grasp of a mode. For example, if one were unsure whether the biotic mode precedes or follows the psychic mode in the order of intermodal succession, one could look for evidence of biotic functioning that opens up under the guidance of psychic functioning and vice versa. Of course, finding such evidence would presuppose a provisional conceptual grasp of what constitutes biotic functioning and psychic functioning.

Dooyeweerd himself often uses the opening-process to verify his own identifications and ordering of the modes, especially in connection with the "normative" modes. For example, as confirmation of his theory that the juridical mode has a retributive nucleus with aesthetic, economic, and social retrocipations and substratum modes, Dooyeweerd points to "the character of most primitive juridical systems of law" (NC 2: 136). Being "primitive," these systems are functionally unopened and generally do not show any traces of anticipatory functions (such as guilt). And yet they do have aesthetic, economic, and social analogies. Since only the primary structure of a mode can be expressed in its unopened state, the presence of these analogies in primitive, functionally unopened legal systems confirms that they are retrocipatory analogies pointing to their respective substratum spheres (cf. NC 2: 136, 182–3). Similarly, the absence of "the juridical moment of guilt" and of "the juridical figures" of good faith, good morals, and equity in primitive legal systems indicates that this moment and these figures are anticipatory, referring ahead to the superstratum ethical or moral and pistic modes (cf. NC 2: 141, 148).

Perhaps this appeal to primitive legal systems and similar arguments in NC indicate the hermeneutic verificational function of the opening-process: if one discovers that differences between opened and unopened functions within a mode of functional coherence tend to disagree with one's conceptualization of this mode within the succession order of the modes, then one should reexamine one's conceptualization. Maybe one's description of the modal nucleus is inadequate or one's location of the mode within the intermodal order is incorrect. If, by way of example, one thinks that the aesthetic mode contains an economical retrocipation pointing to the presupposed economical sphere, but discovers that most "primitive" (unopened) aesthetic activity lacks economization, then one will have to reconsider one's description of the aesthetic nucleus or the place of the aesthetic mode relative to the economical mode. On the other hand, if one should find that differences between opened and unopened functioning tend to agree with one's conceptualization of this mode within the intermodal order, then one should continue to use this conceptualization as a working hypothesis.

I should mention two matters in passing. One is that the verificational use of the opening-process seems to require accepting Dooyeweerd's analysis of this opening-process, with the historical mode functioning as the nodal point. Only on the basis of this analysis can one appeal to "primitive" culture as demonstrating the unopened condition. The other matter is that the circularity of an appeal to primitive culture seems unavoidable: one defines primitive culture as being unopened, and then one finds the unopened condition within that primitive culture. So the use of the opening-process should be recognized for what it is: a means for gathering evidence, not for establishing incontrovertible proofs.

## *5.2 Subject/Object Relations*

The explanation of the functional structure of the subject/object relationship (chapter 5, NC 2: 366–413) indicates that subject/object relations can also serve to verify one's modal analysis. Within the functional coherence of any mode, subject functions and object functions are coordinated and are not interchangeable. The possibility of objectification is primarily bound to the retrocipatory structure of a mode, although a different kind of objectification is possible in the anticipatory structure. An objectification of a subjective modal function belonging to a substratum mode implies the objectification of the subjective modal functions belonging to modes earlier than this substratum mode. For example, the psychical objectification of the subjective biotic function implies the psychical objectification of subjective modal functions within the numerical, spatial, kinematic, and physical modes (cf. NC 2: 373–4). Not only the subject functions but also the subject/object relations belonging to the substratum modes can be objectified within a certain mode.[22] Even an individual subject/object relation within a certain mode can function objectively in another subject/object relation within that same mode (cf. the discussion of "rights to rights," NC 2: 408–9).

A summary of the section on the spatial subject/object relation (NC 2: 383–9) can yield insight into how the functional structure of the subject/object relation serves a verificational role for modal theory. The subject/object relation within the spatial mode is the relation between subjective spatial figures and objective spatial points. A spatial point is an arithmetical analogy functioning within the spatial mode of functional coherence – continuous dimensional extension – without being subjectively extended and without possessing extensive magnitude.[23] Its existence depends on subjective spatial figures; but at the same time a point (such as a terminal point of a straight line) objectively determines the magnitude (subjective numerical analogy) of the subjective spatial figures. As an objective numerical analogy, a point is founded in numerical relations: it is an intensive (non-extensive) objectification of number in space, and the points of a straight line can objectify an infinitesimal series of numbers. The magnitude of a spatial extension between points can be approximated arithmetically by means of the irrational function of number, a function that cannot be identified with either a point or an actual number.

It goes without saying that the discussion of the spatial subject/object relation presupposes the previous examination of the entire spatial mode, where Dooyeweerd undoubtedly followed the three criteria and his intuitive insight. However, the treatment of the spatial subject/object relation tends to clarify and to verify the earlier examination. It allows for a closer scrutiny of the irreducible identity of the spatial mode in contrast to the other modes, especially in contrast to the numerical mode. It makes possible the exposure and avoidance of the antinomy hidden in the conception of a "continuum of points," an antinomy similar to the supposed actual continuity of a numerical series that Dooyeweerd exposed and avoided earlier. It also reaffirms the location of the spatial mode within the irreversible intermodal order: the two-directional relation between the spatial and numerical modes is explained in terms of the point as a numerically founded analogy that intensively objectifies number in space.

The above summary of the section on the spatial subject/object relation, like all of chapter 5 in NC 2, indicates the hermeneutic verificational value of the subject/object relation: (1) If Dooyeweerd's analysis is correct, then all modes other than the numerical mode should display a subject/object relation. If any theoretically isolated mode seems to lack the subject/object relation, then one should reconsider one's theoretical isolation of that mode. On the other hand, if a non-numerical mode does display the subject/object relation, then one has good evidence that one's theorizing is proceeding correctly. (2) If the explanation of modal functioning in terms of the subject/object relation causes the formation of antinomies, one must reconsider not only this explanation but also one's previous account of a mode's nucleus and intermodal location. If the explanation of modal functioning in terms of the subject/object relation helps one to eliminate or to avoid antinomies, then one has evidence verifying the correctness of this explanation and of the theoretical account of a mode that this explanation presupposes. (3) If the most obvious subject/object relations uncovered within a certain way of functional coherence fail to agree with one's analysis of the retrocipatory structure of a mode and of the place of that mode within the intermodal order, then one should reconsider one's analysis. If the structure of the subject/object relations does seem to agree with the retrocipatory structure analyzed, then this agreement tends to verify the modal analysis.[24]

## *5.3 Modal Types of Individuality*

In his brief chapter on the problem of modal individuality (NC 2: 414–26), Dooyeweerd explains that "the modal structures lie at the foundation of the structures of individuality and are individualized by the latter" (NC 2: 414). This individualization does not affect the functional structure maintaining a certain way of functional coherence. Rather the functional structure (nucleus, retrocipations, and anticipations as determined by the cosmic temporal order) both constitutes the condition of all individualization within this way of functional coherence and expresses itself in all individualization.

Thus one can find original (nuclear) types, anticipatory types, and/or retrocipatory types of individuality within any mode. An original type is a modal type not founded in the original types belonging to earlier, substrata modes, even though substrata types functionally anticipate it. An anticipatory type is a modal type belonging to one mode while at the same time being constituted by its anticipatory reference to an original modal type belonging to a later, superstratum mode. A retrocipatory modal type is a modal type that lacks an original character within the mode to which it belongs and that is founded in an original type belonging to an earlier, substratum mode.

Since the discovery and classification of such modal types of individuality presupposes much modal theorizing, it would make little sense to treat the discovery and classification of modal types as a criterion for modal theorizing. Yet the discovery and classification of modal types could help confirm or disconfirm the correctness of one's modal theorizing. Failure to discover original, anticipatory, or retrocipatory types within the functional coherence of a mode should lead to reconsideration. So should a conflict between one's classification of modal types and one's analysis of a mode within the intermodal order. The discovery of modal types and the absence of conflict between classification and analysis tends to confirm the correctness of one's modal theorizing.

## POSTSCRIPT (2015)

This paper, written in 1973 for a graduate research seminar in systematic philosophy, does not draw firm conclusions about the viability of Dooyeweerd's modal theory, nor does it set out to draw such conclusions. Yet it highlights the challenges facing anyone who takes his theory seriously as an ontological and epistemological model for work in the academic disciplines. The challenges arise in part from the theory's intricate and interconnected character: decisions on one question, such as how to circumscribe the nucleus of a mode, immediately affect answers to other equally important questions, such as how to characterize the mode's analogical moments and specify the intermodal order of succession. The challenges also arise, however, from Dooyeweerd's problematic emphasis on theoretical intuition and his insufficient attention to established principles of academic discourse.

It is not surprising, then, that the topic of theoretical intuition returns in my subsequent discussions of Dooyeweerdian philosophy.[25] Nevertheless, I have continued to use modal theory as a heuristic model in my own systematic reflections. Without employing Dooyeweerd's vocabulary, for example, my book *Artistic Truth* identifies "imagination" as the "nuclear moment" of the aesthetic dimension or "mode."[26] I spell out the meaning to this dimension by calling attention to three "moments" that are especially germane to artistic truth: exploration as a technical "retrocipation," and creative interpretation and presentation as lingual and logical "anticipations," respectively. In my view, exploration, presentation, and creative interpretation are central both to what has become differentiated and institutionalized as an aesthetic dimension and to artistic truth. The technical retrocipation (i.e., exploration) has special significance because, like Dooyeweerd and Seerveld, I regard the arts as having a technical founding function ("historical," in Dooyeweerd's terms). The lingual anticipation (i.e., creative interpretation) and logical anticipation (i.e., presentation) are crucial because most debates about artistic truth pertain to the relation of the arts to language and logic. Because I do not regard these debates as completely misguided, I seek to establish within art's qualifying aesthetic function the internal links that provide a social-ontological basis for these debates.

Moreover, what I describe as the aesthetic principle of "imaginative cogency" pertains not only to art's qualifying function but also to the aesthetic dimension as a whole. Imaginative cogency is a historically emergent horizon of expectations concerning what makes aesthetic matters more or less worthwhile. This is my way to characterize what Dooyeweerd would label the "law-side" to the aesthetic modal aspect, although "beautiful harmony" would be closer to his own conception of aesthetic normativity.

Albeit only partial, this modally indebted characterization of the aesthetic dimension is crucial for my theory of artistic truth.[27] Similarly, the emphasis in my social philosophy on the societal principles of solidarity, resourcefulness, and justice derives from a modal understanding of the social, economic, and juridical spheres and of their close mutual proximity within an intermodal order.[28]

Other scholars also have made use of Dooyeweerd's modal theory in various fields and sometimes have refined it. In addition to authors and works already mentioned in this chapter such as Chaplin, Clouser, Hart, and Seerveld, a representative sample of monographs published in English would include ones by Marinus Stafleu in physics and philosophy of science,[29] Elaine Botha and Danie Strauss in philosophy of science,[30] Jacob Klapwijk in philosophy of evolutionary biology,[31] Andrew Basden in computer and information science,[32] Albert Weideman in linguistics,[33] Doug Blomberg in education,[34] and Hendrik Jan van Eikema Hommes in law and legal theory.[35] Modal ontology also shows up in numerous English-language journal articles and collections of essays, not to mention the wealth of resources in Dutch and other languages that have not been translated into English.

In general, reformational scholars have used and refined Dooyeweerd's modal theory without fully addressing the hermeneutic problems I have tried to lay out. For my own part, I have not found it fruitful to do a full-blown structural analysis of, say, the aesthetic, lingual, and logical modes or of the social, economic, and juridical modes. Such an exercise would not seem sufficiently motivated by the issues to which I have given priority – the character and scope of truth, including artistic truth, and the need and potential for a differential transformation of society as a whole in an age of globalization. Nevertheless, I believe this early study of Dooyeweerd's modal theory, in offering a first step toward a critical retrieval of his ontology and epistemology, raises hermeneutic problems that deserve ongoing attention.

# 5

# Fantastic Things: Critical Notes toward a Social Ontology of the Arts

## (1995)

Future historians will note many parallels between the 1930s and the 1990s in Europe and North America. Both decades appear to be times of dramatic cultural upheaval and societal transformation. Indeed, many of the battles fought over capitalism, democracy, and cultural modernism in the 1930s have returned in recent struggles over a global economy, the welfare state, and cultural postmodernism. Hence it may be instructive for contemporary Christian scholars to revisit the seminal texts of European philosophy in the 1930s.[1]

Cultural theorists have long recognized the significance of Martin Heidegger's essay "The Origin of the Work of Art," both as a turning point in his own thinking and as a fundamental challenge to modern aesthetics.[2] Presented as lectures in 1935–36 and first published in German in 1950, the essay develops a conception of artistic truth that breaks entirely with Kantian divisions among epistemology, ethics, and aesthetics. Much less recognized, even among his students and followers, is the significance of Herman Dooyeweerd's discussion of art from around the same time.[3] First published in Dutch in 1936 and then revised and republished in English in 1957, Dooyeweerd's discussion presents a conception of the artwork that reconfigures the Kantian divisions discarded by Heidegger.

My essay presents half of a critical dialogue that I wish to institute between Heidegger's essay and Dooyeweerd's discussion.[4] The dialogue will serve to modify both of their conceptions in ways that are appropriate today. Although I restrict my commentary to Dooyeweerd in what follows, let me briefly suggest how the complete dialogue would go. Then I shall turn directly to Dooyeweerd's discussion of art.

From a Dooyeweerdian perspective, Heidegger draws an illuminating distinction between the typical structure of artworks and the typical structures of physical things (*Naturdinge*), technical objects (*Gebrauchsdinge*), and ordinary products (*Zeug* [equipment]); but Heidegger obscures the distinction between norm and function in a totalizing and mystifying attempt to "think the Being of beings."[5] Dooyeweerd, by contrast, maintains a fruitful distinction between the norms for art and the functions of art; but, from a Heideggerian vantage point, Dooyeweerd reduces artworks to mere things, even while he mistakenly privileges the intentionality of the artist in the origin of the work of art.

Unlike some of Dooyeweerd's other followers, I do not believe that the problems in his account of art are peripheral or accidental, any more than the problems in Heidegger's account are peripheral or accidental. Both accounts play central roles in the authors' attempts to overcome traditional metaphysics and modern epistemology. Moreover, the conclusions they reach in these accounts have troubling implications for their social theories and cultural critiques.[6] For reasons such as these, I would like to arrive at a social ontology of art that makes sense of Heidegger's and Dooyeweerd's insights without accepting their dubious assumptions and problematic conclusions. In particular, I wish to find a path through Heidegger to a normative but de-mystified conception of artistic truth, and through Dooyeweerd to a social and ontological but de-personalized conception of artistic production. The following marks the first loop of the trail.

***

Considered within the entire landscape of *A New Critique of Theoretical Thought*, the placement of Dooyeweerd's discussion of art is striking. On the one hand, the discussion of art in Part I of the third volume provides his first and only extended analysis of a particular thing-structure, his first elaboration of the subject/object relation within the "plastic horizon" of experience, and his first detailed account of enkapsis.[7] To that extent, art plays more than a minor role in the development of his social ontology. Although Dooyeweerd does not provide as thorough an account of art as Heidegger does, and although much of Dooyeweerd's discussion simply uses one sculpture to illustrate some of his ontological categories, yet his actual presentation of those categories occurs by way of his discussion of art.

On the other hand, even though Dooyeweerd regards the artwork as a "secondary radical type"[8] whose expected ontological location would seem to be within society, and even though the concept of enkapsis plays a crucial role in his own social theory, yet he breathes scarcely a word about art when he analyzes societal structures in Part II. When Dooyeweerd returns briefly to the topic of art in Part III, he does so in the context of enkaptic interlacements within and between *thing*-structures (NC 3: 637–41; WW 3: 561–6), in particular those involving plants and animals, not in the context of enkapsis involving *societal* structures. This textual dis/placement indicates a tension in Dooyeweerd's conception, a tension between treating the work of art like a (natural) thing and recognizing that the entire realm of art is historical, cultural, and bound up with societal structures. By restricting his discussion of art to the context of "thing-structures," most of them "natural," however, Dooyeweerd does not deal with the most interesting questions about art's sociohistorical character, and he leaves his understanding of cultural practices and societal structures incomplete.

The peculiar placement of Dooyeweerd's discussion of art leaves interpreters with conflicting options. Most readers play down the importance of Dooyeweerd's discussion, in keeping with his apparent intention to use a sculpture merely to illustrate several ontological issues and to lay out some preliminary distinctions. One might call readings of this sort weak and sympathetic interpretations. A different approach would be to suspend Dooyeweerd's apparent intention, in order to consider what he actually contributes to a philosophy of the arts and what such a contribution implies for his social ontology. This would yield a strong and critical interpretation, which is the sort of reading that I plan to give.

Indeed, I shall suggest that Dooyeweerd's account leads to a fourfold reduction whose ramifications plague not simply his nascent philosophy of art but his entire social theory and cultural critique. I shall identify the four reductions and indicate why each is problematic, discussing in turn the reduction (1) of structure to law, (2) of art to the artwork, (3) of the artwork to a thing, and (4) of the thingly artwork to the artist's aesthetic conception. The upshot of those reductions, in pejorative terms, is that art comes to seem like a preordained collection of unnatural and fantastic things. Nevertheless, one can find seeds in Dooyeweerd's account that, if properly cultivated, could grow into a more productive social ontology of art.

## 1. STRUCTURE AND LAW

Kent Zigterman has demonstrated that Dooyeweerd's theory of individuality structures, as presented in the pages prior to his analysis of art (NC 3: 1–103, WW 3: 1–70), both fails to account for the unity of individual things and "allows no essential difference in internal structure between things, acts, events, and societal relationships."[9] Although these two problems stem, as Zigterman suggests, from Dooyeweerd's opposition to any metaphysics of "substance" that would deny the dependence and referential character of creation, I think they can just as readily be linked with Dooyeweerd's opposition to evolutionism, historicism, and other tendencies to reduce structures to processes.[10] For it is such modern tendencies, and not merely the older metaphysics, that Dooyeweerd credits with eliminating individuality structures from the purview of the academic disciplines: "Special sciences are in a constant danger of surrendering to an evolutionistic or historicistic view which results in an elimination of the structures of individuality. Therefore it is necessary to emphasize that every genetic viewpoint pre-supposes these structures. The latter cannot be subject to genesis and evolution, it is only their *realization* in changeable individuals which permits a genetic investigation according to specific scientific viewpoints" (NC 3: 94).[11] In response to this "constant danger," Dooyeweerd pitches his theory of individuality structures at a very high level of (primarily modal) abstraction, and he treats most such structures, and all structural principles, as invariant laws.

Dooyeweerd's double opposition, to both substance metaphysics and geneticism, generates the reverse sides to his theory of things. On the one hand, he claims, as in the two paragraphs preceding his analysis of "the objective thing-structure of a sculpture," that "thing-reality" (*de dingwerkelijkheid*) is a thoroughly dynamic and "continuous realization [*ver-werkelijking*]" revealing the "inner restlessness of meaning" characteristic of all creation (NC 3: 109, WW 3: 76–7). On the other hand, he also insists, as he does in a telling passage just a few pages earlier, that the structural principles which things continuously realize are "in no way dependent upon the genesis of individuals in which they are realized" but have an *a priori* and determinative character: "they are the structural frame in which alone the process of genesis and decay of individual beings is possible" (NC 3: 106).[12]

According to Zigterman's interpretation of Dooyeweerd, the dynamic "realization" of structural principles in things "is essentially synonymous with a conforming to law, or a being determined by law."[13] Hence it is easy for Dooyeweerd to slide from the claim that structural principles do not depend on the genesis of individual entities, to the quite different claim that structural principles do not come into being, change, or perish. Despite his emphasis on the endless variety and dynamism of creation, Dooyeweerd tends to treat structures and structural principles as invariant laws, regardless of the specificity, scope, and historical, cultural, or societal uniqueness of the structure in question.

Zigterman, ever the charitable exegete, tries to slow Dooyeweerd's slide by introducing terminology derived from a categorial distinction worked out by Hendrik Hart and James Olthuis between "structures-of" and "structures-for." Hoping to avoid the multiple ambiguities in Dooyeweerd's "'structures' 'of' 'individuality'" (*individualiteits-structuren*), Zigterman distinguishes between "factual structures" and "law-structures" (or "typical structures" or "structural types"). The terms signal a categorial distinction between structures that are not laws but are subject to laws, and structures that are not subject to laws but are themselves laws. Factual structures are individual, changing, and transient. They are "actual things with a certain typical make-up in which typical structures [i.e., law-structures] are historically realized." Law-structures, by contrast, are neither individual nor changeable. They "have … no duration but are of an *a priori* determining character."[14] Unfortunately, Dooyeweerd himself is nowhere so clear as this. Moreover, all the problems Zigterman identifies in Dooyeweerd's account of factual structures point in the same direction: Dooyeweerd regularly tends to identify factual structures with law structures, to the detriment of the individuality, variability, and transience that one would expect of factual structures.[15]

Perhaps this tendency helps explain the ease with which Dooyeweerd draws conclusions about the nature of all artworks and of art in general from his analysis of one classical Greek sculpture, the sculpture by Praxiteles of the god Hermes with the boy Dionysus. If structures are laws, then it should not matter much which works or how many works are consulted, so long as the relevant invariant patterns are identified in the phenomenon selected for analysis. And indeed, nearly all of the features identified on the first two pages (NC 3: 111–12, WW 3: 79–80) as belonging to "the internal typical structure" of Praxiteles's sculpture[16] are not peculiar to this particular piece but instead are characteristic of all marble sculptures, or all sculptures, or even all works of art: (1) the last modal subject-function is physico-chemical; (2) this subject-function should express "the internal structure of the objective work of art" (NC

3: 111, WW 3: 79); (3) the sculpture seems to lack an actual biotic function – a source of endless worry for Dooyeweerd, and something he never really lays to rest; (4) all the (other) post-physical structural functions of the sculpture must be objective, corresponding to human subject-functions; and (5) the sensory side of the artist's aesthetic vision of the living human body is objectively depicted (*afgebeeld*) in the artwork's individual structure.[17]

Despite the repeated references to Praxiteles's sculpture in subsequent pages, we learn little more that would be peculiar to this particular piece or its unique structure.[18] The closest Dooyeweerd comes to describing this sculpture as an aesthetic phenomenon is in his comments on the "wonderful technique" Praxiteles employed to present a vital function (NC 3: 117, WW 3: 86). He also details the physical and chemical properties of marble (NC 3: 124, WW 3: 93), but what he says here could be said about any slab of marble. At the same time no other particular sculptures nor any other particular artworks are analyzed. Yet Dooyeweerd derives from his discussion two general norms, one for all artworks (i.e., the inner unity of technical form and aesthetic import – NC 3: 121, WW 3: 91), and the other for all plastic artworks (i.e., the enkaptic unity of natural material and artistic expression – NC 3: 124–5, 640–1; WW 3: 93–5, 564–6). The derivation occurs without examination of the ways in which the Praxiteles sculpture meets such norms, and certainly without consideration of other specific instances in which the norms are either met or missed.

One might be tempted to credit such peculiarities to the oddities of Dooyeweerd's methodology, which, being neither inductive nor deductive, comes across in these pages as a malfunctioning phenomenology. Yet I think the true source of Dooyeweerd's inattention to the details of *Hermes* or of any other artwork lies in his tendency to reduce both structures and structural principles to invariant laws. As I read it, the whole point of Dooyeweerd's discussing the Praxiteles sculpture is not to uncover the structure of this particular piece nor even to unearth the sociohistorically embedded structure of marble sculptures, which simply do not occur in many cultures and societies. Instead the point is to identify the laws governing all "*things qualified by a normative object-function*" (NC 3: 109, WW 3: 77, Dooyeweerd's emphasis) and, by implication, all works of art.

Dooyeweerd's three main conclusions in this context are (1) that all such things have historical founding object-functions and normative qualifying object-functions, (2) that an inner unity between foundation and qualification is crucial to the worth of such things, and (3) that, insofar as such things involve natural materials, an enkaptic unity between the natural material and the thing's own inner unity is essential to the thing's success.[19]

At this point one could say in Dooyeweerd's defence that he simply wants to use the *Hermes* sculpture as an example, and hence one should not expect too much from his analysis. Nevertheless, two problems beset this defence. First, it ignores the arbitrariness of Dooyeweerd's "example," for he could have made most of his main systematic points without ever mentioning the sculpture. Second, the defence ignores the fact that Dooyeweerd himself draws several crucial conclusions about the nature of art from this one example. It is not the critic but Dooyeweerd himself who loads too much into his analysis of the *Hermes* sculpture, even as he ignores most of its particular features and unique structure.

## 2. ART AND ARTWORK

In keeping with the emphasis on invariant laws and the concomitant inattention to particular works and unique structures, Dooyeweerd sidesteps questions about the historical, cultural, and societal settings in which art arises as a relatively independent cultural realm interwoven with relatively independent cultural institutions. Throughout the analysis of *Hermes* he assumes as unproblematic that this sculpture is indeed to be classified as a "work of art," and a "masterpiece" at that.[20] One finds no hint in Dooyeweerd's prose that the categories "artwork" and "masterpiece" are themselves relatively recent products of a convoluted sociohistorical process, or that only much later and outside its original setting did Praxiteles's sculpture come to be regarded as and to function as an "artwork" and a "masterpiece."

When Dooyeweerd does come around to discussing the distinction between fine arts and other arts, he takes a structural and ahistorical approach. In his own terms, the main difference between "free art" or "pure art" and "bound art" or "applied art" occurs at the level of radical types. Whereas free art is aesthetically qualified, bound art is qualified by nonaesthetic functions. "Free art" refers to artworks whose inner structural principle has been liberated (*bevrijd*) from its enkaptic tie to (*binding in*) the structural principle of things not aesthetically qualified (NC 3: 139, WW 3: 110).[21] In "bound art," by contrast, the product's structural principle does not have an aesthetic qualification, and the product's aesthetic function should remain bound in that product's structure, in accordance with the product's own founding and leading functions. Although an architect, for example, must pay attention to aesthetic considerations, the aesthetic side of the architect's conception must be subordinated to the building's structural principle, whose qualifying function is not aesthetic (NC 3: 140, WW 3: 110–11).

If one follows this distinction through to its logical conclusion, however, one must wonder why products of bound art are even considered to be art, since they lack the aesthetic qualification that characterizes all artworks in Dooyeweerd's account. Moreover, although Dooyeweerd indicates that craft has served as a historical occasion (*aanleiding*) for the rise of free art (NC 3: 138, WW 3: 109), and that free art tends to presuppose a differentiated civilization (NC 3: 140, WW 3: 111), he ignores the fact that the rise of free art is also a historical condition for the institutions and categories of bound art. In this sense, the sculpture by Praxiteles, in its original setting, is neither free art nor bound art, neither fine art nor craft, and it is certainly not a "work of art" in the modern sense of the term, which presupposes institutional and categorial distinctions between fine arts and the other arts.

Dooyeweerd, however, plunges directly into an analysis of one sculpture (Why analyze a product rather than a process?), identifies it without hesitation as a work of art (Why not identify it as a cultic object that through the years has turned into a cultural commodity?), analyzes its internal structure (Why examine its status as an independent "thing" rather than its societally imbricated uses and purposes?), and draws conclusions about the nature of art in general – only to find later, but not really to notice, that he has thereby banished all "bound" or "applied" art from the artistic realm, including, for example, liturgical art, most movies, and nearly all folk and popular music. Perhaps this outcome would be less troubling if he were simply giving a philosophically reflective account of the sociohistorically bound category of "fine art," although even then the restriction to "artwork" would be problematic. However, he wants to provide an ontology of one of the "radical types" of human culture, not as a contextualized category, but as a universal structure of reality, and for this purpose he chooses, or rather simply assumes, the relatively recent and limited category "work of art."

Again, one could say in Dooyeweerd's defence that he does not intend to give a thorough analysis of the concept of "art," and thus his discussion of the *Hermes* sculpture should not be read as an account of the concept of "the artwork." And, as a description of Dooyeweerd's intention, the defence is probably correct. The difficulty, however, is that

Dooyeweerd does use his discussion to arrive at claims about the nature of art and artworks, and those claims seem questionable. Moreover, the claims support an account of cultural products ("things qualified by a normative object-function") that divorces their structure from their social and historical settings.

The structure Dooyeweerd discovers is characterized by two of the many functions "internal" to the "thing-structure" of *Hermes*. Against those who would reduce *Hermes* to something serving utilitarian or moral purposes, he argues that the leading function of this particular sculpture is an internal, typical, and aesthetic object-function, namely the presentation (*kunst-uitbeeldsel*) of an intentional, imagined, and aesthetically qualified Hermes-configuration (NC 3: 117, WW 3: 86). Against those who would reduce this and all other artworks to purely aesthetic objects, Dooyeweerd insists that the leading function displays a structurally unbreakable relationship with a typical founding function of an earlier modality (NC 3: 118, WW 3: 86), and that, in the case of works employing natural materials, this relationship is itself grounded in the natural material (NC 3: 640, WW 3: 565).[22] And against those who would reduce *Hermes* to a natural thing, Dooyeweerd argues that the sculpture's typical founding function cannot be located (a) in the physico-chemical function of the unfinished marble, (b) in the sensory fantasy-configuration presented (*uitgebeelde*) and realized (*verwerkelijkte*) in the marble as physical material (*materiaal*), or (c) in the objective sensory configuration of the marble statue (NC 3: 119–20, WW 3: 87–90). Rather, the sculpture's founding function is historical. It is the objective and technical presentational form (*uitbeeldende vorm*) given by the artist to the marble material (NC 3: 121, WW 3: 90).[23]

To summarize, and to extend this account to all artworks: Dooyeweerd holds that technical form and aesthetic import (*aesthetisch gehalte*) are the two functions characterizing every artwork, and that their inner unity is required of every good and mature artwork (NC 3: 121, WW 3: 91).[24] This means that all geno-types of artworks (including, e.g., musical works and literary works) exhibit the same secondary radical type. They are all historically founded and aesthetically qualified (i.e., qualified by an aesthetic object-function) (NC 3: 122–3, WW 3: 91).[25]

Unfortunately, this entire account assumes a relatively recent and Eurocentric sociohistorical process but treats the distinctions thrown up by that process as invariant structures.[26] Dooyeweerd is certainly not alone in that approach. He shares with much of modernist aesthetics the tendency to make the concept "work of art" central to an account of the entire realm of art. More recently, however, numerous studies have shown that the very concept of a "work of art" presupposes the categories and institutions of autonomous art as these crystallized in eighteenth- and early nineteenth-century Europe.[27] To understand this concept, and not simply to assume it as unproblematic, one must see how it serves to shift the emphasis in art making and art enjoyment from process to product, from occasion to commodity, and from use to status. One must also pay attention to how the concept anchors a network of art-related categories whose content and import would shift if the anchor were lifted.

## 3. WORK AND THING

My argument so far is that Dooyeweerd treats the sociohistorically embedded structures of art as ahistorical laws of reality, and he tends to turn the complex and dynamic cultural realm of art into a structurally defined collection of artworks of various types. Both the emphasis on laws and the focus on artworks assume a prior orientation to understanding the structures of "temporal things." The underlying categorial distinction in Dooyeweerd's social ontology is that between "things" (the main topic of Part I) and "societal relationships" (*samenlevingsverhoudingen*, the main topic of Part II).

This distinction was not always obvious, however. The Dutch edition observes that in earlier publications Dooyeweerd had also considered the structures of communities to be "thing-structures." This identification with things, he says, highlighted the real and continuous identity of such societal relationships, their functioning as actual unities in all their modal aspects, and their possessing typical internal structural principles. In addition, calling communities "things" helped distinguish Dooyeweerd's social philosophy from functionalist, substantialist, and dialectical theories. The Dutch edition avoids this terminology simply because it is not "customary" (WW 3: 138–9).

Yet the English edition goes beyond that pragmatic reason. There Dooyeweerd criticizes the "fundamental confusion between the societal structure of an organized community and the thing-structure" in Rudolf Kjellèn's substantialist theory of the state,[28] and he deems it highly "inadequate and confusing" to apply the term "thing-structure" to organized communities (NC 3: 197). More importantly, Dooyeweerd now provides a definition of "thing" that explicitly excludes human communities. A thing is "a structural whole of a relatively permanent character which lacks subject-functions in the logical and post-logical aspects and therefore can be only an 'object' in the typical human societal relationships" (NC 3: 197).[29] An organized human community, by contrast, has subject-functions in all the modes of human experience, "can never be a societal object," and "can only be realized in a ... social coherence of typical human acts and ... modes of ... behaviour" (NC 3: 198).

But what sort of distinction is this, if not one between the human and the nonhuman, between culture and nature, and between "mental" subjects and "real" objects? So far as I can tell, Dooyeweerd nowhere gives an argument for grouping rocks, trees, cats, birds' nests, etc. together under the same ontological category of "thing," other than his repeated claim that human beings and their communities are ontologically different from all of these other entities. The difference hinges on whether or not an entity possesses subject-functions in the post-psychic aspects. That, however, is hardly a compelling argument, since in Dooyeweerd's own terms it establishes no more than the difference between the human and the nonhuman; it says nothing specifically about the purportedly shared identity of all entities called "things." Again, Dooyeweerd nowhere gives a compelling argument for lumping artworks, utensils, books, etc. together with rocks, trees, cats, birds' nests, etc. under the single ontological category of thinghood.

I do not mean to deny the initial plausibility of his intuition that all such entities have a relative wholeness, unity, continuity, individuality, and independence. The problem is that those other entities which he does not want to call things, such as human beings and human communities, also have such characteristics. Hence the crucial difference between "things" and other entities on Dooyeweerd's account lies in the level of subjective functioning, with the primary division occurring between the psychic and post-psychic levels. Although this division plays a large role in Dooyeweerd's ontology, it also spares him a detailed elaboration and justification of one of his own central categories, namely thinghood.

The pitfalls of this division become apparent in Dooyeweerd's account of art. Immediately he must admit that many of the artistic entities he wants to call artworks do not display "the constant actual existence proper to things in the narrower sense" (NC 3: 110, WW 3: 78). Works of music, poetry, and drama lack the relative permanence that characterizes things. So Dooyeweerd allows for artworks *that are not things*, even though he aims to elucidate the *thing-structure* of artworks. He addresses this apparent anomaly by saying that musical works and the like can be "constantly objectified" in scores, books, etc., and that such works always need "subjective actualization" by way of performance. (Presumably "objectification" and "actualization" give such works a degree of "relative permanence" without making them things). The fact that as individuality structures all artworks belong to the same radical type need not imply that all of them have a thing-structure (NC 3: 110–11, WW 3: 78–9).[30]

Given Dooyeweerd's ontological categories, this approach simply defers the question rather than answering it. If works in the performing arts are not things "in the narrower sense," then what are they, and why does Dooyeweerd discuss artworks under the general rubric of "temporal things"? What account would he give of all those performance pieces, whether improvised or sustained by oral traditions, that are not "constantly objectified" in scores and books? Why does Dooyeweerd assume that works in the performing arts are primarily compositions, poems, and plays to be written down and performed rather than the actual occurrences experienced when the music sounds, the poem is uttered, or the play is presented? Doesn't the living presence of human players in such occurrences call for an altogether different category from "thinghood"?[31]

A second problem in the treatment of artworks as things surfaces when Dooyeweerd distinguishes the work's internal structure from its external purposes in order to insist that the artistic radical type be defined in terms of the work's internal structure. The model for this distinction comes from Dooyeweerd's analysis of "natural things" such as the linden tree in his garden. While it makes some sense to say that one's ontology should not lose sight of the tree as such and should not dissolve it into the various purposes it serves within its (cultivated) environment (NC 3: 60, WW 3: 41), the same cannot easily be said of artworks, whose very existence as artworks depends on the ongoing interactions of human beings in their sociohistorical context and institutional settings. Although Dooyeweerd shows a partial awareness of such dependency by analyzing artworks in the context of the subject-*object* relation,[32] he never gets around to discussing artworks in the context of the subject-*subject* relation, nor does he ever do justice to his own insight that artworks are *societal* objects. In fact, the persistent worry about *Hermes*'s apparently absent biotic function could have been quickly laid to rest if Dooyeweerd had simply acknowledged that this sculpture, like all artistic entities, answers to human needs and interests that are malleable and dynamic.[33]

Dooyeweerd overlooks this potential solution, however, because of his preoccupation with the natural material and its connection with the artistic entity. And herein lies a third problem: namely, the treatment of the artwork as a cultural thing wedded to a natural thing. This treatment exemplifies exactly the view Martin Heidegger so thoroughly dismantles in his essay "The Origin of the Work of Art" as he lets the artwork disclose what is thingly about things rather than imposing an inappropriate category of thinghood on the artwork.[34] Dooyeweerd, who appears never to have read Heidegger's essay, assumes in the traditional manner that a sculpture such as *Hermes* has a double identity, and that such a double identity characterizes all artworks that are "things in the narrower sense." His account goes as follows.

When analyzing the Praxiteles sculpture (or any other work of plastic art), one must distinguish two individuality structures: the structure of the physically qualified natural material, and the structure of the aesthetically qualified and historically founded work of art (NC 3: 123, WW 3: 91–2). Although distinct, these two structures are intimately interwoven in the statue, such that the natural marble provides the typical thing-substratum of the marble statue as an artwork. In more general terms, wherever art employs "natural material," a natural thing grounds the artwork (NC 3: 123–4, WW 3: 92–3); the two are bound in an "irreversible enkaptic foundational relation" (NC 3: 640, WW 3: 564).[35] The relation is enkaptic in the sense that one individuality structure (i.e., the artwork) restrictively binds a second structure of a different radical- or geno-type (i.e., the natural marble) without destroying the second structure's peculiar character (NC 3: 125n, WW 3: 94n). The relation is irreversible in the sense that the artwork is "indissolubly bound to the structure of the marble" (NC 3: 640, WW 3: 565) and cannot function separately from its enkaptic interlacement with the marble (NC 3: 128, WW 3: 97). But the same does not apply to the natural material: the marble continues to exist as marble and can function separately from its enkaptic interlacement with the artwork, even though the marble's structure is opened and deepened into "aesthetically expressive material" bound by the artwork's technical form and aesthetic import (NC 3: 124–5, 640–1; WW 3: 93–4, 565–6).

Rather than explain the "thing-structure" of the artwork, Dooyeweerd's account of enkapsis introduces additional complications. Now one must ask what sense it makes to talk about the "sculptural work of art" or the "marble work of art" (NC 3: 123, WW 3: 92–3), when the work of art as such is neither sculptural nor marble. Moreover, the "relative permanence" supposedly characterizing *Hermes* as a thing "in the narrower sense" seems due not to its structure as an artwork but to its connection to a "natural" slab of marble. Also, to talk of the marble as "natural material" is to overlook entirely the extent to which slabs of marble, like pieces of steel, are human *products* dependent on specific economic and technological conditions as well as artistic *media* embedded in specific cultural traditions.

While serving to introduce the notion of enkaptic unity, the discussion of the *Hermes* sculpture further complicates the assumption that artworks are things. On the one hand, Dooyeweerd assigns the artwork a double identity as both an aesthetic-technical thing and an artistic-natural thing. On the other hand, the key to the artwork's unity lies in Dooyeweerd's general conception of things as relatively permanent entities lacking post-psychical subject-functions. Dooyeweerd's discussion implies a double reification of art: the treatment of cultural products as "things in the narrower sense," and the treatment of the artwork proper as an aesthetic-historical structure wedded to a natural thing.

## 4. THING AND CONCEPTION

As if to compensate for this double reification, Dooyeweerd repeatedly underscores the dependence of the artwork's identity upon human consciousness. In particular, the artist's intentional aesthetic conception comes to occupy centre stage. By describing the marble as "expressive material" (*uitdrukkingsmateriaal*) (NC 3: 125, 640; WW 3: 93, 656), for example, Dooyeweerd's account of the artwork's "natural" substructure privileges the artist's intention. He uses similar terms to formulate the enkaptic "normative law" (NC 3: 126; WW 3: 95) for plastic arts: the natural material should become "a complete expression of the artist's conception" (my translation of "een *volledige uitdrukking* … van de conceptie des kunstenaars"), and there should be no disturbing dualism "between the enkaptically bound natural structure … and the objective expression of the aesthetic conception" (NC 3: 125, WW 3: 94). When he returns to *Hermes*'s enkaptic relation in Part III, Dooyeweerd describes this artwork's qualifying function as "the aesthetic conception … objectified in the presentation" (my translation of "de, in uitbeelding *geobjectiveerde, aesthetische conceptie* van de godengestalte"), and he says that the marble's natural lawfulness is made completely serviceable to the aesthetic expression ("Zijn … *eigenwettelijkheid* … in het zichtbare makrobeeld geheel aan de aesthetische uitdrukking is dienstbaar gemaakt") (NC 3: 640–1, WW 3: 565–6).[36]

So too, Dooyeweerd's account of the internal structure of the artwork as such highlights the artist's conception. Against a naturalist aesthetic for which sculptures and other artworks are copies of "real" things, Dooyeweerd argues that, as an objective perceptual image (*waarnemingsbeeld*), the marble statue (*marmerbeeld*) does not simply copy the human model as an objective perceptual image (NC 3: 113, WW 3: 81).[37] Instead the statue expresses the artist's subjective aesthetic conception, which includes a visualization of the artwork's intended sensory configuration (*zinnelijke gestalte*). The statue's sensory configuration is the objective presentation (*uitbeeldsel*) of an intentional fantasy-object (NC 3: 120, WW 3: 89).

According to Dooyeweerd, the artist's aesthetic conception is an "individual, aesthetically qualified total structure" that arises in the artist's productive aesthetic fantasy (*fantasie*) (NC 3: 113, WW 3: 81). The artist's productive aesthetic fantasy, in turn, relies on a (psychic) fantasy-feeling (*fantasiegevoel*) to produce a sensory fantasy-image (*fantasiebeeld*) that becomes part of the artist's aesthetic conception.[38] The object of the artist's aesthetic conception is an intentional object, a fantasied objective thing-structure, and this intentional object gets de-picted (*laat zich afbeelden*) in the artwork, in an actual thing (*een werkelijk ding*). This does not mean, however, that the artwork's aesthetic object-function is simply an objectification of the artist's aesthetic subjectivity. Rather, the artwork's aesthetic object-function is the aesthetic depiction of the artist's merely intentional aesthetic object in the objective and aesthetically qualified structure of a real thing – i.e., in the structure of an artwork (NC 3: 116, WW 3: 84–5).

Accordingly, the *Hermes* sculpture is a thing-reality that has been productively formed in an aesthetic manner (*een productief aesthetisch gevormde ding-werkelijkheid*). It is the aesthetically qualified depiction (*afbeeldsel*) of the original visualization and of the entire aesthetic conception in the artist's productive fantasy.[39] Against those who view such a sculpture as the replica of some particular human being, Dooyeweerd argues that the proper appreciation of this artwork requires more than the universal and receptive aesthetic *beholding* (*de algemeen menschelijke, ontvankelijke, subjectief-aesthetische aanschouwing*) needed to appreciate natural beauty: it requires a reproductive aesthetic *fantasy*, which discloses and deepens such aesthetic beholding (NC 3: 114–15, WW 3: 82–3).[40] Hence, just as the marble is "expressive material" serving the artist's aesthetic conception, so the aesthetic object-function that qualifies the statue as an artwork is itself the depiction of an intentional object of the artist's imaginatively founded aesthetic conception.

In other words, despite Dooyeweerd's emphasis on the artwork's objectivity and its material substratum, he tends to reduce the artwork to a reification of the individual artist's aesthetic fantasy. This reification, however, is indirect, for Dooyeweerd's account inserts an intentional object between the artist's aesthetic conception and the artwork's aesthetic object-function. The problems generated by this account are too numerous and complex to receive adequate treatment here. Let me simply mention several difficulties that show how Dooyeweerd's reduction of the artistic "thing" to the artist's "conception" reinforces the other reductions already described.

In the first place, Dooyeweerd's subjectivizing account of the artwork's aesthetic function reinforces his general tendency to isolate the artistic product from the cultural, societal, and historical conditions under which it arises and within which it continues to function. Although he might seem to correct this deficiency by distinguishing "three figures in the subject-object relation" of cultural "things," his account of these figures simply continues to turn dynamic processes into static structures. I have in mind here Dooyeweerd's distinctions among (1) the intentional depictive relation (*afbeeldingsrelatie*), (2) the opening relation (*ontsluitingsrelatie*), and (3) the actualization relation (*actualiseeringsrelatie*) (NC 3: 143–53, WW 3: 116–28). These distinctions are designed to explain how something created as an aesthetically qualified artwork (intentional depictive relation) calls for, but does not depend on, an appropriately aesthetic response (opening relation). Moreover, the distinctions imply that an artwork does not become a different kind of "thing" when it is treated, say, as a mere commodity, even though its objective aesthetic destination is thereby inactualized (actualization relation). The net effect of applying such distinctions to art, however, is to say: once an artwork, always an artwork, no matter what changes occur in a culture and society. This claim is all the more problematic when one recalls that *Hermes*, Dooyeweerd's prime example, was not even created as an aesthetically qualified work of art.

In the second place, Dooyeweerd's emphasis on the artist's aesthetic conception overlooks entirely the larger realm through whose sociohistorical constitution artists can become artists. At the beginning of "The Origin of the Work of Art," Heidegger correctly observes that neither the artist nor the artwork is the sole origin of the other; instead, art is the origin of both.[41] Dooyeweerd, by contrast, constructs a straightforward genesis from artist to artwork to art, never pausing to consider that neither *artist* nor *artwork* could exist were it not for the categorial and institutional framework of *art*, itself the achievement of a long historical dialectic. While it is the case that Dooyeweerd wants first of all to establish which functions in what aspects characterize artworks as artworks, it is also the case that his account of aesthetic qualification and historical foundation governs everything he has to say about art.[42] In addition, Dooyeweerd's discussion of the relationship between artist and artwork inadvertently overlooks the possibility that artists make creations other than artworks, whether those be art products that are not works (e.g., songs of popular music), or art events (e.g., concerts, exhibitions), or art productions (e.g., recordings, television programs), or art actions (e.g., liturgical dancing). In other words, Dooyeweerd overlooks the possibility that the cultural realm of art calls for a more expansive ontology than one whose primary categories are "thing" and "societal relationship."

In the third place, Dooyeweerd's account of artistry reinforces the reduction of works to things, removing them from the interhuman dialogue that sustains them. His account conjures the picture of the isolated artist, alone with his or her consciousness, and facing inert natural material to be rendered expressive of the artist's aesthetic conception. Yet, for the most part, this is not how the making of art occurs.[43] Artists continually interact with other artists and the world around them. Their efforts aim at certain audiences and take into account various conditions of distribution and reception. And much of their "aesthetic conception" arises from listening intently to humanly constructed media that embody specific traditions or anti-traditions and that speak their own language.

***

My criticisms do not imply that Dooyeweerd's discussion of art is so hopelessly wrong-headed as to be beyond redemption. I think that his account of aesthetic qualification and "historical" foundation can be reconstructed to provide a more expansive and more precise theory of the entire realm of art. But this theory will be a full-fledged social ontology, one that does not tend to reduce structures to laws, or art to artworks, or artworks to things, or things to artistic conceptions. It will acknowledge the cultural, societal, and historical variability that characterizes art, and it will relocate both the artist and the artwork in the interhuman institutions that make art possible.

A brief sketch of this theory would go like this. Art products are imaginative constructions (technical founding function) made to mediate a disclosive presentation (aesthetic qualifying function), and they are used as interpretable expressions (aesthetic qualifying function) grounded in expressive design (technical founding function). The relevant norms for these typical functions are freshness and fit (technical norms) as well as candor and significance (aesthetic norms). In distinction from other art products, the artwork has a peculiar independence from both the making and the enjoying of art, and this independence is made possible by a modern institutional network known as "the art world." Such independence gives rise to a third characterization of typical functions: namely, configured import (aesthetic qualifying function) wedded to allusive configuration (technical founding function), answerable to the norms of (aesthetic) integrity and (technical) authenticity. It is a mistake, however, to hold all art *products* to these norms for art*works*, just as it is a mistake to exempt artworks from the general norms of freshness, fit, candor, and significance, or to consider such norms less important than the more specific norms of authenticity and integrity. Even if artworks as such were to disappear from the map of Western culture, the norms of freshness, fit, etc. would continue to hold for various art products. Moreover, there are many other functions and norms to be considered in addition to the technical and aesthetic ones already mentioned.[44]

What Dooyeweerd provides is an insight into the multidimensional and normative character of all those activities, events, processes, intersubjective relations, and products that make up the artistic realm. With suitable revisions and extensions, his account of the work of art can serve the development of a normative and critical social ontology of the arts.[45]

PART TWO

# Reforming Reason

If the holism, normativity, and radical character of reformational philosophy make the contributions of Dooyeweerd and Vollenhoven important, then these same features generate the tradition's central problems. That becomes apparent in the pathbreaking work of the second-generation reformational scholars with whom I studied at ICS in the 1970s and who shaped my own philosophy, including Hendrik Hart, James Olthuis, Calvin Seerveld, and Al Wolters. The five chapters in Part II take up some of these problems in second-generation reformational philosophy, especially in the work of Hendrik Hart, my predecessor in systematic philosophy at ICS and a source for much of my current work in epistemology and social ontology.

In many ways, the concerns of the second generation flow from the first-generational insights and problems that we considered in Part I. Henk Hart's writings, to be examined in chapters 6–8, take up central issues in Dooyeweerd's transcendental critique and his conception of truth, already explored in chapters 1–3. Cal Seerveld's pioneering work in aesthetics and historiography, briefly discussed in chapter 9, employs and revises both Dooyeweerd's modal theory (chapter 4) and his ontology of the arts (chapter 5). Moreover, second-generation reformational scholars typically retain the first generation's emphasis on the centrality of religion or spirituality to human life, even as they struggle to articulate exactly what this means for the modally diverse ways in which people exist – a topic touched on in chapter 10.

Chapter 6 ("God, Law, and Cosmos") is a critical discussion of Hart's *Understanding Our World* (1984), the book that encapsulates his seminal explorations of ontology and epistemology in the 1970s. *Understanding Our World* remains one of the most important rearticulations of systematic reformational philosophy since the publication of Dooyeweerd's *New Critique* in the 1950s. *Philosophia Reformata* originally published this chapter, under a different title, one year after Hart's book appeared. The chapter probes Hart's account of the relations among creaturely existence, the laws or "nomic conditions" that hold for creaturely existence, and the (divine) origin of both creatures and the laws to which they are subject. Historically, an account of such relations is at the very core of reformational philosophy as a philosophy of the "law idea" (*wetsidee* – Dooyeweerd) or as a "Calvinistic philosophy" for which the distinction between God as sovereign creator and God's creation is a non-negotiable "basic theme" (*grondmotief* – Vollenhoven). Chapter 6 signals two problems in how Hart develops this account. First, by restricting the concept of "existence" to creaturely reality, he raises questions not only about the existence of God and law but also about how anyone can know their existence. Second, by relegating the discussion of his ultimate ontological categories – including the category of (divine) origin – to a "prescientific" Appendix, Hart seems to remove them from philosophical and theological debate – precisely the arena where they arise and where they have the most potential relevance.

What links these two problems is Hart's conception of reason's role in human life and of the relation between reason and faith, a conception he worked out in friendly published debates with the prominent Canadian philosopher Kai Nielsen during the 1980s. I take up Hart's conception in chapter 7. Titled "Artistic Truth, Linguistically Turned," it originally appeared in the Festschrift honouring Hart upon his retirement in 2001, and it gave early expression to ideas about knowledge and truth in my book *Artistic Truth*. The chapter employs these ideas to suggest that, in his legitimate objections to the Western emphasis on rationality, Hart overemphasizes the spirituality of knowledge and underplays the rationality of religion. Nevertheless, I remain deeply indebted to his insights into the dynamic and comprehensive character of knowledge and truth.

Chapter 8, titled "The Inner Reformation of Reason," goes into greater detail about Hart's conception of faith and reason. First presented in 2004 at an ICS symposium devoted to issues raised in the Hart Festschrift, it elicited a lively discussion from Henk Hart and the other two panelists: James Olthuis, his friend and close colleague, and Vaden House, his first doctoral student at ICS. The chapter argues that Hart's conception has three limitations. First, he characterizes rationality as an explicit grasping of order. Second, he holds that the ultimate objects of faith lie beyond the order that rationality can grasp. Third, he does not give adequate attention to how the practices of rationality, including those that occur within the life of faith, are embedded in ordinary linguistic practices. Drawing on the work of Jürgen Habermas, I propose instead an account that emphasizes intersubjective validity rather than nonsubjective order, regards the practices of communicative rationality as intrinsic to faith, and makes faith both a topic and a resource for normative criticisms of contemporary society, including religious organizations and practices.[1]

In the background to these chapters on Hart's philosophy, as well as the previous chapters on Dooyeweerd and Vollenhoven, lies an approach to the history of philosophy that took shape during three years of doctoral research and writing on Theodor Adorno in West Berlin during the late 1970s. Although the opening pages of my doctoral dissertation give a compressed account,[2] I first elaborated this approach in 1985 when I presented a paper at ICS titled "Metacritique in the Historiography of Philosophy." Never previously submitted for publication,[3] the paper, significantly revised, appears here as chapter 9, titled "Metacritique: Adorno, Vollenhoven, and the Problem-Historical Method." This chapter examines Vollenhoven's distinction between systematic philosophy and the historiography of philosophy, and it argues that metacritique is the centre from which these two lines of inquiry should proceed. In making this case, I take up different appropriations of Vollenhoven's "problem-historical method" proposed by Al Wolters and Calvin Seerveld, both of whom helped shape my own understanding of the history of philosophy.

Although chapter 10 ("Defining Humankind"), on the philosophical anthropologies of phenomenologist Max Scheler and cultural philosopher Ernst Cassirer, is too brief to illustrate all that a metacritique entails, it does attempt the movement from immanent criticism to metacritical reflection that, on my view, should characterize historically informed systematic philosophy. Originally presented in a shorter version at the 1988 World Congress of Philosophy in Brighton, England, the chapter rearticulates a reformational insight about humankind for a general philosophical audience. As Dooyeweerd, Vollenhoven, Hart, Olthuis, Seerveld, and Wolters all agree, no single function or group of functions defines human existence – neither reason nor politics, neither work nor play. Rather, all of our distinct functions cohere in a unity – the heart – that exceeds them and through which we are related both to our origin and destiny and to all other creatures. Despite my criticisms of Dooyeweerd's transcendental critique, Vollenhoven's problem-historical method, and Hart's critique of rationality, I take this emphasis on the "hearted" character of all human existence to be central to the reformational tradition and a key to its philosophical contributions.

6

# God, Law, and Cosmos: Issues in Hendrik Hart's Ontology

(1985)

The publication of *Understanding Our World: An Integral Ontology* has been eagerly awaited by scholars acquainted with the Institute for Christian Studies in Toronto.[1] We have not been disappointed. This book is a significant achievement for its author, Hendrik Hart, and for the Institute where he has taught systematic philosophy for more than fifteen years. The first major work in ontology to come from North American students of H. Evan Runner, Herman Dooyeweerd, and D.H.Th. Vollenhoven, *Understanding Our World* provides a fresh paradigm for Calvinian scholars in the school of cosmonomic philosophy. Hart's approach is neither provincial nor pedantic, however; he recognizes contributions from other traditions and revises cosmonomic categories when these fail to meet contemporary problems.

According to the Introduction, the book has several aims: to help renew systematic philosophy; to "promote Christian philosophical thinking"; and to "construct an integral ontology" that is "dependent on a Christian worldview." Meeting these aims is required "to integrate scholarship and to relate it integrally to the rest of human culture."[2] Indeed, as the subtitle of the book indicates, integrality is the book's main concern, just as integrity is a dominant quality of Hart's philosophical style.

Hart notes several obstacles to integrality. One is a frequent failure among Christians to achieve consistency between their worldview and the philosophical categories employed in their scholarship. Another obstacle comes from the venerable but moribund tradition of considering reason autonomous with respect to fundamental commitments. An additional barrier emerges from the primacy of epistemology over ontology in modern philosophy. To achieve integrality, according to Hart, "we need to explore epistemology in the context of ontology, and ontology in the context of the history of our deepest convictions."[3] *Understanding Our World* provides such an exploration and preludes a planned study in epistemology.

Given the book's aims and the obstacles to their achievement, we may expect a demanding discussion. Hart takes a "high altitude" approach. An approach at lower altitudes would have turned each chapter into a separate monograph. Fortunately, what the book lacks in detailed analysis and sustained argument, it compensates for by the coherence and sweep of a comprehensive survey. The *topoi* scrutinized are central to contemporary ontology and cosmonomic philosophy. These include universality and order (chapters 1 and 2), actors and actions (chapters 3 and 4), relations (chapter 5), humanity (chapter 7), and the categories of unity, diversity, coherence, totality, and time (chapter 6). "A Concluding Prescientific Postscript" presents Hart's "ultimate assumptions" and their roles in his ontology.

Aside from a few aphorisms, which either perplex or provoke further thought, the writing is usually clear and sometimes eloquent. Hart is a master of everyday examples. Occasionally these seem quaint, as in the opening sentence of chapter 1: "Our universe ... is populated by little girls, white-tailed deer, yellow lady slippers, planets and many other things."[4] Most often, however, the examples make illuminating connections with human experience. Another strength of the writing is found in the notes and glossary. These Germanic additions to the main text often extend Hart's analysis and clarify his terminology. I do wish, however, that an alphabetical list had been provided for abbreviated titles. Without it the checking of references becomes tedious.

That complaint aside, I find the book reflects solid, painstaking scholarship. The book is significant, demanding, and of excellent calibre. It will reward careful reading and provoke fruitful debate. To contribute to such reading and debate, I wish to discuss several issues in Hart's ontology. These are not the only issues. Certainly they are not the only ones I find interesting or important. But I suspect they are the ones that will shape the initial reception of this book. They will be discussed under the following six headings: (1) the status of an ontology; (2) the question of existence; (3) the reality of nomic conditions; (4) the origin of nomic conditions; (5) philosophy and God; and (6) commitment and ontology.

## 1. THE STATUS OF ONTOLOGY

It is no secret that for most of our century metaphysics has been considered dead. Many philosophers have seen it as either a backwater to be avoided by progressive analysis or a barrier to be overcome by original thought. Historians might differ as to whether Hegel or Nietzsche or even Heidegger was the last metaphysician, but few of them would view metaphysics as central in twentieth-century philosophy.

If ontology has been the crux of traditional metaphysics, which itself has fallen out of fashion, then contemporary ontological pursuits require some justification. We have already noted that Hart considers ontology crucial for renewing systematic philosophy and for achieving academic integration. In themselves, however, such considerations offer little more than a pragmatic rationale. Upon reading the high claims made for an ontology's potential contributions, we may wonder about the status of this ontology. How does it address its predecessors? How is it situated in its own historical context? Why does it develop certain categories and not others? Furthermore we may expect some answers in the Introduction. Thus the brevity of Hart's comments along these lines may seem puzzling or disappointing.

The Introduction mentions Dooyeweerd, Dewey, Polanyi, and persons in the analytic tradition as having shaped the book's "curious mixture of continental European and analytic approaches."[5] It becomes clear in the first two chapters that Hart's primary distinction between order and existence reworks Dooyeweerd's distinction between law-side and subject-side and Dewey's notion of conjugate relations. This is done in conversation with two parts of analytic philosophy. These parts are "realist" ontologies of universals and particulars (Armstrong, Loux, Quinton, Wolterstorff) and "deductivist" treatments of laws (Hempel, Popper) and systems (Laszlo) in philosophy of the natural sciences. Although neither a realist nor a deductivist, Hart cannot avoid having such discussion partners set some of his own agenda.

One can only speculate about the shape this book would have taken if it had begun in conversation with Hegel, Nietzsche, or Heidegger, none of whose works are cited in the bibliography. Many scholars in the humanities and social sciences probably would have preferred a dialogue with Adorno, Gadamer, Habermas, or Ricoeur, whose works are cited but seldom addressed. In any case, what seems "curious" about the book's mixture is that an approach obviously indebted to the continental school of cosmonomic philosophy can be so ascetic toward other continental approaches and so selective in its dialogue with analytic approaches. There is even surprisingly little discussion of Dewey's work, in which Hart is well versed.

I do not seek to dispute Hart's style but to ask about the status of his ontology. It seems this is not an attempt to come to terms with the broad, battered tradition of metaphysics. Instead, Hart's book is an attempt to develop those ontological categories he considers necessary for a new epistemology and philosophy of science. Hart's central theme is a cosmonomic concern over rationality and commitment;[6] his primary challenge is to develop this theme in language intelligible to contemporary realists and deductivists in the analytic tradition. Given Hart's theme and challenge, we cannot expect him to address worries about ontology's reification of Being (Heidegger), the question of human finitude and fallibility (Ricoeur), the linguistic character of human existence (Gadamer), theories of social evolution (Habermas), or the problem of intersubjectivity in social ontology (Theunissen). Given the broader context of twentieth-century philosophy, however, we may wish such topics had been addressed, or at least we may wish the author had told us why they were being omitted. Where one begins, and which categories one develops, are crucial and perennial problems in ontology. At this level *Understanding Our World* may be expected to go further than it does.

## 2. THE QUESTION OF EXISTENCE

Hart tells us that chapters 1 and 2 "deal with the problem of how to account for the fact that things are both unique and similar to other things."[7] Against realists he argues that universals do not exist. Against nominalists he argues that apparent universality is not simply a function of names or concepts. Hart associates universality with the law-like conditions central to Hempel's account of deductive-nomological explanation in the natural sciences. Universality is nomic, as are the kinds, categories, properties, and relations normally subsumed under the traditional "problem of universals." Calling universality "nomic" or "law-like" allows Hart to say that universality is real but universals are not.

Summarizing his hypothesis about universality, Hart writes: "Both individuality and universality are real. They are also mutually irreducible and correlative. They are in fact traits of a relationship … between the nomic conditions that hold universally for what exists and the empirical existents that individually and subjectively meet those conditions or are subject to them. And understanding what something is, is grasping in a concept what the conditions for its existence are."[8] This summary incorporates a fundamental distinction between "nomic conditions" and "subjective existence." First developed in chapter 2, the distinction is gradually subsumed under an even broader distinction between order and world, where "order" refers to "the totality of all nomic conditions in their coherent interrelations."[9] In the context of the philosophy of science, which dominates chapter 2, Hart postulates "that we all experience an ordered world, that in science we conceptualize and name the order of our world, that whatever it is that we so conceive and name is a reality, and that in appealing to that reality we can both successfully explain our world and account for that explanation."[10]

After developing this position in considerable detail, Hart returns to "the problem of universals" – the question of whether and in what manner universals exist. His position allows us, he says, "to reject the existence of things which are universals, and also the existence of things which are purely individual. Whatever ... has the universality of a universal will not be found among the entities, objects, things, that we find in our empirical, subjective world of individual existents. And an individual will bear evidence of universality."[11]

By connecting ontology and philosophy of science, Hart's approach opens exciting avenues for further investigation. There is a sense, however, in which he has not addressed the problem of universals but simply transposed it into the universe of discourse about conditions. Saying that conditions obtain universally allows Hart to deny the existence of universals. Universals, he says, are "reified conditions characterized by the way in which they relate" to that which they condition.[12] In denying the existence of universals, however, Hart also denies the existence of conditions. These are real but do not exist, since existents are subject to conditions but conditions cannot themselves be conditioned. Were this denial simply a function of Hart's peculiar definition of existence as entailing subjection to conditions, we could accept the denial despite its counterintuitive ring. But there seems to be a genuine problem here. Following the same line of reasoning, for example, we would have to conclude that, since God is not subject to conditions, God does not exist. This, I submit, would be an unacceptable conclusion for Hart's own philosophy.

The problem at stake, it seems to me, stems from an inadequate ontology of existence. If the existence of universals is our initial question, then surely we should get clear what is meant by "existence." This is, in fact, one of the oldest problems in ontology. It will not simply disappear when a new definition of "existence" is posited. Within Hart's own approach there are at least three angles from which the question of existence could be pursued further. The first, and by far the most radical, would be to avoid all talk of existence and reality. From this angle the world and its order would be neither existent nor nonexistent, neither real nor unreal. Order would "order" and world would "world," and both would do so in irreducible correlation. Unfortunately the clarity of such an approach would be offset by its unintelligibility to most other philosophical traditions. A second angle would be to say that conditions and order do not exist in the manner of entities, objects, and things. Hart suggests this angle at one point,[13] but fails to explore other manners of existence. Could it be, for example, that while not existing in the manner of things, conditions exist in the manner of processes? Perhaps Hart's own analysis of time as "the integral interrelation of conditionality and subjectivity"[14] would make this second angle worth considering. In the third place, we could reexamine the reasons given for distinguishing existence and reality and for restricting "existence" to whatever is subject to conditions. Since this third angle takes us into the crux of Hart's ontology, let me discuss it at greater length in a separate section.

## 3. THE REALITY OF NOMIC CONDITIONS

Hart describes "existence" as "a basic term which indicates the reality of whatever is subject to conditions. Rules obtain, while what is subject to rules ... exists."[15] By "conditions" Hart means nomic conditions: rules, laws, or standards that obtain universally and necessarily for what exists. The irreducible correlate of nomic conditions is subjective existence. "Subjective existence" includes everything that exists; according to Hart, nothing can exist except in subjection to nomic conditions. Thus the term "subjective existence" is redundant: by definition all existence is subjective – subject to nomic conditions – and no subjectivity is nonexistent.

The intent of these definitions seems to be to avoid subsuming irreducible correlates (conditionality and subjectivity) under a single category such as existence. Hart does not wish logical operations appropriate to one side of the correlation to be applied without reservation to the other side. To do this would permit the realism he wants to circumvent. It is not clear, however, that Hart's intent has been accomplished. After all, he does apply the single term "reality" to both conditions and subjectivity, to both order and world.

Let us pursue the matter a little further. Hart's definition of existence is supposed to express the claim that conditionality and subjectivity are irreducible correlates. By "irreducible correlates" Hart means that we cannot have the one without the other, but neither one can ever be legitimately reduced to the other. In itself this formal description tells us little about the ontological status of conditions.

Fortunately chapter 2 tells us considerably more. We learn that nomic conditions are "real" in the sense that they "cannot be disregarded or ignored with impunity."[16] But they are unlike any existents. Against various types of realism Hart argues that nomic conditions, though real, are unlike such existents as things, states, circumstances, and events, as well as words, sentences, concepts, and propositions. At the same time, Hart insists against nominalists that nomic conditions are known and experienced, and that semantic and conceptual levels of existence are the conduits of such knowledge and experience. To be known and experienced, however, nomic conditions must be present to us in the existences for which they hold. Otherwise they would remain inaccessible. Their reality, which is unlike subjective or existent reality, but which is known and experienced, is the reality of holding universally and without exception for the kinds of existents that nomic conditions make possible. To use Hart's examples, for every frog or for every traffic pattern there is a nomic condition or set of nomic conditions prescribing what it takes for anything to be a frog or to be a traffic pattern of that kind. Through conceptual analysis of frogs and other existents we learn what is required – what conditions must be met – for these existents to be what they are to be.

Hart's account of nomic conditions is fascinating; by pointing out problems I do not mean to suggest otherwise. Still I cannot help continuing to wonder about the "reality" of nomic conditions. Hart tells us that the term "reality" simply "indicates that whatever we name as real must be accepted by us on its own terms."[17] What would it mean for us to accept nomic conditions on their own terms? Among the statements Hart makes about nomic conditions are several that are difficult to understand without further explanation or argument. These statements can be boiled down to an epistemological question, a question in the very area for which Hart's ontology seems designed. The question is whether and in what sense nomic conditions can be known to be real.

This question arises at three levels in chapter 2. In the first place we must find a way to bridge the gap between real conditions and existents, which the conditions are unlike. It would seem that the knowable and the known tend to coincide with existence. We know about frogs and traffic patterns, for example. But how do we move from such knowledge to knowledge of the real nomic conditions holding for frogs and traffic patterns? Even if we suppose that we are talking about two distinct kinds of knowledge, the question remains as to how these kinds are connected. Hart recognizes this problem and tries to address it by distinguishing "conditions-1" (nomic conditions) and "conditions-2" (patterns and structures displayed by existents and evidencing the fulfillment of nomic conditions).[18] The distinction is not entirely clear, however, nor is the manner in which conditions-1 become known in conditions-2. Hart's account seems open to the objection that the existence of conditions-2 renders superfluous the postulated reality of nomic conditions.[19] In addition, the displaying of regularity might not in itself provide epistemic access to *regulae*.

Epistemological questions arise at a second level as well. Hart wishes to say that nomic conditions are known and experienced in their reality. An important epistemological question at this point is how such knowledge and experience are possible, a question not unlike the guiding concern of Immanuel Kant's critical philosophy. In Hartian language the question would read, "What real nomic conditions make possible knowledge of real nomic conditions?" The gist of Hart's answer is that such knowledge is made possible by the nomic conditions holding for conceptual and semantic "experience." Words and sentences, especially assertions, refer to concepts and propositions, in which nomic conditions are grasped. According to Hart, "the rules for analysis, its nomic conditions, if met in the actual analysis of *x*, are destined to lead to the nomic conditions obtaining for *x*."[20] This answer makes two major claims: (1) that nomic conditions can be conceptually grasped and semantically asserted; and (2) that such conceiving and asserting are made possible by the conditions holding for conceptualization and assertion. Taken together, the two claims amount to a version of a familiar epistemological circle: to know that nomic conditions can be conceptually grasped, we need to know that nomic conditions make such conceptualizing possible; but to know that nomic conditions make such conceptualizing possible, we need to have a conceptual grasp of nomic conditions. The circle is not vicious, however, and for the most part chapter 2 enters and leaves the circle gracefully.

The price for this movement through the circle is to give logic a privileged position among the academic disciplines. For only in logic, according to Hart, does the analysis of certain conditions-2 (such as the rules of inference) lead to a conceptual grasp of those nomic conditions (logical conditions) that make possible any and every conceptual grasp of any and every nomic condition. Although privileging logic in this manner does justice to a large part of the philosophical tradition, I am not sure it does justice to the deepest impulses for Hart's challenge to the tradition. To find out we may need to turn to Hart's subsequent work on epistemology, for *Understanding Our World* contains no detailed discussion of logic. The book has even less to say about semantics, semiotics, and linguistics, even though Hart's comments on semantic access to nomic conditions seem to make these disciplines nearly as crucial as logic.

To my mind the privileging of logic becomes most problematic when Hart makes a third claim. This claim is formulated somewhat vaguely. At one point Hart writes that nomic conditions "are explicitly known only as a result of our conceptual activity."[21] Later he says that "one cannot focus attention on conditions or principles except by way of words and concepts."[22] The terms "explicitly" and "focus attention on" are not delimited further. Perhaps Hart is claiming no more than that we cannot have *conceptual* knowledge of nomic conditions except by way of conceptual activities and results. If so, then his claim would be unproblematic but tautologous.

I take it that Hart's claim is stronger: namely, that conceptualizing and assertion are the only ways in which we can know nomic conditions. This claim, or one like it, would be problematic. If nomic conditions are real in the sense that they obtain for whatever they make possible, then why would there be no other ways of knowing nomic conditions? Why, for example, could we not imagine nomic conditions, and in this imagining come to know them? Is not such imagining of nomic conditions an essential feature of artistic activity as well as of the hypothetical element in scholarship? Or, to use other examples, why could we not sense and feel nomic conditions and in our sensing and feeling come to know them? Why could we not give shape to nomic conditions, and in this formative activity come to know them? I consider these important questions for the simple reason that nomic conditions would hardly seem "real" if they could not be experienced in preconceptual and presemantic ways. If they were experienced in these ways, then there would be less need to call our experience of them "indirect" and less compulsion to argue that conceptual activity can "count as experience."[23] In addition, without, some such modification, Hart's approach threatens to intellectualize the "reality" of nomic conditions in a manner not unlike that of Plato.

The third level of epistemological questioning pertains to the origin of nomic conditions. Knowledge of their origin would seem to be significant for determining whether and in what sense nomic conditions can be known to be real. Because this topic has peculiar problems attached to it, I shall treat it in a separate section.

## 4. THE ORIGIN OF NOMIC CONDITIONS

With respect to nomic conditions, Hart wonders whether the following questions are legitimate or meaningful: "How are we to conceive of the origin of ... conditional order? ... How are the limits of possibility made possible? Is there a limit to order?"[24] He suggests these are ambiguous questions. If we are asking whether nomic conditions are conditioned, then we seem to have the "contradictory" assumption that nomic conditions, which can never be subjective or existent, are somehow "subject to other conditions."[25] If we are asking about the origin of nomic conditions, then we are asking a different question, one that is not legitimately or appropriately pursued in philosophy.[26] Whatever we say about the origin of nomic conditions is so dependent on our "deep-seated commitments" that a philosophical discussion of the origin cannot be simply philosophical. Hart himself wishes to say no more at this point than "that the positing of the reality of a world order ... is a reasonable theoretical move." With respect to origin, the order of our world cannot be explained philosophically, even though "in our culture, if we cannot explain it, we will not be inclined to accept it."[27] As Hart himself recognizes, by avoiding a philosophical discussion of the origin, his position on nomic conditions risks being unacceptable, no matter how reasonable it might be.[28]

I for one find Hart's position difficult to accept. It seems to endorse truncated philosophy, given the centrality of the question of origins in traditional ontology and epistemology. If explanation were no more than the subsumption of an explanandum under nomic statements à la Carl Hempel, then indeed the reality of nomic conditions could not be explained with respect to their origin. Hempel's account is one of natural scientific explanation, however, and even in philosophy of science his account is not without plausible rivals. But why would a *philosophical* explanation have to take a deductive-nomological form? To explain need mean no more than to give a credible philosophical account. Surely this is not too much to expect or to receive from an integral ontology.

Our epistemological concern now is all the greater. For with no account of the origin of nomic conditions, we are even more perplexed about knowing them to be real. To say they are there without saying how they got there is little more than a deictic gesture. Such a move seems to assume that the reality of nomic conditions can be known apart from knowledge of their origin. Admittedly there is a sense in which we can know things without knowing their origins. We can know a great deal about frogs, for example, without knowing where they came from or how they came into existence. But few biologists have been satisfied with such knowledge. Similarly, few philosophers would be satisfied with positing the reality of nomic conditions without having philosophical knowledge about their origins.

As Hart's own questions indicate, two issues merit further attention. The first issue has to do with relationships among nomic conditions. Even if we accept Hart's thesis of an irreducible correlation between conditionality and subjectivity, we may wonder whether there is any order of priority among nomic conditions. Hart postulates that each condition holds universally and necessarily for the existents it makes possible. But this postulate need not entail that the holding of each condition is equivalent to the holding of every other condition. Thus, for example, the conditions holding for frogs would seem to be less extensive than the conditions holding for all animals. Without suggesting that certain conditions limit other conditions, we can still suppose that some conditions hold less extensively than do others, and that these others might be more original. Some such supposition seems to operate in the natural sciences, from which Hart derives evidence for the reality of nomic conditions. A similar supposition seems implied by distinctions among the various dimensions of the horizon of human experience in volume 2 of Dooyeweerd's *A New Critique of Theoretical Thought*. To suppose that conditions hold more or less extensively would allow us to refine our picture of the universality with which, according to Hart, every condition obtains. We might also discover the legitimacy of asking whether nomic conditions are limited and how they are made possible.

A second issue worth further pursuit pertains to the real origin of nomic conditions. The traditional problem of universals revolved around the question of their origin or location. Thus we can hardly address this problem without discussing the question of origins. Despite Hart's hesitancy to discuss origins, let me suggest that as soon as philosophers know something about nomic conditions they already know something about the origin of nomic conditions. For example, if we know that nomic conditions are not subjective, then we already know that their origin can hardly be subjective. If nomic conditions are thought never to hold for themselves, then their origin can hardly be thought to be a nomic condition. If nomic conditions are real but not existent, then their origin might be real but probably will not be existent. If the origin of nomic conditions is other than those conditions, then the origin is probably unconditioned. And if the conditions in question are best characterized as being "nomic," then we may expect them to originate in a reality that can best be conceived along the lines of legal authority.

No doubt such conclusions would have to be kept tentative, be elaborated in dialogue with other ontologies, and be checked against our own "deep-seated commitments." But there seems to be little reason to cut off philosophical analysis at the point of asking about origins. If we know something about the limits, then we know something about what is beyond them, including their origin. Conversely, if our philosophy cannot say anything about the origin of nomic conditions, then it is questionable whether our philosophy is entitled to say much about nomic conditions. At least the refusal to talk philosophically about the origin casts doubt on the supposed reality of nomic conditions, making us wonder how we can know them to be real.

## 5. PHILOSOPHY AND GOD

Although chapter 2 refuses to account for the origin of nomic conditions, subsequent chapters employ the concept of origin at crucial points. Chapter 4, for example, says that the modal order displays a reference to the "origin of all that is relative." This origin is the "ultimate unity" of actors and actions.[29] Chapter 7 explains the "exceptional place of humanity" in terms of the functional openness of human experience to the "origin and destiny of the universe."[30] Later in the same chapter, the dualism of body and soul is contrasted with Hart's assumption of "the fundamental unity of the world in its origin and in its subjection to an order of the same origin."[31] Detailed discussion of origins is reserved, however, for the "prescientific" Appendix and for a transition[32] to the Appendix. When we finally learn what Hart understands about the origin, we also learn that he considers the presentation of this understanding to be something other than philosophy properly so called.

In other words, Hart does discuss the origin, which he equates with the God of Christianity, but he considers his discussion nonphilosophical. His approach raises two sets of issues, one about the status of philosophy, and the other about the role of "ultimate assumptions" in philosophy. The issues are indicated by the two lines of argument attached to Hart's insistence on nonphilosophical talk about the origin. The first line has to do with limits to philosophical discourse. The second line has to do with connections between philosophy and commitment. I shall explore the first line of argument first and save the second line for a separate, concluding section. In both sections, the question of origins will serve as a test case for Hart's conception of philosophy.

Hart is aware that his opposition to philosophizing about God is not without problems: "Theorizing without commitment is impossible, but so is a theory of the ultimate ground of one's commitment. For this reason I have saved some of my final declarations about important problems for the Appendix ... Although we need to be committed in philosophy, we cannot philosophically analyze the ultimate ground of our commitment. How can we resolve this problem?"[33] The first approach to a solution is Hart's explanation of why God, like the content of other ultimate assumptions, cannot be "philosophically analyzed." The explanation can be reduced to three claims.[34] (1) Because "the structure of analysis is bound by the order of the world," therefore "it is only possible to analyze whatever is within those bounds." (2) God could be analyzed philosophically only if God were subject to the order of the world, or at least subject to logical order. (3) As "the origin of order," God is not subject to any order.

Restating the first claim, we can say that philosophy, being subject to nomic conditions, cannot analyze their origin. But why would the subjectivity of philosophy preclude philosophical analysis of the origin? This subjectivity does not prevent philosophy from grasping nomic conditions; why should it prevent the grasping of origins?[35] In critique of Kant, Hegel has made the important point that for thought a limit is simultaneously an opening beyond itself.[36] Applying Hegel's insight to the question of God as origin, we could propose that being "bound by the order of the world" need not exclude analysis from grasping God. Rather, when grasping God, analysis is restricted to doing so in subjection to the order of analysis. In fact, following other lines similar to Hart's might force us to conclude that God's presence cannot be sensed, and God's faithfulness cannot be trusted. Sensing and trusting are no less "bound by order" than analysis. The conclusion of such lines of argument would seem to be agnosticism: human knowledge, being bound by order, cannot in any way know whatever lies beyond the bounds, and therefore we cannot have knowledge of God. This I take to be the gist of Immanuel Kant's position when he said our idea of God cannot be a concept.

Since Hart's own commitment militates against agnosticism, let us see whether his second and third claims lay this problem to rest. Kant wished to allow for thinking about God even though we cannot have knowledge of God. Hart's next claims seem to deny that we can philosophize about

God even though we can have knowledge of God. The crux of these claims is the thesis that God is not subject to logical laws. The motivation for Hart's thesis seems to be criticism and avoidance of a certain type of speculation about God: "If we allow for subjection of God to logical rules, then theology and philosophy will autonomously decide on the nature of God, guided by arbitrary, philosophical, and logical prejudices."[37] One could, of course, share Hart's concern without assuming his thesis to be necessary or effective for avoiding arbitrary speculation. But to understand the thesis we shall need to remember its motivation.

The question of God's subjection to logical laws, like Hart's answer, is too complex to receive its due in this essay.[38] Let me simply summarize what I take to be Hart's position and point out some problems. Hart's position can be reconstructed as follows:[39] (1) Valid theoretical assertions and concepts concerning God would require that God be subject to rules of inference, have a nature, and be of some kind. (2) For God to be so subject etc., God would have to be subject to logical laws. (3) As the Creator of logical (and all other) laws, God cannot be subject to them. (4) Since God cannot be subject to logical laws, there can be no valid theoretical assertions and concepts concerning God. (5) As a theoretical pursuit, philosophy cannot legitimately be about God.

To the obvious objection that this position is itself a philosophy about God, Hart's apparent response is that he has simply given philosophical expression to contextualized, non-theoretical discourse about God, discourse that is tied to God's self-revelation within the order of creation: "So we can experience God concretely and contextually, but when we speak or think generally and out of context we lose the *right* to speak and think. So this makes a theory of God, as a description of the structures which define God, impossible and any statements here become theoretically invalid. My remarks are not simply theory, however, but a means of drawing out the meaning of some beliefs I confess to hold."[40] This response is less convincing than it is illustrative of three problems with Hart's position. Let us see what they are.

In the first place, it is unclear whether all theories about God are illegitimate, or whether merely certain types of theories – those pursued in abstraction and out of context – are invalid or tend to become invalid. It could be that in criticizing a certain type of speculation Hart has hastily shut the door on all theories about God, except his own theoretical criticism. If so, then the onus is on his theoretical criticism to show either its non-theoretical character or its concrete, contextual origins. Whether the Appendix shows this I will let other readers decide.

In the second place, within Hart's system there is little reason to think that what he says about theoretical assertions would not apply with equal force to non-theoretical assertions. If all assertions are subject to rules of inference and express concepts and propositions about "natures" and "kinds," then how can Hart allow for the validity of any assertions about God? Perhaps Hart's reply is that non-theoretical assertions about God are actually about God's "creatiomorphic revelation" but not about God as such.[41] But then why could there not be valid theoretical assertions about such revelation? Furthermore, would not this restriction argue for a mild agnosticism in the area of assertions, concepts, and propositions: i.e., we cannot validly think about God, but only about God's self-revelation?

The third problem with Hart's position is by far the most complex. In arguing against theories about God, Hart assumes the legitimacy of his own ontology of conditionality and analysis. Indeed, just as, according to Hart, Wolterstorff's book *On Universals* was written to argue a position on the Creator/creature distinction,[42] much of *Understanding Our World* might have been written to argue a different position. Hart's discussion of God is heavily dependent on chapters 1 and 2. To challenge this discussion is to disagree with some conclusions reached in those earlier chapters. The specific focus of disagreement will be whether any reality must be subject to logical laws in order to be the topic of valid theories. The disagreement will not be fruitful, however, unless we are clear about the meaning of "being subject to logical laws." On this matter, Hart's discussion about God has surprisingly little to say.

From his earlier chapters we may infer that to be subject to logical laws is to exist in correlation with the nomic conditions governing the logical possibilities for whatever is so subject. What types of existences would Hart consider subject to logical nomic conditions? Concepts, propositions, and arguments, undoubtedly, as well as such activities as conceiving and arguing, would be subject to logical conditions. But would all the realities about which we think have to be subject to logical laws? Must frogs, for example, be subject to logical laws? How about the conditions that make possible frog-like existence? Are they subject to logical laws? I do not see how Hart could answer yes without endorsing the logicism he opposes. I do not think he wants to say that any and every existence or that any and every nomic condition is made possible by logical laws. Nor do I believe he wants to claim that we can think about existences and their nomic conditions only because logical laws make them logically possible. If I am correct, then why would God have to be subject to logical laws in order for us to have valid theories about God? The minimum to which Hart's ontology obligates him is that valid theories about God require concepts, propositions, arguments, etc. that are subject to logical laws. This would be a non-controversial stance.

Perhaps Hart intended to argue that valid theories about God would require that God be subject to some nomic conditions. This argument would have agreed with his view that conceptualization is the conditioned grasping of nomic conditions. Indeed, this argument is implied by his claim that God has no nature and is not of any kind. Let us assume that the argument "God cannot be subject to logical laws" really means "God cannot be subject to any nomic conditions such as are grasped conceptually." From here we have at least three options. Either we can agree, and then ask Hart to be consistent by excluding the possibility of any valid conceptualizing of God, whether theoretical or not. Or we can agree, but suggest the fallaciousness of any account of conceptualization that precludes valid conceptualizing of God. Or we can disagree, and ask for an account of God that does not force untenable conclusions about the validity of conceptualizing God. In any case, the position advanced at the end of chapter 7 remains hard to accept in its present form. The purported limits of philosophy with respect to God seem to require further reflection.

## 6. COMMITMENT AND ONTOLOGY

We have examined the first line of argument for Hart's insistence on the non-philosophical character of his talk about God. This line is that philosophical theories about God cannot be valid. The second line concerns the role of "ultimate assumptions" in philosophy. Hart explains that "the ultimate assumptions of a theory do not belong to the theory in the sense that they can be theoretically explained and accounted for. They are the foundation for one's analysis and they cannot themselves be analytically justified."[43] Implied by this explanation is an account of connections between commitment and philosophy. Noting Hart's desire for integrality and his indebtedness to Dooyeweerd's transcendental critique, we may suppose that the book stands or falls with this account, even though it is relegated to the Appendix. Rather than analyzing everything in Hart's account, I will again use the question of origins as a test case for his position.

The Appendix connects commitment and philosophy primarily by way of the "ultimate categories" of an ontology and the "ultimate assumptions" of an ontologist's "ultimate commitment."[44] The categories are implied by the ultimate assumptions and "directly related to" them; the assumptions are reflected by the ultimate categories.[45] Ultimate categories such as "order" and "world" are basic and fundamentally irreducible positions in philosophy. Ultimate assumptions such as "God's sovereignty" are fundamental, non-philosophical beliefs of commitment. Such assumptions belong to our "ultimate commitment to the ultimate." They are "constitutive" of that commitment, and they provide final grounds for our accepting or rejecting other beliefs.[46] Because ultimate assumptions are so fundamental, they cannot be rationally "explained" or "justified"; they are held in the trust of an ultimate commitment, and they are already assumed in any discussion of ultimate assumptions. Nevertheless philosophers, especially ontologists, ought to be articulate and open about their ultimate assumptions. Such articulateness and openness are attempted in the Appendix. Hart is presenting his ultimate assumptions not *as* philosophy but *for* philosophy: he is presenting them in order to display connections between his ultimate assumptions and his ultimate categories.

There can be no mistaking the ring of integrity in Hart's presentation. Philosophers, however, being the perennial questioners they are, will wonder about his account of ultimate assumptions in philosophy. At least four questions come to mind: (1) Why ought ultimate assumptions to be presented by philosophers? (2) May such presentations be anything other than philosophical? (3) Are ultimate assumptions as ultimate as Hart suggests? (4) Is ultimate commitment the only non-philosophical source of ultimate categories? Before examining one of Hart's ultimate assumptions, let us consider each of these questions.

The first question is important for the philosophical reception of *Understanding Our World*. Unless other philosophers learn why any philosopher ought to present ultimate assumptions, it will be easy for them to ignore Hart's presentation as a mere idiosyncrasy. Indeed, they would be justified in so doing. The reason for this is that there is little in the recent tradition of philosophical self-reflection to suggest that ultimate assumptions are as fundamental to philosophy as Hart claims with respect to his own philosophy. When inserting his ontology into this tradition, Hart is obliged to show that the structure of assumptions and categories in his philosophy is not peculiar to this philosophy. Despite a few comments along these lines,[47] Hart does not go far beyond simply depicting the structure of his own position. We receive no sustained argument similar to Dooyeweerd's persistent critique of the "pretended autonomy" of theoretical thought. Though not without its own problems, Dooyeweerd's approach had the merit of demanding philosophical attention for the purported religious conditions of any philosophy. This demand threatens to become a personal confession in the Appendix of *Understanding Our World*.

It will not be surprising, then, if other philosophers wonder about the character of this Appendix. Hart tells us his presentation of ultimate assumptions is not a meditation or sermon, but "neither is it philosophy."[48] It is not theology either. What character does his presentation have? Perhaps we may say it has the character of "worldview" or "faith talk."[49] But this discourse is unusual compared to most worldview talk. Hart's presentation is not embedded in the making of concrete decisions, adopting specific policies or strategies, or explaining and defending such decisions, policies, or strategies. Instead, the presentation occurs in abstraction from any context other than that of accounting for ultimate philosophical categories. In addition, the presentation is plainly systematic, even though its tone is somewhat informal. Do not these characteristics suggest that we are reading a product of considerable scholarship? And can this product be anything other than philosophical?

Hart considers these pages pre-philosophical and calls them nonphilosophical. His apparent reason for calling them nonphilosophical is to avoid the impression that ultimate assumptions are merely philosophical. This is an important point, one which many other philosophers would accept. But the extra-philosophical character of ultimate assumptions need not exclude legitimate philosophical discourse about them. What we read is discourse by a philosopher, in a philosophical book, about ultimate assumptions supposedly having profound philosophical implications. Is not such discourse philosophical? May this sort of discourse be anything other than philosophical? These are not idle questions of classification. Their answers would tell us what sorts of expectations are appropriate to such discourse on ultimate assumptions. May we have philosophical reservations and objections? May we require philosophical explanations and arguments with other philosophical positions? Or must we simply accept the presentation as a report on the worldview of one person who, among other things, is a philosopher?

The third question raised earlier is whether ultimate assumptions are as ultimate as Hart suggests. The "ultimacy" of ultimate assumptions refers to at least four overlapping characteristics: (1) being the most broadly fundamental of all beliefs; (2) being accepted "not on grounds but as ground"[50] – because of the way in which they support our experience; (3) providing final grounds for justifiable beliefs; and (4) being directed to "the ultimate," to whatever is given "ultimate allegiance." The first characteristic would make ultimate assumptions similar to Dooyeweerd's three "transcendental ideas."[51] The fourth characteristic would make them similar to Dooyeweerd's "religious ground motives." Taken together, the second and third characteristics could allow ultimate assumptions to be viewed as basic "control beliefs" in Wolterstorff's sense of the term.[52] Whether all four characteristics can be intelligibly ascribed to the same type of belief would be worth further investigation.

In any case, I wish to ask how ultimate these ultimate assumptions are. There are two reasons for asking. In the first place, it is not initially clear what "being directed to the ultimate" has to do with the supposedly foundational role of these assumptions within experience and within a network of beliefs. For example, many Christians whose allegiance is to God would not count their belief in God as foundational among their scholarly beliefs. Presumably this situation is the real burden of Hart's talk about ultimate assumptions. He, for one, finds belief in God to be foundational for his philosophy. But do others? Ought they? Must they? These questions are not clarified by assuming that beliefs directed to "the ultimate" are equivalent to foundational beliefs.

In the second place, I wonder how any belief can be ultimate. If "the ultimate" is indeed ultimate, then how can any human belief be ultimate? I realize, of course, that Hart is describing certain beliefs with a view to their role in human experience. I also think, however, that he does not wish to ascribe ultimacy to any part of human experience. Is not some such ascription implied by his conception of ultimate assumptions? For example, Hart says an ultimate assumption is "much more an accepted belief than an understood fact." It is accepted not with reference to other things we know but "because of our commitment," through which the ultimate becomes known.[53] Do not such formulations ascribe to human assumptions and human commitment an ultimacy bordering on the irrational? To accept a belief *because* of our commitment would seem to render the belief impervious not only to interhuman discourse but also to ultimate presence.

These potential problems might be compounded by Hart's manner of connecting ultimate commitment and ultimate ontological categories. Without stating it in so many words, Hart leaves the distinct impression that, via ultimate assumptions, ultimate commitment is the only source of his ultimate categories, and perhaps of any ultimate categories. If this is in fact his position, then I must express misgivings. The position would seem not only inaccurate but also detrimental to Hart's own project.

The concern about inaccuracy arises from my hypothesis that philosophical propositions, including "ultimate categories," seldom have a single source. It could be that ultimate categories are "implied" by the assumptions of ultimate commitment. But why would ultimate assumptions be the only source of such categories or even the most pervasive or determinative of various sources? Hart's assumption seems to be that, because commitment is a "terminal level" of human functioning and is characterized by "ultimate acceptance of what is ultimate,"[54] ultimate categories must be derived from ultimate assumptions of commitment. Is this in fact the case? Let us imagine, for example, a philosopher who is an African-American woman with a working-class background. Though she is a Christian just as Hart is, might not her ultimate categories turn out to be quite different from Hart's? Must these differences be attributable to differences in ultimate commitment, such as those between a Calvinist emphasis on God's sovereignty and a Lutheran emphasis on God's liberating love?[55] Might they not be more plausibly assigned to differences in class consciousness, gender roles, and racial and national experience? If a belief in God's sovereignty seemed to help legitimate an oppressive social order, might not members of an oppressed minority be interested in emphasizing some other belief about God? Would such an interest simply be the outcome of an ultimate commitment? Furthermore, might not such an interest itself help generate ultimate categories that are quite different from Hart's? The point of this example is to suggest that besides ultimate assumptions many other elements of experience "imply" ultimate categories and are "reflected" by them. Perhaps Hart would reply that these elements play such a role only to the extent that they enter ultimate assumptions or function as ultimate assumptions. I do not think this is so, nor do I see why this must be so.

Indeed, one of my misgivings is that Hart's emphasis on the assumptions of ultimate commitment might be detrimental to his own project. On the one hand, it might prevent his project from establishing contact with kindred criticisms of supposedly autonomous rationality, criticisms not primarily motivated by religious concerns. I have in mind the work of Thomas Kuhn, Jürgen Habermas, Hans-Georg Gadamer, and others. On the other hand, Hart's emphasis might force him to load so much philosophy into his stated assumptions of commitment that few Christians could accept these as statements of authentic Christian commitment. The consequence of overloading the ultimate assumptions might be that the ultimate categories come to seem unacceptable to persons of common commitment. The categories could then be easily rejected for nonphilosophical reasons, even when the rejection is couched in philosophical language.

Hart's discussion of "the sovereign God"[56] and "the radical distinction"[57] may serve to test the legitimacy of my questions about ultimate assumptions in philosophy. The sovereign God is one of Hart's ultimate assumptions, one of his fundamental, nonphilosophical beliefs of commitment. In his purportedly nonphilosophical descriptions of this ultimate assumption, Hart makes a number of claims about God. God is the Creator, origin, and supreme ruler of creation. God transcends creation but is not absolute. God is not arbitrary but is faithful to "self, Word, and work."[58] God is the only source of true knowledge about God and creation. God makes such knowledge available through God's Word, of which God is "origin, speaker, and author."[59] This Word is the way in which the creation is ordered by God. Because God is not subject to the order of creation, to which human beings are subject, God is beyond our control and grasp. God sets limits and bounds to everything, but no laws hold coeternally with God, not even the laws of logic. "A belief in such coeternal laws is in conflict with belief in God's sovereignty."[60]

No doubt many Christians will recognize their own beliefs in one or another of Hart's claims. At the same time, some of them might hesitate about an emphasis on transcendence rather than immanence. Others might be puzzled about God as sole source of true knowledge. Objections could be lodged against the identification of God's Word with creation's order. And exception could be taken to a view of sovereignty that equates it with there being nothing outside of God's control and nothing that controls God.[61]

It seems to me that these Christians would be entitled to disagree and to frame their disagreement in philosophical language. My reason for saying this is that the notion of God's sovereignty as presented by Hart is not simply a nonphilosophical belief. It is, as a matter of fact, a stance on one of the most troublesome sets of issues in philosophy of religion and Christian theology. The language Hart uses is not simply the language of faith or worldview. "Origin," "transcendence," "Word as order" are philosophical terms with philosophical and theological histories. Furthermore, Hart has presented the notion of God's sovereignty in such a way that it makes one of his most important and contentious philosophical points, namely that God's sovereignty precludes God's being subject to logical order. If my assessment is correct, then it does indeed seem legitimate to ask whether a philosopher's presentation of ultimate assumptions may be or can be anything other than philosophical. At least we may suppose that most ultimate assumptions held by a philosopher will be informed to a significant degree by that philosopher's ontology. On this supposition we may ask that beliefs about such matters as God's sovereignty be presented in dialogue with other philosophical positions. Such a presentation could hardly avoid being philosophical.

The ultimate ontological category implied by the ultimate assumption of God's sovereignty, according to Hart, is what he calls "the radical distinction."[62] In conjunction with other ultimate assumptions about "the covenant relation between Creator and creation through Word and Spirit,"[63] God's sovereignty implies a radical distinction among origin, order, and world. This is "the ultimate distinction." It is not a normal categorical distinction "since the realities named are not susceptible to normal definition or conceptualization."[64] Hart claims that on purely philosophical grounds we could just as well hold that the world is its own origin or that the world is either not ordered or not distinct from its order. But on the basis of his ultimate assumptions he considers these three realities irreducibly distinct but not discontinuous. Their continuity is ensured by the claim that the world's origin is related to the world through an order originating in the same origin but holding for the world. Other than these three realities there is nothing else that is real or knowable. These positions, Hart tells us, are "founded on a prior belief rooted in commitment to God the Creator, God's Word and Spirit, and God's creation."[65]

If Hart were simply telling us how he connects some of his personal assumptions with some of his ontological categories, there would be few philosophical reasons to object, even if one held different positions. The problem is that we would also have few philosophical reasons to take Hart's positions seriously. In light of this problem, I must assume that Hart is not simply making a personal statement, but is commending an ontological position as being one worth our consideration. I must also assume he is recommending that other Christian philosophers consider whether "the radical distinction" might not be a good way or even a preferable way to link our ontologies with certain tenets of the Christian faith.

I find many attractive features to Hart's radical distinction. This fact is hardly surprising, given my own training in cosmonomic philosophy with Hart at the Institute for Christian Studies. My difficulty, which others will no doubt share, is that other Christian philosophers of integrity over centuries of reflection have not found their commitments leading them to this radical distinction. I need mention no more than various

Christian realists who distinguish creator and creature but do not posit a mediating order. Why have their commitments not led them to the radical distinction? It will not do simply to attribute the disagreement to differences in philosophical traditions, although these differences are significant. Differences in tradition will not help us decide which positions are more or less correct or more or less commendable with respect to Christian faith. Are we simply to check our own commitments to decide which positions to prefer? How are debates at this crucial level of ontology to be waged and adjudicated?

Concerns along these lines lead me to think we may legitimately ask about the ultimacy of ultimate assumptions and about non-philosophical sources of ultimate categories. It would seem the better part of wisdom – and a requirement of contemporary philosophical self-reflection – to stress the relativity of our ultimate assumptions and the multiplicity of sources for ultimate ontological categories. This is said not to endorse relativistic eclecticism but to encourage constructive dialogue. Hart himself wishes such dialogue. The great merit of *Understanding Our World* is that, by laying its confessional cards on the table, it invites other philosophies to do the same. Not only is this an important move, but also Hart's entire ontological strategy is one that deserves sustained scrutiny and discussion.

# 7

# Artistic Truth, Linguistically Turned: Variations on a Theme from Adorno, Habermas, and Hart

(2001)

All dimensions of experience may help us know truth.

Hendrik Hart[1]

All aesthetic questions terminate in those of the truth content of artworks.

Theodor W. Adorno[2]

The aesthetic "validity" ... that we attribute to a work [of art] refers to its singularly illuminating power ... to disclose anew an apparently familiar reality.

Jürgen Habermas[3]

## 1. INTRODUCTION

Hendrik Hart's 1972–73 graduate seminar in systematic philosophy marks a turning point in my intellectual life. I had arrived in Toronto that fall to study philosophical aesthetics with Calvin G. Seerveld, who set his students to work on Immanuel Kant's *Critique of Judgment*. Henk dedicated his own seminar to a thorough study of Herman Dooyeweerd's massive *A New Critique of Theoretical Thought*, a work I had begun to read at Dordt College. Students led nearly every session in this year-long seminar, and we became a formidable team of Dooyeweerd experts and critics. Henk's manner of directing the seminar and his own insights inspired our best efforts. Together with Cal's pioneering in the relatively unplowed field of aesthetics,[4] Henk's innovative work in systematic philosophy has provided a focus for much of my subsequent scholarship.

Henk and Cal would have their debates, especially over whether one needs to identify an aesthetic dimension to life, culture, and society. Their debates added a sense of urgency to my own inquiries. Deeper down, however, Henk and Cal shared a comprehensive conception of knowledge and truth, one that encompassed more than theory, logic, and propositions and could accommodate the indirect, nondiscursive, and allusive character of much modern and contemporary art. Each in his own way continued Dooyeweerd's critique of "the pretended autonomy of theoretical thought" as a project of utmost significance to culture, religious practice, and Western society.

Looking back, I see just how formative this combination of interests has proven. The final and longest chapter in my master's thesis treats Kant's "dialectic of taste" as a profound but unsuccessful attempt to ground the truth character of aesthetic judgments.[5] The language of the concluding section, subtitled "Aesthetic Truth in Kant's Perspective," has many a Hartian inflection. Not long afterwards, at a 1977 ICS summer seminar in aesthetics organized by Cal Seerveld, I presented a paper on "Musical and Musicological Knowing" whose systematic reflections on analysis, theory, and knowledge plainly derive from Henk's work in epistemology. My subsequent study of Theodor W. Adorno's negative dialectic and aesthetic theory drew from Henk's critique of rationality, although Adorno helped me introduce a more explicitly social and political edge than I found in Henk's writings at the time.

This is not to say that I have embraced Henk's work uncritically. One issue in particular has troubled me. It shows up in reports to my doctoral committee (on which he served), in correspondence and conversations, and in my 1985 essay on his book *Understanding Our World*. The issue has to do with the connection between analysis and critique; between the logical dimension of knowledge, on the one hand, and human awareness of norms and their violation, of order and disorder, and of good and evil, on the other. The issue surfaces early on, in my master's thesis, where, taking a cue from Seerveld's emphasis on "imaginativity" and "allusivity," I suggest that aesthetic awareness, albeit non-identificatory, is "the *most elemental* way" in which people have self-reflective consciousness of a coherence between subject and object.[6] This implies an aesthetic way of knowing "order" that can be more or less truthful, even though, in Hartian or Seerveldian terms, it is pre-logical or pre-analytical. The issue receives a more forceful formulation in a proposition accompanying my doctoral dissertation, which responds to Hart's "The Impasse of Rationality Today"[7] as follows: "That we must follow logical order in our *explicitly* knowing order does not entail that our knowing order is logical: if we follow nonlogical order in our *implicitly* knowing order, then at least some of our knowing order may not be logical." This topic returns in my essay on *Understanding Our World*, where I posed questions about Henk's tendency to claim that conceptual and semantic modes of experience are the only ways in which "nomic conditions" can be known.[8] I raised such questions to resist a potential intellectualizing of the "reality" of nomic conditions (à la Plato, for example) and to suggest that they "would hardly seem 'real' if they could not be experienced in preconceptual and presemantic ways."[9]

In the meantime, of course, Henk has revised his views on nearly every topic that provoked my interest in the first place. At the time of his retirement from ICS, he probably would have had fewer counter-objections to my old worries and criticisms than he had in the 1970s and early 1980s. In the essay quoted at the outset, for example, he mentions poetry, novels, films, and music as providing "truth and knowledge not available to … conceptual knowing," without conceding, however, that such artistic knowledge could afford valid insights into nomic conditions (or what the essay calls "regularity and structure in reality" and "an order of sameness").[10] At the same time, in moving away from his older account of analysis and order, he may have landed in anti-rationalist territory that I find equally problematic, although for different reasons.[11]

Enough of autobiography. My point is simply to acknowledge the formative role Henk Hart has played in my own intellectual life, and to thank him publicly for the creative and discerning directions in which he has taken the Kuyperian tradition in philosophy. Also, I wanted to set a context for the topic of this chapter. Although it does not discuss Henk's writings at length, I owe to him my interest in developing a broader conception of knowledge and truth and my sense that the topic of "artistic truth" is still worth pursuing, despite a long-standing aversion to this topic in Anglo-American philosophy, and despite recent challenges to the idea of truth within poststructural and postanalytical philosophy.

There is no way to do justice to such a complex and contentious topic in a single essay or even to indicate how my own conception of artistic truth relates to crucial formulations by Hegel, Nietzsche, Heidegger, Gadamer, and Derrida. Let me instead make some remarks on the history and significance of the topic and then sketch the beginning of an approach derived in part from Adorno and Habermas. In the conclusion

I indicate how my approach might complement the systematic philosophy of Hendrik Hart.

## 2. TRUTH IN ART

The Western philosophical debate about truth in art goes back to Plato and Aristotle. Whereas Book X of Plato's *Republic*, on a non-ironical reading, denies the arts of his day any capacity to carry truth, Aristotle's *Poetics* suggests that Greek tragedy (and, by extension, all the "imitative arts") can provide true insight into the sorts of events and characters that could occur under certain conditions. The difference between Plato and his most famous student turns on their contrasting accounts of the nature and location of universal "forms," and on corresponding differences in their theories of knowledge and mimesis or representation. My own worries about a Hartian tendency to privilege analysis as the way to grasp order have their historical origins in this debate.

The Plato/Aristotle debate in its many versions lasted until the eighteenth century, when new theories of art as expression drastically changed the ways in which truth is attributed to art. From then on the most forceful advocates of "artistic truth" would link it with creativity, imagination, and the expression of that which exceeds the grasp of ordinary or scientific understanding. One glimpses this new tendency in Kant's account of artistic "genius" as an imaginative capacity for presenting "aesthetical ideas," even though he would have found puzzling or downright dangerous subsequent Romantic claims that art's imaginative character makes it a "higher" source of truth than are science and bourgeois morality – a higher source alongside philosophy and religion, in Hegel's account of "absolute spirit." Hart's recent manner of attributing truth capacity to the arts reminds one of the Romantic emphasis on imagination and expression.

The debate shifts once more with the so-called "linguistic turn" in twentieth-century philosophy.[12] Although many traces remain of both pre-modern accounts of representation and post-Kantian emphases on expression, a philosophy whose head is linguistically turned cannot easily posit direct dis/connections either between (representational) art and reality or between (expressive) art and the inner self. Increasingly the questions of whether art can carry truth, and whether this capacity or its lack is crucial to art's significance, get posed in one of two ways: (1) Can arts-related conversation (interpretation, evaluation, criticism, historiography, and the like) be true or false? (2) Are the arts themselves languages, such that, depending on one's response to this question and one's theory of language, the arts lack or possess truth-capacities in the way that languages do?[13]

If the debate over truth in art, in its shifting guises, were merely the concern of philosophers, we might find it interesting but not all that relevant. This is particularly so of the way the debate has proceeded since philosophy became institutionalized as an academic profession and began to doubt its own relevance to contemporary society and culture. Yet I believe the topic is highly significant at a time when mass media, entertainment industries, and new computer technologies have become driving forces for an increasingly globalized consumer capitalist economy. A deep ambivalence pervades contemporary Western societies concerning the role of visual imagery, literature, and public performances in human life. Many people regard these as "mere entertainment" providing diversion for consumers and profits for producers and investors. Others, however, worry about the pedagogical, political, or moral impact of the arts and at times hold these to unyielding standards that the critics cannot meet in their own lives. Neither side seems to grasp what enables the arts to provide either the "entertainment" or the "instruction" that people find satisfying or troubling, as the case may be. Yet everyone turns to visual imagery, literature, and performing arts to find orientation and to confirm or disconfirm orientations already found. Gaining orientation is essential to the acquaintance, recognition, understanding, and know-how that belong to "knowledge" in a broad sense. To that extent, it is not esoteric to regard the arts as ways of acquiring and testing knowledge, nor to consider specific works or events or experiences of art more or less truthful. The challenge for philosophers is to give an account of artistic truth that illuminates the contemporary cultural scene and provides theoretical insight of use to those who develop public policies, educational strategies, and personal or group decisions in connection with the arts.

Unfortunately, many standard theories of truth prove deficient in this regard. I do not have the space to review them here.[14] Perhaps the easiest way to indicate their inadequacy is to observe that they restrict their attention to linguistic and conceptual bearers of truth. Richard Kirkham lists the following as candidates for the sorts of things that Anglo-American philosophers have considered capable of being true or false: "beliefs, propositions, judgments, assertions, statements, theories, remarks, ideas, acts of thought, utterances, sentence tokens, sentence types, sentences (unspecified), and speech acts." Although Kirkham urges tolerance about which candidates to admit, arguing that "there is no sort of entity that cannot in principle bear truth values," he does not actually expand the field beyond linguistic and conceptual entities.[15] So long as the class of truth bearers is restricted in these ways, it will be difficult to construct a theory of truth in art.

Difficult, but not impossible. I can think, for example, of two ways to regard propositions as vehicles of artistic truth. One way is to say that works of art simply *are* propositions or that artworks can be true or false only insofar as they function as objects of logical discrimination, in both production and reception. Reminiscent of early Wittgenstein's description of propositions as pictures, this first approach says nothing about the unique manner in which art "carries" truth or falsehood. Another way to locate artistic truth in propositions is to say art *embodies* propositions in a variety of artistic phenomena and media. On this approach, artistic truth exists independently of its embodiment, even though the approach could allow certain propositions to be unique to art in the sense that they cannot be expressed or communicated except by way of art.[16] The disadvantage to this second approach is that it reifies a logical object function into a thing in itself, as if propositions are independent and eternal universals simply waiting to be instantiated. Not only is this a questionable view of propositions, but also it ignores the social, historical, and political character of artistic truth.

Although some other version may be possible, and although I have not given a detailed account of the two versions mentioned, I think the propositional view of artistic truth is beyond redemption. If there is truth in art, it will have to be located in something other than propositions. The same applies to the other conceptual and linguistic contenders – judgments, sentences, utterances, assertions, and the like. For what distinguishes much of art, as it has developed historically in various societies and under various political conditions, is its tendency to favour the nonconceptual, nonlinguistic, and nonpropositional. In fact, partly because Western societies have privileged science and technology but have failed to find meaning in instrumental rationality, much of twentieth-century art became anti-propositional. To expect of such art that its truth be propositional would misread much of recent history. A better approach is that recommended by Adorno: to try to understand such art's incomprehensibility.

Before turning to Adorno, let me note one anti-propositional approach that might seem compatible with a theory of artistic truth but actually undermines the entire project. Some philosophers have used speech act theory to propound a deflationary thesis to the effect that "is true" is not a genuine predicate. Consequently, "there are no such properties as truth and falsity" and "nothing can bear truth values."[17] The deflationary thesis has one potentially salutary effect – namely, to break a fixation on conceptual and linguistic entities as privileged bearers of truth. But this potential is purchased at the price of rendering theories of truth superfluous, and that would apply to a theory of artistic truth as well. The deflationary thesis is a parallel in the analytic tradition to the questioning of the very idea of truth within some French poststructuralism.

## 3. ADORNO AND HABERMAS

Although the characterization of truth bearers forms only part of an adequate theory, it is decisive for the question whether truth can be meaningfully attributed to art. That is why I find Theodor W. Adorno's conception of truth content (*Wahrheitsgehalt*) so instructive. Adorno's conception allows one to attribute a nonpropositional import to artistic phenomena that is true or false but is neither representational along either Platonic or Aristotelian lines nor expressive in the manner proposed by Romantic theories. Once that fundamental point is granted, one can address the other questions of truth theory: roughly, what truth is, what it means, and what it does.[18]

Adorno clears the deck of all remnants of logical positivism when he describes the truth content of artworks as neither factual nor propositional yet perceptible and structural: "They have truth content and they do not have it. Positive science and the philosophy derived from it do not attain it. It is neither the work's factual content nor its fragile and self-suspendable logicality … What transcends the factual in the artwork, its spiritual content, cannot be pinned down to what is individually, sensually given but is, rather, constituted by way of this empirical givenness … [A]rtworks transcend their factuality through their facture, through the consistency of their elaboration."[19] Can we give a fuller and more positive characterization of truth in art? In one sense we cannot, since the truth content of each artwork is unique to it and cannot be cleanly extracted from it: "The truth content of artworks cannot be immediately identified. Just as it is known only mediately, it is mediated in itself."[20] Yet Adorno's discussion allows for a number of additional characterizations, such as these:[21] (1) Truth in art has historical, societal, and political dimensions. Truth content is not a metaphysical idea or essence, for it is bound to specific historical stages, societal formations, and political contexts. (2) Truth in art is not merely a human construct, even though it would not be available in art were it not for the production and reception of particular works in specific media. (3) Truth in art emerges from the interaction between artists' intentions and artistic materials. It is the materialization of the most advanced consciousness of contradictions within the horizon of possible reconciliation. (4) Truth in art depends both on the successful mediation of content and form and on the suspension of form on behalf of that which exceeds this mediation. (5) Truth in art is nonpropositional, yet it invites and needs critical interpretation. (6) Truth in art is never available in a directly nonillusory way: "Art has truth as the semblance of the illusionless."[22]

To summarize Adorno's conception: truth in art is carried by sociohistorical meaning that emerges from artistic production, depends on the mediation of content and form, resides in particular works, transcends them, and invites critical interpretation. Perhaps not every work has truth content (*Wahrheitsgehalt*), but every work having import (*Gehalt*) calls for judgments about the truth or falsity of its import. In a sense, then, truth in art has a double location. First, it is located in the truth content of autonomous works of art.[23] The concept of truth content suggests that truth is *in* artworks and not simply prompted or denoted by them. Second, truth is located in a reciprocation between critical interpretation and artistic phenomena, a reciprocation that occurs by way of the truth content of particular works.

The advantage to Adorno's approach is twofold. First, it refuses to divorce truth from the phenomena of art, insisting instead that truth is thoroughly mediated by the phenomena. Second, it resists the philosopher's temptation to read into art whatever truth the philosopher wishes to find there. But this advantage comes with a double disadvantage. Not only does Adorno privilege autonomous art, specifically *autonomous artworks*, as the site of truth in art, but also he privileges philosophy, specifically *negative dialectical philosophy*, as the most authoritative interpreter of artistic truth.[24]

Admittedly it is difficult to give a philosophical account of artistic truth that does not fall into one of these two traps. Like Albrecht Wellmer,[25] I have found Jürgen Habermas's theory of communicative action particularly helpful in that regard. Let me briefly summarize elements of Habermas that are relevant for a theory of truth. Then I shall propose an approach that combines the best insights of Adorno and Habermas, but in a language that does not merely derive from either one.

Habermas retains propositions as bearers of truth, but he turns the claim to truth into an intersubjective validity claim.[26] He speaks in this connection of shifting from a subject/object to a subject/subject paradigm. Habermas regards the claim to truth (*Wahrheit*) as one of three validity claims for which every speaker is accountable when she or he uses language to reach an understanding. The other two validity claims are normative legitimacy or rightness (*Richtigkeit*) and sincerity or authenticity (*Wahrhaftigkeit*). As is illustrated in the table, the three validity claims correspond to three universal pragmatic functions of language: to represent something in the world, to establish interpersonal relations, and to express the speaker's intentions, respectively. These functions can be derived by considering the three types of illocutionary force that, according to Habermas, speech acts can have: constative (assert, inform, etc.), regulative (promise, request, etc.), and expressive (wish, avow, etc.). Truth is the primary validity claim that we attach to constative speech acts.

Habermas's Correlations of Validity Claims, Language Functions, and Speech Acts

| *Validity claims* | *Universal pragmatic language functions* | *Types of speech acts* |
|---|---|---|
| propositional truth | representing a world | constative |
| normative legitimacy | establishing interpersonal relations | regulative |
| sincerity or authenticity | expressing intentions | expressive |

Habermas says that language users raise a claim to truth whenever they make utterances as a way of asserting, informing, describing, and the like. In ordinary conversation this claim often accompanies language use without calling attention to itself. Truth becomes an issue, however, when an asserted proposition is called into question. At this point it becomes apparent that the speaker has raised a truth claim when asserting the proposition. The only way to "redeem" this truth claim is to engage in discourse. Habermas distinguishes "discourse" (*Diskurs*) from communicative action (*Handlung*). In *communicative action* we silently presuppose and accept the validity claims implicit in our utterances. In *discourse*, by contrast, we engage in argumentation, thematizing validity claims that have become problematic and investigating their legitimation (*Berechtigung*). In discourse we do not exchange "informations" as we might in an ordinary conversation about the weather, but rather we exchange arguments that serve to ground or refute validity claims that have been problematized. For the most part, "facts" become a topic in discourse, not in conversation.[27]

Habermas tends to regard *aesthetic* validity claims as expressive rather than constative or regulative. In other words, when people call something beautiful or publicly judge the quality of a musical performance or literary work, they are primarily[28] expressing their own experience and raising a claim to be sincere or truthful in that expression. Such a claim can, of course, be challenged by any conversation partner. The sorting-out of such challenges would characterize aesthetic discourse. Habermas also tends to characterize art and art criticism as a differentiated value sphere in which expressive validity claims can be thematized. Science/technology and law/morality, by contrast, are differentiated value spheres for the thematizing of constative and regulative validity claims, respectively.

Because Habermas grounds his theory in a reconstruction of social theory and of ordinary language, his approach privileges neither autonomous artworks as the site of truth in art nor philosophy as the most authoritative interpreter of artistic truth. This provides a worthwhile correction to Adorno's approach. Unfortunately, it comes at the expense of nearly eliminating art's capacity to carry truth. At best, in a modification borrowed from Albrecht Wellmer, Habermas accords artworks a "truth potential" as a singular power "to disclose anew an apparently familiar reality" and thereby to address ordinary experience, in which the three validity domains intermesh.[29] This account implies that art is not entirely locked up in an autonomous sphere of aesthetic validity overseen by professional artists and expert critics, but can directly stimulate transformed relations among ordinary selves or between them and the world. Nevertheless, given the distance Habermas himself has pointed out between ordinary experience and the expert culture of the aesthetic domain, his appeal to artistic truth potential is not grounded in a social-theoretical account of how this potential could be actualized.

This problem is linked to Habermas's tendency to underestimate the disclosive functions of ordinary language, as Charles Taylor suggests.[30] Although Habermas grants Taylor the point that ordinary language serves to open up new perspectives on the world, interpersonal relations, and one's self, he does not treat this as a central function of language. Rather, linguistic disclosure is a pre-staging, as it were, of the communicative action in which validity claims are raised.[31]

Indeed, Habermas considers the truth potential of artworks and the disclosive function of language to be similar in precisely this regard: "To the extent that experiences with their inner nature gain independence in an aesthetic sphere of its own, the works of autonomous art take on the role of eye-opening objects that provoke new modes of perceiving, new attitudes and forms of behavior. Aesthetic experiences are not linked to particular practices; they are not related to cognitive-instrumental skills and moral beliefs that grow out of innerworldly learning processes; they are bound up with the world-constituting, world-disclosing function of language."[32] This has prompted sympathetic critics such as Maeve Cooke to propose that Habermas admit additional types of validity claims beyond the three he identifies, and to expand his conception of communicative action to include the sorts of interpretation and formulation that occur not only in art but also in ordinary language.[33]

## 4. ART TALK AND IMAGINATIVE DISCLOSURE

This is not the place to sort out such Habermasian debates. Instead let me propose an approach to artistic truth that combines Adorno's insight into artistic "truth content" with Habermas's insight into the differentiated character of validity claims. My suggestion is to consider artistic truth to be internal to artistic phenomena, as Adorno claims, yet differentiated into three dimensions, in a manner reminiscent of Habermas. As I shall explain, these dimensions can be understood in terms either of three relationships that artistic phenomena sustain or of three levels at which they function. Moreover, the prevalence of one or another dimension correlates with the historically conditioned status of the phenomenon – i.e., whether or not it is constituted as a work of art.[34]

Let us suppose that all the art we know of, whether "high" or "low," whether "popular" or "esoteric," whether "mass art" or "folk art," has as one of its tasks to proffer and provoke imaginative insight. To be imaginative, such insight cannot be divorced from the media of imagination – images, stories, metaphors, musical compositions, dramatic enactments, and the like. To be insightful, such media of imagination cannot be deployed in either arbitrary or rigid ways. Perhaps, to avoid the static and visual metaphor of "insight," we should speak of imaginative inseeings, imaginative inhearings, imaginative intouchings, and the like. As a generic term I shall use the word "disclosure" rather than "insight."[35]

I take it that when people talk about truth in art, they are referring to how art discloses something of vital importance that is hard to pin down. When philosophers disagree about how to theorize truth in art, their disputes usually concern what art does or can disclose, how this disclosure takes place, and whether this disclosure is important, legitimate, preferable, and the like. Philosophers also disagree as to whether this disclosure is also a concealment (Heidegger), and, if so, how the process of disclosure and concealment contributes to human knowledge.

Art can be true in the sense that its imaginative disclosures can uncover what needs to be uncovered. Art can be false in the sense that its imaginative disclosures can cover up what needs to be uncovered. Once we realize what is at stake in artistic truth or falsehood, it will not do to say "This is merely imaginative; just playful or ironic or parodic exploration; the work of creative genius." Such special pleadings have the inadvertent effect of making art seem irrelevant or frivolous, as if imagination has little to do with disclosure. But it also will not suffice simply to attack disturbing art as "blatantly immoral" or "sacrilegious" or "repressive." Such hyperbolic accusations inadvertently make art seem more directly effective than the imaginative character of its truth or falsity permits, as if artistic disclosure is not tied to imagination.

Philosophers who reflect on contemporary art, and who engage in cultural and social critique, must ask, What needs to be disclosed in an imaginative way? This is not so different from the question facing every artist of integrity. There is no way to answer the question once and for all, especially not when one is an artist, since that which needs disclosure is continually changing, as are the media of imaginative disclosure. In the broadest terms, a philosopher must appeal to a general understanding of good and evil. At various stages of social history, one or another pathology may have priority. Hence, for example, Adorno may have been right to connect the truth of modern art with the memory of suffering and the exposure of antagonisms in a society that erases this memory and resists such exposure while it multiplies suffering and deepens antagonisms. Nevertheless, where imaginative disclosure is genuinely needed, what needs to be disclosed cannot be limited to autonomous artworks, nor can the identification of these needs be the sole prerogative of philosophy.

It is crucial, I think, that imaginative disclosure occurs in art itself, and not merely in people's lives when they experience it, talk about it, and engage in arts-related discourse. At the same time, however, I see little reason to restrict imaginative disclosure to the "import" of autonomous works of art. Every artistic phenomenon, whether or not it is constituted as a work of art, occurs in contexts of production and use. Accordingly, the idea of imaginative disclosure can be differentiated into concepts of mediated expression, configured import, and interpretable presentation.

"Mediated expression" indicates a relationship to the context of production. It pertains to the phenomenon's status as an imaginative artifact. "Interpretable presentation" indicates a relationship to the context of use. It pertains to the phenomenon's status as an imaginative object of appreciation, interpretation, and criticism. "Configured import," however, indicates the phenomenon's relationship to its own internal demands, and it may well be peculiar to artworks. In traditional terms, which Adorno also uses, import has to do with the relationship between content and form within phenomena that are institutionally constituted as works of art.

This implies that an artistic phenomenon can be true in three respects: true with respect to the artist's intentions, true with respect to the audience's expectations, and true with respect to an artwork's internal demands. It also implies that an artistic phenomenon succeeding in one or two respects can nonetheless fail in another, just as a well-formed speech act asserting a proposition can be inappropriate, for example, or a genuine act of promising can be misinterpreted. I designate these three dimensions of artistic truth with the terms authenticity (vis-à-vis the artist's intentions), significance (vis-à-vis the audience's expectations), and integrity (vis-à-vis the work's internal demands). Perhaps "great works of art" tend to display all three of these, and continue to display them in new contexts of use.

One can also take such dimensions of truth to mark different levels of functioning. Thus, for example, authenticity pertains to the expression of intentions, significance to the establishing of interpersonal relations, and integrity to the presenting of a world, all within a process of imaginative disclosure.[36] If this is right, then one can postulate more precise links between artistic truth and the sorts of speech acts that commonly occur when people engage in art appreciation, interpretation, and criticism – more precise than a diffuse entering into ordinary experience where three validity domains intermesh, as described by Wellmer and Habermas. To indicate these links, I need to introduce one more set of terms.

It is common knowledge, and a basis for much of analytic aesthetics, that language usage pervades ordinary experiences of art. Viewers, listeners, and readers talk about art, write and read about it, watch videos and television programs about art, read reviews, listen to their acquaintances talk about art, and so forth. Let me introduce the phrase "art talk" as a way of summarizing all these sorts of language usage.[37] When art talk occurs as a relatively unproblematic use of language to reach an understanding, it can be called "art conversation." When it enters a more "reflective" mode, however, and implicit validity claims become an explicit topic of discussion, art talk can be called "art discourse."[38] In everyday art talk, people regularly and almost imperceptibly slide between conversation and discourse. There are many possible topics (depending on the artistic medium, the background and experience of the participants, and the setting and occasion), and many different dimensions to art can provide points of entry: technical, economic, political, ethical, etc. Here I am singling out the topic of truth as approached via art's aesthetic dimension. My proposal is as follows.

Like language usage in most other contexts, art conversation tends not to thematize the validity claims implicit in speech acts, but it does make the truth dimensions of art available for art discourse. Conversations about art address, among other topics, the artist's intentions, the audience's expectations, and the artwork's internal demands. These conversations shift readily across descriptive, interpretive, explanatory, evaluative, and prescriptive registers. Frequently one discussion partner or another will find a particular art phenomenon lacking in authenticity or significance or integrity, saying this painting is not genuine or that piece of music doesn't do anything for me or that film is a piece of trash. If someone else disagrees, then the implicit "norms" of authenticity, significance, and integrity can themselves become topics of discussion. Someone, for example, may ask you why you do not find the painting genuine, or why you think it should be genuine, or what you mean by "genuine," and you might respond by appealing to some notion of authenticity. When you give reasons for your judgment and explain your criteria, your conversation tends to turn into discourse.

Art discourse does more than thematize the dimensions of artistic truth, however. It also thematizes the validity dimensions of art conversation itself. Hence the topic for discursive consideration might very well be not simply the authenticity, significance, or integrity of the artistic phenomenon but the sincerity or appropriateness or correctness of a discussant's claims about it. Often, in fact, the topics of art discourse jump back and forth between artistic truth and conversational validity claims. I might assert that a painting by Norman Rockwell presents too rosy a picture of American family life. You might dispute my assertion and ask me to defend or explain it. I might reply by appealing to certain facts – the clean-scrubbed look of the children, the sentimental happiness of the dog, etc. You might grant these facts, but say they do not make up a rosy picture. Or you might grant that they make up a rosy picture, but you might deny that such a picture is too rosy. Very soon we might find ourselves discussing what Rockwell "was trying to depict" (intention) and how others have interpreted this depiction (significance). And so it would go.

At a minimum, this dispute would have two inseparable and simultaneous poles: the painting's import, and the asserted proposition. To reach agreement concerning the first pole, we would need to look at the painting together and try to see "what the painting is all about." To reach agreement concerning the second pole, we would need to establish whether certain shared facts bear out the asserted proposition. If we had not both looked at the painting with an eye to its import, we would be hard-pressed to find sufficient shared facts relevant to the disputed proposition. Facts are funded (not founded) by objects as experienced, even though, according to Habermas, facts play a role only in discourse.

So I wish to postulate not simply a general connection between artistic truth and conversational validity claims, but more specific links between each of the three dimensions of artistic truth and each of the three validity claims: between artistic authenticity and expressive sincerity, between artistic significance and normative legitimacy, and between artistic integrity and propositional truth. Moreover, the links are dyadic. In the first place, art conversations cannot get at artistic authenticity without raising a conversational claim to sincerity; they cannot get at artistic significance without raising a conversational claim to normative legitimacy; and they cannot get at artistic integrity without raising a conversational claim to propositional truth.[39] In the second place, our experience with issues of authenticity, significance, and integrity in art, and our art conversation about these issues, are part of the lived matrix from which the content of the correlative validity claims arises.

If these links and their dyadic structure could be demonstrated in sufficient detail, that would help show that imaginative disclosure is neither esoteric (Adorno) nor peripheral (Habermas). It would also provide a way to build disclosure into the very fabric of communicative action, rather than relegating it to a preliminary stage within language usage. My proposal might even offer a different perspective on propositional truth, both by tying it more closely to imaginative disclosure than standard truth theories allow and by indicating truth itself to be a multidimensional idea whose reduction to propositional truth leads to theoretical impoverishment and practical dead ends.

I must finish on that promissory note, hoping to redeem some of my more ambitious claims in the book *Artistic Truth*. Let me conclude with comments about the relevance of my approach to Hart's work in epistemology.

## 5. KNOWING OTHERWISE

Earlier I indicated my long-standing reservations with the way in which Henk Hart's writings link analysis and critique. If conceptual and semantic modes of experience are the primary or exclusive ways in which order is known, as Hart seems to think, then this puts rationality in a privileged position, contrary to the gist of his own criticisms of what he calls the rationality tradition. As is apparent from nearly all his writings, those criticisms are motivated by a religious conviction that knowledge and truth are not only multidimensional but also guided by a deep spiritual trust with respect to "the existential boundary issues of experience: life and death, origin and destiny, meaning and happiness, good and evil."[40] In these respects he is a faithful follower of Dooyeweerd, despite the differences in their vocabularies. Both of them propose holistic epistemologies based on anti-reductionist ontologies and motivated by religious concerns.

In Hart's later writings, however, his criticisms of the rationality tradition generate a problematic account of religion. Opposing a tendency to reduce Christianity and other religions to systems of propositions and beliefs (which can then be rejected as irrational by enlightened critics), Hart describes religion as a community's living out of trust, guided by a historically narrative wisdom.[41] That leads to what I consider to be an overly spiritualized epistemology and an insufficiently rational spirituality. I shall sketch what this means, and then suggest how my own approach to the topic of artistic truth could provide fruitful revisions. For brevity's sake, let me restrict my discussion to the essay "Conceptual Understanding and Knowing *Other*-wise."

This essay describes rationality as the "capacity to reach a conceptual understanding of regularity and structure in reality which gives us a general grasp of things."[42] The measure of worth for conceptual insights is their usefulness in dealing with reality: "If [concepts] are true in our experience this can at most mean that with their help we have been able to make better adjustments to real relationships in our real experience. They help us to control disease, improve crops, spread wealth, and do many other wonderful things that could not have been done without them."[43] Whether such uses are themselves worthwhile depends, in turn, on their integration with a spiritual way of life: "[Rational knowledge] gives potentially beneficial powers to our culture, even though such power can be ... abused ... Hence we [Westerners] face a serious call to responsibility in knowing how to deploy our rational powers ... The power is not as such evil, nor is it automatically good. Only what we do with it in our spiritual journey determines the good and the evil."[44]

These passages, and many others like them, express what I would call an overly spiritualized epistemology. By that, in this context, I mean an account of "rational knowledge" that first reduces the validity dimensions of communicative action to propositional truth, then reduces propositional truth to a matter of practical effects, and finally subsumes the question of practical effectiveness under a post-rational spirituality. I have more to say about "post-rational spirituality" below. First I need to explain why I see two reductions, and why I consider them problematic.

I find Hart's account of "rational knowledge" unduly restrictive in light of the "rationality tradition" he criticizes. Since I have already discussed Habermas, I shall return to him, even though one could just as easily go back to Kant's tripartite discussion of rationality (understanding [*Verstand*], practical reason [*Vernunft*], and reflective judgment [*Urteilskraft*]). Kant's discussion is the obvious predecessor to Habermas's differentiation of communicative rationality into cognitive-instrumental, moral-practical, and aesthetic-practical rationality, with their correlated validity claims of propositional truth, normative legitimacy, and expressive sincerity. It seems to me that Hart credits only the first of these moments of communicative rationality and ignores the other two altogether. This helps explain why he tends to link analysis and order, since, historically, cognitive-instrumental rationality has been concerned with uncovering laws, patterns, and the like. But he also overlooks the critical side of cognitive-instrumental rationality, which Kant adumbrated in his discussion of reason (*Vernunft*) in its theoretical employment, and which Habermas stresses by pointing to the communicative preconditions that make such rationality possible. Instead Hart loads critical capacities into other, "nonrational" dimensions of knowledge that trump, as it were, the deliverances of (propositionally restricted) rationality. Hence there can be no criteria internal to "rational knowledge" that help us adjudicate the truth or falsity of its discoveries and assertions, but only the external criterion of a conceptual insight's potential benefit for human life. Since Hart does not deal with questions about how to "rationally" sort out the priorities of different potential benefits or how to distinguish genuine benefits from bogus ones, but assumes these questions will be adequately answered by our spiritual orientation, I reluctantly but ineluctably conclude that he has proposed an overly spiritualized epistemology.

The flip side of this, as I have already hinted, is an insufficiently rational spirituality, or what I described in passing as a postrational spirituality. In "Conceptual Understanding and Knowing *Other*-wise," Hart describes "spiritual knowing" as "knowing focused in hope and trust." It "seeks to embrace an open vision of hope in embodied trust, without domination or totalization." It allows people to "come to know our future, our comfort, our neighbor in ways that give shape to communal traditions in narratives which direct, edify, and comfort us." The faith-talk appropriate to such spiritual knowing is "metaphorical" in the sense that it "breaks through the limits of given language to remain open to saying what lies beyond being said." So too the beliefs of faith – a rational dimension within spiritual knowing, according to Hart – are "an imaginative articulation of how trusted forces speak to us as they guide us."[45]

As these passages illustrate, Hart does not advocate a totally irrational spirituality. This would be very difficult to do so long as one speaks of spiritual *knowing*, gives rationality a (limited) role in full-fledged, multidimensional, and integral knowledge, and recognizes a place for faith-talk and beliefs of faith within spirituality. My worry, therefore, is not that Hart has rendered spirituality *irrational* but rather that he has made it *insufficiently rational*. It is telling, I think, that he seldom raises the question of false or destructive spirituality, other than in his caustic and astute comments on the latent spirituality of the rationality tradition. Yet if spirituality is truly a way of knowing, then there must be differences between better and worse instances of it, and there must be ways to tell the difference. Not every object of hope and trust is worthy of such, as the Hebrew prophets made abundantly clear. Not every communal narrative tradition shaped by spiritual knowing promotes human flourishing, as the sordid history of nationalist, racist, and imperialist mythologies in the twentieth century makes painfully plain. Nor will it suffice at such points of deep critique simply to appeal to the story guiding one's own community of faith, which as often as not has squandered whatever hope and trust it receives and has perpetuated the destruction it decries. What is needed is a spirituality that is both critical and self-critical, and for this neither metaphorical faith talk nor imaginative beliefs are adequate. As described by Hart, they are not sufficiently rational to support criticism and self-criticism. Moreover, because these are the only elements of rationality he admits into spiritual knowing, the spirituality he describes is insufficiently rational.

To prevent misunderstanding, let me hasten to add that the missing elements of rationality of most concern here are not Hart's truncated version of rationality as the conceptual understanding of order. Instead I surmise that the pressure created by Hart's restricted notion of rationality drives other elements of rationality from his account of spirituality. If rationality were conceived instead as communicative, hence intersubjective, rather than monological, and as oriented toward a plurality of validity claims rather than toward a (constructed) order of reality, then a richer account of the rationality within spirituality could be given, and the necessity of spiritual discernment and discourse could be fully acknowledged.

Here my own account of artistic truth might help. Much earlier I mentioned the Romantic flavour to Hart's manner of attributing truth capacity to the arts in this essay. He seems to have an expressive theory of art, according to which art discloses the higher truths of the inner self, or at least ones that are "not available to discursive conceptual knowing."[46] In retrospect, this *notion* of artistic truth seems available only to a *philosophy* that has not completed the linguistic turn. An incomplete linguistic turn also affects Hart's accounts of rationality and spirituality, both of which assume a type of immediacy between subject and object, even when the object is a mystery of faith. More specifically, it affects Hart's account of the elements of rationality within spiritual knowing, namely faith talk and beliefs of faith. When he describes faith talk as "metaphorical," the implied concept of metaphor is the Romantic symbol, which directly expresses the ineffable without the intervention of ordinary language.[47] Similarly, when he characterizes beliefs of faith as "imaginative articulations," the implied concept of imagination is Romantic creative intuition, which directly captures what ordinary understanding cannot grasp.

Such nonrational immediacy disappears, however, if one postulates an internally differentiated idea of artistic truth and links the dimensions of artistic truth with validity dimensions in art conversation, which themselves can be discursively thematized. Then imaginative disclosures, such as one finds in art, appear to contain important elements of (communicative) rationality: discussable norms, if you will, of authenticity, significance, and integrity. It also appears that such elements call for conversation and discourse that have their own elements of rationality: the validity claims of expressive sincerity, normative legitimacy, and propositional truth. Moreover, the rationality of both art and art talk are dialogical rather than monological, so that the possibility of criticism and self-criticism is built into the very fabric of imaginative disclosure.

Similar points can and should be made about faith talk and beliefs of faith. One can grant that these are metaphorical and imaginative without thereby pitting them against or placing them above rationality. If faith talk and beliefs of faith function as means of imaginative disclosure within spirituality, on my account of imaginative disclosure they will be open to assessments of their authenticity, significance, and integrity. If they function as means of trustful conversation, on my account of conversation they will imply discussable validity claims to sincerity, legitimacy, and propositional truth. And if faith talk and beliefs of faith involve both imaginative disclosure and trustful conversation, as I suspect they do, then they will display a nexus of disclosive truth and communicative rationality very similar to the linkages I have mapped for art and art talk.

In this proposed revision of Hartian philosophy, spirituality would no longer seem *insufficiently* rational, but *appropriately* rational. Spirituality construed along these lines will preserve the unique character of "spiritual knowing," but it will not threaten to turn "knowing otherwise" into something that is otherwise than knowing. Perhaps, then, the long journey of exploration that Henk Hart helped me launch decades ago will have turned up a few discoveries that he, too, finds beneficial for a spirituality he has so generously nurtured, exemplified, and studied as a systematic philosopher in the Kuyperian tradition.[48]

# 8

# The Inner Reformation of Reason: Issues in Hendrik Hart's Epistemology

## (2004)

Reformational philosophers have long talked about "the inner reformation of science." Central to this reformational task has been exposing and rejecting "the pretended autonomy of theoretical thought," to use Dooyeweerd's phrase. Henk Hart has done more to carry out this project of exposure and rejection than any other member of the second generation of reformational philosophy. As a member of the third generation, and his appreciative former student, I gratefully acknowledge my debt to this mode of critical engagement with the entire tradition of Western philosophy.

Yet I want to suggest that the time has come for an "inner reformation of reason." Like Dooyeweerd and Vollenhoven, Hart employs a conception of reason that is both outdated and internally problematic. In Hart's formulation, he and his reformational predecessors regard reason as "the absolutized logical/analytic function of our experience and its special relation to the (logically conceived) order of reality."[1] Their critiques of reason aim to show that such absolutization is both illegitimate and religiously motivated. Nevertheless, the way in which they characterize this absolutized function itself draws heavily from problematic sources within the "rationality tradition" they criticize.

The question I wish to pursue is what a better account of rationality would look like, an account that neither absolutizes one function nor obsesses about a religious commitment to reason. Briefly, I want to suggest that a better account would have three characteristics: (1) it would connect rationality with the notion of communicative validity rather than the notion of world order; (2) it would call attention to the inescapable rationality of faith within modern societies and postmodern cultures; and (3) it would demonstrate the necessity of rational criticism in matters of faith and spirituality.[2]

The three characteristics just mentioned parallel in reverse the three topics that Hart's symposium paper describes as critical issues. I begin with his third issue because I agree that here the deepest differences lie. But I do not accept his suggestion that the other two issues involve primarily semantic differences. I think they are equally substantive. I hope this will become apparent if I start with the third issue he has so helpfully identified.

## 1. VALIDITY, NOT ORDER

Hart claims that "our analytic functioning focuses on order." It enables us "to grasp some [of] reality's regularities and their implications," and it gives us "explicitly understood access to the world's order, its patterned continuity."[3] He seems to suggest that because animals lack analytic functioning they have no access to the world's order.[4] Moreover, he claims that connecting analytic functioning with an access to order is "not only the view of reformational philosophy ... but also of the continuous Western rationality tradition."[5] Precisely! And if both reformational philosophy and the rationality tradition are misguided on this score, then both need to undergo inner reformation.

Why do I say this? First, because this account of rationality cannot avoid the dilemma of realism. To assert that analytic functioning focuses on order immediately frames rationality as a matter of epistemic access to a mind-independent reality. When one then rejects realist accounts of such access, as Hart has done, one almost unavoidably slides into the equally unwelcome arms of anti-realism. Thanks to a phenomenological notion of intentionality, Dooyeweerd found a way to slip past this dilemma. But most of his followers have been less agile. Certainly the wider community of self-identified Christian philosophers in North America remains impaled on the horns of a realism dilemma.

Second, an emphasis on order does not encourage us to pursue Vollenhoven and Dooyeweerd's underdeveloped insight into modal laws as the differentiation of one central call to love God above all and our neighbours as ourselves. An emphasis on order also inappropriately reduces the Trinitarian complexity of God's relationships to creation, turning these into the sorts of regularities and patterns studied in the natural sciences (for a certain construal of "natural science"). When the order-emphasis turns out to be problematic, one then runs the risk of pitting it against a notion of non-order such as an "ethos of compassion."[6] Thus does a realism dilemma carry over into the problems of ethical emotivism.

Third, the notion of order to which Hart appeals presupposes a problematic conception of a single (objective) world. Ever since Kant, philosophers have been keenly aware of a need to distinguish world concepts: Kant's phenomenal and noumenal realms; Hegel's subjective, objective, and absolute spirit; Heidegger's being-in-the-world, being-with, and being-in; Habermas's objective, social, and subjective or personal worlds. Such differentiation in world concepts calls for a differentiation in types of rationality. To that extent, the claim that analytic functioning focuses on "the world's order" begs important questions about the sort of world and the sort of order in focus.

Beyond such problems with "order," however, my main point is that rationality has more to do with communicative validity than with world order. In modern societies, what marks practices as rational is not so much whether they lead to an analytic grasp of order as whether they raise claims to validity, can back up these claims with reasons, and can remain open to criticism. Claims to validity can be claims to factual accuracy, or to propositional correctness, or to practical rightness, or to expressive sincerity.[7] In the standard cases such claims arise intersubjectively, in an interchange among two or more people. So the validity in question is intrinsically intersubjective and communicative. And it is indexed to a plurality of worlds, depending on the claim being raised and discussed, such that assertoric claims about the weather forecast have a different ontological status from that of expressive claims about how I am feeling.

## 2. RATIONALITY OF FAITH

This implies a different notion of rationality from one where the primary relationship resides between an epistemic subject and an epistemic object. Hart's notion of rationality is of the latter sort. Even when he defends himself on this score, saying that "the disclosure of so-called objective states of affairs is a subjective process,"[8] he still talks about subjects in relation to objects, not subjects in relation to other subjects. This subject/object paradigm steers his account of the relation between faith and rationality.

As I understand it, Hart's account of this relation claims three things: first, that faith and rationality are mutually irreducible; second, that rational practices unavoidably have a moment of faith built into them; and third, that "beliefs of faith," as the "rational dimensions of the life of faith," "depend on the life of faith."[9] Taken together, the weight of these three claims privileges faith over reason. I think it is time to rebalance the scales.

To get at this, let me ask why "beliefs of faith" should be regarded as the "rational dimensions of the life of faith." Perhaps Hart's answer would be that beliefs of faith give propositional expression to that which we hold in a supra-propositional mode of trust. But he would hasten to add that "in its functional core faith transcends understanding."[10] I think he has two systematic reasons why he hastens to add this: first, because he construes rationality as giving epistemic access to order, and second, because he holds that the ultimate objects of faith always exceed the boundaries of the order to which we have rational access.

If one gives up that account of rationality, however, the worry over whether faith transcends understanding disappears, and so does the identification of faith's rational moments with "beliefs of faith." For it is not certain propositions or certain propositional look-alikes that make up the rationality of faith, but certain practices in which validity claims are raised, contested, revised, and borne out. These are the elements of rationality to which Hart's account of faith is insufficiently attentive. For example, he concludes at one point that "faith on some levels in practice resists critical argument."[11] In the context, he clearly takes this to reinforce his earlier claim that "faith transcends understanding." But I would take it quite differently. I would say that, to the extent that faith resists critical argument, the faithful in modern societies need more critical discourse rather than less. For contemporary practices of faith in which validity claims cannot be raised, contested, revised, and borne out are insufficiently rational to deal adequately with fundamental issues of life and death, of good and evil, and of hope amid suffering.

## 3. RATIONAL CRITICISM

That brings us to my third topic: namely, the necessity of rational criticism in matters of faith and spirituality. So far I have suggested that rationality is not primarily about the world's order. It is about communicative validity. Whereas order would be something given or constructed, validity is both discovered and contested. I have also suggested that, in modern societies, rationality is a legitimate and unavoidable element within any practice or institution of faith. That is part of what it means for a society to be modern or a culture to be postmodern. Now I need to say more about the notion of rationality in order to show why rational criticism is necessary in matters of faith.

Let me begin with the modal location of rational practices. Both Vollenhoven and Dooyeweerd regard rationality as prelinguistic, and they link rational practices very closely to perception, sensation, and memory. Although in principle Henk Hart regards rationality as postlinguistic (or postsymbolic, in his own terminology), he often writes as if rationality is prelinguistic.[12] For example, in the essay "Whither Reason and Religion?" he speaks of language as "the soil into which we implant our understandings." Language is the "vehicle of communication" that "gives us access to our shared conceptual understanding."[13] This makes it seem as if we arrive at understandings prelinguistically and then somehow transport these understandings into language. But that account runs directly contrary to one of the most important discoveries of twentieth-century philosophy, a discovery central to the so-called "linguistic" and "interpretive" turns. Twentieth-century philosophy discovered that the practices of rationality are always already linguistic and hermeneutical. They cannot occur outside the practices of language and interpretation.

The postlinguistic character of rational practices requires several revisions in reformational epistemology. The first pertains to God-talk and God-concepts. On this topic Henk Hart, Jim Olthuis, and I all three disagree. Whereas Hart tends to deny our having any concepts of God, and Olthuis doubts "the possibility of strictly theoretic concepts of God,"[14] I want to affirm our having concepts of God. The God-concepts we have can function in many different contexts, including scholarly contexts, and they can also be abused in just as many contexts. Precisely because we do have God-concepts that can be abused, they need always to be subject to critique and self-criticism. My position here is consistent with the postlinguistic character of rationality. To put the point bluntly: whatever can be discussed can also be conceived. Hence it would be inconsistent to admit God-talk, on the one hand, but disallow concepts and propositions and arguments about God, on the other. Further, if one allows ordinary God-concepts, one must allow scholarly God-concepts as well.

My position here relies on a second revision in reformational epistemology. Both Hart and Olthuis employ a distinction between "theoretical" and "non-theoretical" or "pre-theoretical" that goes back to

Dooyeweerd's transcendental critique of theoretical thought. After the linguistic turn, however, Dooyeweerd's structural and phenomenological distinction between theoretical and pre-theoretical needs to be redescribed. It needs to be redescribed as an institutional and sociological distinction between scholarly and non-scholarly or between academic and non-academic. Here Vaden House and I are on the same page. If something like the "Gegenstand relation" characterizes the theoretical element in academic work, this is not because of how thought itself is ontologically structured. Rather it is because of how academic work is institutionalized in universities, disciplines, and the like. Such institutionalization allows certain types of abstraction, reflection, experimentation, and debate to occur that otherwise would be difficult to achieve. That is the sort of context in which theoretical God-talk and scholarly God-concepts emerge. If we think certain abuses of God-talk and God-concepts regularly beset academic discourse, then we should focus our critique on the institutions in which such discourse occurs, rather than try ontologically to rule such discourse out of order.

One target of my own critique, which I find oddly missing in both Hart's account of theory and House's account of science, is the instrumentalization of rationality in the modern academy. This is a huge topic, of course, to which I cannot do justice here. But let me simply say that I find it extremely problematic to describe the "truth of science" as the "truth of control,"[15] or to suggest that most of science properly aims at developing "conceptual tools and technical instruments in the interest of effective action in the world."[16] Such fundamentally Baconian notions of science, in which knowledge is power, marginalize the elements of dialogue, interpretation, and self-criticism in science. But precisely those elements would be required for the practices of "justice, morality, frugal caring, [and] vulnerable trust" to genuinely "*in-form*" science,[17] or for the claim of science actually to be "limited for the sake of the fullness of life."[18]

More generally, I think we misunderstand the tasks of normative critique if, like Hart, we construe rationality as primarily a matter of concepts and propositions. His construal derives from Dooyeweerd and Vollenhoven, both of whom, in locating rationality as postpsychic and prelinguistic, make the recognition of norms dependent on the availability of concepts and propositions. Given my own view of rationality as postlinguistic, I cannot simply continue their account of the relation between normativity and logical functioning. Yet their account offers an insight that should remain central to reformational philosophy. In my own vocabulary, their insight is that in modern societies a critique of antinormative tendencies cannot be legitimate unless it relies on rational practices and remains open to rational responses. That is to say, a normative critique cannot be legitimate if it does not raise validity claims and does not stand ready to back them up in public. Such reliance on rational practices and such openness to rational responses do not guarantee the legitimacy of a normative critique. But they do count as necessary conditions for a legitimate normative critique in modern societies.

Hence the practices of faith cannot be exempted from the rationality requirement either. Yet I fear Hart's approach bestows precisely such an exemption, despite his protests to the contrary, and despite his criticisms of his own faith tradition. The basis for my worry comes through in Hart's characterizations of "religion" and "religious truth."[19] At one point he describes religion as "the institutionalized form in which we ritually cultivate the human experience of trust to enable us to rely on our intimations of transcendence and ultimacy to order our lives." He makes clear that by "transcendence" he means "surpassing understanding."[20] A little later he describes religious truth as "the power of symbols to reveal the meaning of our surrender in trust to the ultimate mystery of our existence." He explicitly contrasts this to "the adequacy of conceptual grasp."[21] These descriptions certainly sound to me as if the practices of faith always already trump any rational critique that could be offered them. How can one legitimately criticize an "experience of trust" or "intimations of transcendence"? What would motivate one who has such experience and intimations to offer discussable claims about them? How would the experience of religious truth, as revealing the meaning of trustful surrender to an ultimate mystery, become an actual truth claim in a public language? And what purchase would such experience give for a normative critique of both faith and other practices or institutions in contemporary society?

Our challenge now, it seems to me, is to offer an account of faith practices that frees them from a subject/object paradigm in which the ultimate object of faith lies ever beyond the grasp of order-oriented concepts and propositions. For this a different account of rationality is required. We need an account that emphasizes validity rather than order; an account that shows the practices of communicative rationality to be intrinsic to faith within modern societies; and an account that makes faith both a topic and a resource for normative critique. In short, we need an inner reformation of reason.

# 9

# Metacritique: Adorno, Vollenhoven, and the Problem-Historical Method

## (1985)

Tensions pervade the study of the history of philosophy. To contribute to philosophy, such study must be philosophical. To live up to its name, however, it must also be historical. How can philosophy and history be combined? I wish to explore this question by developing the notion of a metacritique. I shall argue that metacritique is central to the study of philosophy's history,[1] and I shall develop this argument by discussing the work of Dirk Vollenhoven (1892–1976) and Theodor W. Adorno (1903–69).

## 1. INTRODUCTION

Historical inquiry is essential to the interpretation of Adorno's philosophy. Like the work of Martin Heidegger, the philosophical writings of Theodor W. Adorno pose numerous obstacles to adequate interpretation. Many of these obstacles stem from the unusual methodological, stylistic, and conceptual strategies Adorno employs. The resultant difficulties are so great that one writer has said of Adorno: "What he once complained about in Heidegger could perhaps … be extended to him as well: 'He lays around himself the taboo that any understanding of him would simultaneously be falsification.'"[2] The stormy reception given Adorno's work after his death in 1969 compounds our difficulties. There were numerous partisan debates among Marxist-Leninists, existentialists, critical rationalists, and Adorno's loyal or disgruntled students. While highlighting problems in Adorno's work, these debates also generated frequent misinterpretations.

Gradually, however, historical studies have calmed the turbulent atmosphere and corrected partisan misinterpretations. Most of these studies are of two types: commentaries, which help clarify Adorno's concepts and methods, and intellectual histories, which help elucidate the contexts of his philosophy. In themselves, however, such approaches are not fully philosophical, nor can they do complete justice to Adorno's philosophical writings. Indeed, sometimes the net effect has been to domesticate and relativize Adorno's most provocative and significant contributions, many of which were the focus for partisan debates. What is needed in addition to commentaries and intellectual histories, it seems to me, is a historical approach that is thoroughly philosophical. Otherwise Adorno's philosophical contributions will not receive the philosophical attention they deserve, nor will the other types of reception enrich our philosophical understanding.

There are, of course, numerous areas of interpretation in common among philosophical historiography and other historical studies. In the case of Adorno's philosophy, every historian will need to make sense of Adorno's writings and present a credible account. Many of the difficulties mentioned earlier lie at this common level of interpretation. How are any of us to develop and present credible interpretations of a philosophy that deliberately resists paraphrase? Like Heidegger, Adorno challenges historians to reexamine their methodological preconceptions and exegetical inclinations during the very process of interpreting his writings.

At the same time, philosophical historiography has a unique area of interpretation, and it makes a unique contribution to our understanding of a philosophy. Unlike the history of ideas (a close cousin, so to speak), the historiography of philosophy attempts to be not only historiographic but also philosophical. Unlike other historians, historians of philosophy are expected to develop and present philosophical positions on the philosophical writings and issues they examine. The fact that not all historians of philosophy meet this expectation does not eliminate the expectation, although such a failure might help explain why many Anglo-American philosophers have not considered philosophical historiography a subdiscipline of philosophy.

As soon as we claim that historiography of philosophy is expected to be philosophical, however, we confront a perennial problem of philosophy: What are philosophy's legitimate tasks in terms of which we may specify the philosophical character of the historiography of philosophy? If we expect such historical inquiry to be philosophical, then we cannot avoid requiring that every historian of philosophy have some idea of philosophy's legitimate tasks. As is well known, philosophers often have mutually incompatible ideas along these lines. Their lack of agreement is a main reason why the question of philosophy's tasks is a perennial problem. Historians of philosophy can hardly avoid the problem, even when they give an account of the problem's history.

This self-reflexive character, I suggest, helps distinguish philosophical historiography from other histories, even where these concern philosophical writings. A thoughtful historian of ideas will no doubt reflect on methodology, presentational strategies, and criteria of selection, just as a thoughtful historian of philosophy will. But the historian of philosophy will also be expected to reflect philosophically on the legitimate tasks of philosophy. Furthermore, only historians of philosophy will be expected to show how philosophical reflections on philosophy inform their historical accounts.

This chapter attempts to engage in such reflection with reference to the notion of metacritique. Given my own idea of philosophy's contemporary calling, metacritique seems central to the study of philosophy's history. Metacritique seems central in this sense: it provides a crucial link between history as history and philosophy as philosophy, and without it the historiography of philosophy might fail to be simultaneously historical and philosophical.

The chapter develops the notion of metacritique and argues for its centrality in several stages. First I introduce this notion by way of example and historical precedent. Next I explore distinctions in the levels and directions of philosophical discourse. Then, after clarifying some key terms and concepts, including "metacritique," I draw two conclusions: genuine metacritique must be genuinely historical, and metacritique is essential to the philosophical character of philosophical historiography.

## 2. METACRITICISM, METACRITIQUE, AND VOLLENHOVEN'S METHOD

### 2.1 *Metacriticism and Metacritique*

Before considering *metacritique* itself, let us discuss a related concept: the concept of *metacriticism* in the study of aesthetics. George Dickie suggests that contemporary aesthetics includes three areas. He lists these as theory of the aesthetic, philosophy of art, and metacriticism or philosophy of criticism; and he describes metacriticism as the philosophical analyzing and clarifying of the basic concepts used by art critics to discuss particular works of art. According to Dickie, "The development in philosophy which led to metacriticism in aesthetics was the widespread influence of analytic, linguistic philosophy, which conceives of philosophy as a second-order activity taking as its subject matter the language of some first-order activity."[3] In aesthetics this development has led to an emphasis on metacriticism, on the philosophical criticism of the language of art criticism.[4]

Metacriticism in aesthetics illustrates two minimal criteria of metacriticism as a general function of philosophy. (1) To count as an instance of metacriticism, something must be theoretical discourse about discourse of some specific type. (2) To count as an instance of metacriticism, such theoretical discourse must give philosophical attention to basic concepts and criteria in some type of discourse. Although metacriticism is not the only function of philosophy, it would seem to be characteristic of much philosophy.

*Metacritique* is a heightened version of *metacriticism*. If, for example, we asked about the criteria whereby philosophers subject art criticism to metacriticism, then we would take metacriticism one step further. We would enter the area of metacritique. In effect we would be engaging in philosophical discourse about basic criteria in philosophical discourse about criteria in one type of non-philosophical discourse. It is in this area of heightened metacriticism – call it third-order discourse, if you wish – that I aim to find a crucial link between history and philosophy. For it seems to me that, to be philosophical, a historiography of philosophy must engage in third-order discourse. Historiography of philosophy is, among other things, philosophical discourse about philosophical texts. These texts in turn are often about basic concepts and criteria in other philosophies or in non-philosophical forms of discourse.

By way of illustration, consider a philosophical-historical account of Adorno's *Negative Dialectics*. The number of ways to give a historiographic account might be as great as the number of persons who cared to give one. For example, we could trace certain emphases back to Adorno's intellectual biography, beginning with his gifted childhood, his subsequent training in music and philosophy, his exile from Nazi Germany, and concluding with his final twenty years as one of Germany's most influential sociocultural critics. We could do a philological study of key terms such as "dialectics," "negation," and "truth," uncovering their historical antecedents and their functions in *Negative Dialectics* and in earlier writings by Adorno. We could explore the process of Adorno's writing, the drafts of various passages, and the final outcome. We could also interpret the text in terms of the social, political, and economic circumstances under which it was written. The ways of historical interpretation seem endless. None of the ways I have mentioned is philosophical, however, even though philosophical historiography cannot afford to ignore these ways. What, then, would a philosophical-historical account be like?

Such an account would focus on the philosophical issues Adorno has raised. The philosophical historian would interpret these issues with respect to the positions of other philosophers on similar issues, especially those philosophers with whom Adorno expresses agreement or disagreement. Moreover, the philosophical historian would assess Adorno's approach to such issues in terms of the contributions he has made to philosophical understanding. Such a philosophical-historical account would have two overriding aims: to interpret the philosophical issues in a philosophical text, and to assess the philosopher's contribution with respect to these issues. To meet either aim, historians of philosophy would seem obliged to engage in a metacritique. At the very least, they would seem obliged to engage in some version of third-order discourse. They would have to write or speak about a philosophical text that discusses basic concepts and criteria in other philosophies and in non-philosophical forms of discourse.

Thus far I have suggested that metacritique is a form of third-order discourse. I have not established what is distinctive about this form. But I have begun to describe the type of historiography in which metacritique seems central. Such historiography emphasizes philosophical interpretation and assessment of philosophical issues. To describe this type of historiography, let me next discuss one of its historical sources. Later I will show it to be a historical source of the notion of metacritique in philosophical historiography. The actual sources are complex and varied. But the one most relevant in the present context is Dirk Vollenhoven's "consistent problem-historical method" (*consequent probleemhistorische methode*). My account will simplify Vollenhoven's method but, I hope, will not distort it.[5]

## 2.2 *Vollenhoven's Problem-Historical Method*

To the historian of philosophy, according to Vollenhoven, the history of philosophy is a process of immanent criticism. The history of philosophy is to be viewed as a process of disagreement and agreement about fundamental philosophical questions. The main continuity in this process lies in the philosophical problems treated and the manner of their treatment. The main discontinuity lies in periodic shifts, mainly with respect to questions about creation's laws and their location.

Vollenhoven describes the lines of continuity as "types" of conceptions about ontological problems such as unity and diversity or being and becoming. What is typical about various conceptions in one period can recur and often does recur in later periods, although individual conceptions as such do not recur. During one historical period, common problems unite significantly different conceptions. Philosophers with various conceptions frame their agreements and disagreements with one another in terms of such common problems. Although Vollenhoven thinks the usual common problem is one concerning creation's laws, he also allows for other sources of periodic unity. In "pre-Platonic" philosophy, for example, the relationship of philosophy to myths was a problem shared by all philosophers.[6] Correlatively, what unites conceptions in one period tends to differ from what unites conceptions in subsequent periods. Vollenhoven attributes the main discontinuities in the history of philosophy to this difference. "Time-stream" (*tijdstroom*) is his technical term for the unity of a period and its fundamental difference from other periods.

Vollenhoven's method is not without its own problems. One sympathetic critic has suggested that Vollenhoven's method shares with neo-Kantian philosophers a tendency to subordinate historical study to systematic study.[7] The main problem with Vollenhoven's method, according to Al Wolters, is that it reduces both the history of philosophy and the historiographic method to logical matters. Vollenhoven's approach treats only the logical element of philosophical problems and solutions, says Wolters, and, by categorizing and conceptualizing philosophical conceptions, it treats this element only in a logical manner. Wolters wonders "what is then the specifically *historical* of this 'problem-historical' method, if the extra-logical factors in the history of philosophy, such as social, economic and political conditions, are deliberately excluded?"[8] The only answer seems to be that Vollenhoven emphasizes the common framing of problems among philosophical contemporaries and distinguishes periods with reference to the question of law. This answer seems unsatisfactory, however, since the common framing of problems still strikes Wolters as a "systematic" or "logical" matter.[9]

Two facts are worth noting about Wolters' line of questioning. One is that he proceeds by locating and pursuing problems in Vollenhoven's approach. This fact is noteworthy because it tends to demonstrate

Vollenhoven's point – namely, that philosophers tend to engage in immanent criticism. The history of philosophy is one of problems and solutions. The second significant fact is that the questions raised by Wolters assume a fundamental distinction between the historiography of philosophy and systematic philosophy. Strictly speaking, the distinction is not Wolters's own but derives from Vollenhoven. What is a distinction for Vollenhoven, however, seems to become a disjunction for Wolters. Here we have a good example of the type of historical change Vollenhoven wished to understand. We also come upon one source of the notion of metacritique I am trying to develop: namely, a disputed distinction between historiography and systematics in Vollenhoven's philosophy. Let's take a closer look at this distinction with a view to developing the notion of metacritique. We shall examine some of the levels and directions of philosophical discourse.

## 3. LEVELS AND DIRECTIONS OF PHILOSOPHICAL DISCOURSE

### *3.1 First-, Second-, and Third-Order Discourse*

Vollenhoven distinguishes between systematic philosophy and historiography of philosophy. Methodologically, systematic philosophy generates "primary concepts" about reality, he says; historiography of philosophy generates "secondary concepts" about the conceptual results of philosophical activities. Ontologically, systematic philosophy concerns "the structure of creatures and their ontic genesis"; historiography of philosophy concerns "the genesis of a subdivision of human culture."[10] Vollenhoven goes on to say that, though clearly distinguishable, the two parts of philosophy need each other.

As Wolters notes, there are some problems with Vollenhoven's distinction. Vollenhoven seems to ignore the "nonconceptual" activity that goes into philosophizing, and he poses an unsatisfactory distinction between structure and culture.[11] The more significant difficulty, it seems to me, is that Vollenhoven overlooks the extent to which all philosophy is at least second-order discourse, and the extent to which historiography of philosophy is third-order discourse. The concepts in "systematic philosophy" are not simply "primary concepts," nor are these concepts simply about the structure and genesis of creatures. Such concepts are simultaneously "secondary concepts" about other concepts, both philosophical and non-philosophical. A philosophical history of systematic philosophies will require "tertiary concepts" about the secondary concepts of systematic philosophies.

It is somewhat puzzling to think that Vollenhoven did not recognize the "second-order" level of most philosophical discourse. This is puzzling, given Vollenhoven's emphasis on immanent criticism. Already in 1922, according to Wolters, Vollenhoven objected to T. Hoekstra's *History of Philosophy I* because it lacked sufficient immanent criticism.[12] Vollenhoven argued that rejecting another philosophy must always be based on indicating internal difficulties in the philosophy rejected. Such indicating of internal difficulties is what Vollenhoven means by "immanent criticism." The lack of immanent criticism leads Hoekstra's book to ignore the dialectic of philosophy's history. In contrast, Vollenhoven thinks that immanent criticism is the primary means by which philosophers arrive at their positions. Immanent criticism is also the primary way in which continuity and discontinuity are generated in the history of philosophy. Not even historians of philosophy may dispense with immanent criticism of the positions they interpret. Wolters correctly takes this emphasis on immanent criticism to be a constant feature in Vollenhoven's historical accounts and in his problem-historical method.

Given Vollenhoven's emphasis, we may expect him to recognize that no philosophy, no matter how systematic, is simply about the structure and genesis of creatures. To the extent that immanent criticism is central to the philosophical enterprise, to that same extent even the most systematic philosophy will be about other philosophies. Furthermore, the distinction between "systematic" philosophy and historiography of philosophy is not as dramatic as Vollenhoven suggests; for in both areas there is philosophical discourse about other philosophies, and in both areas immanent criticism is a central manner of such discourse.

### *3.2 Systematic and Historical Directions*

Perhaps we can better view systematics and history not as distinct, complementary parts of philosophy but as two directions in which philosophical inquiry proceeds. Moreover, these might not be the only directions. There may be topical or thematic studies, for example, whose primary direction is neither systematic nor historical. Leaving this possibility aside, we must try to get a clearer picture of the relationship between the systematic and historical directions. It seems to me that the historical direction is necessary and legitimate in philosophy as a whole and in every philosophical subdiscipline: philosophy of religion, ethics, philosophy of law, social philosophy, philosophy of language, epistemology, philosophy of science, philosophy of art, philosophy of education, and so on. Is the historical direction of philosophy and its subdisciplines significantly different from the systematic direction?

In certain important respects my answer is no. In both directions, philosophy aims to give a general account of the world and of human life within it. In both directions, philosophy relies heavily on immanent criticism among various positions. And in both directions, philosophy involves discourse and concepts that are not directly about the phenomena for which philosophy aims to account. The discourse seldom is first-order discourse, and the concepts seldom are primary concepts.

Perhaps returning to our earlier illustration will help us see how indistinct the historical and systematic directions are. We noted that one can distinguish three areas within aesthetics: theory of the aesthetic, philosophy of art, and metacriticism. Metacriticism involves philosophical discourse about the basic concepts of art criticism. Now I want to propose that the other two areas also require philosophical discourse about basic concepts in various forms of discourse. Theory of the aesthetic is not simply about the aesthetic dimension of existence and experience. Certainly philosophical aesthetics aims to give an account of this dimension. To the extent that aesthetics is philosophical, however, it gives such an account both by analyzing the concepts people use to describe aesthetic phenomena and by engaging in immanent criticism of other philosophical positions on the aesthetic. Similarly, philosophy of art is not simply about art but also about the concepts and positions people have with respect to art.

Furthermore, in each area of aesthetics, philosophers are able to take an additional step. They are able to ask about the criteria and categories employed when philosophers analyze aesthetic concepts, discuss concepts of art, and clarify the language of art criticism. In other words, philosophers are able to engage in the third-order discourse characteristic of what I have called metacritique. Whereas philosophical aesthetics, philosophy of art, and metacriticism render problematic established discourse about aesthetic and artistic phenomena, metacritique renders problematic the manner in which philosophers pose problems in the three areas of aesthetics itself.

How is this done? How do we engage in a metacritique of aesthetics? It seems to me that philosophers do this both historiographically and systematically. To put the matter more accurately, metacritique is so thoroughly historical-systematic that here the historiographic and systematic directions become indistinct. Take, for example, the concept of "art." If, instead of asking about concepts of art, we ask about the criteria for philosophizing about such concepts, we enter an inquiry that is neither distinctly historiographic nor distinctly systematic. On the one hand, to grasp the relevant criteria we need to examine the criteria to which philosophers have actually appealed to legitimate their discussions. On the other hand, to determine the validity of any such criteria, we need to develop our own position about them. In both activities we need to render problematic the ways in which other philosophies have legitimated their own discussions of the concept of art.

The primary means for rendering other legitimations problematic seems to be immanent criticism. Is immanent criticism at this level for the sake of historical interpretation or for the sake of systematic theorizing? The answer seems to be neither and both. As a method of metacritique, immanent criticism seems neither distinctly historiographic nor distinctly systematic. Metacritique itself seems so thoroughly historical-systematic that the historical and systematic directions become indistinct.

Does this tentative conclusion imply that we should abandon the distinction between historiography and systematics? I think not, although I do believe we should distinguish them as directions rather than as parts or areas of philosophy. We can picture philosophy as a two-directional arrow. In one direction the arrow is historiographic. In the other direction the arrow is systematic. Somewhere near the centre, where it would be hard to tell in which direction the arrow is pointing, lies the enterprise of metacritique. But there is much more to the arrow than metacritique. The further we are from the centre, the more clear becomes the distinction between the historical and systematic directions. Moving away from the centre, we can observe a difference between immanent criticism by a philosophical historian and immanent criticism by a systematic philosopher. This difference corresponds to a difference in the levels of discourse at which immanent criticism occurs. The historiography of philosophy tends to occur one additional step away from some of the phenomena for which systematic philosophers try to account.

## *3.3 The Problem of Induction*

Take, as an example, the so-called "problem of induction" in philosophy of science.[13] Many philosophers since the nineteenth century have held that scientific discoveries are made inductively and ought to be made inductively. According to these philosophers, scientists properly proceed from particular observations and observation statements to more general statements, theories, and laws. Proper scientific procedure in the context of discovery is to induce from the particular to the general. From the observation of many swans, for example, we may gradually arrive at the inductive conclusion that all swans are white.

This position about scientific discovery has run into problems, however, because the principle of induction cannot itself be logically justified. To say that inductive arguments are necessarily valid is obviously incorrect. No induced conclusion, no matter how carefully it is made, is necessarily correct. This fact is quickly illustrated when we discover black swans in New Zealand. The most that can be claimed for an inductive conclusion is some degree of probability. Having observed many swans, and having never learned of black swans, I can legitimately conclude that swans *probably* are white. The universal conclusion "All swans are white" *might* be correct but need not be correct.

Even though inductive arguments cannot be necessarily valid, we might wish to justify them through an inductive argument. We might say, for example, that we have observed that inductive arguments, properly constructed, always yield correct conclusions. This was substantially the justification given in John Stuart Mill's *A System of Logic*. The problem with this justification, and the real "problem of induction," is that such a justification is itself an inductive argument. Thus the justification is a case of circular reasoning, with the added disadvantage of taking a form that cannot be necessarily valid.

The "problem of induction" would seem to be a genuine problem, one worth philosophical scrutiny. The philosophical historian's approach to this problem, however, differs significantly from that of a more systematic philosopher of science. The historian will be more concerned about the traditions informing the problem and the most significant attempts that have been made to pose and resolve it. For example, the historian would wish to consider the tradition of empiricism and the positions on induction taken by Aristotle, Francis Bacon, John Locke, David Hume, and John Stuart Mill. For the historian, understanding recent debates about induction in science will require understanding the traditions and positions tacitly or explicitly informing those debates. Thus, for example, Kant's reply to Hume would merit the historian's attention because it provides an important source for many subsequent anti-empiricist moves such as those by N.R. Hanson and Thomas Kuhn.

In contrast, more systematic philosophers of science tend to work within the context of recent and current debates. They will pay attention to traditions and precursors, but with an eye for strategic arguments and concepts rather than for historical connections. The systematic philosopher will be concerned primarily to address the problem directly, either to propose a solution or to show how the problem can be avoided. The systematic approach to a problem will be relatively direct, even though second-order discourse about other positions will be prevalent.

The historical philosopher's approach to a problem will be less direct. The historian's primary interest will not be to tackle the problem in the context of contemporary debate but to trace its development in a tradition of philosophical discourse about other philosophical discourse. Whereas philosophical systematists use immanent criticism of other positions to work out their own positions, philosophical historians trace the lines of immanent criticism along which the problem has acquired a certain shape.[14] Historiography of philosophy tends to occur one additional step away from phenomena such as inductive discoveries in science.

Despite such differences, I wish to submit that the historian, far from simply presenting lines of immanent criticism, should be expected to offer criticism of the lines presented. The historian should be expected to say when a position is more or less correct, more or less fruitful, and more or less significant within the line being presented. Saying this is initially a matter of immanent criticism. Another way of putting the matter is to claim that in presenting the history of philosophy, the historian should become a creative participant, a history-maker, and in this participation should do philosophy. Crucial to such participation is the enterprise of metacritique, in which the historical and systematic directions of philosophy become indistinct.

## 4. PROBLEMS, IMMANENT CRITICISM, AND METACRITIQUE

Up to now I have used several terms and concepts that may seem ill-defined. Three in particular require further attention: "problem," "immanent criticism," and "metacritique." Let me discuss each in turn.

### 4.1 *Philosophical Problems*

Wolters takes Vollenhoven's usage of "problem" to refer to logical matters: a problem is a logical difficulty. Yet a problem need not be taken as a merely logical difficulty. This is clear from another one of Vollenhoven's sympathetic critics. Calvin Seerveld does not think Vollenhoven reduced history and historiography to logical matters. Instead Seerveld objects to Vollenhoven's apparent tendency to treat problems as unchanging paradigms inherited from Greek philosophy. Seerveld attempts to "forge a more impassioned historiographic method which will push back to *creational problems as historical givens*." Greek philosophers gave Greek responses, but the problems themselves are "neither essentially Greek *problems* ... nor quasi timeless fixations." Instead they are "perennial *historical challenges* ... and have staying power through the ages *because* they are *creational structural affairs*."[15] Every philosophy, according to Seerveld, is challenged to give an account of the coherence and diversity of creation, for example; the two mistaken ways of doing so are dualism and monism in their numerous varieties.[16] For Seerveld, the problems indicated by Vollenhoven's historiographic categories are not simply logical difficulties.

Without entering questions of how to interpret Vollenhoven, I wish to propose that neither Wolters nor Seerveld has hit upon a satisfactory formulation. Contra Wolters, and regardless of what Vollenhoven himself thought, most philosophical problems are not simply nor primarily logical. Besides such obviously logical difficulties as inconsistency or invalid argumentation, there are several other levels where philosophical problems arise. In debates between philosophies, misinterpretations and misunderstandings often occur. Within a philosophy there can be terminological confusion or rigidity. A philosophy can be misinformed, can misconstrue the phenomena it tries to explain, or can seem implausible. The list could go on. My only point is that philosophical problems are not reducible to logical difficulties, even though logical difficulties often signal difficulties at other levels. So too, attempts to address philosophical problems are not simply logical operations.

On this point I agree with Seerveld, who notes the breadth and depth of philosophical problems and does not reduce these to logical difficulties. Yet Seerveld seems to overstate his case. I grant that it is questionable whether large classifications such as "monism" and "dualism" indicate paradigmatic Greek problems and solutions. Yet I also find it puzzling to think of them as pointing to "creational problems" that challenge each new generation of philosophers. On the one hand, the notion of *creational* problems seems to suggest the inevitable inadequacy of any *philosophical* solution. On the other hand, this notion seems to ignore the fact that historiographic categories such as "monism" and "dualism" are forged in particular historical circumstances, during the process of critically interpreting philosophical problems and the philosophies in which these take shape. The precise Vollenhovian categories of "monism" and "dualism" arose in a particular twentieth-century philosophy that employed immanent criticism on specific historical connections of immanent criticism. To say that such categories indicate creational problems would seem to make illegitimate any significant revision of the categories. What if, for example, historical research should indicate that the supposed problems of monism and dualism are not live issues for contemporary philosophy? Should we nevertheless persist in trying to classify recent philosophies as either monist or dualist? Perhaps recent philosophies are so pluralist that "monism" and "dualism"are inadequate or irrelevant ways to classify or interpret them.

As is now apparent, the notion of a philosophical "problem" is itself problematic. We may say that philosophical problems are neither merely logical difficulties nor enduring challenges embedded in the structure of creation. But we have not yet said exactly what the term "philosophical problem" means. More precisely, we have not spelled out any criteria by which to recognize or identify philosophical problems as philosophical problems. Yet any problem-historical method will assume such criteria. Unfortunately, making such criteria explicit would require a metacritique beyond the scope of this chapter.[17]

## 4.2 *Immanent Criticism*

The location, discussion, and attempted solution of problems in another philosophy characterize "immanent criticism." Here, again, differences between formulations of Vollenhoven's method may help us understand a central term. Wolters reports that Vollenhoven regarded immanent criticism as the indicating of logical inconsistencies or terminological confusion within another position. Transcendent criticism, in contrast, highlights errors as these are viewed outside the position criticized, from the critic's own standpoint.[18] Seerveld, however, thinks "Vollenhoven points beyond the usual combination of immanent critique … and transcendent criticism" toward a "truly transcendental christian critique of other philosophies."[19] Using Vollenhoven's method and categories, one neither simply stands outside the other position nor temporarily suspends one's own position. Instead one "asks christian questions within the other thinker's assumed framework." The approach of transcendental criticism provides opportunity for "listening intently to the (checkmated) contribution of nonchristian philosophies to our (faulty) christian understanding of reality."[20] Seerveld's article attempts to show how Vollenhoven's categories provide such an opportunity.

Vollenhoven's own methodological reflections seem to corroborate Wolters's emphasis on immanent criticism. Vollenhoven's article of 1961 stresses immanence in two respects. In the first place, Vollenhoven insists that his method gradually arose in the process of treating historical subject matter. Vollenhoven seems to think this is the most desirable way to develop a historiographic method. Otherwise the method risks being inappropriate to the subject matter.[21] In the second place, Vollenhoven says he developed categories such as monism and dualism in response to the terminological, conceptual, and classificatory problems he found in other accounts of Greek philosophy.[22] Immanent criticism of Greek philosophies and immanent criticism of modern historiographies seem for Vollenhoven to be the most potent sources of his own method.

Yet Vollenhoven clearly did not consider immanent criticism self-sufficient. It is also unlikely that he was satisfied with a split between or a combination of immanent and transcendent criticism. It would seem then, that Seerveld's emphasis on "transcendental criticism" has some merit. Nevertheless, his descriptions of transcendental criticism seem incompatible with Vollenhoven's actual method and methodology. Where Seerveld emphasizes a Christian understanding of reality to which other philosophies are to contribute, Vollenhoven emphasizes the actual problems and solutions that philosophers have addressed. Where Seerveld wishes to ask Christian questions "within the other thinker's assumed framework," Vollenhoven attempts to understand that framework in the context of historical continuity and discontinuity. Thus immanent criticism remains important in Vollenhoven's method, even though the actual role and limitations of immanent criticism need to be clarified.

To clarify the role of immanent criticism would require better criteria for philosophical problems than either Vollenhoven or his sympathetic critics have provided. Short of specifying such criteria, my own position is that immanent criticism is a process of discussing, arguing with, and evaluating a philosophical position. Immanent criticism attempts to locate, elucidate, and resolve the argumentative, conceptual, terminological, methodological, and other inadequacies within a stated position. The position being criticized usually provides the criteria used in this process. Immanent criticism characterizes much of philosophical debate. Historians of philosophy should attempt to reconstruct philosophical debates with an eye to the immanent criticism involved. At the same time, historians of philosophy should not take such debates at face value, but should engage in their own immanent criticisms of the various positions taken.

### 4.3 *Metacritique*

The limits to the historian's own immanent criticism lie in the area of metacritique. Although "metacritique" is not synonymous with Seerveld's notion of "transcendental criticism," the two terms are closely related: both refer to the movement between immanent criticism and the presentation of one's own position. The main difference comes from varying views about the dependence of one's own position on the positions that are being criticized.

Seerveld's notion of transcendental criticism assumes the prior presence of a full-fledged systematic philosophy. Transcendental criticism amounts to an evaluation of another philosophy's contribution to one's own system. The idea of metacritique, by contrast, is less thetical, more dialectical, than Seerveld's notion of transcendental criticism. A metacritique will always openly depend on the positions subjected to immanent criticism. This description holds both for the metacritique present in other positions and for the metacritique carried out by the historian interpreting those positions. To be sure, dependence on criticized positions is only one dimension of metacritique. Metacritique is also a movement beyond the positions subjected to immanent criticism.[23] The essential point, however, is that, unlike Seerveldian transcendental criticism, metacritique openly depends on the criticized positions it supersedes.

Recalling earlier stages in our discussion, we may describe metacritique as immanent criticism in the dependent process of rendering problematic the manner in which a criticized position poses its problems. In a metacritique, immanent criticism no longer simply accepts a criticized position's criteria, even though it acknowledges its reliance on them. Such descriptions must apply to an instance of philosophical historiography in order for this to count as a genuine instance of metacritique. Without self-reflection and self-transcendence, the historiographer's immanent criticism will not disclose its own dependence on the position criticized. Reflecting on an immanent criticism's own problems and criteria, the historiographer will note the degree to which these belong to the position that is being criticized. By pushing beyond such problems and criteria, the historiographer may note the degree to which any genuine solutions and alternative criteria are discovered through struggle with the position being criticized and with the issues it raises. Recognition of dependence is not enough, however; ways must also be found to question, fundamentally and irrevocably, the problems and criteria of the position criticized. Otherwise the historiographer's work will not contribute significantly to our philosophical grasp of the phenomena addressed by the criticized position. To be genuine, a metacritique must live up to a double expectation. It must recognize the degree to which the historiographer's immanent criticism depends on the object of criticism, but it must nevertheless go beyond both the object and the immanent criticism.

## 5. HISTORICAL METACRITIQUE IN PHILOSOPHICAL HISTORIOGRAPHY

### *5.1 Historical Metacritique*

Another way to put this double expectation is to say that, to be genuine, a historiographer's metacritique must be genuinely historical. By "genuinely historical" I mean that the metacritique must participate creatively in the history being reported. Thomas McIntire has suggested that "the history of something is the actual temporal course of the phenomenon in its process of becoming, being, and ceasing."[24] Historical study tries to account for such history. In the case of human beings and human phenomena, the histories to be studied are creative processes of "bringing things into being, modifying them, and bringing them appropriately to an end."[25] In McIntire's terms, then, the historiography of philosophy would study the creative processes whereby philosophical concepts, terms, debates, positions, texts, schools, etc. are initiated, continued, changed, and terminated. For a problem-historical method, the main subject matter for such study would be the processes of posing and solving problems.[26] If the writing of philosophical history is itself historical, however, then philosophical historiography is itself a creative process whereby philosophical matters are initiated, continued, changed, or terminated. Metacritique would seem to be a fountain of creativity in philosophical historiography, provided it is genuinely historical. To be genuinely historical, the historiographer's metacritique must itself initiate, continue, change, or terminate the problems and solutions located through immanent criticism.

Moreover, a metacritique must manifest the triple relationship characteristic of historicity in McIntire's account. This relationship, one of past, present, and future, is "a whole in which at no present moment is past entirely past, nor is future merely in the future." Instead, "at any present moment the past is present in the form of tendencies and the possibilities for what may occur."[27] For the historian of human phenomena this relationship implies a possible "fusion of horizons," to use Hans-Georg Gadamer's phrase. Not only are the historian's "past-present-future" and the historical subject's "past-present-future" related as "parts of one historical process,"[28] but also this relationship may become manifest within the historian's account. For such a fusion of horizons to occur, the historiographer's account must take up the subject matter's "past-present-future" into the account's own "past-present-future." In historiography of philosophy, this sublation is primarily a function of metacritique. To be genuinely historical, a metacritique must take the subject matter's "past-present-future" into the "past-present-future" of the philosophical historiographer.

What would such a sublation look like? How would it be carried out? In a problem-historical approach, the fusion of horizons would occur at several simultaneous levels. In the first place, a problem or solution in one position would be shown to have more than antecedents and a context of contemporaneous debate. The problem or solution would also be shown to have historical fulfillments reaching into the historiographer's own day. Second, a position's problem or solution would be shown to have become a problem or solution for the historiographer and to hold possibilities for the future of the historiographer's own philosophy and of the historiographer's generation. Third, neither the position's problem or solution nor the historiographer's reception thereof would be treated as matters of strict logical necessity. The possibilities of correction, reformulation, reinterpretation, and reevaluation would be continuously open as we move into the future. Problems would not seem irrevocably beyond redemption, nor would solutions appear to be permanently settled. In new circumstances the previous problem could make a fundamental contribution, just as an apparent solution could become inadequate. So too, previous problems and solutions could help create noticeably new circumstances.

I have described metacritique in philosophical historiography as the self-transcending of immanent criticism and as the rendering problematic of problems and criteria in a criticized position. A metacritique must not only recognize dependence on the object of immanent criticism, but also go beyond both the object and the immanent criticism. Described in this manner, historiographic metacritique is crucial to the fusion of historical horizons. By both acknowledging dependence and going beyond, a metacritique makes evident the historiographer's historical connections to the position criticized. Made evident is how this position, with its past-present-future, is part of the historiographer's own past-present-future. Also made evident, however, are ways in which this position and the historiographer's reception might become part of a subsequent history. A metacritique can show how the historical fulfillments of a position's problems or solutions are present in the historiographer's own day and hold possibilities for the future. Accordingly, we should not view the problems discussed in immanent criticism as Greek paradigms (Vollenhoven) or creational problems (Seerveld). Instead we should treat them as historical achievements in an ongoing process of redemption. The fulfillment of this process comes to us from a future in which both the position criticized and the criticism itself are called to participate.

To be genuine, then, a metacritique must be genuinely historical in a double sense. It must participate creatively in the reported history by initiating, continuing, changing, or terminating the problems and solutions located through immanent criticism, and it must take the subject matter's history into the historiographer's own history.[29]

## 5.2 *The Centrality of Metacritique*

I began by asking how philosophy and history can be combined. How can the historiography of philosophy be both philosophic and historiographic? Although I have not given a complete answer, I hope some important reasons for asking this question have become clear. I hope as well that the centrality of metacritique to philosophical historiography has become more evident. I have argued that the philosophical historian's challenge is not so much to combine philosophy and historiography as to pursue critically the historiographic direction of philosophy without ignoring its systematic direction. Unlike other types of historical study, the historiography of philosophy is philosophical. The historiographer of philosophy does philosophy, although not primarily in a systematic fashion. At the same time, the historiographer of philosophy does history, although primarily in a philosophical fashion. The philosophical historian does history in the double sense of giving a historiographic account of the history of philosophy and creatively participating in that history. Both the report and the participation are primarily philosophical.

Mediating between the historiographic and systematic directions of immanent criticism, metacritique is central to philosophical historiography. Without metacritical mediation, the historiographer's immanent criticism remains locked into the problems, solutions, and criteria provided by earlier positions. Locked in, the historiographer's account cannot give us a fundamentally new or transformed philosophical grasp of the positions in question or the phenomena they have tried to make intelligible. Historical relativism or eclecticism is the most likely outcome of historiographic immanent criticism cut off from metacritique. Yet metacritique is equally central to systematic philosophy. Without metacritical mediation, one of two problems tends to occur in systematic philosophy. Either a chasm emerges between immanent criticisms and the systematician's own position, or no distinct position is developed. Either dogmatism or skepticism seems the most likely outcome of systematic immanent criticism cut off from metacritique. Metacritique is an agency for transforming both one's own position and one's immanent criticism of other positions, whether that criticism be historiographic or systematic in orientation.

Metacritique is not the sum total of philosophical historiography. Nor have I presented a complete discussion of either metacritique or philosophical historiography. In fact, I have ignored several significant questions. One such question concerns the extent to which historiography of philosophy is tied to philosophical writings. Another question pertains to the cognitive status of historiographic categories. In addition, I have not spelled out either criteria for identifying problems and solutions or criteria for their significance and fruitfulness.

### *5.3 Historiography and History*

One other important question, however, merits some concluding comments. Earlier I claimed that historians can write many types of histories about Adorno's philosophical writings, but only a philosophical historiography can do complete justice to them. In claiming this, I made the double assumption that philosophical histories are distinct from other types of histories, and that one type of historiography will be more appropriate than other types to a certain sort of history. Granted these assumptions, we still face an interesting question. How are philosophical histories related to other types of histories? This question is similar to one Wolters has raised about Vollenhoven's problem-historical method.

Adorno's philosophy provides clues to an answer. Within the history of philosophy, he claims, something of the movement of history as a whole appears.[30] In his own studies of writings by Kierkegaard, Husserl, and Hegel, Adorno attempted to disclose something of this larger historical movement.[31] Most important for our present discussion, however, is Adorno's claim, not his attempts to realize the claim. How might his claim help us understand the relationship between philosophical and other histories?

Adorno's claim is instructive in three respects. First, it suggests that the history of philosophy has acquired its own integrity, which is not to be confused with either autonomy or isolation. This integrity needs to be respected in the historical process of philosophy as well as in the philosophical historiography whereby a philosopher takes part in this process.

Second, Adorno's claim eliminates problematic separations between "philosophical history" and "other sorts of history." Instead he emphasizes how internal to philosophical history the entire movement of history is. This emphasis implies that comprehending philosophical history requires comprehending something of the entire historical movement that encompasses philosophical history. The best way to do this, according to Adorno, is not to turn to biographical, intellectual, economic, and other histories, but to engage in philosophical critique.[32] Carried out with sufficient rigour and imagination, philosophical critique will disclose something of the entire movement of history: although treated philosophically, philosophical problems will not be understood as *merely* philosophical problems.

In the third place, Adorno's claim does not suggest that philosophical historiography of philosophical history is itself sufficient for comprehending the entire movement of history. "Something" of that movement appears within the history of philosophy, but full comprehension requires more than philosophical historiography. From the side of the history studied, let me suggest, even more is taking place than what all the various general and specialized historiographies study. From the side of historiography itself, no study and no combination of studies will be adequate for fully comprehending the entire movement of history. Historiographic study, like any other academic work, is fundamentally a derivative life practice.[33] Such study helps shape the historical dialectic it studies, but the historical dialectic also continually shapes such study. Full comprehension eludes historiography because neither historiography nor the movement of history has reached fulfillment. Furthermore, historiography is always subject to reorientation by the other life practices to which it is tied.

In this connection, let me propose one final description of metacritique. Metacritique is a conscious attempt to maintain philosophical integrity in philosophical historiography without ignoring the entire historical movement. Metacritique is a conscious attempt to maintain such integrity without acting as if philosophical historiography or any other historiography can be comprehensive or self-sufficient. The time has not yet come for the owl of Minerva to spread its wings. Were this time to arrive, it would not be dusk, but the dawn of a new day. Philosophers are called to work towards the light, letting it shine in anticipation on their own work. When the light dawns, a new day will begin. Then Minerva's owl will take flight in joy.

# 10

# Defining Humankind: Scheler, Cassirer, and Hart

## (1988)

A crisis in self-knowledge motivates two seminal writings in twentieth-century philosophical anthropology. In *Man's Place in Nature* (1928), Max Scheler (1874–1928) applauds attempts by philosophers, biologists, and social scientists to construct a new model for humanity's "essential structure." Yet he says we are a greater mystery to ourselves now than ever before.[1] Ernst Cassirer (1874–1945) makes a similar observation in *An Essay on Man* (1944). The sciences have given us abundant information and sophisticated methods for understanding ourselves, Cassirer says, but our theoretical self-understanding has "lost its intellectual center." We have become rich in facts but poor in thoughts, to the detriment not only of scholarship but also of "our ethical and cultural life."[2] Such concerns are common among thoughtful people today. Despite all our specialized knowledge, we seem to lack wisdom about ourselves.

The crisis in self-knowledge has many dimensions. The most important ones may be neither scientific nor philosophical. Indeed, the age of nuclear geopolitics makes the remarks of Scheler and Cassirer seem almost quaint. Yet a philosophical dimension remains in the crisis of self-knowledge, one worth addressing, provided we harbour no grand illusions about its impact.

Central here is a problem of definition discussed by both Scheler and Cassirer. Let me reconstruct parts of their solutions in order to propose an alternative approach. I shall focus on attempts to define human beings in relation to animals, leaving aside relationships with other creatures as well as questions about self-relation, interhuman processes, and the origin and destiny of human existence. My argument is that Scheler and Cassirer correctly criticize essential definitions of humanity, but they confuse differences in function with differences in kind. To avoid such confusion, we need to propose transfunctional definitions of humankind.

## 1. FUNCTIONAL DEFINITIONS

Traditionally, Western philosophers have tried to define the essence of human existence. Usually they have found this essence in some substance or some set of essential properties. This was then assumed to be the essence of one type of animal. Well-known phrases such as "rational animal" and "political animal" summarize these traditional definitions.

Nineteenth-century idealism and positivism, each in its own way, challenged the essentialist project, and Darwinian biology strengthened this challenge. Gradually functional definitions arose: *homo creator* (Friedrich Nietzsche), *homo faber* (Friedrich Engels), *homo ludens* (Johan Huizinga). Now the problem of definition was not what human beings are but what we do, not which essential properties we possess but how we become human. Moreover, the burden was not so much to differentiate between the animal and the human as to explain their continuity. In such functional definitions, human beings are not so much a distinct type of animal as an emergent species.

### *1.1 Max Scheler: Life and Spirit*

Max Scheler's book recapitulates the shift from essential to functional definitions. Scheler says we have two concepts of humankind: as a small subclass of the vertebrates and mammals, and as a being whose characteristics "must be sharply distinguished from the concept 'animal.'"[3] The first concept, from the natural sciences, does not note any qualitative differences between animals and human beings. The second concept, by contrast, indicates our "essential nature" and notes differences in kind. At first Scheler seems to attempt an essential definition of humankind. Upon further reflection, however, it becomes clear that he interprets both concepts as functional concepts that one must connect in a functional definition.

Scheler's terms for the two concepts are "life" (*Leben*) and "spirit" (*Geist*), respectively. Life is the process of living. It manifests itself in four stages or forms that together comprise the "overall structure of the biological-psychological world."[4] The four forms, from "lowest" to "highest," are vital impulse (*Gefühlsdrang*), instinctual behaviour, habitual behaviour, and practical intelligence. Whereas plants manifest only the first form, animals and human beings manifest all four forms of life. Hence human life differs from animal life only in degree, not in kind.[5] Human life displays the same kinds of functions that we find in animals.

Nevertheless, human beings are not simply a type of animal. Whereas animal existence coincides with animal life, human existence manifests a "new principle." The new principle is "not a stage of life ... but a principle opposed to life as such, even to life in man."[6] Scheler calls this principle "spirit." Our qualitative difference from animals consists in the fact that we are spiritual beings.

It would be easy to think of spirit as the substance or essence of human beings. That, however, would violate Scheler's explicit intention, and it would do so for two reasons. First, Scheler characterizes spirit in functional terms. Spirit is a structure of intellectual, emotional, and voluntary acts whose centre, the person, is "a continuously self-executing, ordered structure of acts. The person is only in and through [the person's] acts."[7] In the second place, Scheler claims that spirit and the person are neither objects nor substances. Although our spiritual acts objectify phenomena in the organic world, including our own life, the acts themselves cannot be objectified. Persons cannot be objectified either. Accordingly, persons and spiritual acts cannot be treated as substances or defined in terms of essences.[8] That is why Scheler characterizes spirit in functional terms and insists that spirit is not a substance, and his discussion of spirit is not an attempt to give an essential definition of humankind. Instead of defining the essence of humanity, Scheler's discussion of spirit describes various functions that help distinguish us from animals. Both "life" and "spirit" indicate functional concepts, with spirit regarded as the higher structure of functioning.

Given his sharp distinction between life and spirit, Scheler must account for their relationship. As I suggested earlier, he describes the relationship between spirit and life in functional terms. The relationship is not one of evolution or causality, however. Instead it is one of actualization and sublimation. Being inherently impotent, spirit must actualize itself by directing (*Lenkung*) and guiding (*Leitung*) the vital impulses.[9] The blind energy of life must be sublimated into spiritual activity.[10]

Now we can state Scheler's functional definition of humankind: human beings are those finite beings who are in the continuous process of actualizing spirit and sublimating life. This functional definition marks not only our qualitative difference from animals but also the special place of humanity in the cosmos. According to Scheler, our place is to be the primary diplomat for a fusion between the spiritual principle and the vital impulse, both of which belong to the Ground of Being.[11] Such diplomacy implies that humanity, and only humanity, cooperates with the Ground of Being in the creation of God[12] and perhaps in the re-creation of the world.[13]

### *1.2 Ernst Cassirer: Symbolic Forms*

Scheler's functional definition is not without internal problems. Ernst Cassirer raises several in his "'Spirit' and 'Life' in Contemporary Philosophy" (1930).[14] Cassirer asks three questions directly relevant for our discussion. First, how can life and spirit cooperate in "constructing the specifically human world"?[15] Second, doesn't Scheler's view of spirit as inherently impotent overlook the form-creating power of the human spirit?[16] Third, by anchoring both life and spirit in the Ground of Being, doesn't Scheler transform a "purely functional antithesis" into a "substantial one"?[17]

As Cassirer's questions suggest, his own definition of humanity will be even more thoroughly functional and anti-substantial than Scheler's. Life and spirit are not "substantial essences set over against one another," Cassirer writes. They are purely functional activities that in their mutual opposition "seek and demand each other."[18] Symbolic forms such as language and art are the protean media of this transaction. Life gives birth to spirit when life "gathers itself together into enduring forms." Spirit expresses life by creating the forms into which life is gathered.[19]

The relevance of these formulations for defining humanity becomes clear in *An Essay on Man*. There Cassirer explicitly seeks a functional definition of humankind: "[I]f there is any definition of the nature or 'essence' of man, this definition can only be understood as a functional one, not a substantial one. We cannot define man by any inherent principle which constitutes his metaphysical essence – nor can we define him by any inborn faculty or instinct that may be ascertained by empirical observation. Man's outstanding characteristic … is not his metaphysical or physical nature – but his work."[20]

Lest we mistake Cassirer for either a latent Aristotelian or a closet Marxist, we should note that by "work" he does not mean craft, manufacture, or wage labour. Instead he means a "system of human activities" whose constituents include myth, religion, language, art, historiography, and science – all of which Cassirer calls "symbolic forms."[21] Notably absent from his list are ordinary activities of production and procreation as well as social, political, and economic institutions. He tries to define humanity in terms of certain cultural forms. His strategy is to uncover a basic function for each form – sympathy (myth and religion), communication (language), formal intuition (art), cultural renewal (historiography), and order (science). The forms find their unity in the creative process flowing through them;[22] their functions find unity in a common end, namely the "progressive self-liberation" of humanity.[23]

Like Scheler, Cassirer regards "spirit" as the key to our humanity. Whereas Scheler's "spirit" indicates a functional structure of intentional acts, however, Cassirer's "spirit" indicates certain cultural forms and functions in their unity. Such unity is a Heraclitean harmony in opposition, a "dialectic unity" rather than a "substantial unity." And precisely for this reason we should not attempt an essential definition of humankind, he says: "Here we are under no obligation to prove the substantial unity of man. Man is no longer considered as a simple substance which exists in itself and is to be known by itself. His unity is conceived as a functional unity. Such a unity does not presuppose a homogeneity of the various elements of which it consists. Not merely does it admit of, it even requires, a multiplicity and multiformity of its constituent parts. For this is a dialectic unity, a coexistence of contraries."[24] The multiformity and multifunctionality within spirit seem to prevent a straightforward definition of humankind; Cassirer's definition seems to unfold across the entire process traversed by his phenomenology of spirit. Nevertheless, human spirit clearly distinguishes human beings from animals and other creatures in his approach. The main disagreement between Cassirer and Scheler, other than their mutually incompatible concepts of "spirit," is that Cassirer insists on the *mediation* of spirit and life, while Scheler insists on their *separation*.

Cassirer's discussion of animals illustrates his affinity with Scheler's position. Cassirer's search for a clue to human nature begins with the biology of Johannes von Uexküll. According to Uexküll, animals have a functional circle (*Funktionskreis*) made up of a receptor system (*Merknetz*) for receiving stimuli and an effector system (*Wirknetz*) for reacting to stimuli. Cassirer adds that human beings, although they are subject to the same biological rules governing other organisms, have an additional system for adapting to their environment. This additional system is the symbolic system, which introduces a "qualitative change" in the functional circle and "transforms the whole of human life." So the clue to human nature lies in the system of symbolic forms, and we can provisionally describe humankind as an *animal symbolicum*.[25] In other words, a Schelerian assumption lies behind Cassirer's functional definition: as organisms, human beings are (like) animals; but as cultural beings, human beings are qualitatively different from animals.

This assumption motivates Cassirer's attempt to show the qualitative difference between apparently symbolic behaviour among animals and the genuinely symbolic behaviour of human beings. Cassirer argues that animals have a language of the emotions, but they lack propositional language. They have practical, problem-solving intelligence but not properly symbolic intelligence. They have an awareness of relations but are unable to consider relations in their abstract meaning. The objective reference, universal applicability, and abstraction that characterize human language distinguish human symbolism from animal quasi-symbolism. Without genuine symbolism, he says, our life would be "confined within the limits of ... biological needs and ... practical interests." Human life would lack "access to the 'ideal world' which is opened ... by religion, art, philosophy, science."[26] Since animals lack genuine symbolism, they are confined within biological limits.

### *1.3 Deep Affinity*

Although Cassirer does not discuss biologically limited behaviour in human beings, whereas Scheler does, and although Scheler emphasizes (inter)personal consciousness, whereas Cassirer does not, there is a deep affinity in their attempts to distinguish human beings from animals. Both of them look to certain "spiritual" functions as the marks of humanity and the means to transcend biological limits. For both authors, such transcendence seems to rely primarily on characteristics traditionally associated with rationality, whether objectification (Scheler) or objective reference, universality, and abstraction (Cassirer). Both of them functionalize the classical definition of humankind as an *animal rationale*, but neither author completely abandons its contents. Although they rightly reject essential definitions, their functional definitions do not eliminate the traditional problem of explaining how we can be both animal and properly human and yet have unity to our existence.

If philosophical anthropologists want to respect and scrutinize the findings of contemporary science, as I do, then rejecting essential definitions of humankind seems inevitable. For, as Cassirer argues in other writings, the primary concepts of the natural and social sciences are functional concepts. An essential definition of humankind is incompatible with the conceptual apparatus of contemporary science. Both Scheler and Cassirer were keenly aware of this incompatibility. Their fruitful solution was to propose functional definitions. Yet their definitions retain the classical view of the human being as a creature of two kinds, both animal and properly human. Thus both Scheler and Cassirer retain the traditional problem of explaining how these two kinds can fit together in one kind of creature. Scheler constructs a chasm between our intentional consciousness and our vital existence, a chasm seemingly bridged by actualization and sublimation. Trying to eliminate the chasm, Cassirer posits a harmonious opposition between our culture and our biology. Yet the question of our unity remains, and no amount of metaphysical speculation or dialectical maneuvering will conjure the question away.

## 2. THREE PROBLEMS

It would be naïve to think that the failure to answer the question of our unity is merely a philosophical failure. The unresolved question of human unity has deep roots in Western society and culture. It would be equally naïve, however, to think we can simply attribute the philosophical failure to extraphilosophical factors. Philosophers themselves have contributed to the problem by trying to define humankind as a creature of two kinds. Hence it will be worth our while to examine the matter more carefully and propose an approach that may lead to a more satisfactory answer.

Both Scheler and Cassirer go wrong, it seems to me, when they equate similarities and differences in function with similarities and differences in kind. This move forces them to see human beings as animals in those "vital" or "natural" dimensions (physical, organic, and sentient) where human beings seem to function similarly to animals. By contrast, human beings are seen as properly human in those "spiritual" or "cultural" dimensions where human beings seem to function differently from animals. Human beings are then defined as being both animal and properly human and as ever struggling to transcend and humanize their own animality.

Such definitions obscure the unity of humankind as a distinct kind, and they do so in three ways. First, they fail to account for the specifically human quality of our physical, organic, and sentient functions. Second, such definitions ignore our reciprocity with animals in certain "cultural" dimensions that purportedly are only human. Third, the definitions give rise to unnecessary paradoxes about human existence. Let me discuss each problem in turn.

### 2.1 *Human Biology*

Traditional Western philosophy tends to see the "body" and "bodily" functions as not peculiarly human. This tendency remains in Scheler and Cassirer. Consider Scheler's account. He claims that vital existence holds no differences in kind between animals and human beings. We do not even find a qualitative difference in practical intelligence or problem-solving behaviour. Scheler's position seems to entail that our "life" is not really human, except to the extent that it becomes sublimated under the guidance of the human spirit.

But how plausible would such a conclusion be? Consider the following analogy. Both plants and animals have reproductive systems and functions. Yet biologists do not regard animal reproduction as a type of plant reproduction. Why, then, would the fact that both animals and human beings have "vital" functions lead philosophers to regard human impulses, instincts, memory, and practical intelligence as a type of animal vitality? Are not human needs specifically human needs? Is not human sexuality qualitatively different from animal sexuality? Are not human sensations and feelings distinctly human? Why should every similarity in vital functioning be taken to indicate the animality of our vital existence? Is it not more plausible to assume that human life is distinctly human, and that similarities with the vital functions of animals are no more than similarities? Would not this assumption be equally capable of documentation by research in various branches of biology and psychology? At the very least, such documentation seems like a worthwhile research project for empirical and experimental scientists. Scheler fails to adequately consider the specifically human quality of human life.

### 2.2 *Animal Culture*

This failure creates considerable pressure to regard "cultural" functions as exclusively human and to ignore the reciprocity between animals and humans in these dimensions. For both Scheler and Cassirer, "spiritual" or "cultural" functions provide the key to our humanity. Scheler barely raises the question whether animals also display such functions. Cassirer raises the question, but his answer makes "cultural" dimensions exclusively human and generates internal problems for his philosophy.

Consider, for example, Cassirer's account of language. Cassirer proposes "*animal symbolicum*" as a correction of the classical "*animal rationale*." One of his reasons is that the identification of language with reason fails to cover the emotional and imaginative side of language: "For side by side with conceptual language there is an emotional language; side by side with logical or scientific language there is a language of poetic imagination. Primarily language does not express thought or ideas, but feelings and affections."[27] Yet Cassirer separates animal language from genuinely human language by saying that animals have *merely emotional language* and lack propositional language: "The difference between *propositional language* and *emotional language* is the real landmark between the human and the animal worlds."[28] His analysis is obviously incomplete, although Cassirer seems not to notice this. Suppose someone posits qualitative differences between animal emotional language and human emotional language. How might Cassirer respond? He might agree, but explain these differences in terms of propositional language, thereby undermining his earlier insistence on the multidimensionality of human language. Or he could deny that there are qualitative differences in emotional language, thereby implying that human emotional language is not genuinely human, again contrary to his explicit intention.

Such problems of internal inconsistency may indicate that Cassirer ignores important phenomena because of the pressure to regard "cultural" functions as exclusively human. Are not the cry of an infant, the laughter of a child, and the body language of an adult genuine instances of human language? If so, how do they compare with the whimpers, growls, and tail-waggings of various animals? Further, how is it possible that animals interpret the human baby's cry or that human beings almost intuitively tell the difference between a dog's growl of delight and its growl of warning? Don't such phenomena indicate both qualitative differences and genuine reciprocity between animals and human beings as linguistic agents?

Instead of struggling to show that animal language and similar phenomena are not genuine, perhaps philosophers should assume that animals take subjective initiative in nearly all the dimensions that Cassirer and Scheler wish to reserve for human beings. Cassirer is right not to ignore altogether animal language and animal societies.[29] One could easily add the production and play of various animals. Such phenomena highlight the inadequacy of attempts to define human existence in terms of unique dimensions or functions (e.g., *homo faber*, *homo ludens*, *animal symbolicum*, *animal sociale*). Scientific research may eventually show that animals are agents in all the dimensions that at one time seemed uniquely and exclusively human. The philosophical conclusion to be drawn from such research need not be that animals and human beings are one and the same. Instead one could conclude that previous philosophers have misinterpreted animal behaviour, failed to grasp the uniqueness of human beings in all their dimensions, and ignored our reciprocity with animals as productive, playful, communicating, and sociable creatures. We need to understand, for example, what is uniquely animal about animal language and what is uniquely human about human language. But we also need to understand the process of communication between animals and human beings as users of distinct kinds of language.

### 2.3 *Irresolvable Tension*

The equation of differences in function with differences in kind gives rise to unnecessary paradoxes about human existence. Cassirer, for example, seems to suggest both that our "emotional language" is human and that it is not really as human as our "propositional language." Scheler claims both that our life is human and that it is not (yet) authentically human. He also claims that the human spirit is inherently impotent, yet somehow it guides our vital impulses. One could easily expand the list of apparent contradictions. At bottom such paradoxes document an irresolvable tension in functional definitions of humankind.

The tension occurs among three claims, each of them asserted with equal force. (1) Human beings instantiate two kinds of existence, one natural and the other cultural, or one animal and the other not animal. (2) One of these two kinds is genuinely human, whereas the other is not. (3) Human beings belong to a unified and qualitatively distinct kind of existence. Taken together, these three claims assert the following: Humankind consists of two kinds, of which only one is the genuinely human kind. This assertion seems both logically untenable and phenomenologically doubtful. Moreover it tends to establish a hierarchy of value such that certain human functions seem vastly more important than they really are, while other human functions are denigrated. This hierarchy of value usually links with a hierarchy of being whereby human beings transcend creation rather than remaining part of the cosmic fabric. Although such hierarchies are more obvious in an explicitly metaphysical approach such as Scheler's, they can remain just as powerfully in effect in a nonmetaphysical approach such as Cassirer's. For Cassirer, culture is the salvation of nature, and symbolic forms are avenues for the "self-revelation" of human spirit.[30]

This is not to suggest that philosophers should return to essential definitions. Essentialism cannot eliminate the paradox. Nor will it uncover the specifically human quality of our vitality or the reciprocity we have with animals in so-called cultural dimensions. The reason is simple. All three problems pertaining to the unity of humankind occur in traditional essential definitions. Scheler and Cassirer replace substances with functions without removing the fundamental duality in traditional definitions. Two kinds of functions replace two kinds of substances, but two kinds remain. Although Scheler and Cassirer are right to reject essentialism, their functional definitions prove inadequate, partly because they preserve the content of essential definitions.

## 3. TRANSFUNCTIONAL DEFINITIONS

Instead of returning to essential definitions, philosophical anthropology should move toward transfunctional definitions, as Hendrik Hart has proposed. I have chosen the term "transfunctional" for four reasons.[31] First, the term indicates that the content of the definition must span all the functions of human beings and all the dimensions in which human beings function. No one function or group of functions will be considered any more human or less human than any other. Human beings are just as characteristically human in their "vital" or "natural" existence as they are in their "spiritual" or "cultural" existence. Second, the definition must comport well with functional analyses in a broad range of disciplines. The definition must support research organized around functional concepts, and it must receive support from such research. Third, a transfunctional definition will go beyond specific functions and beyond the findings of specific disciplines. Because no function or group of functions will be definitive, the definition will posit totality concepts of humankind. The totality will not be conceived as a substance of which all functions are properties, however. It will be considered a horizon without which humanity's unity, uniqueness, and cosmic position would remain philosophically unintelligible.

Finally, "transfunctional" suggests a change in the functional understandings gained in various disciplines. Functional understandings will come to appear incomplete. By reminding biologists, psychologists, linguists, economists, and all other specialists that no specific functional understanding fully accounts for human existence, totality concepts will encourage interdisciplinary investigations. Such concepts will also serve as reminders, especially urgent today, that humanity belongs to a cosmic fabric that is still being woven, and our uniqueness is inextricable from multiple relations that carry us beyond merely human existence.

To go beyond these formal descriptions would be to embark on the journey the term "transfunctional" announces. Recalling previous travellers and examining their maps readies one for departure. My criticisms of Scheler and Cassirer are preparations for further explorations. Perhaps the notion of a transfunctional definition will help disclose a different landscape.

## POSTSCRIPT (2015)

The somewhat abrupt ending to this essay reflects its origins as a necessarily brief conference paper. Although the essay calls for a transfunctional definition that posits totality concepts of humankind, it does not give such a definition, nor does it offer any totality concepts for consideration. Moreover, although the essay mentions Hendrik Hart's *Understanding Our World* as a source for the proposed approach, it does not discuss the wider reformational tradition.

There are two reasons for the restriction to Hart's work, beyond the constraints of a conference paper. First, much of the important new work in philosophical anthropology by reformational scholars occurred after the paper was presented at the World Congress of Philosophy in 2008. Here the most relevant writings in English, in chronological order, include publications by Stafleu (1991),[32] Geertsema (1993),[33] Olthuis (1993 and 2000),[34] Klapwijk (2008),[35] and Glas (2010).[36]

Second, to my mind, Hart's discussion of "The Special Place of Humankind"[37] was – and remains – the most important attempt in the generation after Dooyeweerd and Vollenhoven to provide an ontological framework for reformational anthropology. His discussion systematizes and extends the models proposed earlier by other influential figures in the Toronto School of reformational philosophy, if I may call it that,[38] and it decisively breaks with the most problematic aspects of Dooyeweerd and Vollenhoven's philosophical anthropologies. Whereas Dooyeweerd[39] introduces an unwieldy hierarchy of four enkaptically interlaced "individuality structures" internal to the "human body" – i.e., physico-chemical, biotic, and psychic substructures, plus an "act structure" somewhat reminiscent of Scheler's account[40] – Hart takes the simpler and sociologically more plausible approach of saying that different types of human practices have different functional qualifications in relation to different types of social institutions. Further, whereas Vollenhoven rarely elaborates the fundamental relation between the prefunctional human heart, as "that which determines the direction" of one's life, and the multidimensional human body, as "the entire cloak of the functions,"[41] Hart provides a substantial and lucid account of how the *entire human being* is both body and spirit, both ever corporeally engaged in diverse relations and activities and ever oriented in spirit to the origin and destiny of creation, both "bodily spirit" and "spiritual body."[42]

From Hart's approach emerges a transfunctional definition of humankind as that realm of creatures which, in relation to the other realms of creatures (i.e., physical things, organisms, and animals), "is called to be an agent for the direction of the world."[43] At every level of functioning, and in every relationship to themselves and others and to other creatures, human beings are both responsive to and responsible for the directing of creation toward what calls it into existence and what promises creaturely flourishing. This definition, in turn, suggests that totality concepts such as love, truth, and goodness are more comprehensively decisive for what it means to be human than are the various functional concepts uncovered by the scientific enterprise. Such totality concepts point to an all-encompassing call that is in effect at every level of human practice and institutional organization.

An anthropological approach along Hartian lines has much to commend it. First, it allows one to acknowledge the *responsive/responsible* character of human existence, as emphasized by Geertsema and Olthuis. As Olthuis says, to be and to become human is to be and become both gifted and called to love God, others, ourselves, and all creation.[44] Second, a Hartian approach supports an emphasis on the *directionality* of human existence – i.e., that human existence is always already oriented with respect to its origin and destiny, as both Dooyeweerd and Vollenhoven insist, each in his own way. Yet it neither separates questions of direction (e.g., good versus evil) from questions of structure (e.g., the "nature" of rationality) and process (e.g., historical development), nor collapses directional questions into either matters of structure (e.g., as when rationality is declared intrinsically good or bad) or matters of process (e.g., as when historical progress is simply affirmed or denied). Third, given such an understanding of both responsiveness and directionality, this approach can take up the questions of an *I-self relation* highlighted by Glas and Olthuis, while simultaneously acknowledging the social and cultural character of personal identity. Fourth and perhaps most important, given the history of reformational philosophy, Hart's approach, unlike either Dooyeweerd's or Vollenhoven's, allows for a theory of *emergent evolution* along the lines first suggested by Stafleu and then elaborated by Klapwijk, according to which qualitatively distinct levels of human functioning have emerged innovatively from previously existing levels, and humankind itself has emerged innovatively from prehuman forms of life.[45] This, despite the fact that Hart does not take up questions of evolutionary theory in *Understanding Our World*.

In all of these ways, a transfunctional definition of humankind worked out along Hartian lines would retain the central holistic emphasis that sets the reformational tradition in opposition to both dualism (e.g., Scheler) and monism (e.g., Cassirer) not only in ontology but also in philosophical anthropology. For, as Hart, Dooyeweerd, and Vollenhoven agree, the unity and uniqueness of human existence do not lie in certain levels of human functioning but in how all of our functions flow from and to our hearts, from and to our orientation with respect to creation's origin and destiny, from and to that which sets the direction for our lives and calls for our response. Our unity and uniqueness as human beings are not due to some metaphysical essence. They are not due to certain distinctive capacities or traits or practices, certain distinctive functions. The unity and uniqueness of humankind are due to the responsive and directed way in which all of our capacities and traits and practices are oriented and continually undergo (re-)orientation.

To my understanding, such holistic pluralism frees the reformational philosopher to consider seriously the scientific evidence for evolution both between realms and within the line of development from hominids to human beings.[46] Correlatively, holistic pluralism frees the reformational philosopher to make genuinely original and helpful contributions to debates about neuroscience, ecology, and personal identity that too often remain stuck in outmoded but persistent patterns of ontological reduction, primarily of a dualist or monist sort. Obviously, the proof for any of this will have to be in the pudding. Yet we already have the ingredients for a better recipe. That, at least, is what my all-too-brief essay has tried to suggest.

PART THREE

# Social Transformation

Whereas the chapters in Parts I and II primarily sort out contributions from the first and second generations of reformational philosophy, respectively, Part III aims more directly to advance a third-generational re-articulation of this tradition. These essays take up the themes highlighted in the 2003 ICS inaugural address that concludes this volume: societal evil, spiritual struggle, and social critique. The chapters also show how my own appropriation of the reformational tradition relates to other important strands of Western philosophy.

Chapter 11 ("Good Cities or Cities of the Good?") compares Dooyeweerd's normative critique of modern Western society with the stances of Graham Ward and John Milbank. Originally presented in 2003 during a conference at Calvin College on Radical Orthodoxy and the Reformed tradition and published in 2005, this chapter suggests that neither traditional reformational philosophy nor radically orthodox theology provides an adequate critique of the societal evil manifested in contemporary conflicts and global injustice. At the same time, however, I caution against any critique that fails to appreciate the genuine social, cultural, and intellectual progress contributed by modernity.

In sorting out such matters, questions unavoidably arise about the proper role of organized religion in contemporary society. Do religious communities have important contributions to make in public debates about politics, economics, and social policy? Or, as Richard Rorty once argued, does religion serve primarily as a public "conversation-stopper"? Chapter 12 addresses such questions by examining elements of Hegel's social philosophy. Titled "Religion in Public," and first published in the inaugural issue of the *University of Toronto Journal for Jewish Thought*, this chapter provides a normative account of religion, the state, and their relationship. Religion should have both critical and utopian roles toward the state, I argue, and it should both support and disturb civil society. Religious truth, as I describe it in this essay, is not at odds with democratic communication; religion need not be a conversation-stopper.

A social critique along reformational lines also raises questions about the normative basis for such a critique and the vision of societal goodness that sustains it. Such questions are intrinsic to what Abraham Kuyper once described as an "architectonic critique" of society in its general structure. The normative basis for Kuyper's social critique, and for Dooyeweerd's and Vollenhoven's too, is an idea of creational ordinances. This idea has become problematic in the second and third generations of reformational thought, as evidenced by the title of the 2011 international conference – "The Future of Creation Order" – that celebrated the 75th anniversary of the Association for Reformational Philosophy (originally the Association for Calvinist Philosophy), a conference held at the VU University Amsterdam, which Kuyper and his followers established in 1880. I first presented chapter 13 ("Macrostructures and Societal Principles") as an invited keynote lecture at this conference. Asking what role the idea of creational ordinances should play in a reformational understanding and evaluation of the contemporary social order, the chapter tries to retrieve this idea for an architectonic critique of Western society. First it maps three societal macrostructures that organize much of contemporary social life – civil society, the proprietary economy, and the administrative state. Then it discusses solidarity, resourcefulness, and justice as societal principles that can sustain a critique of societal macrostructures. Next it identifies normative deficiencies within and between these macrostructures. On the basis of this architectonic critique, the chapter concludes by calling for a normative and emancipatory transformation of Western society as a whole.

The transformation I envision embodies a holistic and normative conception of truth, one that arises from the critical retrieval of reformational philosophy begun in Parts I and II. The transformation of Western society as a whole requires a dynamic correlation of societal principles and societal disclosure, and truth itself is such a correlation. I present this general conception of truth in chapter 14, titled "Unfinished Business: Toward a Reformational Conception of Truth." Originally published by *Philosophia Reformata* in 2009, this chapter gives the gist of an ongoing attempt to develop a transformational conception of truth, in dialogue with both analytic and continental philosophy. After comparing the method of critical retrieval with other reformational models of critique, the chapter proposes to think of truth as a dynamic correlation between (1) human fidelity to societal principles and (2) a life-giving disclosure of society. This conception both recontextualizes the notion of propositional truth and links it with an emphasis on bearing witness to truth.

Chapter 15 ("Science, Society, and Culture"), the final chapter, explores what such a conception of truth might imply for academic work today. Taking issue with the deflationary view of truth in Joseph Rouse's politics of science, and reclaiming insights from Martin Heidegger's hermeneutical conception of truth, the chapter argues that the pursuit of propositional truth, properly understood, is central to the academic enterprise. Indeed, in a reformational understanding of truth, all the sciences, including the humanities and social sciences, should serve human fidelity and societal disclosure precisely by way of pursuing propositional truth – that is how they should contribute to truth in its most comprehensive sense. First presented as an invited lecture in 2004 and 2005 at three North American schools in the Reformed tradition and then as the 2007 Kenneth Konyndyk Memorial Lecture to the Society of Christian Philosophers, this chapter rearticulates the idea that religiously inspired philosophy should contribute to the "inner reformation of the sciences." In my understanding of this central reformational idea, such academic rebirth needs both to accompany and to support the transformation of society as a whole. I hope a transformed and transforming conception of truth will contribute to both academic and societal renewal.

# 11

# Good Cities or Cities of the Good? Radical Augustinian Social Criticism

## (2005)

Christian scholars have a modernity complex.[1] We had it long before disenchantment with the Enlightenment came to pervade many academic disciplines. And we shall have it long after Protestant intellectuals, ever trendy in a belated fashion, grow weary of polemics over postmodernism. To reflect on this complex will help us find our bearings for the years ahead.

Toward that end, let me discuss two radical Augustinian critiques of modern society. First I illustrate the modernity complex in reformational thought. Next I summarize and evaluate the social critique of the reformational philosopher and legal theorist Herman Dooyeweerd. Then I turn to two texts by the radically orthodox theologians John Milbank and Graham Ward. I conclude by indicating why Christian scholars cannot simply embrace or reject the project of modernity.

### 1. MODERNITY COMPLEX

Radical Orthodoxy and reformational thought share a concern about the eighteenth-century Enlightenment and its role in Western society.[2] Both schools contain a deep anti-Enlightenment strain, just as anti-intellectual undertones reverberate in North American evangelicalism. These tendencies help explain both an enthusiastic embrace of so-called postmodernism by some Christian scholars and an uninformed rejection thereof by many others. Both sides of this postmodernism polemic play out an unresolved script from the past.

Let me mention several signs of anti-Enlightenment fervour in the reformational tradition. *Unbelief and Revolution*, Groen van Prinsterer's most influential book, portrays the French Revolution as a societal disaster driven by Enlightenment apostasy.[3] Following Groen, Abraham Kuyper, in his famous Stone Lectures at Princeton in 1898, depicts Enlightenment-inspired "Modernism" as the enemy of Christianity, to which only the Calvinist worldview can provide a fully viable alternative.[4] H. Evan Runner aimed his vigourous warnings against "synthesis thinking" at uncritical borrowings from modern philosophy.[5] Similarly, Hendrik Hart, not known as a conservative, has spent most of his career criticizing an Enlightenment faith in reason.[6]

Calvin Seerveld, to his credit, has always looked for the positive contributions of Enlightenment thought, while warning about its pitfalls. Nevertheless he regularly adopts a stance of antithesis, for example, when he points to "the enormity of our Enlightenment evil" in order to call students to "take up [their] cross of scholarly cultural power."[7] Notice, however, that he says "*our* Enlightenment evil." Implicitly here, and more explicitly elsewhere, Seerveld acknowledges that the Enlightenment has some Christian sources, and that it remains inescapably entwined with Christianity in the West.

Merold Westphal has taken this even farther, urging Christians to read post-Enlightenment atheists as insightful critics of idolatrous tendencies within Western Christianity: "The first task of Christian thinkers as they face the likes of Marx, Nietzsche, and Freud is not to refute or discredit them. It is to acknowledge that their critique is *all too true all too much of the time* and to seek to discover just where the shoe fits, not 'them' but ourselves."[8] Yet even Westphal's advice falls short, it seems to me. To be sure, using the "masters of suspicion" for Lenten purposes is better than the narrow rejection practiced by too many conservative Christians and carried over into easy dismissals of "postmodernism." It also improves on the open-armed acceptance voiced by more progressive Christians and continued in eager appropriations of postmodern thought. But the contemporary challenge of Christian scholarship is larger than this. We need in addition a nuanced sifting of what is intrinsically worthwhile and intrinsically problematic in supposedly "secular" ideas. We also need equally careful judgments about the better and worse roles these ideas play in society. Christian scholars must take seriously not only the "antithesis" between good and evil but also the abundance of God's "common grace." And we must do so with a view to both God's intentions for creation and the promise of a new Earth. To explore what this might mean, let us consider two radical Augustinian critiques of modern society.

## 2. ROOTS OF WESTERN CULTURE: HERMAN DOOYEWEERD

In a series of editorial articles written during the 1940s for the Dutch weekly *Nieuw Nederland*, Herman Dooyeweerd addresses the challenges of reconstructing European society after the Second World War. These articles have been collected as a book translated into English under the title *Roots of Western Culture: Pagan, Secular, and Christian Options*.[9] The book's subtitle indicates that Dooyeweerd sees these as the three options for the direction postwar reconstruction could take. Advocating the third direction, he aims to distinguish this from the "third way" advanced by the Dutch National Movement (*Nederlandse Volksbeweging*), which sought a more ecumenical and confessionally less restricted approach. Two themes stand out in Dooyeweerd's critique of modern society and in his proposals for reconstruction: namely, his emphasis on the spiritual antithesis, and his embrace of structural differentiation. Let me summarize each theme in turn.

### 2.1 *Spiritual Antithesis*

Dooyeweerd defines the antithesis as "the unrelenting battle between two spiritual principles that impacts the nation and indeed all of humankind."[10] His understanding of this spiritual struggle recalls Augustine's famous reflections on the world-historical conflict between the "earthly city" and the "city of God." Like Augustine, Dooyeweerd sees the antithesis as universal, comprehensive, and deeply spiritual. It is universal in the sense that no individual and no group stands outside this unrelenting battle. The most fundamental divide in society is not simply between, say, Christians and humanists, nor simply between, say, devout Calvinists and secular socialists. The divide "runs right through the Christian life itself."[11] The antithesis is also comprehensive: nothing in human life, society, and culture stands outside it, neither economics nor politics, neither art nor health care, neither schooling nor worship. And the reason why the antithesis is so universal and comprehensive is that it is deeply spiritual.

Dooyeweerd explains the deeply spiritual character of the antithesis in terms of "religious ground motives" that pervade an entire society and come into conflict with one another. He describes a ground motive as "a spiritual mainspring in human society." It is "an absolutely central driving force" that "governs temporal expressions [of human religion] and points towards the real or supposed origin of all existence. In the profoundest possible sense it determines a society's entire life- and worldview. It puts its indelible stamp on the culture, [the] science, and the social structure of a given period."[12]

Accordingly, Dooyeweerd sees the challenge to reconstruct society after the devastations of World War II as fundamentally a struggle over which ground motives will hold sway among those that have helped shape Western civilization. At bottom the battle lies between a spiritual orientation for which life, culture, and society are God's redeemed and redeemable creation, and one for which God's creative and redemptive work are irrelevant or nonexistent. The rest of his book traces the historical origins and contemporary significance of this spiritual struggle.

### 2.2 *Structural Differentiation*

Dooyeweerd's second central theme is that of structural differentiation. He introduces this theme using the term coined by Abraham Kuyper: sphere sovereignty. Kuyper understood "sphere sovereignty" to mean that there is a legitimate God-given diversity among distinct kinds of social institutions and cultural sectors, and that each kind receives its own norms, authority, and tasks from God and not from any other sphere. This was especially important in Kuyper's crusade to create political space for independent schools and a Free University established on Calvinist principles: they needed to be free from both state and church control. The task Kuyper posed for Dooyeweerd's social philosophy was to articulate the legitimate authority and task of each sphere, the norms or principles governing it, and how it should relate to the other spheres.

In taking up this task, Dooyeweerd deepens Kuyper's understanding in two respects. First Dooyeweerd argues that sphere sovereignty is not merely a societal principle but a creation-wide principle. He secures this argument through an elaborate theory of modal aspects, and an equally complex theory of societal structures. The result is a social theory that endorses the differentiation of institutions in the modern West but resists the secular spirit that helps drive this process. This positions Dooyeweerd's reconstructive project against both modern political totalitarianism and premodern ecclesiastical supremacy, but without aligning him with mainstream liberalism.

He also deepens Kuyper's understanding by arguing for "sphere universality" as a correlate to sphere sovereignty among the modal aspects. Dooyeweerd recognizes that the distinctiveness of different modal aspects is not enough. "Inner connection" and "inseparable coherence" are also required.[13] Similarly, in his theory of societal structures, Dooyeweerd sees that the gradual differentiation of distinct institutions and sectors can go wrong if it is not accompanied by their integration into a larger societal cohesion. Although Dooyeweerd seems to think such cohesion can be fully attained only when society is no longer riven by spiritual conflict, that does not prevent him from applying the norm of integration in his evaluation of various societies past and present.[14]

### *2.3 Dilemma of Normative Critique*

Together an embrace of structural differentiation and an emphasis on spiritual antithesis sustain Dooyeweerd's critique of modern Western society. On the one hand, he claims that modern structural differentiations among, say, the church, the state, the economy, and civil society are historical achievements worth preserving and advancing. On the other hand, he decries the secular spirit that seems to permeate and propel this process, urging instead that it be imbued with a holy spirit. Nor does he make this urging a mere appeal. Rather he tries to discover in detail what the God-given norms of justice, stewardship, and solidarity require in the institutions and cultural fabric of contemporary society. His critique of modern society is a normative critique, one that takes seriously the historical achievements of modern Western society.

All of this makes for a comprehensive and attractive social vision. Yet a certain awkwardness afflicts the way in which Dooyeweerd combines his two themes. The apparent dominance of a secular spirit since the eighteenth-century Enlightenment raises the question of whether modern Western differentiation might be more deeply misdirected than Dooyeweerd recognizes. At the same time, the apparent legitimacy of modern Western differentiation raises the question of whether spiritual redirection is as crucial to societal well-being as he insists. I do not think Dooyeweerd successfully resolves this dilemma. Not surprisingly, some of the social critiques launched by his successors go down two different paths. Those who are distressed at the spiritual malaise of the West tend to become reactionaries who see little of worth in contemporary society. Others who are enthusiastic about modern differentiation end up whitewashing the evil that besets Western societies and that these societies inflict on others. And neither side has grasped any better than Dooyeweerd did the spiritual and societal damage done by an ever-globalizing capitalist economy.[15]

Here Radical Orthodoxy can offer important corrections to the reformational tradition. For Radical Orthodoxy has deep suspicions of modern differentiation, even as it struggles to be fully contemporary in the way it articulates that suspicion. Let me briefly explore this in two texts that, like Dooyeweerd's book, take Augustine's social vision as their source of inspiration. I want to comment on the concluding chapters of Graham Ward's *Cities of God* and John Milbank's *Theology and Social Theory*. Because I assume greater familiarity with these texts on the part of my readers, my discussion will be more provocative and less summative than was my treatment of Dooyeweerd.

## 3. CITIES OF GOD: RADICAL ORTHODOXY

Whereas Dooyeweerd describes the "spiritual crisis" of postwar Europe as a struggle between competing religious ground motives, Milbank and Ward see it as a growing nihilism that only an "analogical worldview" can resist. Their diagnosis emphasizes spiritual fragmentation rather than an antithesis between two culturally embedded and societally effective spiritual principles. This emphasis informs their own appropriation of Augustine's tale of two cities.

### 3.1 *Spiritual Nihilism: Graham Ward*

The last chapter in Graham Ward's *Cities of God* is especially instructive in this regard. Titled "Cities of the Good," this chapter rereads Augustine's *De Civitate Dei* with a view to "the redemption of cyberspace." On Ward's reading of Augustine, what unites the earthly and heavenly cities – love – is also what divides them – self-love versus love of God. Until the final separation of the tares from the wheat, the two loves are inextricably bound together (*permixtum*). Hence Ward cautions against our trying to separate God's city from the secular city. He says that none of us knows the extent to which the two cities are independent, and "none of us can know the extent to which any activity we are engaged in is a work in God."[16]

Yet the city of God is "to be historically realised." Here my first question arises. Given "our" partial ignorance, one wonders how, *historically*, this realizing of God's city is to happen, by way of which *historical* agencies, and on the basis of which *historical* conditions. Ward answers that the requisite institutional structures and societal arrangements must emerge from "the good practices" that "responses to God's grace" call "into existence." So, to the extent that such practices already occur and have already occurred, the city of God is always already being historically realized. I take it that Ward has this "always alreadiness" in mind when he says the city of God "is immanent to the forms of all cities" and "makes possible" everyday cities and their "redemption."[17]

This suggests something important about the social positioning of Ward's own theory. Apparently his theory can depict a relationship *between* the two cities to the extent that the theory inhabits *both*, and does so as a "good practice" in response to God's grace. Part of the goodness to such a theoretical practice is not to presume too much about the relationship between the two cities, other than the fundamentally Platonizing assumption that whatever goodness "everyday cities" display owes itself to participation in the redemptive and (always already) historically realized pattern of the city of God. So modesty and confidence embrace: epistemic modesty in making specific judgments concerning the goodness of existing institutions and structures, and ontological confidence in asserting analogy as the key to redemptive history.

More emphatically, Ward's Augustine asserts that a lust for domination characterizes the earthly city and is a "perverse imitation" of loving service in the heavenly city.[18] Ward's Augustine associates lust for domination with "perverse individualism" as "the source of social atomism." Likewise he associates loving service with sociable communitarianism as "concern for 'the common good for the sake of the heavenly society.'"[19] Yet this Augustine also resists either translating "God's kingdom into sociological, historical and political practices" or identifying "the Church with the Heavenly city." The reason for the second resistance is that the Church's members are themselves "subject to the same desires and temptations as those [who are] espoused to the *civitas terrena*."[20]

In a sense, I would have to say this is all well and good. Reformational thinkers, too, claim that the antithesis between good and evil cuts through all human endeavours and through every human heart. But why should acknowledging the pervasiveness of evil lead to "our" withholding judgment about current institutions and societal structures? Why would it not be instead an urgent reason to pass such judgments? And might not the hesitation to pass judgment be itself a form of sociological, historical, and indeed political judgment, one in which current institutions and societal structures as such do not count, but only the love with which people enter them and thereby participate in "the city of God"?

Augustine/Ward's confident modesty arises from a weaving together of the "logic of analogy" with "the logic of parody and the doctrine of the fall."[21] As I understand Ward's exposition here, the fundamental norms for human life and society "were part of the order of creation." After the fall, however, these norms became "virtual" (rather than "real"?). In the postlapsarian condition, these virtual norms make possible their own parodies, the perverse imitations of justice and love and sociability that show up in the *civitas terrena*. The norms make their own parodies possible only by virtue of their eschatological "meaning." And this meaning will never break fully into current society until the eschaton, although it is an open question whether, in Ward's ontology, the eschatological city of God will or would or could ever be a current society.

Ward's precise language is instructive: "For when love, justice, society and peace are predicates of the *civitas terrena* then they are parodies of predicates of the *civitas dei*; they find their true significance in relation to Christian eschatology ... the use of these terms parodically in the *civitas terrena* is made possible by the reality of what these terms mean eschatologically."[22] Notice the phrase "the reality of what these terms mean." Insofar as what the terms mean is eschatological, their meaning is not ever-sustaining creational reality nor current historical reality. This implies that, prior to the eschaton, a just society cannot be truly just, and a good city cannot be truly good.

Again there is a sense in which I would agree. But I would not agree that a pre-eschatologically just society must be perversely imitative of justice or that an ordinarily good city must be perversely imitative of goodness. I would not agree, even though I appreciate the eschatological emphasis as a corrective to, say, reformational fixations on creational ordinances or Thomistic fixations on natural law. I would disagree because I think it is a fundamental mistake in ontology to equate norms with ideals. Norms are dynamic and historically unfolding guidelines that require human responses in order to have effect. They are, in Bob Goudzwaard's words, "pointers that guide us along ... passable roads. Apart from norms our paths run amok."[23] Ideals, by contrast, are static models – whether in Plato's intelligible world or in Augustine's mind of God – whose supposed effects necessarily trump all human efforts to approximate them either in theory or in practice.

An ontology such as Augustine/Ward's threatens to render pointless conversations about "good cities" – real, current, inhabited cities that are relatively better and relatively worse in various specifiable respects. This ontology pushes the radically orthodox toward talking about all cities (and no cities) as "cities of the good." All cities, in that sense, are either virtual cities or parodies of a virtual city – namely, parodies of "the" city "of God." As a result, we can talk about good cities only with reference to that virtual reality, not with reference to other currently inhabited cities.[24] Comparative judgments among cities, such as one makes when deciding where to live or such as citizens make when deciding how to improve their cities, are, if not precluded, then rendered pointless. For according to Augustine/Ward, only in pointing to "the theological difference" or to "trinitarian participation" can civic judgments of any sort find the transcendent anchor they need: "Only theology can ... give to secularism a legitimacy that saves it from nihilistic self-consumption, from the atomism of *amor sui*, from the drift into the disorders of the *nihil*. Protestantism at the Reformation lost sight of this, and we now need to retrieve it."[25] As we shall see, structural sacralization is the radically orthodox response to what is perceived as spiritual nihilism.

### *3.2 Structural Sacralization: John Milbank*

An emphasis on structural sacralization pervades "The Other City," the last chapter of John Milbank's *Theology and Social Theory: Beyond Secular Reason*. The chapter begins with a provocative act of renaming and rebaptizing. Milbank renames theology "a social science" and rebaptizes it "the queen of the sciences." But it is not altogether clear which witnesses are supposed to attend this ceremony of rechristenation, to coin a phrase. Are only those inhabitants of the "other city" invited who are "on pilgrimage through this temporary world"[26] and for whom theology will be scientific queen? Or do the congregants include everyone in the academy as such, for whom theology shall be the supreme social science? Similar questions can be posed with reference to the book's subtitle: what would it mean to be "beyond secular reason," and for whom would such beyondness have significance? Or, to make my questions more pointed: Is theology to be a social science in a way that is recognizable as social science to contemporary social scientists, who are wary not only of theology but also of philosophy and of any other pretenders to the academic throne?[27]

I have dwelt on the opening paragraph at some length because it crystallizes both the insights in Milbank's project and the issues it raises for reformational thought. Whereas the reformational tradition has affirmed modern structural differentiation – also in the academy – while worrying about directional secularization, radical orthodoxy tends to resist modern directional pluralism – the proliferation of religions and antireligions – while promoting structural sacralization. Two key issues lie between them: first, the role and legitimation of modern structural differentiation, an issue reformational thinkers will tend to pose for the radically orthodox; and, second, the structural consequences of directional secularization, an issue the radically orthodox will tend to pose for reformational thinkers. Both traditions are "radical" in their critique of what Dooyeweerd called "the pretended autonomy of theoretical thought" and, more generally, the pretended autonomy of modern persons, cultural practices, and social institutions. But only one tradition wants to be "orthodox" in the sense of reverting to pre-modern understandings of church, society, and culture. Dooyeweerd and company have instead pushed for an "inner reformation" of modern sciences, practices, and institutions, rather than either rigid rejection or automatic accommodation.

Not surprisingly, then, Milbank's account of theology "as a social science" troubles my reformational sense of propriety. While recognizing valid objections to the Eurocentric optimism in Dooyeweerd's embrace of differentiation, I remain an unreconstructed or undeconstructed modernist in this regard. Despite the undeniable pathology in the development of modern Western societies, I regard the differentiation of distinct academic disciplines, cultural regions, and societal spheres as relatively good for human beings, including those "on pilgrimage" to and in the *altera civitas*. The same holds for modernity's concomitant relativizing of theology, religious worldviews, and ecclesiastical institutions. Professor Milbank, I take it, would beg to differ.

In this connection he rightly resists the tendency among contemporary theologians and other Christian scholars to borrow their global theories of society and history "from elsewhere." He urges instead that "theology itself" provide the global theory needed, and do so "on the basis of its own particular, and historically specific faith." This global theory must explicate "a distinguishable Christian mode of action." Milbank ties this directly to "the Church" as a "distinct society" that "defines itself, in its practice, as in continuity and discontinuity" with "other human societies." So theology is a (regal) social theory (and a social science)[28] primarily as "an *ecclesiology*."[29]

Reformational scholars will find that Milbank's insightful critique of social-theoretical "synthesis" elides a number of crucial distinctions. First, he equates the entire project of Christian scholarship with "theology." This makes theology more than the purported queen of the social sciences. In effect, theology becomes the *only* science in which faith-oriented scholarship can take place. I agree with Milbank that Christian scholars should provide a "counter-theory" of society and history, or, more modestly, should work together in that direction. But I worry that, on his approach, any efforts along such lines by philosophers, political scientists, or cultural theorists would immediately need to be rechristened as "theology" in order to fit the project of Christian scholarship.

Second, Milbank carries out a double elision at the level of social theory. First, he equates certain social institutions (churches) and a societal relationship (the worship community) with "a society." Second, he fails to distinguish between the body of Christ (*ecclesia*) and the reign of God (God's "kingdom," in an older vocabulary). Only this double elision makes it possible to consider "the Church" a "distinct society" and to describe Christian social theory as "first and foremost an *ecclesiology*." For Milbank, "the Church" is not one social institution among many, nor is it one type of societal relationship among many. As "a society" his Church, in principle, encompasses all the distinct social institutions and societal relationships that would make up a full-fledged society. Moreover, he tends to equate this *ecclesia* with the *civitas dei*, or, in my own terminology, with the reign of God. He thinks that God's reign occurs either only in or only through "the Church." That is why he can bemoan the Church's failure "to bring about salvation"[30] and can give inordinate world-historical weight to this purported failure: "[E]ither the Church enacts the vision of paradisal community ... or else it promotes a hellish society beyond any terrors known to antiquity ... For the Christian interruption of history 'decoded' antique virtue, yet thereby helped to unleash first liberalism and then nihilism."[31] But was "the Christian interruption" really all that powerful? Did not other factors play an equal role, including economic, technological, and political forces that were not simply intellectual or ethical? And to what extent does the triune God really need "the Church" in order globally to fulfill the prayer Jesus taught his disciples ("your kingdom come, your will be done")?

### 3.3 *Dilemma of Critical Normativity*

Despite significant differences between Ward's and Milbank's appropriations of Augustine, with Ward being less inclined to crown theology as the supreme social science or to regard "the Church" as the city of God, they share a stance toward normativity that characterizes Radical Orthodoxy as a whole.[32] This shared stance has two characteristics. First, it locates the source of societal goodness in an ideal pattern that lies outside human history. Second, it restricts the effectiveness of this pattern within human history to certain practices developed within an ecclesial community. There the central practice mediating God's ideal pattern to contemporary life and society is not the preaching of the Word, as many Protestants have thought, but the celebration of the Eucharist. Both Ward and Milbank propose a sacramental approach to social critique that seems oddly out of step with contemporary realities.

Being out of step is not necessarily a bad thing. Jesus, too, like the Hebrew prophets before him, was no social chameleon, although they did not stand on liturgical ceremony. The problem with a radically orthodox approach arises because it wishes to provide a critique of contemporary society but has few theoretical resources with which to make nuanced judgments about better and worse tendencies. By emphasizing that all cities should be cities of the good, it has little to say about what makes specific cities relatively good. This, I submit, points up a dilemma of critical normativity. On the one hand, all social institutions and societal structures are held up to the divine pattern of "self-forgetting conviviality"[33] or sociable love[34] and are found wanting. On the other hand, the historically embedded and enacted ecclesial community that purportedly mediates this pattern to society as a whole has itself forgotten or ignored or rejected the pattern it was supposed to instantiate. So we are left, for the most part, with abstract norms that have little historical effect and historical developments that have little normative promise: either a city of the good, but no good cities, or potentially good cities that are never good enough.

## 4. THE CHALLENGE OF MODERNITY

Radical Orthodoxy's dilemma of critical normativity forms an obverse to the dilemma of normative critique that faces reformational thought. Whereas Radical Orthodoxy makes the norms of justice, stewardship, and solidarity historically unattainable, reformational thought makes them too easily and nonhistorically attained. In the terms of Kuyperian theology, radical orthodoxy makes all grace special, and reformational thought makes too much of it common. Our mutual difficulty is to address at a deeper level the historical dynamics of societal evil. That, it seems to me, is the greatest challenge of modernity.

A good place to begin a response would be to ask hard questions about systemic deformation. As I have indicated elsewhere, "systemic deformation" refers to "a large-scale historical structure and process that permeates a society, equally affects conflicting groups within that society, and fundamentally violates human life before the face of God."[35]

Let us suppose, as Nicholas Wolterstorff claimed in 1983, that the "widening gap" between rich and poor nations "is not an anomaly but a continuing basic mechanism of the operation of the world-economy."[36] If the effects of that mechanism persistently violate human aspirations as well as fundamental norms, then we confront a systemic deformation of global proportions. If at the same time Western ideals of freedom and democracy have turned into a way to help maintain this economic mechanism, then these ideals have become highly problematic. An appeal to them might invoke the legacy of liberation to reinforce oppression, or it might posit the fact of democracy to subvert the same. Have Western ideals become a form of false consciousness? Have they become a way to justify our own positions in a deformed system, and a way of ignoring what cries out for systemic transformation?

If this is how matters stand, then either endorsing modern structural differentiation or appealing to a divine pattern beyond history might hide the deepest problems in contemporary society. Hidden would be the real injustice and lack of solidarity in relationships between so-called "developed" and "developing" nations. Nor would tracing a spiritual antithesis or exposing spiritual nihilism in the West suffice as a diagnosis of this global condition. The condition exceeds the categorical confines of a radical Augustinian critique, even though saying this implies the sort of self-criticism that Augustine made central to Western Christianity.

That brings us back to the "modernity complex" with which this essay began. Like many other scholars today, reformational and radically orthodox thinkers can see the dark side of Greek philosophy: how its notions of logos and order ratify a social hierarchy built on slavery and the oppression of women, for example; or how a Greek emphasis on democratic dialogue allows only some partners into the conversation. Similarly, I would say, we need to recognize that medieval wonder at God's mysteries occurred in a world where illiteracy, poverty, disease, and human servitude ran rampant, and where neither Jews nor Muslims were considered to be God's children.

Against this backdrop, modernity contributes some genuine progress. The growth of modern science and technology, the demise of church control over culture, the fitful rise of political democracy and constitutional law, and even, in a qualified sense, the opening of new markets, international trade, and large-scale manufacturing – all provide welcome relief. Moreover, for all its shortcomings, and despite the religious wars that followed, the Protestant Reformation helped usher in this unprecedented transformation of society and culture as a whole. Those of us who belong to Protestant traditions can take some credit and some blame for modernity.

But, the antithetical Kuyperians and radically orthodox among us might ask, what about Bacon's empiricism and Descartes's rationalism? What about their dismissal of textual traditions and communal wisdom? What about their quest for absolute certainty that is methodically secured and anchored in the decontextualized human mind? What about their limiting legitimate knowledge to the natural sciences and to whatever science can support? What about Descartes's reduction of human nature to "a thing that thinks"? What about Bacon's equating knowledge with power? Surely, they say, these moves are excessive, unwarranted, even destructive. Surely, the sooner we leave foundationalism and epistemic subjectivism and scientism on the scrap heap of modern history the better off we'll be, as scholars, as participants in traditions of religion and spirituality, as citizens of the world.

Well, I want to reply, in good dialectical fashion, yes and no. So much depends – as methodological pluralists and theoretical poststructuralists and academic contextualists would have to agree. So much depends on how modern thought corrects or fails to correct medieval and classical thought. So much depends on how modern thought interacts with other trends in society and culture. So much depends on the insights and blind spots that arise because of modern thought or in opposition to modern thought.

Consider, for example, the efforts of Bacon and Descartes to construct a subject-position stripped of all prior ties to textual tradition, communal wisdom, and ecclesiastical or political authority – to achieve the famous "view from nowhere." I would join Heidegger or Derrida in finding these efforts misguided and internally problematic. Yet I would want to make a few claims on their behalf. Historically, neither Heidegger's "Being-in-the-world" nor the poststructuralist notion of subject positions would be possible without the modern construction of an epistemic subject. Culturally, modern subjectivism puts a heavier emphasis on human responsibility than one finds in medieval or classical culture, and it gives an impetus to cultural self-criticism of the sort that postmodern thinkers can only continue. And spiritually, although modern subjectivism seems to move us away from trust and reverence toward that which sustains and renews all creation, nevertheless it also powerfully awakens us to the creative potential that God has given to even the most ordinary of human beings. In all these ways, we who inhabit a postmodern culture are deeply indebted to modern thought, even as we seek ways to escape its destructive dilemmas.

So the challenge modernity sets before us is to be postmodern without becoming antimodern, and to recover medieval humility and ancient wonder without embracing the narrow parochialism and rigid stratification of a premodern world. Those of us who find our deepest wisdom in God's creative will, in scripture, and in the Word made flesh must bring to this challenge the best resources of our own traditions. We shall need to bring the story of a good creation, a God who loves justice and mercy, and the promise of a new heaven and a new Earth. And we shall need to observe the Feast of Unleavened Bread, while turning aside, in good Lenten fashion, from the ways in which our own traditions have participated, and continue to participate, in destroying God's world.

# 12

# Religion in Public: Passages from Hegel's *Philosophy of Right*

## (2010)

"In political discussion with those outside the relevant religious community," Richard Rorty once claimed, religion is "a conversation-stopper." That is why "religion needs to be privatized."[1] In advancing this claim, Rorty reinforces a popular misconception of religion as personal and private. I would argue by contrast that religion is a public matter. Its public character becomes manifest in the relationships that contemporary religion has to the state and to civil society. The discussion proceeds in two stages. First, taking up some claims in Hegel's *Philosophy of Right*, I give a normative account of religion, the state, and their relationship.[2] Then I examine the role of religion in civil society, focusing primarily on political and economic questions. By the end it should have become clear why I characterize religion as a public matter.

### 1. RELIGION AND THE STATE

Section 270 in Hegel's *Philosophy of Right* advances four claims concerning the state's relation to religion. First, religion provides a justificatory ground for the state by pointing to God "as the unlimited foundation and cause on which everything depends," including "the state, laws, and duties."[3] Second, any attempt to make religion "the essentially valid and determining factor" in relation to the state destabilizes the state and "leads to religious *fanaticism*."[4] Third, as institutionalized worship that "consists in *actions* and in *doctrine*," religion needs and deserves state "assistance and protection."[5] Fourth, religion and the state are properly distinct and independent, such that the state must guard the right of citizens to have their own "insight and conviction" when religious communities assert "unlimited and unconditional *authority*" in society.[6] I want to suggest that each of Hegel's claims is roughly right, but for the wrong reasons. The wrongness of his reasons stems from how he characterizes both religion and the state.

### *1.1 Religion*

In the passage quoted, Hegel portrays religion as both inward and outward, both personal and public. On the one hand, the content of religion is "absolute truth." Religion has this content in the subjective mode of faith, feeling, and representational cognition (*vorstellende Erkenntnis*) "whose concern is with God as the unlimited foundation and cause on which everything depends."[7] On the other hand, as institutionalized worship, religion has a public side. A religious community carries out actions of worship on the basis of appropriate "*possessions* and *property*" and via "*individuals* dedicated to the *service* of the community."[8] The religious community's actions and property place it under the jurisdiction of the state and its laws. Religious teaching or doctrine (*Lehre*), by contrast, is primarily a matter of conscience and, as such, lies outside the state's purview. Insofar as religious teaching pertains to "ethical principles" and "the laws of the state," however, the state must uphold its own "self-conscious, objective rationality" against religiously motivated refusals of the state's authority or attacks upon it.[9]

Despite emphasizing the double-sidedness of religion, Hegel characterizes religion as a *subjective* rationality, in contrast to the *objective* rationality of the state. In separating the state from religion, for example, the addition to §270 emphasizes the inwardness [*die Innerlichkeit*] of religion: "emotion, feeling [*Empfindung*], and representational thought are the ground on which [the content of religion] rests. On this ground, everything has the form of subjectivity."[10] It is this characterization of religion that I wish to modify. Although it is the case that modern religions involve faith, feeling, and representational thought, this is not all that they involve, nor are faith, feeling, and representational thought primarily subjective. Nor are the actions and teachings of a religious community best regarded as the "expression" of an inner realm of faith, feeling, and representational thought. I would argue instead that religion is primarily a distinctive array of practices and organizations, that the practices of religion are always already institutionalized, and that they are thoroughly intersubjective. That is why it is a mistake to regard religion as personal and private.

Here it helps to distinguish two concepts of religion that we often confuse. The first concept is that of religion as *spirituality*. Religion as spirituality is the all-encompassing orientation or direction of people's lives and of their culture and society. It has to do with what we find most important, what matters most. Certainly the orientation or direction of our lives will show up in institutionalized religious practices. But it does not require such practices in order to show up, and it can and does show up in many other organizations and practices – political, economic, artistic, academic, and the like. The so-called secularization of Western society may well have shaken the ability of religious organizations to shape people's spirituality. That does not mean, however, that spirituality has weakened or disappeared. Instead, either other institutions have stepped into the breach (the nation-state, for example, in connection with nationalism, or the market economy, in connection with consumerism as a way of life) or individuals have sought non-institutional and anti-institutional pathways for their spiritual quests (nature mysticism, for example, or an ethic of personal authenticity).

The second concept of religion is that of *institutionalized worship and faith*. We employ this concept when we speak of religious traditions and world religions. Religion in this second sense involves a distinctive array of practices and organizations that have their own legitimacy and worth in relationship to other institutions – not only the state but also institutions of kinship, economy, education, and the like. Whereas religion as spiritual orientation *shows up* in many different institutions and practices, including organized religion, religion as institutionalized worship *intersects* other institutions and practices but maintains its own legitimacy and worth. From here on I use the term "religion" to refer to this second concept, to religion as institutionalized worship and faith, and reserve the term "spirituality" for the first concept, for religion as all-encompassing orientation or direction.[11]

Like Hegel, I believe the content of religion lies in religious truth. Unlike Hegel, I do not regard religious truth as absolute. Nor, however, do I consider religious truth to be mainly subjective, even though, like Hegel, I also do not regard it as primarily propositional. I understand religious truth to be a process of worshipful disclosure in dynamic correlation with human fidelity to the societal principle of faith as hopeful trust. In the practices of religion, people disclose the meaning of their lives and of the institutions, communities, cultures, and societies they inhabit. The meaning to be disclosed pertains to what ultimately sustains them in the face of both good and evil, whether personal and interpersonal or cultural and societal or historical and transhistorical. In disclosing such meaning, people place their hope and trust – their faith – in a source of ultimate sustenance. That source can have various names, and it can show up in diverse ways. Many people name the source of their ultimate sustenance "God."

Religious communities often find and have found "God" speaking to them in the stories of their faith, both oral and written. Religions such as Judaism, Christianity, and Islam, for which certain "sacred writings" provide an authoritative touchstone, can be called scriptural religions. In a scriptural religion, the activities and symbols of worship typically orient themselves to the stories of faith told in that religion's sacred writings or scriptures. For adherents of such religions, to interpret scriptures, whether informally or formally, is to retell inscripturated stories of faith in a contemporary context.

Every religion, whether scriptural or not, also develops and passes on certain rituals. Rituals are ways in which a religious community finds "God" showing up. Rituals are how a religious community appropriates the hopeful and trustful disclosure of ultimate meaning that occurs in the activities and experiences of its members. Within a religious context, to participate in the rituals of worship is to reenact faith-ful disclosure, to remember and celebrate the source of ultimate sustenance, to participate in "God's" appearance.

To this point I have avoided the term "revelation." If "God" speaks in the stories of faith and in their retelling, however, and shows up in the rituals of worship and their reenactment, then such stories and rituals are media of "God's" being revealed.[12] They are not the only ways in which "God" is revealed: people can find "God" showing up or speaking in any of their practices, regardless of whether these occur within a "faithing" frame. Unlike other media of "divine" revelation, however, the stories of faith and rituals of worship are singularly oriented toward worshipful disclosure in hopeful trust, and they acquire their full meaning within a religious community. They acquire full meaning there because people must *expect* "God" to speak or show up in such stories and rituals and must retell and reenact them in order to *find* "God" speaking or showing up in them. That in turn requires the encouragement and support of others who also take this approach – something that usually occurs within a community of faithful and worshipful participants. A religious community finds the meaning of its stories and rituals to be significant when these address the community's need for worshipful disclosure of the source of ultimate sustenance in which the community places its faith. Teachings are attempts to summarize the meaning that a religious community has found significant over the generations and continues to find significant. Doctrines are attempts to render explicit the significant meaning of a community's stories of faith and rituals of worship. The propositional truth of teachings and doctrines is indexed to such significant meaning. That is why, like Hegel, I do not consider religious truth to be primarily propositional, even though I also do not regard it as mainly subjective.

### *1.2 The State*

We have seen that Hegel develops a dialectical account of the state's relation to religion. On the one hand, religion points to God as the state's ultimate justificatory foundation and merits state assistance and protection. On the other hand, the state must ward off any attempt to put religion in control of the state and must protect citizens from religious imperialism. In developing this account, Hegel appeals to his own conception of the state as the most comprehensive source of societal integration under the conditions of modernity. As he puts it at the end of *Philosophy of Right*, the present "has cast off its barbarism and unjust [*unrechtliche*] arbitrariness, and truth has cast off its otherworldliness and contingent force, so that the true reconciliation, which reveals the *state* as the image and actuality of reason, has become objective."[13]

Without discussing Hegel's conception of the state in detail, which would require a separate treatment, let me simply assert once again that I think Hegel is more or less right, but for the wrong reasons. The reason why the state – or, more precisely, the constitutional democratic state – needs to sustain a dialectical relation with religion is not because the state is the most comprehensive source of societal integration, but because of the specific type of societal integration the modern democratic state provides: namely, political and legal integration. This becomes clear if we consider the primary normative task of the state. The state's primary normative task is, through legislation, administration, and judicial decisions, to achieve and maintain public justice for all the individuals, communities, and institutions within its jurisdiction. When the state lives up to its normative task, it is the most important institutional framework within which matters of public justice can be addressed.

Matters of public justice occur in three domains. One is the plurality of distinctive institutions – religious, ethical, economic, educational, and the like – that need societal space to pursue their own legitimate tasks and that have a claim to state protection from illegitimate incursions by other institutions. I shall call this the domain of institutional pluralism. The second domain of public justice is that of cultural pluralism. Many different cultural communities have claims to public recognition from other communities. Such claims need to be adjudicated within the context of statewide legislation. The third domain of public justice pertains to the diverse needs and concerns of all the individuals who live within a state's jurisdiction. The state must protect persons from gross injustices at the hands of others, and they can expect a rightful share in the benefits afforded by government policies and programs.

It is not easy to reconcile this normative conception of the constitutional democratic state with the fact that national governments today take the shape of an administrative system – a system of governance in which the primary political power resides not in the legislature or judiciary but in a complex and self-regulating bureaucracy largely impervious to influence from citizens.[14] The administrative system makes it more difficult to see how the state can be an institutional framework for public justice and not simply a hegemonic centre of political power. Yet the power of the administrative state is not unlimited, nor is the task of achieving and maintaining public justice unconstrained. Rather, the state's power is always subject to the requirement of public justification. State power needs to prove justifiable before the court of public opinion if it is to be sustained. Moreover, matters of public justice come into the state's purview only insofar as enforceable laws and policies – themselves subject to the requirement of public justification – can address such matters. Like Habermas, I believe that democratic communication is the source of public justification.[15] Even as an administrative system, then, the state's task is to pursue enforceable public justice on the basis of publicly justifiable force. That is how the state provides political and legal integration in a pluralist society. Contra Hegel, however, *political* integration is not a *comprehensive* integration of society.

### *1.3 Dialectic of State and Religion*

Now we are in a position to reconsider the dialectical relation between state and religion. Religion and the state each provide what the other lacks, and, in making such provision, each inflects the scope of the other's mandate. As institutionalized faith and worship, religion calls the state to account. Indeed, it calls all other institutions to account. At its best, religion holds open possibilities for human flourishing and either relativizes or calls into question the specific ways in which people, in their cultural practices and social institutions, try to follow discrete societal principles such as solidarity and justice. It does so by calling adherents to hopeful trust in a source of ultimate sustenance that cannot be limited to any current practices and institutions, whether in isolation or in combination. The allegedly "transcendent" character of religions does not lie in their pointing toward a completely other world, toward a so-called "spiritual" realm, but rather in their holding open possibilities for a greater degree of interconnected flourishing in the contemporary world. So too, the supposedly "absolute" character of religions does not lie in their offering a source of dogmatic certainty, but rather in their placing in question contemporary attempts or failures to pursue solidarity and justice.

Hence religion can perform both a critical and a utopian role with respect to the state. On the one hand, religious communities can challenge the operations of state power and can ask whether the state is in fact achieving public justice for the diverse institutions, communities, and individuals within the state's jurisdiction. One sees this potential, for example, in the history of Judaism, when prophets such as Isaiah, speaking on behalf of their people and religion, criticized their rulers for failing to defend the widows and orphans. Decoupled from the state through modern differentiation, contemporary religions can achieve a new degree of freedom: not the subjective freedom of Hegelian inwardness, but a critical freedom to envision what justice requires, to resist state-sponsored injustice, and to lend a voice to the marginalized and oppressed in society. Religions can do this in the very practices of faith and worship that make up their distinctive texture.

On the other hand, religious communities can also hold open the prospect of a society in which the state, along with other institutions, truly sustains the interconnected flourishing of all human beings and the Earth they inhabit. Images of such a society occur in every world religion: the messianic condition in Jewish prophetic literature, for example, and the new Earth in the apocalypse of Saint John – images that recall the promises of reconciliation (Genesis) and liberation (Exodus) in the earliest books of the Jewish and Christian scriptures. By itself, the state is powerless to pursue such a social vision. When the state tries to pursue it on its own, the state exceeds its normative task, with disastrous results. Yet the state needs religious reminders that there is more to societal well-being than the state can provide, and that what the state does provide is never enough. In other words, religion can offer an eschatological horizon that relativizes the state's accomplishments and mandate.

The state, in turn, needs to call religion to account, protecting it from illegitimate incursions from other institutions, to be sure, but also counteracting religion's own worst tendencies with respect to public justice. Hegel is surely right to say that the state should not allow religious communities to dominate the political and legal framework of public justice and should protect citizens from religious coercion. In adjudicating conflicting demands from religious and nonreligious institutions, and in weighing the claims of diverse cultural communities, some of which have religious roots, the state must adhere to a nonreligious and publicly accessible conception of public justice. Otherwise injustice toward nonreligious institutions and communities will inhere in the integrating framework of public justice. This is not to deny that the state must secure political and legal space for religious organizations and practices, a space that allows faith and worship to have their own legitimacy and worth and not to succumb to the dictates of the state, the marketplace, or any other institution. In securing this space, however, the state also needs to resist the tendencies of religious communities to collapse social critique into ideological assertion and to turn eschatological vision into political imposition. No contemporary religious community has the right, in a public setting, to proclaim its own critique of other institutions and practices to be the only right way. Nor does any contemporary religious community have the duty to achieve its social vision by political force. A state that resists such tendencies can help remind religious communities that reinterpretation and reenactment lie at the heart of their own religious practices.

In the dialectical relation between state and religion, then, religion provides a critique of state power with a view to what justice requires, and it relativizes the state's accomplishments and mandate. The state, in turn, secures the political and legal space in which religious critique and relativization occur, while protecting itself and other institutions from religious incursions that would also undermine the legitimacy of religious practices. It is in protecting itself and other nonreligious institutions, paradoxically, that the state lends assistance to religion. Seen through the lens of this dialectical relation, religion necessarily has a public character.

## 2. RELIGION AND CIVIL SOCIETY

The public character of religion goes beyond its relation to the state, however. For religion also sustains a dialectical relation with civil society. To uncover this relation, let me first describe my conception of civil society. Then I shall explore the role of religion at two points of intersection among civil society, the economy, and the state.

## 2.1 *Civil Society*

I regard civil society as one of three macrostructures in contemporary Western societies.[16] The other two macrostructures are the for-profit (or proprietary) economy and the administrative state. Whereas the economy and the state are highly integrated systems that operate according to their own logics, civil society is a more diffuse array of organizations and social movements. It is the space of social interaction and interpersonal communication where cultural and economic alternatives can thrive and where informal political publics can take root.

The intersections between civil society and the proprietary economy, on the one hand, and between civil society and the administrative state, on the other, have special significance for the role of religion in civil society. I call the first of these intersections "the civic sector." "Civic sector" refers to the economic zone of cooperative, nonprofit, and mutual benefit organizations within national and international economies. The civic sector is the primary way in which civil society achieves economic differentiation and economic integration toward the proprietary economy and the administrative state. The civic sector is the region in society that is most conducive to what some have labelled a "social economy" – an economy in which considerations of solidarity take precedence over efficiency, productivity, and maximal consumption.

I call the second intersection – that between civil society and the state – "the public sphere." The public sphere is a continually shifting network of practices and media of communication by which social groups and individuals seek wider recognition, social movements and classes struggle for liberation, and cultural products and events achieve general circulation. The public sphere supports wide-ranging discussions about justice and the common good, and it sustains widespread participation in the shaping of societal structures.

Philosophically, religion as institutionalized faith and worship has had an uncertain status with respect to civil society. Neither Hegel nor Habermas, for example, gives sustained attention to religion when they lay out their conceptions of civil society. Yet both of them clearly think religion has a role to play in the formation and continuation of civil society. How should that role be understood?

I propose that we regard religion as both an incubator of civil-societal organizations and a disturber of civil-societal patterns. Religious communities, in their disclosure of ultimate meaning, can help give birth to artistic, educational, and other organizations and movements that contribute to cultural, economic, and political change. One sees this, for example, in the history of North American schools and universities, in struggles to expand the electoral franchise, and in the Civil Rights Movement. Religious communities, in their refusal to find ultimate meaning in any existing practices and institutions, can also disturb the current array of organizations in civil society or challenge the direction in which civil society is heading. This disruptive role becomes most readily apparent when religious communities take a fundamentalist turn, as is evident from contemporary efforts in the United States to restrict the teaching of evolutionary biology in public schools and to resist environmentalism. Historically, however, religious communities have also opened spaces in civil society for scientific inquiry and have helped redirect civil society toward environmental concerns.

Unlike other critics of fundamentalism, I do not think that all religious disturbance of civil society is problematic. Moreover, insofar as fundamentalism's disruptive tendency is problematic, I would trace the source of the problem back to normative deficiencies in fundamentalists' understanding and practice of religion. Rather than pursue worshipful disclosure in hopeful trust, fundamentalism tends to substitute its own scriptures and rituals for the source of ultimate sustenance. While purporting to worship "God," fundamentalism fetishizes its own religious practices: its interpretation of sacred writings becomes sacrosanct, and its enactment of religious rituals becomes an ultimate authority. Consequently, anyone who worships differently or not at all becomes an object of suspicion and an occasion for despair. Such subversion of hopeful trust often translates into efforts either to reject or to dominate civil society.

The critique of fundamentalism has particular relevance for the civic sector and the public sphere, where religion's dual role as incubator and disturber acquires its greatest societal significance. Let me next discuss religion and the civic sector and then consider religion and the public sphere.

### 2.2 *Religion and the Civic Sector*

Hegel correctly observes that religious communities have an economic dimension. They have "possessions and property," he says, and this fact places them within "the province of the state."[17] But Hegel does not ask about the peculiar character of religious ownership, nor does he reflect on how religious ownership relates to larger economic patterns. Hegel does not note that the economic organization of religious communities exemplifies an economy that cannot be reduced either to a proprietary market economy or to a governmental political economy. In a religious economy,[18] resources are supposed to be held in trust for the community as a whole and cannot legitimately be deployed to the advantage of only select members of the community. Moreover, every member of the community is expected, where able, to contribute resources, whether time, money, or specific possessions, to the ongoing life of the religious community.

A pattern of communalizing resources is necessary for the type of institution that religion is. Because institutionalized faith and worship require mutual encouragement and support among members of a religious community, the appropriate economy cannot operate either on the principle of private profit or on the principle of impartial allocation. The guiding economic principle must be one of mutual service on behalf of the community and all of its members – what some religionists call "stewardship."

This guiding principle for a religious economy places religious communities in both proximity to and tension with the economy of civil society. Elsewhere I have identified three normative expectations as predominant in the civic sector: sociality, open communication, and resource sharing.[19] "Sociality" is the expectation that civic-sector organizations should provide socially significant goods of collective benefit. "Open communication" refers to the expectation that participants in such organizations will have a say in the decisions, policies, and strategies that affect them. "Resource sharing" identifies an imperative to gather and tend sociocultural goods on behalf of others and without assurance of private gain. Together these three expectations point toward a mode of economic organization in which solidarity has priority – i.e., toward a social economy.

The priority of solidarity as a societal principle in the economy of civic-sector organizations helps explain both the proximity and the tension in which religious communities stand toward the civic sector. Economically, both religious communities and civic-sector organizations give normative priority to a "common good" rather than to either "private" or "public" goods. Yet this similarity harbours an important difference. Whereas the common good emphasized by religious communities is first of all the good of their own communities of faith and worship, the common good emphasized by civic-sector organizations is more diffuse, a good that in principle would be tended and provided for all who need it, regardless of their community memberships.[20] From the perspective of civil society, religious organizations can appear unduly parochial. From the perspective of religion, civic-sector organizations can appear unduly open-ended.

Nevertheless, interactions between religious and civic-sector organizations can open up religion. If the addressee of religious faith and worship is indeed a source of ultimate sustenance, then religious communities cannot properly be concerned about only their own well-being. What ultimately sustains members of a religious community in the face of both good and evil would not be ultimate if it sustained only them. Furthermore, the people who make up a religious community are not simply members of a religious community. They are citizens, family members, workers, consumers, and so forth. Under contemporary conditions of institutional and cultural pluralism, they share tasks and challenges with others who do not belong to their religious community. If the point of their religious practices is to disclose the meaning of their lives, that will include the meaning of nonreligious relationships. Religious practices are unavoidably about more than religion. To be parochial with respect to the religious community's resources would violate the ultimacy of its source of sustenance and would subvert the import of the community's religious practices.

Accordingly, participation in the civic sector can help remind religious adherents of a religion's inherent potential for inclusiveness and generosity. Civic-sector organizations can also challenge religious adherents to relativize their own religious community, to regard religious truth as not their exclusive possession and the community's resources as not exclusively theirs, to recognize that the good is more common than a devout religionist might expect, and that the goods a religious community holds in common are also for the common good.

### *2.3 Religion and the Public Sphere*

Just as Hegel acknowledges but attenuates the economic dimension of religious communities, so he recognizes but resists their political dimension. Although he constructs a dialectical relation between religion and state, he has little to say about the role of religion in the practices and media of communication where political interests and advocacy take shape. Yet it is precisely here, in the political public sphere or, better, in the political dimension of the public sphere, that many contemporary concerns about religion and the state arise.

Lying at the intersection between civil society and the state, the public sphere is both a societal structure and a normative principle. As a structure, it encompasses formal publics (e.g., parliaments) and informal publics (e.g., advocacy groups) and allows two-way traffic to flow between the state and civil society. As a normative principle, the public sphere embodies the promise, built into the operating assumptions of various organizations, that communication and decision-making about matters of general concern such as health care and the environment will be genuinely democratic. This principle of democratic communication implies that groups should demonstrate universal respect and egalitarian reciprocity when they call attention to matters of general concern and should be prepared to justify their procedures in that regard.[21]

On the face of it, this principle of democratic communication seems incompatible with the process of religious truth. Do not religious practices unavoidably lift matters of general concern out of the public arena and into a place where democratic communication is either impossible or inappropriate? Conversely, if religious communities try to bring the worshipfully disclosed meaning of their lives to bear on matters of general concern, will they not automatically violate the principle of democratic communication?

The apparent incompatibility between democratic communication and religious truth has two conceptual sources. One is an overly constricted notion of truth. Many religionists, like their contemporary critics, restrict the character of truth to propositional truth. They thereby tend to reduce the import of institutionalized faith and worship to whatever can be stated in propositional form – to teachings, creeds, and doctrines, for example. Although such formulations do have a legitimate role to play in religious communities, it is a mistake, in my view, to reduce faithful and worshipful disclosure of ultimate meaning to statements about it.

The other source of apparent incompatibility is inattention to the democratic presuppositions of religious life. Inattention arises from how religionists and their critics understand and practice the justification of religious beliefs. We tend to view such justification as primarily or exclusively a discursive procedure, as a matter of arguing for the validity of linguistic claims. Combined with the restriction of truth to propositional statements, this tendency undermines the disclosive character of religious truth and removes the justification of religious beliefs from the practical contexts where such a discursive procedure has significant meaning.

It would be better, it seems to me, to regard the justification of religious beliefs as just one element within a more comprehensive process that I call the "authentication of truth." By "authentication" I mean the ways in which people bear witness to truth.[22] Authentication of religious truth is the process whereby religious communities attest in practice to a dynamic correlation between the worshipful disclosure of what ultimately sustains them and their hopeful trust in this source of ultimate sustenance. Religious communities can attest to such religious truth in retelling the stories of their faith and in reenacting the rituals of their worship. They can also bear witness economically in their organization and deployment of communal resources. And they can testify to religious truth in how they discursively justify their religious beliefs. If such justification becomes isolated from other modes of authentication, however, or if discursive justification becomes the full extent of a religious community's authentication, that will impede a community's ability to live out the content of its religion.

Moreover, the authentication of truth, whether religious or otherwise, is invitational and public. It openly invites others to recognize what truth requires, and it welcomes a response from those invited, a response of uncoerced acceptance or rejection or inattention. Hence the principle of democratic communication is intrinsic to genuine authentication. More specifically, the principle of democratic communication is intrinsic to the authentication of religious truth. Democratic communication is thereby also intrinsic to the discursive justification of religious beliefs that makes up one element within religious authentication. The apparent incompatibility between religious truth and democratic communication is just that: it is merely apparent, even though failures in democratic communication are all too common in the actual conduct of religious communities.

No doubt many will object to how I have characterized religious truth and religious authentication. On one side will be those who object to my relativizing propositional truth to just one dimension of religious truth and to my treating discursive justification as just one element in the authentication of religious truth. Surely, they will say, these characterizations either render religion irrational or exempt religionists from the standards of public accountability. Do not my characterizations of truth and authentication permit or even encourage the sort of dogmatism that makes religion what Richard Rorty calls a "conversation-stopper"?

On the other side will be those who consider the truth of their religion to be the only truth. They hold that this truth is indeed propositional, that it can be discursively justified within their own religious community, and that it does not need to be discursively justified outside that community. For these "true believers," my characterization of religious truth will be much too open-ended, and my characterization of religious authentication will be excessively democratic.

Now I think one can answer these two sets of objections. Answering them, however, would require an account of how propositional truth relates to more comprehensive truth and how justification relates to more comprehensive authentication, and giving such an account here would take us too far afield.[23] Of the greatest interest in the present context is how both sides give priority to propositional truth and discursive justification. They simply disagree about the compatibility of religion with propositional truth and about the discursive justifiability of religious beliefs. Furthermore, this disagreement truncates their debate about the role of religion in the public sphere. For both sides, the debate comes down to whether and how religious beliefs and their discursive justification can enter public debates about government programs, policies, and legislation.

I have suggested, by contrast, that religion is first and foremost a matter of retelling stories of faith and reenacting rituals of worship. If these stories and rituals have a bearing on matters of general concern – as they surely do and must – then contemporary religious communities need to communicate the meaning of their stories and rituals in ways that show respect for others and remain open to being accepted, rejected, or ignored. There will be no knockdown arguments for religious beliefs in the public sphere, for the point of such arguments will not be to knock down the opposition. But there will also be no refusal to give arguments, because arguments are intrinsic to respectful and open communication in the public sphere.

Yet the most important "arguments" to be given by religion in public will not be merely discursive justifications. They will be demonstrations in practice that a religious source of ultimate sustenance truly deserves hopeful trust. The prophet Micah summarized as follows what the religion of his community comes to: "to do justice, and to love kindness, and to walk humbly with your God" (Micah 6:8, NRSV). If contemporary religions were to follow this injunction in their dealings with others, they would not be conversation-stoppers. They would be worthy conversation partners in the public sphere.

13

# Macrostructures and Societal Principles: An Architectonic Critique[1]

## (2011/2015)

"[A *social* question] does not exist for you until you exercise an *architectonic* critique of human society itself and hence desire a different arrangement of the social order and think it possible."

Abraham Kuyper

Addressing the First Christian Social Congress in 1891, Abraham Kuyper urged his audience to take up the pressing social question of their day: namely, the problem of economic injustice. A social question arises, he said, when people have serious doubts about "the *soundness of the social structure in which we live*" and disagree about the basis for "a more appropriate and more livable social order." The violence and poverty that accompany capitalism lay at the centre of Kuyper's concern. To address these manifestations of societal evil, he said, heightened piety and greater charity are not enough. Rather, Christians need to engage in an "*architectonic* critique of human society." Such a critique will help people "desire a different arrangement of the social order and think it possible."[2] His own critique pointed toward a uniquely Kuyperian form of Christian socialism, toward an organic national society that is "a God-willed community."[3]

Four features stand out in the social philosophy Kuyper presented in 1891. First, compassion toward those who suffer and solidarity with fellow human beings motivate his critique of the existing social order. Second, he bases this critique on an appeal to God's will and ordinances for human life. Third, Kuyper takes seriously the patterns of historical development that give rise to specific social arrangements. Fourth, he believes that human beings can transform the existing social order – they can "repattern" society "according to God's Word."[4] But he does not work out the tensions these features involve: for example, between compassion and obedience, or between the past and the future.

One hundred and twenty years later, and seventy-five years after Kuyper's followers founded the Association for Reformational Philosophy, the need for an architectonic critique of the social order remains urgent. At the same time, the tensions in Kuyper's social vision, which he passed along to his reformational successors, also need to be addressed. I wish to take up this challenge by proposing an approach that emphasizes societal macrostructures and societal principles. Let me begin by commenting on the notion of creational ordinances, around which the tensions in Kuyper's social philosophy revolve.

## 1. CREATIONAL ORDINANCES

Kuyper bequeathed to his followers a robustly normative vision and critique of the social order. By "robustly normative" I mean the following: how society is organized, and how this organization emerges and changes, are not merely matters to be described and explained. Rather, in addition to descriptions and explanations, and in the very process of describing and explaining, we need to evaluate a society's organization and point out how it can be improved. For a society's organization makes a real difference to the quality of human life and the well-being of other creatures.

Such a robustly normative project raises questions about the basis for evaluation and advocacy with respect to the social order. In response, Kuyper and his followers often appeal to the notion of creational ordinances, to the notion that the divine Creator has mandated from the very beginning, and continues to mandate, how society should be organized, and that these mandates are given in the very structure of creation. In Herman Dooyeweerd's social philosophy, for example, this notion underlies his emphasis on universal modal principles that humans must positivize as norms, his account of societal disclosure as a process of differentiation and integration, and his insistence that each of the major social institutions of modern society – such as the state, the family, and the organized religious community ("church") – needs to fulfill and uphold its own "structural principle." The notion of divine creational ordinances also pervades Dooyeweerd's account of the fundamental social conflict of his day as a directional "antithesis" between either serving God or serving an idol.

### 1.1 Recent Debates

Recent debates within reformational philosophy indicate that the notion of creational ordinances needs to be reexamined. Three features of the classical Kuyperian conception have especially come into question. Ontologically, it has become hard to reconcile the supposed "givenness" of creational ordinances with the evolutionary path of human development and the historical character of society itself. Epistemologically, doubts have arisen about our ability to discern what the relevant creational ordinances are and what they mean. Theologically, the appeal to creational ordinances has come to seem insufficiently Christological, pneumatological, and eschatological, as if a salutary emphasis on a good creation has come at the expense of sufficient attention to redemption and fulfillment.

Such debates leave several options for contemporary social philosophers in the reformational tradition. We can uphold the classical Kuyperian conception and simply modify it to accommodate some of the criticisms. Or we can abandon this conception and perhaps find new formulations for whatever insights it offered. Or we can incorporate the classical conception into a new understanding that addresses the most persuasive objections to it. One can label these options as defence, rejection, and critical retrieval. I propose to take the path of critical retrieval.

### 1.2 Three Concerns

Three concerns are central to the critical retrieval I wish to pursue. First, when it comes to social order, it is problematic to regard so-called creational ordinances as straightforwardly "given" in an ontological sense. If human existence is itself the outcome of a long evolutionary process of hominization, and if the social organization of human life undergoes distinct historical stages and takes many discrete forms, then we need an evolutionary and historical conception of how God's will for human life emerges over time and within the changing fabric of social existence. For such a conception, the notion of creational ordinances as the Creator's original mandates is too simple and too static. Nor do I think that Jonathan Chaplin's otherwise congenial suggestion goes far enough when he proposes to anchor the "normative design of social structures" in the "given, stable, but dynamically unfolding, created structure of the human person,"[5] for two reasons. First, what it means to be a human person is inextricably tied to the gradual emergence of certain social structures, minimally of a legal and ethical sort. Second, human personhood is not so much a "created structure" as it is a historical achievement: hominids have become human over a long process in which they themselves have taken an active and creative role.

My second concern pertains to the epistemology of creational ordinances. Traditionally Kuyperians have said that God reveals God's will for human life in three interconnected ways: in creation, in scripture, and in Jesus Christ. This threefold emphasis helps distinguish the Kuyperian tradition from both "fundamentalist" and "modernist" forms of Protestant Christianity. More ecumenically oriented Kuyperians might add other revelatory sources to the list: human wisdom, for example, or church teachings, or the work of the Holy Spirit. No matter how short or long one's list, however, all such sources of revelation unavoidably need to be interpreted. Moreover, so long as there are two or more sources, they each need to be interpreted in light of the others. In addition, "creation" is an expansive notion in the Kuyperian tradition. It includes not only the so-called natural world but also culture, society, and human life. So when one turns to creation for insight into what God wills for human life, one inevitably turns to intrinsically hermeneutical matters – to cultural practices, social institutions, and human relationships that embody interpretations of who we are, what we need, and what our lives mean. Hence the discovery and enactment of so-called creational ordinances are hermeneutical through and through, and it is a fundamental mistake to treat these as epistemological "givens." Although we may be confident that, all things considered, a specific decision or action or mode of organization is in line with God's will, such confidence must be won rather than assumed, arrived at through nuanced interpretation rather than postulated as the starting point for deliberation.

Theologically, Kuyperians recognize their most encompassing hermeneutical situation to be a good, broken, and redeemed creation headed toward the eschaton. But we have not always known how to let this hermeneutical situation, in all its complexity, inform how we talk about God's will for human life. This leads to my third central concern – namely, that the traditional Kuyperian notion of creational ordinances is soteriologically static and eschatologically thin. It does not sufficiently acknowledge the redemptive unfolding of God's will in response to human suffering and the promissory character of God's will in relation to God's own future. God's will for human life is not simply what God has mandated or, better, taught from the very beginning. It is also what God asks us to be and do in the midst of creation-wide brokenness, and it is what God promises as the fulfillment of creation-wide and historically developed potentials. That is why, in line with Vollenhoven's Trinitarian conception of the "threefold law," I prefer to speak of God's will as divine instruction and invitation and guidance.[6] It is also why, in keeping with James Olthuis's eschatologically informed theology, I think of God's will as both God's gift and God's call.[7]

Each of the three concerns just mentioned is comprehensive, such that to elaborate them and respond to them would require a longer discussion of ontology, epistemology, and theology. But that is not my brief in this essay. So let me turn from these introductory remarks to my main topic: namely, an architectonic critique of the social order. I hope to show how one can have a robustly normative, reformational vision and critique of the social order without employing the Kuyperian conception of creational ordinances *in its classical form*.

This is not to say, however, that I simply abandon the Kuyperian conception. Rather, I seek to incorporate it, through critical retrieval, into a new conception of societal principles and differential transformation. In what follows I first describe the macrostructures that organize much of human life in Western societies. Next I discuss three societal principles that must be in effect in order for these macrostructures to foster the interconnected flourishing of all creatures. Employing these principles, I then point out normative deficiencies both within each of the macrostructures and between them. I conclude by calling for a thorough transformation of all three macrostructures in their interrelation.[8]

## 2. SOCIETAL MACROSTRUCTURES

I should say at the outset that my systematic description of societal macrostructures has a normative horizon. The concept of social order is fundamentally about how human life in society is organized. As Kuyper recognized, this is not merely a descriptive notion. The concept of social order is unavoidably linked to normative questions. In Kuyper's terms, one can always ask about a social order whether it is "sound" and whether "a more appropriate and more livable social order" can be envisaged and achieved.

Certainly, for purposes of analysis, one can distinguish a more descriptive approach from more historiographic and evaluative approaches. But these approaches feed into each other. In *A New Critique of Theoretical Thought*, for example, Dooyeweerd introduces several systematic distinctions in order to think about how (modern) society is organized: distinctions between modal laws and positivized or positivizable norms; between structural principles and societal forms; between institutional communities and voluntary associations; between interlinkages and enkaptic interlacements; and, within the category of institutional communities, between natural communities (e.g., the family) and organized communities (e.g., the state).[9] So too, Hegel's *Philosophy of Right* draws systematic distinctions between persons and things, between morality and ethical life, and, within the realm of ethical life, among the family, civil society, and the state.[10] Yet these systematic distinctions have historiographic underpinnings and a normative point. In Dooyeweerd's social philosophy, the distinctions rest upon a story of cultural development in which criteria of differentiation and integration play a crucial role, and structural and confessional pluralism provide the story's normative point. Hegel's systematic distinctions, by contrast, draw upon a historiographic account of ever-expanding freedom, and the reintegration of modern society serves as a normative telos. Similarly, as will become apparent, a historiographic dialectic between structural differentiation and normative distortion undergirds my own systematic distinctions, and the prospect of interconnected flourishing is the dialectic's normative horizon. Now let me introduce some systematic distinctions and describe three societal macrostructures.

## *2.1 A Triaxial Model*

To answer the question of how life is organized in contemporary differentiated societies, I begin with the following premise: human persons exist in relation to others, and these relations are constitutive of who they are. We could call this the premise of interpersonal identity.[11] Accordingly, I give social-theoretical priority to the category of intersubjective "interaction" over such categories as individual "action" and "behaviour."

Assuming this premise of interpersonal identity, I have developed a triaxial model of contemporary Western societies. The model distinguishes three vectors along each of three axes. The three axes of society, which intersect, are the *levels* at which interaction in society is configured, the *macrostructures* within which social life occurs, and the *societal principles* that obtain for social life in its configuration and structuration. The three levels of interaction are institutions, practices, and interpersonal relations. The macrostructures of contemporary social life consist of economy, polity, and civil society, along with the interfaces or intersections among them. And the most relevant societal principles that obtain for social life at these levels and within these macrostructures are ones of resourcefulness, justice, and solidarity.

So far as I can tell, there are no clear precedents in Kuyper, Vollenhoven, and Dooyeweerd for the notion of societal macrostructures. Because of a shared systematic emphasis on sphere sovereignty, a social-critical concern to uphold societal differentiation and structural pluralism, and the state of social theory when they wrote, they do not ask whether distinct social institutions, for example, in the areas of art, education, economy, polity, kinship, and faith life might themselves belong to larger patterns of organization. If, however, we wish reformational social philosophy to be "integrally empirical," to borrow a phrase from Dooyeweerd,[12] and if we want to address both current social problems and the contemporary state of social theory, then we cannot avoid asking this question. For claims about societal differentiation and advocacy of structural pluralism will come to little if in fact contemporary society, as currently theorized, does not fit the projected pattern of multiple differentiated spheres.

## 2.2 *Economy, State, Civil Society*

After reflecting on this question for many years, I have come to the conclusion that, for better and for worse, contemporary differentiated societies such as we find in Europe and North America are indeed organized into three macrostructures: namely, the for-profit or proprietary economy, the administrative state, and civil society.[13] These macrostructures might not encompass all social institutions: kinship patterns and faith communities, for example, might be encompassed either only partially or not at all. Yet I do not think we can adequately grasp or critique the contemporary social order, at least in Europe and North America, if we do not understand the pervasive role of these macrostructures.[14]

To describe the three macrostructures, I need to introduce a distinction between systemic and informal macrostructures. The economic and political macrostructures are systemic, but civil society is not. This means that the proprietary economy and administrative state are operationally self-contained. In Habermas's terms, they follow their own "logics" and have their own "steering media" – money, in the proprietary economy, and power, in the administrative state. The advantage to this systemic mode of organization is that proprietary-economic and state-administrative operations can proceed without continual communicative interaction by human agents. The disadvantage, however, is that these systems are prone to nearly intractable crisis tendencies and resistant to normatively motivated critique and redirection.[15]

Civil society, by contrast, is not a system. It is not operationally self-contained, it does not follow its own "logic," and it does not have its own "steering medium." Instead it is a diffuse array of organizations, institutions, and social movements that have a variety of tasks and retain direct ties to cultural practices and interpersonal relations. Yet civil society is a macrostructure, a large-scale structuration of contemporary social life. Schools, museums, public media, non-commercial arts organizations, non-governmental social agencies, and advocacy groups are just a few examples of agencies within civil society. The advantage to civil society's informal mode of organization is that it engenders communicative interaction among those who participate in it. But the disadvantage is that civil society is vulnerable to systemic pressures of an economic and political sort and is often unable to have its legitimate concerns registered by the proprietary economy and the administrative state.[16]

### 2.3 *Civic Sector and Public Sphere*

The intersections between civil society and the proprietary economy and between civil society and the administrative state are especially important for an architectonic critique of contemporary society, as we shall see.[17] The first of these intersections is what I call "the civic sector," an economic zone of cooperative, nonprofit, and mutual benefit organizations. Via the civic sector, civil society achieves both economic differentiation from and economic integration with economic and political systems. Compared with these systems, the civic sector is more conducive to a "social economy" where considerations of solidarity take precedence over efficiency, productivity, and maximal consumption.

The second intersection – between civil society and the state – is what I call "the public sphere," a vast network of discourses and media of communication that serves to promote democratic communication about social justice and the common good. The public sphere sustains widespread participation in the shaping of societal structures, and it facilitates challenges to the operations of the economic system and the administrative state.

The proprietary economy and administrative state are complementary systems heavily dependent upon each other. Contemporary capitalism requires a high degree of state regulation, intervention, and support, as ongoing attempts to deal with a global financial crisis have shown, and governments have much of their agenda set by the demands of maintaining national and global economies.[18] Hence, whatever flows from civil society toward the proprietary economy via the civic sector – such as new modes of organic farming – has direct implications for the public sphere – such as advocacy for new agricultural policies and health regulations. Similarly, whatever flows from civil society toward the administrative state via the public sphere has direct implications for the civic sector. The same holds for movements in the opposite direction, from the proprietary economy through the civic sector and from the administrative state through the public sphere. In order for civil society to remain intact, and not simply to become a pawn of economic and political systems, the interfaces among these macrostructures must maintain their identity and integrity. Specifically, the civic sector and the public sphere must remain responsive to the imperatives of civil society and not become fully colonized by the proprietary economy and administrative state.

To forestall possible misunderstandings, let me add two remarks about economic and political systems. First, I specify the economic macrostructure as the for-profit or *proprietary* economy. But I do not think the proprietary economy is all-inclusive. Rather, countries in Europe and North America have a mixed economy that includes, along with the proprietary economy, a governmental economy and a social economy. One can say something similar about the global economy. So, although the proprietary economy is systemic and dominant, it is not the only way in which economic life is organized. Second, although I use the label "administrative state," I do not regard constitutional democratic states as merely administrative institutions. They *are* administrative institutions, to be sure, and bureaucratic control tends to be a dominant imperative within them. But they are also institutions for public justice, and securing and maintaining public justice is their primary normative task. Taken together, these two remarks suggest that tensions might inhere within and between the macrostructural systems of contemporary society. These tensions could provide sites for normative critique and redirection. At the centre of such critique lie the societal principles I discuss next.

## 3. SOCIETAL PRINCIPLES

### *3.1 Solidarity, Resourcefulness, Justice*

Three societal principles are central to the critique I wish to propose – namely, solidarity, resourcefulness or stewardship, and justice. Although not the only relevant societal principles, these three need special attention in an architectonic critique of contemporary macrostructures. By "solidarity" I mean "the expectation, indigenous to modern democratic societies, that no individual, group, or community should be excluded from the recognition we owe each other as fellow human beings."[19] "Resourcefulness" refers to our "carefully stewarding human and nonhuman potentials for the sake of interconnected flourishing."[20] "Justice" is the requirement that the legitimate interests of every bearer of rights and responsibilities, whether individual, communal, or institutional, should be honoured in proper relationship to the interests of others.[21]

These descriptions of solidarity, resourcefulness, and justice are not intended to be comprehensive definitions. They are preliminary approximations for the purpose of further discussion. And this is how it should be, given my general conception of societal principles as historically emergent, hermeneutically textured, and eschatologically open. Let me discuss each of these characteristics.

### *3.2 Three Characteristics*

First, societal principles are historically emergent. This means that they are not creational ordinances *as understood by Kuyper*. They are not simply what the divine Creator has mandated from the very beginning and in the very structure of creation. Rather, they have taken shape and gone into effect as human beings have responded to God's gift and call – the call to love God, themselves, fellow human beings, and all creation – and have given responses within their cultural practices and social institutions. What various societal principles mean and how we should enact what they require emerge historically in our attempts to be faithful to them. What solidarity means and requires today, for example, would have been unavailable and incomprehensible in a premodern world, even though one can trace its emerging meaning and effect back to premodern societal formations.[22]

From the vantage point of systematic reformational philosophy, one can best regard societal principles as "modal principles" rather than as individual or typical "structural principles." The societal principle of justice, for example, pertains to all levels of interaction and all societal macrostructures, not simply to, say, political organizations and the administrative state. Yet, unlike Dooyeweerd and Vollenhoven, but in keeping with my own stance on "creational ordinances," I do not regard justice as a divinely given principle that must then be "positivized" by human effort. Rather, God comes to call us to justice and to gift us with justice as, within historically emergent practices and institutions, human beings work out the flourishing to which they are invited. Human responses to God's gift and call become constitutive of what justice means and what it requires.

This suggests, in turn, that societal principles are hermeneutically textured. Not only do we need to interpret them in order to be faithful to them, but also they themselves embody human interpretations of who we are, what we need, and what our lives mean. I try to get at this hermeneutical texture by describing societal principles as both commonly holding and commonly held. We experience justice, for example, as something in which everyone has a stake and to which everyone can contribute. We also experience it as a site of social struggle, however, such that the task of doing justice is never finished, and what justice means and requires is always in need of interpretation. As I have said elsewhere, "human fidelity to societal principles is ongoing and never finished, and part of such fidelity is to continue giving shape to societal principles. The ways in which people hold principles in common are significant for how societal principles hold people in common. What people actually hold in common at a particular time might not be in line with such principles. Yet they cannot hold something in common without appealing or gesturing toward societal principles, no matter how self-serving the appeal or how ideologically distorted the gesture. Conversely, in order for a principle to hold people in common, they must hold something in common." Hence, fidelity to societal principles "always involves people struggling over principles for human existence. At stake in the struggle is whether the commonly holding/held sustains and promotes life."[23]

Historically emergent and hermeneutically textured, societal principles are also eschatologically open to a future we do not control. We do not know now what solidarity, resourcefulness, and justice will mean and require in a hundred years. Yet being faithful to these societal principles now has implications for the future: such fidelity is a way in which God redeems suffering humanity and a broken creation and ushers in an advent of interconnected flourishing that we can barely imagine. That is why I think fidelity to societal principles properly occurs in dynamic correlation with a life-giving disclosure of society. Societal principles themselves, which have emerged historically through human interpretation, manifest the call of God's own future, a future when, as the psalmist promises, justice and peace embrace.

Yet this call from the future addresses us now. Perhaps reformational social philosophy partially articulates that futural address in Dooyeweerd's notions of "sphere universality" and the "opening process" and in the idea of a "simultaneous realization of norms" used by Bob Goudzwaard. In my own terms, the dynamic correlation of societal principles and societal disclosure means that solidarity, resourcefulness, and justice, as well as other societal principles, need to be in effect across the board in contemporary society, and that we cannot be fully faithful to one without being fully faithful to the others. Let me call this dynamic correlation "the nexus of faithful disclosure." The nexus of faithful disclosure plays a crucial role in my critique of normative deficiencies and my vision of differential transformation.

## 4. NORMATIVE DEFICIENCIES

Many critics of the contemporary social order take a functionalist approach. The economy or the state or civil society is not working well, they say, and we need to improve the internal operations of these macrostructures. Some critics will go farther than this and identify dysfunctional relations between macrostructures – for example, the failure of governments and international agencies to regulate the proprietary economy or the tendency of the proprietary economy to undermine and dominate civil society. Relatively few critics offer substantial normative criticisms of all three macrostructures in their interrelations. That, however, is central to a reformational architectonic critique.

Three general claims sustain this critique. First, each of the three macrostructures suffers from normative deficiencies. Second, these deficiencies are complementary and mutually reinforcing, such that to address one we must simultaneously address the others. Third, to remove such deficiencies will require both a normative redirection of all three macrostructures and a structural transformation of society as a whole. So an architectonic critique must indicate the normative deficiencies, demonstrate their complementarity, and point toward normative redirection and structural transformation.

### *4.1 The Proprietary Economy*

I begin with the proprietary economy, which, so far as I can tell, has become the dominant macrostructure in contemporary society. Its dominance is not surprising, given two prominent features of capitalism. First, capitalism has an inexorably expansive character: it needs to keep growing in order to survive, and it is very effective at finding new ways to grow, new resources to develop, new markets to create and control. This drive to expand presupposes a second feature: namely, the imperative to channel "intrinsically collective and public goods into private and privileged pockets ... [Capitalism] must continually generate excess returns for those who occupy positions of economic power, whether they be individual investors, transnational corporations, or the most prosperous countries in the world economy. Attempts to rectify resulting imbalances in the distribution of wealth – charity, progressive taxation, debt relief, foreign aid, and the like – do not challenge the continuation of this inherently exploitative system."[24]

Taken together, the expansive and exploitative features of capitalism go a long way toward explaining the normative deficiency of the contemporary economic system. This deficiency involves two mutually reinforcing normative failures. First, as Bob Goudzwaard has argued, the economic system gives priority to certain sorts of economic expansion and technological innovation, and it does so at the expense of justice and solidarity, turning such considerations into mere means to achieve so-called progress. Second, the capitalist economic system also distorts the societal principle of resourcefulness. Instead of fostering a society where human and nonhuman potentials are carefully stewarded so that all the Earth's inhabitants can flourish, contemporary capitalism twists the principle of resourcefulness "in the direction of efficiency, productivity, and maximal consumption for their own sakes." The second failure reinforces the first, for it turns considerations of justice and solidarity into "economic afterthoughts" – into "belated attempts to alleviate the damage necessarily done by a system that does not prize resourcefulness in the first place."[25] When unrestrained, contemporary capitalism shows itself to be an exploitative and unsustainable system.

### 4.2 *The Administrative State and Civil Society*

Often the critics of capitalism turn to either the administrative state or civil society to make up for normative deficiencies in the economic system. Unfortunately this not only helps secure the economic system as it is but also presupposes that the state or civil society is itself normatively intact. I see little reason to endorse this presupposition. Both the contemporary state and today's civil society suffer from normative deficiencies that complement those of the economic system. Just as capitalism prioritizes "growth" at the expense of justice and solidarity, distorting the meaning of resourcefulness, so the administrative state gives priority to certain types of bureaucratic control at the expense of resourcefulness and solidarity. In tandem with this failure, the contemporary administrative state also distorts the societal principle of justice. Instead of providing legal frameworks and democratic governance that would ensure just distributions of resources and meaningful participation in the affairs of state, it redirects the justice it should uphold toward positions of power and privilege.

So too, contemporary civil society gives priority to diversity and charity and thereby distorts the societal principle of solidarity. Rather than provide a robust array of avenues for intercultural dialogue and social inclusion, organizations in contemporary civil society tend to equate solidarity with tolerance and kindness.[26] This tendency not only undermines democratic participation and recognition, but also gives short shrift to considerations of resourcefulness and justice that cannot simply be relegated to the proprietary system and administrative state.[27]

### 4.3 *Mutual Complementarity*

In other words, the three macrostructures suffer from two types of mutually complementary normative deficiencies. They distort the meaning of resourcefulness, justice, and solidarity, and they make it less likely for these societal principles to be in effect across society as a whole. Instead, the principles are relegated to separate zones, as if, for example, justice is of little concern to proprietary businesses, or solidarity does not count in governmental matters, or resourcefulness need not be an important consideration in civil society. In fact, the two types of deficiency reinforce each other, for resourcefulness, justice, and solidarity themselves are mutually complementary: the intrinsic meaning of each societal principle depends on the others also being in effect at the same time. Instead of mutual normative complementarity, we have a society whose macrostructures both distort the meaning of specific societal principles and render other societal principles inoperative. The economic system distorts resourcefulness while downplaying justice and solidarity. The political system disfigures public justice while thinning out the meaning of resourcefulness and solidarity. Civil society reduces the scope of solidarity while underemphasizing considerations of resourcefulness and justice.

Yet the three societal principles at issue here cannot have equally decisive roles in all three macrostructures. Just as resourcefulness and justice set the primary tasks of the institutions within economic and political systems, respectively, so solidarity is the primary normative consideration within civil society. An economic system that gave greater weight to considerations of solidarity or justice than to careful mobilization of the Earth's resources would be no less problematic than one that blindly pursues efficiency, productivity, and maximal consumption, no matter what the social and political costs. Similarly, a political system that gave greater weight to considerations of resourcefulness or solidarity than to achieving and maintaining public justice would be no less flawed than one that pursues administrative power for its own sake. So too, a civil society that made resourcefulness or justice its highest consideration would quickly turn into an economic system or administrative state. That would be no less destructive of civil society than is diluting solidarity into the mere promotion of tolerance and kindness.

In other words, what Goudzwaard calls "the simultaneous realization of norms"[28] cannot mean that the three societal principles have equal weight in all three macrostructures. But it does mean that the decisive weight of solidarity, resourcefulness, and justice, respectively, in civil society, economy, and state cannot come at the expense of the other societal principles. That is why normative redirection and structural transformation must go hand in hand, in a process I call "differential transformation."

## 5. DIFFERENTIAL TRANSFORMATION

By "differential transformation" I mean a process of significant change in contemporary society as a whole that occurs at differing levels, across various structural interfaces, and with respect to distinct societal principles. As I indicated earlier, the primary levels in question are social institutions, cultural practices, and interpersonal relations. The primary structural interfaces lie among economy, polity, and civil society. The most relevant societal principles in this context are those of resourcefulness, justice, and solidarity. Because no single societal site can suffice as an arena in which to promote creaturely flourishing, and because the various levels and macrostructures intersect, the change must occur in society as a whole.

Yet changes in many diverse sites also will not suffice if they do not move in mutually reinforcing directions. Hence the change in society as a whole needs to be an internally differentiated and complementary process. And, given the role of macrostructures in organizing social life and their mutually reinforcing normative deficiencies, this process must involve both structural transformation and normative redirection. I believe that the differentiation of levels, macrostructures, and principles in Western society provides a historical basis for such a process. Let me illustrate the required structural transformation by discussing interfaces among civil society, the proprietary economy, and the administrative state. Then I will consider normative redirection.

### *5.1 Structural Transformation*

Arguably an achievement of modernization has been to create societal macrostructures that follow their own imperatives. The result is a society in which, for example, law and politics are not supposed to serve merely private economic interests, and the organizations and agencies of civil society are not supposed to serve merely the interests of state. Admittedly, the integrity of these macrostructures is under constant threat. Indeed, the economically and politically powerful regularly subvert it in their pursuit of greater wealth and control. Yet the macrostructures remain mostly intact, and their boundaries are relatively clear.

This provides a basis for evaluating patterns of social order. As Habermas's thesis about the "colonization of the life world" suggests, patterns that subsume one macrostructure under another are inherently destructive and unstable. Two obvious examples are economic imperialism and political authoritarianism. Yet a critique of imperialism and authoritarianism needs to go beyond simply identifying and rejecting violence. It must insist on the integrity of distinct macrostructures, and it must detect those spots where structural interfaces have been weakened or overridden. For a macrostructure cannot maintain its integrity if it does not open in appropriate ways to the imperatives of other macrostructures. Here the civic sector and the public sphere, as intersections between civil society and the proprietary economy and administrative state, become especially important for structural differentiation and integration. To achieve sufficient focus, let me concentrate my remarks on the civic sector and leave the public sphere out of consideration.

### STRUCTURAL INTEGRATION

The apparent dominance of the economic macrostructure in contemporary society raises questions about the relationship between differentiation and integration. Some types of integration, while allowing for functional differentiation, can nevertheless hollow out differentiated spheres, destroy the Earth, and foster oppression on a massive scale. This seems to characterize contemporary turbocapitalism. It provides global integration that sparks and supports functional differentiation, but in a hollowing, destructive, and oppressive fashion. So how are we to conceive of a proper structural integration under conditions of economic globalization?

In line with my previous comments about "the nexus of faithful disclosure," I think a proper structural integration will have as its horizon a life-giving disclosure of society: a historical process "in which human beings and other creatures come to flourish, and not just some human beings or certain creatures, but all of them in their interconnections."[29] This idea of societal disclosure relativizes the achievements of functional differentiation. It encourages us to ask to what extent and in which respects the current array of differentiated levels and macrostructures supports, promotes, hinders, or prevents the interconnected flourishing of human beings and other creatures. The idea also enables one to engage in an internal critique of specific differentiated levels or macrostructures with a view to the larger historical process and structural constellation in which they participate and to which they contribute.

All of this has implications for how we understand the civic sector's social economy. Although it is an economy, and neither a polity nor a set of values, the social economy of the civic sector is one in which solidarity needs to inflect considerations of resourcefulness and justice – just as resourcefulness needs to inflect considerations of justice and solidarity in the proprietary economy, and justice needs to inflect considerations of resourcefulness and solidarity in the political economy of the administrative state. From a normative perspective, then, one can distinguish between a social economy of solidarity-inflected resourcefulness and a political economy of justice-inflected resourcefulness. In the proprietary economy, by contrast, resourcefulness should play the leading role, inflecting considerations of solidarity and justice.

This normative understanding supports a more-than-pragmatic conception of how the three economies would properly intersect. Intersections with the civic sector's social economy would not be thought to arise as mere responses to what economists call "market failure." Rather, we would regard the social economy as the sort of economy that is especially appropriate for the civic sector – one that enables civic-sector organizations to foster solidarity in society, always with a view to considerations of resourcefulness and justice, but not as a substitute for what the proprietary economy and administrative state should properly accomplish. Because the latter systems are normatively deficient, as is civil society too, pressures have built for civic-sector organizations to take on what these systems fail to provide, such as sustainable sources of energy or universal health care. It would be better for agencies of civil society to call these systems to account than to act as the de facto dumping ground for systemically generated problems.

### THE SUBMERGED SOCIAL ECONOMY

Part of calling economic and political systems to account is pointing out the social economy submerged within them. I realize it is controversial to claim that these systems have a hidden social economy; initially the claim might strike other social theorists as implausible. Nevertheless, I think a hidden social economy is what gives some credence, for example, to American sociologist Jon Van Til's concept of the "social entrepreneur." Van Til cites the example of the University College of Cape Breton. In the 1990s it developed an array of collaborative partnerships with businesses, nonprofit organizations, and government agencies and thereby helped revitalize the economy of a traditionally impoverished region in Nova Scotia.[30] A hidden social economy also confers some plausibility to Jeremy Rifkin's proposal that governments should forge a new partnership with the civic sector via tax deductions for the time workers volunteer to tax-exempt organizations and via "a social wage for community service" that would provide the unemployed with "meaningful work ... in the [civic] sector to help rebuild their own neighborhoods and local infrastructures."[31] But Van Til does not comment on the macrostructural conditions that allowed the Cape Breton experiment to succeed. Nor does Rifkin uncover sufficient impetus within the administrative state for forging his new partnership.

In my judgment, Van Til's social entrepreneurial experiment would not succeed if proprietary businesses had only their financial "bottom lines" in view. Nor could Rifkin's two-sector partnership thrive if government agencies sought only to extend the economic reach of their administrative power. There must be something like a social economy submerged in the proprietary and political economies – submerged both because the imperatives of such systems do not allow them to make solidarity their primary focus and because the reduction of resourcefulness and justice within them hides from view the need for solidarity to be in effect there at the same time.[32]

Yet one can find evidence of a submerged social economy in both systems.[33] Thanks in part to examples and advocacy stemming from the civic sector, proprietary businesses often use the language of "social responsibility." They develop procedures of social accounting and undertake social audits. They also adopt voluntary codes of conduct within specific branches of industry and commerce that go beyond business ethics toward something like a social ethic. In other words, there is a growing recognition, at least among socially enlightened firms, that the proprietary economy has a social-economic moment – that showing solidarity toward the workers, customers, and communities that sustain these enterprises and are affected by them cannot be an economic afterthought. So too, government agencies regularly use the language of "community involvement." They develop procedures of consultation with stakeholders and undertake impact studies before launching new projects. They also put in place self-regulatory guidelines that go beyond minimal legal requirements toward something like a social ethic. In these ways politicians and civil servants, at least in some branches and departments of government, demonstrate awareness that the political economy has a social-economic moment – that showing solidarity with citizens and with the beneficiaries of government programs cannot remain on the margin of government operations.

To point out this hidden social economy in economic and political systems is not to deny that they need redirection. Nor is it to suggest that systemic economies should become full-fledged social economies. The point instead is to indicate a social-economic basis within economic and political systems for giving appropriate weight to considerations of solidarity, considerations that their own focus on efficiency-reduced resourcefulness and administratively diminished justice would seem to preclude. There is a social-economic basis within the proprietary and political economies for a differential transformation of all three macrostructures and their interfaces. Civic-sector organizations need to highlight this social-economic basis. They need to call for significant restructuration of both systems, even as they pursue a redirection of the civic sector.

## *5.2 Normative Redirection*

My critique of normative deficiencies in societal macrostructures envisions a different social order. The social order I envision would promote the interconnected flourishing of all Earth's inhabitants. To move toward such a social order will require normative redirection throughout society, and especially within and across society's macrostructures. The societal principles of solidarity, resourcefulness, and justice provide substantial guidelines for the normative redirection required. Let me describe this normative redirection first *within*, then *across*, and finally *beyond* societal macrostructures.

### INTERNAL REDIRECTION

I said earlier that solidarity is the decisive societal principle for civil society, and I criticized contemporary civil society for reducing the scope of solidarity and underemphasizing considerations of resourcefulness and justice. There are many sources to such normative deficiencies, some of them internal to the organizations that make up civil society, and others stemming from external pressures exerted by the proprietary economy and the administrative state. Philosophically, however, the dynamic that most undermines solidarity in civil society today is a dialectic between abstract individualism and identity politics. Organizations in civil society find themselves pushed and pulled between individuals pursuing their own self-interests and cultural or religious groups promoting their own agendas. The typical response from those who see the destructive consequences of this dialectic has been to promote greater tolerance among the various groups and more charity toward individuals who have fewer chances to pursue their own self-interests. Unfortunately, this response fails to challenge the mistaken approaches to individuality and community that underlie the dialectic.

I believe that solidarity requires a new direction in civil society. If every individual, group, and community deserves recognition, then our schools, arts organizations, and media of communication need to develop patterns of critical and creative dialogue where all are welcome to participate. In education, for example, the old division between state-funded and faith-based schools is outmoded, even when supplemented by interest-based charter schools and commercial learning centres. We need to envision a different way to organize truly public and inclusive schooling, and this will not occur unless other organizations in civil society also embrace a vision of robust solidarity.

I have also claimed that resourcefulness is the decisive societal principle for the economic system, and I have criticized the current proprietary economy for distorting the meaning of resourcefulness while downplaying considerations of justice and solidarity. One way to counter these deficiencies is, as I suggested, to strengthen the system's hidden elements of a social economy through social accounting and voluntary codes of conduct. Yet the central problem from a normative perspective is that the proprietary economy pursues the twin goals of continuous growth and private profit. Nor do I think that the classical socialist approach of state ownership can solve this problem: it does not challenge the goal of continuous growth, and it introduces patterns of administrative coercion that run counter to genuine resourcefulness. So we need to imagine a different economic order, one where stewardship for the sake of interconnected flourishing, not continuous growth or private profit, is the overriding consideration.

Similarly, I have suggested that justice is the decisive societal principle for the political system, and I have criticized the administrative state for disfiguring public justice while thinning out the meaning of resourcefulness and solidarity. Again, normative redirection is required, and for this we need a normative vision of the state's task in contemporary society. In my own view, which derives primarily from the work of Dooyeweerd and Chaplin, the state's primary normative task is to achieve and maintain public justice, and to do so in the domains of interpersonal, cultural, and institutional pluralism.[34] Moreover, even though national governments today take the shape of an administrative system where the primary political power resides in a complex and self-regulating bureaucracy, the power of a constitutional democratic state remains subject to the requirement of public justification. Even as an administrative system, such a state must pursue enforceable public justice, pursue it on the basis of publicly justifiable force, and thereby provide political and legal integration in a pluralist society.

### INTERLINKED REDIRECTION

The public sphere, as the intersection between state and civil society, is crucial in this regard. This fact is just one indication that normative redirection must occur *across* the interlinked macrostructures and not simply *within* them. That this is so follows from the claim that each societal principle holds for all three macrostructures and that these principles are mutually complementary. But it also follows from the practical challenges of pursuing normative redirection within existing organizations and interpersonal relations.

Perhaps I can illustrate the challenges with reference to "art in public," the topic of my book by that title. According to this book, noncommercial arts organizations make important cultural, economic, and political contributions to society, but cultural, economic, and political pressures threaten their ability to make these contributions. The proper response to such pressures, I argue, is for arts organizations to pursue their properly artistic tasks by participating in the social economy of the civic sector and by fostering democratic communication in the public sphere. To do this, I claim, arts organizations need to resist the normative deficiencies of civil society, the proprietary economy, and the administrative state, and, in their very structure and operations, to provide creative alternatives to such deficiencies.

Yet it is readily apparent that arts organizations cannot provide these alternatives all on their own. They need compatible efforts by other organizations in the civic sector. They also need appropriate support from organizations in the proprietary economy and the administrative state. Government funding for the arts can be one channel of such support, provided the rationale and delivery of such funding do not simply reinscribe "business as usual." Similarly enlightened corporate and foundation funding would also help. In turn, civic-sector arts organizations, seeking to remain true to the principle of solidarity, can expose elements of a social economy lying latent in economic and political systems.

This example illustrates that the societal principles of solidarity, resourcefulness, and justice pertain to all of the levels and macrostructures of a differentiated society, even though each principle holds in a special way for a distinct range of levels and macrostructures. The theoretical challenge, and a practical one as well, is to envision normative integration across these differentiated zones without either allowing one to dominate the others or exempting any zone from the requirements of all three principles. In other words, we need to pursue normative redirection not only within but also across all three macrostructures.

### FAITHFUL DISCLOSURE

The sheer scope of the redirection required raises the question of whether it is historically possible. That question forces us to look beyond the current social order both toward the past and toward the future. Looking toward the past, we can see that no social order has been inevitable or permanent, and that our own social order has emerged from a complex process of social change. This insight allows us to ask whether and to what extent the current patterns of macrostructural differentiation and integration are historical achievements or historical failures. Looking to the future, we can envision possibilities for structural transformation and normative redirection that build on the historical achievements and repair or remove the historical failures. In the midst of such historical orientation and reorientation, people can hear a call to life-giving disclosure that resonates in historically embedded societal principles and in our attempts to be faithful to them. In other words, within our organizations, institutions, and interpersonal relations, we can undertake faithful disclosure.[35]

Yet, given the preponderance of normatively deficient macrostructures in the current social order, and the extensive ways in which they organize all of social life, faithful disclosure cannot be the prerogative of one community or tradition. It requires the concerted efforts, and what Theodor Adorno called the "transparent solidarity," of humanity as a whole.[36] Unlike Adorno, I do not believe such efforts in solidarity are in short supply. Rather, along with economic globalization and transnational governance, we are witnessing the gradual emergence of a global civil society in which many communities and traditions can fashion and enact a global ethic. This emergence holds potential for both structural transformation and normative redirection in countries around the world.

Reformational social philosophers can contribute to this process by articulating societal principles in the direction of life-giving disclosure. We can present a vision of significant social change. The change I have envisioned would be a society-wide transformation and not simply a modification at one level or one structural interface. Yet this transformation would be differential, involving mutually reinforcing developments across the various levels and interfaces and strengthening the legitimate differentiation of macrostructures and societal principles that, in my view, is a historic achievement in Western society.

Normatively, differential transformation would redirect the proprietary economy away from the maximization of private profit toward the societal principle of resourcefulness. It would redirect the administrative state away from merely bureaucratic power toward a genuinely democratic pursuit of public justice. It would also allow societal principles such as resourcefulness, justice, and solidarity, which are distinct and pervasive, to be in effect across the board and not to be relegated to separate zones within society. The envisioned redirection of economic and political macrostructures, along with complementary changes in civil society, would generate freedom to pursue a life-giving disclosure of society.

Structurally, political and economic systems would become more open to the legitimate concerns of civil society. But they would also foster within themselves elements of democratic communication and a social economy that are mostly latent at present. If the state would place priority on the task of promoting and securing public justice, it could give appropriate attention to concerns for economic resourcefulness and social solidarity as well. So too, if the economic system would give priority to pursuing resourcefulness and not to exploiting people and habitats for private gain, then hidden elements of a social economy could become stronger, and considerations of economic justice could find their proper place.

In tandem with these structural transformations and normative redirections of the political and economic systems, the institutions of civil society would need to become robust sites for social solidarity and not be mere release valves for the pressures generated by normative deficiencies in the administrative state and proprietary economy. In its networks of public communication and its social economy, civil society would provide solidaristic inflections to justice and resourcefulness that political and economic systems need but cannot themselves fully provide. A differential transformation along these lines would result in a more genuinely life-giving society across the board, within and among all three macrostructures.

In the end, the question all members of society face, as citizens, as workers and consumers, and as educators, artists, and scholars, is whether we want a life-giving society. Such a society would go beyond one in which the state is formally democratic to one where the state pursues and maintains justice for all. It would be a society in which the resources everyone needs in order to flourish do not continually flow into the private coffers of the most wealthy and powerful. It would also be a society where the solidaristic norms of participation and recognition prevail in the institutions and organizations of civil society. The macrostructures of such a society would have undergone internal transformation; the conflicts among them would have been resolved; and people would enjoy justice, resourcefulness, and solidarity across the entire range of their social lives. We might not arrive at such a society in the foreseeable future. Imagining it, however, and disclosing the potential of a life-giving society, will remain worthwhile endeavours.

Contemporary reformational social philosophers might not seek an organic national society that is a "God-willed community," as Kuyper did. But we do desire a social order where, in the words Jesus taught his disciples, God's will is done.

14

# Unfinished Business: Toward a Reformational Conception of Truth

## (2009)

Theoretical thought never finishes its task. Anyone who believes to have created a philosophical system that can be adopted unchanged by every ensuing generation shows no insight into *the historical contingency [gebondenheit] of all theoretical thought.*

Herman Dooyeweerd[1]

How should one undertake a critical retrieval of Dooyeweerd's conception of truth? My book on *Artistic Truth* proposes a theory of truth in art. It also sketches in preliminary fashion a more comprehensive conception of truth. Both the proposed theory and the preliminary sketch have raised questions among reformational philosophers. In a March 2005 book symposium, Adrienne Dengerink Chaplin and Calvin Seerveld asked how my book's theory of artistic truth relates to the main lines of reformational ontology. A year later, in a review published in *Philosophia Reformata*, Sander Griffioen posed similar questions.[2] Both Seerveld and Griffioen also wondered whether the book lacks the depth of criticism and structural insight that comes with the reformational project of transcendental critique.

Building on a previous article,[3] the current essay explains in five stages how my emerging conception of truth appropriates Dooyeweerd's conception. First I comment on how my approach differs from other reformational models of critique. Then I indicate how my theory of artistic truth incorporates reformational ontology. Next I show how my general conception of truth responds to issues in Dooyeweerd's conception.

Then I take up the topic of propositional truth. Finally I show how my account of "authentication" incorporates insights from Dooyeweerd's emphasis on "standing in the Truth."

## 1. CRITICAL HERMENEUTICS

Let me first discuss how I am working out my conception of truth in critical dialogue with other philosophers. Like Dooyeweerd, I aim to address a contemporary philosophical audience. Yet my audience differs significantly from his. In North America, and increasingly in Europe, the philosophical world divides into primarily analytic and primarily continental thinkers. This "continental divide," as I call it, poses a challenge to communicating with one's peers. My response is deliberately to cross philosophical divides: divides between analytic and continental philosophy, and, within continental philosophy, between Heideggerian thinking and Critical Theory. A primary question when I write is how to address this internally divided audience in terms they will understand.

That means, among other things, keeping unexplained jargon and religiously fraught language to a minimum. Yet any reader who is attentive should be able to figure out where I am coming from. The Preface and Introduction to *Artistic Truth*,[4] for example, clearly signal my religious affiliations; I dedicate the book to three philosophers in the Reformed tradition; and I name reformational sources at strategic points in the argument. I hope readers will pay attention to the reformational orientation of my work. If they find what I write genuinely worth their while, perhaps they will want to find out more about its orientation.

The desire to offer something substantial to an internally divided audience helps explain my manner of engaging the work of other philosophers. I employ two methodological assumptions: first, that one should understand such work from the inside out, and, second, that one should call upon a philosopher's best opponents to help develop one's position with regard to the issues at stake. These assumptions are motivated by a desire to develop my own position in critical dialogue with others. What sort of approach is this? Is it a version of immanent critique? Transcendental critique? Perhaps even thetical or transcendent critique? I would say it is all of these and none of them at once. My own label for it is "critical hermeneutics."

Perhaps I can explain this approach using language from the Introduction to an earlier book on Theodor W. Adorno's *Aesthetic Theory*. There, after describing the models of transcendent, transcendental, and immanent critique, I call my approach to Adorno's text *an immanent critique with metacritical intent.*[5] Such an approach takes seriously Adorno's own issues, expectations, and criteria, but it moves beyond these when his text fails to meet its own criteria. As the book moves beyond Adorno's position, however, it continues to depend openly on his position, so that the movement beyond takes on the character of self-criticism. The more recent book on *Artistic Truth* simply adds one feature to "immanent criticism with metacritical intent": namely, to call upon already existing oppositions within philosophy to sharpen one's understanding of the alternatives and to formulate one's own position.

In other words, I do not follow the thetical approach of Vollenhoven's systematic philosophy.[6] Nor do I simply take the route of immanent criticism emphasized in his historiography of philosophy.[7] Neither do I follow the path of either transcendental critique à la Dooyeweerd or transformational critique à la Jacob Klapwijk.[8] What I attempt instead is a critical hermeneutics. I seek the contributions and limitations of a philosopher's position by trying to understand it from within his or her writings. And I assume that considering another philosopher's opposing position, and constructing a dialectical dialogue between the two positions, will yield greater nuance in one's understanding of both positions and stronger articulation for one's own position.

Behind this approach lies a posture of epistemic openness, a readiness to learn from others, regardless of their religious or philosophical convictions. But there also lies a recognition that various positions are better and worse in different respects, and that the task of a reformational philosopher is to sort these matters out – critically, to be sure, but with help from others. I believe this posture is in line with what truth requires in a pluralistic and public setting. Unfortunately, Dooyeweerd's conception of truth, and his mode of carrying out a transcendental critique, do not encourage such a posture. That is an important reason why, as I have argued elsewhere,[9] Dooyeweerd's epistemology requires a critical retrieval.

## 2. REFORMATIONAL ONTOLOGY AND ARTISTIC TRUTH

Implicitly the book *Artistic Truth* has already launched this critical retrieval. Although it does not examine the work of reformational philosophers, it begins with two intuitions shared by Dooyeweerd and Vollenhoven and explicitly stated by my mentors Calvin Seerveld[10] and Hendrik Hart[11] – namely, that human knowledge is multidimensional, and that the arts are ways in which human beings acquire and revise their knowledge. If art is a form of knowledge, and if knowledge seeks truth, then questions arise about whether and in which respects the arts are capable of truth. It seems to me that the available answers, whether reformational or not, are not satisfactory, and that many contemporary philosophers, both analytic and continental, have abandoned these questions altogether. One reason for such shared inarticulacy is that we lack a general conception of truth within which the notion of artistic truth could make sense. Propositionally inflected correspondence theories of truth are perhaps the least plausible in this regard, and they have dominated Anglo-American aesthetics. The challenge, then, is to explain how artistic truth can be neither propositional nor governed by a correspondence with "reality" or "facts" or "states of affairs," yet still be true.

My response to this challenge has two stages.[12] First I characterize what reformational philosophers regard as the "qualifying function" of the arts.[13] Then I employ this characterization of the aesthetic dimension to propose a nonpropositional and noncorrespondence theory of artistic truth.[14] The result is a trilateral conception of authenticity, significance, and integrity that gives as much weight to mediated intersubjective relations among artists and their publics as to the relational import internal to a work of art. This trilateral conception of artistic truth allows one to show how prominent figures in Anglo-American aesthetics ignore or misconstrue one or another of these relations. And it provides a systematic basis for understanding what I call "art in public."[15]

Dooyeweerd's ontology provides a sturdy scaffold upon which to construct this conception. The fundamental distinction between "aesthetic" and "artistic" goes back to his distinction between modal and individual horizons. My characterization of the aesthetic dimension relies on a modal theory and refuses to collapse the "law-side" into the "subject-side." My account of the three relations of artistic truth employs a distinction inherent to Dooyeweerd's ontology, although not fully worked out there, among subject/object, subject/subject, and subject/product relations. I link these three relations with the aesthetic mode's techno-formative, lingual, and logical analogies as well as with the x/y pattern to structures of individuality:[16] authenticity pertains to an imaginative artifact's mediated expression, significance pertains to the interpretable presentation it makes as an imaginative object of use, and integrity pertains to its configured import when it achieves relative independence as an artwork.

Yet my approach differs from Dooyeweerd's in several important respects. First, I consider the law-side to be historical when it pertains to human affairs. That is a stronger claim than Dooyeweerd's insistence that the law-side is temporal. Accordingly, I describe principles of validity, such as the aesthetic principle of "imaginative cogency," as *historical* horizons, and not simply as belonging to the temporal horizon. Second, I do not think of these principles as "creational ordinances" or "divine laws." Rather I characterize them as "societal principles" through which God's call to love can be heard. Imaginative cogency is a societal principle, and so is the principle of logical validity. Third, I am wary about construing ontological structures as fully transcultural and transhistorical. Epistemic openness will acknowledge that one uncovers ontological structures within the societal formation one inhabits, and that one does not have the exhaustive knowledge needed to claim that they occur in precisely this way within other societal formations. Fourth, rather than speak of subjects and objects first, I speak of processes in which subjects and objects participate. I do this partly to recover the intersubjectivity that goes underground in Dooyeweerd, and partly to break with modern subject-centred tendencies that recur in Dooyeweerd. Finally, my characterization of the aesthetic dimension is much closer to Seerveld[17] than to Dooyeweerd.

My account of artistic truth has two implications for truth theory in general. First, it allows one to forge significant links between imaginative disclosure and propositional truth, rather than holding them in either opposition or isolation, as many philosophers do. Second, my account suggests that truth in general is multidimensional, as Dooyeweerd understood. Indeed, reducing truth to propositional truth bearers and to a correspondence between propositions and facts leads to impoverished theories and practical dead ends. Hence the account points toward a conception of truth that would not be a correspondence theory, yet would address the concerns of propositionally inflected correspondence theories. At the same time, this account of artistic truth draws upon an emerging general conception of truth, my primary research project in the years ahead. I turn to that general conception next.

## 3. FIDELITY AND DISCLOSURE

I propose to think of truth in its most comprehensive sense as a dynamic correlation between (1) human fidelity to societal principles and (2) a life-giving disclosure of society. Before I explicate each axis in this correlation, let me make two general comparisons with Dooyeweerd's conception.

First, by "truth in its most comprehensive sense" I mean something like Dooyeweerd's "fullness of truth." Like Dooyeweerd, I believe that theorists can and should propose a comprehensive conception of truth. Indeed, this effort belongs to the proper tasks of philosophy. While understandable, contemporary "postmetaphysical" efforts to avoid this task, in both continental and analytic philosophy, are misguided.[18] Nevertheless a special challenge confronts attempts to propose a comprehensive conception of truth, for one must both presuppose and appeal to what one is conceiving. So the project has an unavoidable circularity. Because this circularity is unavoidable, however, the key is not to step outside the circle, by pointing with Dooyeweerd to "transcendent truth," for example. Rather, as Martin Heidegger says in a different context, the key is to enter the circle in the right way.[19]

Second, in characterizing truth as a "dynamic correlation," I mean to distinguish it from any static structure. As Hegel recognized, truth is a historical process that unfolds in time. Consequently I depart rather dramatically from Platonic and Aristotelian conceptions of truth. I do not regard comprehensive truth to be either an unchanging form or a fixed property. Dooyeweerd's conception embarks on a similar departure, for his "Truth" comes down to a proper relationship that is religious in character. Yet he structuralizes this relationship and construes it as supra-temporal, thereby eliminating any possibility that it could be a temporal process, not to mention a historical one. While acknowledging continuities with Dooyeweerd's approach, then, I must candidly state that to regard truth as a historical process also marks a departure from his conception. Now let me fill in the two axes to truth as a dynamic correlation.

### *3.1 Societal Principles*

On each axis one finds a relation between "law-side" and "subject-side." The relation is more explicit on the first axis, where I speak of human fidelity (subject-side) to societal principles (law-side). Although I *distinguish* human responses from the "nomic conditions"[20] that make them possible, I do not keep these *separate*. Societal principles, which are always already in effect, take some of their shape from the ways in which we are faithful to them, and our efforts to enact what these principles require are always already informed by the shape they have taken in the societal formation we inhabit. This is why I describe societal principles both as "that which people hold in common" and as that which "holds them in common" or, more succinctly, as the "commonly holding/held."[21] People hold these principles, and are held by them, within historically developed cultural practices and social institutions. Here I have in mind what Dooyeweerd calls the "law-side" of modal aspects – resourcefulness, justice, and solidarity, for example, the "law-side," respectively, of the economic, juridical, and social aspects.[22] But I do not *separate* the law-side from the subject-side in the way Dooyeweerd does. Instead I revise his ontology of principles, characterizing societal principles as historical horizons that people learn, achieve, contest, reformulate, and ignore in the midst of social struggle.

An "ontology of principles" is an account of the status and meaning of the conditions that obtain for normative practices and institutions. "Normative practices and institutions" are ones that can be better or worse for human flourishing and can be experienced as better or worse for human flourishing. Many reformational philosophers, like Dooyeweerd, wish to anchor such conditions in God's creational ordinances. By contrast, I describe such conditions as "societal principles" and call attention to their historical embeddedness, their eschatological openness, and their vocational character.

I thereby revise the cosmonomic notion of "norm" in three respects. First, I claim that societal principles such as solidarity and justice are not in effect prior to their formation by human beings within cultural practices and social institutions. Second, societal principles were not simply given or fixed when human beings were created, but they emerge during the course of human history and could change in the future. Justice, for example, is continually contested and historically unfolded as a way to work out the flourishing to which human beings are called within their cultural practices and social institutions. Third, societal principles manifest God's instruction and invitation and guidance, God's call to love, addressed to societally constituted human beings and continually calling for their response. So I regard societal principles as historical horizons that cannot be anchored in creational ordinances outside human history, and I also regard them as "future-oriented callings in which the voice of God can be heard and traces of a new Earth can appear."[23] Hence human fidelity to societal principles is an ongoing process in which we continue to give shape to societal principles.

From Dooyeweerd's perspective, my account of societal principles calls up the spectre of historicism. He would worry that a principle such as justice will come to be regarded as valid only for a historically limited time and place. And he would think that his anchoring justice in creational ordinances counteracts such a limitation, since presumably creational ordinances hold for all times and places. But if one locates creational ordinances outside human history, then one needs to explain how they become effective *within* human history, raising the threat of an infinite regress. Still, Dooyeweerd could wonder whether my talk of societal principles as historical horizons makes their content arbitrary. And he might insist that we have to regard the ontic grounding for human endeavour as real if we would avoid historicism, which he described in postwar Europe as the "fatal illness of our 'dynamic' times."[24]

Although adequately answering these worries would require a lengthy response, I can at least indicate how the answer would go. First, the historical-horizonal character of societal principles such as justice and solidarity does not make their content arbitrary. It *does* mean that their content is never fixed once and for all, but ever emerges as history unfolds. As their content emerges, God's transhistorical call to love meets human responses, to which God responds in turn. Second, I do not say that societal principles *will come to be* commonly held. I say they *are* held in common, even as they *do* hold people in common. Further, if they were not commonly held, neither would they commonly hold. I follow Hegel in refusing to lift such principles out of the historical process to be either unchanging absolutes or merely regulative ideas. Finally, I have no problem calling societal principles "real," if we do not mean by "real" that they "exist" in the manner that concrete entities, communities, and institutions exist. Societal principles are real because they are always already in effect, and their being always already in effect is part of what it means to call them historical. Through them God calls human endeavour to account, even as human endeavour gives them shape. I take this conception to be in tune with scriptural teaching about God's ongoing and dialogical direction for human affairs. It is also not that far removed from Dooyeweerd's own insistence on the temporal character of the "law-side" to creation.

### *3.2 Life-Giving Disclosure*

The relation between "law-side" and "subject-side" is less explicit on the second axis. I characterize this axis as the "life-giving disclosure of society." By "disclosure" I mean a historical process of opening up society. This process is "life-giving" when human beings and other creatures come to flourish in their interconnections. Here the "subject-side" has to do with the contributions human beings make, within and through their cultural practices and social institutions, to opening society in a life-giving fashion. The "law-side" has to do with what Dooyeweerd calls the "central religious law": the call to love God and neighbour, suitably expanded to include the call to take care of creation – the so-called "cultural mandate." To foster the flourishing of all creatures is to hear and live out this call.

At first glance, the notion of life-giving disclosure may seem foreign to Dooyeweerd's conception of truth. Yet it reworks his idea of the "opening process" (*ontsluitingsproces*) in order to forge a link with truth at which he hints in a few places. Dooyeweerd's account of the opening process is primarily structural rather than genetic. Modally, it has to do with modal aspects' disclosing their meaning in an anticipatory fashion within the transcendental direction of time (NC 2: 181–365, WW 2: 126–300). Societally, it has to do with how, on the basis of opened historical foundations, societal formations and the cultural practices and social institutions within them acquire enriched normative and structural meaning.[25] He does not emphasize what I take to be the telos of disclosure: namely, the flourishing of all creatures in their interconnections.[26]

Introducing the notion of interconnected flourishing serves to destructuralize Dooyeweerd's account and render it both historical and eschatological. Once one transforms the crucial temporal horizon into something historical and postulates interconnected flourishing as the telos of history, the notion of disclosure turns away from a "transcendent horizon" toward an eschatological future – *Van boven naar voren* ("From above to ahead"), to borrow the title of Henk Geertsema's 1980 dissertation on Jürgen Moltmann. This helps one avoid problems that beset Dooyeweerd's account of the opening process, such as his odd notion of sinful disharmony on the law-side (NC 2: 334–7, WW 2: 265–8), his tendency to install Western societal differentiation as a "structural hypernorm" for historical development,[27] his under-appreciation of relative goodness within so-called "primitive" cultures,[28] and his conflicted stance toward so-called "apostate" cultures, where false faith leads to genuine achievements. Today, in a world that is simultaneously globalizing and breaking apart along political and confessional fault lines, it is crucial to rethink his account, especially in the fields of social ethics and international law.

### *3.3 Dynamic Correlation*

Truth in its most comprehensive sense is not the same as disclosure. Nor is it identical with human fidelity. Rather it is a dynamic correlation between two "law/subject" axes, between human fidelity to societal principles, on the one hand, and a life-giving disclosure of society, on the other. In Dooyeweerd's terms, although significantly modified, this means that truth involves an "accordance" between human responses to "modal laws" and the direction that the results of these responses take – the direction they take both with respect to the "central religious law" and with respect to the God who calls creation into existence and who meets human beings from an inexpressible future.

Like Dooyeweerd's conception of the fullness of truth, the conception of a dynamic correlation gives truth a speculative reach that much of contemporary philosophy rejects or neglects. This speculative reach is eschatological, however, not transcendent. My conception of truth brings together a normative critique of societal evil with historically informed hope for God's inexpressible future. Truth, we could say, is a gathering of hopeful critique. Yet one should not restrict truth to its speculative dimension. Reformational philosophers need to deal modestly and attentively with a complex interplay between normativity and eschatology.

Because of truth's eschatological dimension, history cannot be the "final horizon" or "ultimate horizon," nor can human beings have such a horizon "in view." Rather, all the views we have occur within the historical horizons of societal principles that, being dynamic and comprehensive, always already inform whatever notions we have of "life" and "societal disclosure." As a dynamic correlation, truth calls for our faithfulness to societal principles such as solidarity and justice. It also calls forth the flourishing of all creatures in their interconnections. This dynamic correlation is open to a future we have difficulty imagining or conceiving. Strictly speaking, and contrary to Dooyeweerd's problematic notion of a "transcendent horizon," there is no ultimate *horizon*.[29]

It might seem from such descriptions that my conception of truth is completely circular. I seem to define societal principles in terms of creaturely flourishing, and to define creaturely flourishing in terms of societal principles. Although I do not think my definitions of the two axes and their correlation are circular, I do regard fidelity to societal principles and life-giving disclosure to be indissoluble correlates. The point of such fidelity is to promote a process in which human beings and other creatures come to flourish. Correlatively, life-giving disclosure depends upon the degree to which cultural practices, social institutions, and entire societal formations align with principles such as solidarity and justice. Life-giving disclosure occurs in part by way of people being true – pursuing fidelity – in the various dimensions of their social existence.

But only in part, for disclosure also occurs both beyond and despite our principles and alignment. As Dooyeweerd also acknowledges, there is always more to truth than our "being in the truth," whether theoretically, politically, or in any other way. Consequently one must appeal to the notion of creaturely flourishing to motivate such fidelity, and one must employ societal principles to evaluate the extent and quality of creaturely flourishing. Again, the hermeneutical key is not to avoid this circle but to enter it in the right way.

Central to my conception, then, is that truth is a dynamic process, not a fixed pattern, and that no practices, institutions, or communities either stand outside this process or have exclusive access to it. Closely connected with this central point is that the effectivity of, say, the call to be just depends on human fidelity to the societal principle of justice, yet human fidelity is never enough to bring about justice. Hence it becomes impossible to talk about truth in its most comprehensive sense as either structural or directional. As Dooyeweerd recognizes in his own way, truth is both structural and directional. One's conception of truth needs to acknowledge the dynamic this intersection opens up. Part of acknowledging this dynamic in one's philosophy is not to be overly prescriptive at first about the content of societal principles or the meaning of creaturely flourishing. There is always more to say about such content and meaning, and one needs other voices in order to say this. One should not present a comprehensive conception of truth as the absolute truth about absolute truth, but rather as an invitation to discussion. In this sense, too, "theoretical thought never finishes its task" (NC 2: 556, WW 2: 487).

## 4. PROPOSITIONAL TRUTH

Elsewhere I have criticized Dooyeweerd's account of theoretical truth for ignoring the question of objectivity.[30] It might appear that my own conception of truth falls into the same trap. That appearance could arise because I have said nothing specific about propositional truth or, as I prefer to call it, assertoric correctness. Although it would be premature to attempt a full-blown theory of propositional truth and objectivity, let me begin to fill the gap.[31]

### *4.1 Heidegger's Contribution*

My account of assertoric correctness derives from a critical dialogue with the hermeneutical conception of truth in Heidegger's *Sein und*

*Zeit*.[32] To make sense of his conception, it helps to regard it as a deepening and transformation of correspondence theories. The mainstream of Western philosophy since Plato and Aristotle has been dominated by propositionally inflected correspondence theories of truth. Correspondence theories of truth hold "that there are truth bearers and that a truth bearer is true if and only if it corresponds to a state of affairs that obtains. They differ concerning the class of truth bearers (e.g., beliefs, propositions, sentences, or statements), the nature of states of affairs (whether they are facts, and whether they are mind-independent, as realists hold), and the type of correspondence required [congruence (e.g., Bertrand Russell) or correlation (e.g., J.L. Austin)]. In addition, most correspondence theories are propositionally inflected ... 'Propositionally inflected' theories ... regard propositions as the sole or the primary bearers of truth."[33] In a correspondence theory, then, to say that the proposition "The cat is on the mat" is true is to say that it corresponds to what is the case – i.e., that kitty really is on the mat. When combined with logical empiricism, such a theory tends to treat propositions as "self-sufficient," facts as "uninterpreted," and the relation between them as timeless.[34]

Heidegger transforms propositionally inflected correspondence theories via three theses. First, he says that assertions or propositions, the supposed bearers of truth, derive from more fundamental processes and practices of interpretation and acquire their truth via interpretation. Second, he claims that the "states of affairs" to which a true assertion or proposition must "correspond" are themselves embedded in contexts of relevance, and their "truth-making" capacities stem from such embeddedness. Third, he regards the so-called "correspondence" between, say, propositions and facts, not as a fixed congruence or correlation but rather as deriving from the dynamic ontological condition he calls the "disclosedness of Dasein" (see below). So the "propositions" are not self-sufficient, the "facts" are not uninterpreted, and the relationship between them is not a timeless "correspondence."

When Heidegger calls assertions a derivative mode of interpretation[35] – his first thesis – I take him to be saying three things. First, that making assertions is one of the many ways in which we make sense of what we can do and be. Second, that the practice of making assertions tends, in a universalizing and decontextualizing way, to draw our attention away from other practical involvements. And that, third, because of this tendency, assertions and propositions come to seem as if they were totally context-transcending claims about isolated objects and their "universal" properties. In Heidegger's own vocabulary, the making of assertions involves a transition from "handiness" to "objective presence." By insisting that assertions are a *derivative* mode of interpretation, Heidegger reminds us that they could be neither "true" nor "false" if they lacked meaning within the relationships we have with ourselves, with other human beings, and with other creatures. Although he overstates the supposed tendency of assertions to cover up these relationships and to be cut off from other human involvements with the world, he is surely right to regard assertions as ways in which we make sense of what we can do and be. I also think it is correct to say that they play a universalizing and decontextualizing role in human understanding.

Heidegger's second thesis is that the truth-making capacity of the entities about which an assertion can be made stems from their being embedded in contexts of relevance.[36] Heidegger's term for this truth-making capacity is "discoveredness" (*Entdecktheit*). He says the discoveredness of entities depends on the more comprehensive "disclosedness" (*Erschlossenheit*) of the world to which they belong. Similarly, an assertion's capacity to discover an entity – an assertion's "discovering-ness" (*Entdeckend-sein*) – depends on the more comprehensive "disclosedness" of the being that makes assertions – it depends on Dasein's disclosedness.

Hence the truth of an assertion, and the truth of the asserted entity, are not fixed properties of isolated things that somehow "correspond." Rather, they are dynamic tendencies embedded in larger contexts of relevance without which neither the assertion nor the asserted entity would make sense. This implies that the truth-making capacity of asserted entities stems from their embeddedness in contexts of relevance. Asserted entities must show themselves to us in the right way, and they can do this only in connection with other of their aspects and together with other entities with which they are connected. Heidegger's point, in my own terminology, is that the correctness of our assertions depends to a significant extent on how "an entity, in its predicative availability, offers or manifests itself in relevant accord with nonpredicative aspects of its availability."[37] From now on I shall use the term "correctness" to indicate the truth of assertions and propositions.

Heidegger's third thesis is that the so-called correspondence between assertions and asserted entities, or between propositions and facts, derives from a more "primordial" ontological condition – namely, the "disclosedness of Dasein."[38] "Dasein" is his term for what we might call "human existence." Its "disclosedness" refers to the fact that human existence is fundamentally open to other creatures and oriented toward its own future possibilities. My version of this thesis is that assertoric correctness (i.e., propositional truth) is one mode of a more comprehensive truth. Suitably modified in a reformational fashion, Heidegger's three theses bear directly on the question of objectivity.

### 4.2 *Predicative Availability*

The question of objectivity has two parts. One concerns logical objectivity as such. The other concerns the relation between logical objectivity and nonlogical objectivity.[39] Dooyeweerd and Vollenhoven agree that, in general, objectivity has to do with functions that certain creatures fulfill in relation to other creatures. A bird's nest, for example, functions as a biotic object in relation to the bird as a biotic subject. It functions as a psychic object in relation to animals or human beings that can sense it and have feelings toward it. So too, any creature that can be known in a logical fashion functions as a logical object in relation to human logical subjects. These object functions are not simply created or assigned by the biotic or psychic or logical subject. In some sense they are inherent to the creature that functions as an object in a specific subject/object relation.

Yet the founders of reformational philosophy have significantly different accounts of the relation between concepts and logical objects. Dooyeweerd regards concepts as having an "intentional logical content." Logical subjects must employ this content in order to disclose logical object functions that would otherwise remain hidden in temporal meaning-coherence. Moreover, logical objectivity requires our achieving a conceptual synthesis that accords with the logical "objective connectedness" in reality's "systatic meaning-coherence" (NC 2: 389–90, WW 2: 321–2). Vollenhoven, by contrast, makes no mention of the "intentional content" of concepts. In fact he regards the logical subject function not as "conception" but as "perception," along with the "interrelations" of "recollection" and "expectation."[40] Concepts, for Vollenhoven, are not the intentional means of logical knowing. Instead they are its achieved results. Hence his primary consideration regarding logical objectivity is that the "[logical] subject has to direct itself in the first place to the [logical] perception of the [logical] object."[41] The concepts we form through such activity can be about either conceptual or nonconceptual "states of affairs." And these concepts, like the judgments (*oordelen*) they enter, are "determined" not only by the logical norm of noncontradiction but also by the knowable and by the activity of knowing.[42]

Without attempting to adjudicate this implicit dispute over logical objectivity, let me say that I account for similar matters with the notions of predicative availability and predicative self-disclosure. Unlike Dooyeweerd and Vollenhoven, I do not consider the logical dimension to be directly post-psychic. It presupposes the technical, aesthetic, and lingual dimensions as well. Accordingly my point of entry to the logical dimension is neither intentional concepts (Dooyeweerd) nor perception (Vollenhoven) but assertion as a speech act in which predication plays a more prominent role than it does in other speech acts such as promising, requesting, or confessing. Like Heidegger, I distinguish between "assertion" and "the asserted." Thanks to Vollenhoven, I also distinguish more carefully than Heidegger does between the practice of *asserting* and the *assertion* that results.

One of Heidegger's insights is that the relation between *asserting* and the asserted is direct: it does not need the intermediary of a mental representation. He derives this insight from Edmund Husserl's notion of "self-givenness," and Dooyeweerd and Vollenhoven in their distinctive ways would agree.[43] The relation between accomplished *assertions* and the asserted is not direct, however. As Vollenhoven puts this, "between what is knowable and the related result, there is always the analysis of the person thinking, who analyzes what is knowable correctly or not and, in turn, comes to knowledge concerning what is knowable."[44]

In order for either the direct asserting/asserted relation or the indirect assertion/asserted relation to be in effect, Heidegger says, the asserted must show itself in an appropriate fashion. In order for the asserting and the assertion to be true (i.e., correct), the asserted entity must show itself to be just as it was asserted to be: "That an assertion *is true* means that it discovers an entity [as it is] in itself. The [true] assertion asserts, points out, 'lets be seen' (*apophansis*) the entity in its discoveredness [*Entdecktheit*]."[45] Although there are some problems with this formulation, Heidegger argues correctly that the accomplished assertion is about an entity (or a range of entities) in a certain mode of its givenness. This "aboutness" indicates a mutual mediation between the practice of asserting and the "object" of this practice. The object – i.e., the entity asserted – not only allows itself to be asserted but also calls forth the assertion.

To get at an asserted entity's "givenness," or, in Dooyeweerd and Vollenhoven's terms, a logical or analytic object function, let me introduce the term "predicative availability." As both Heidegger and the founders of reformational philosophy recognize, entities are available

(Heidegger: at hand) for human practices in many ways. One way is for entities to let us make assertions about them. An entity's offering itself for our asserting is its predicative availability. This is only one of the many ways in which entities can engage us. We do not impose predicative availability upon them, nor does our asserting create their identity, even though it can help shape their identity, for better or worse.

### *4.3 Predicative Self-Disclosure*

By itself such "logical objectivity" does not account for assertoric correctness, however. For that, one must explain how an "object's" predicative availability relates to other ways in which it is available. Dooyeweerd might have this in view when he speaks of a systatic "objective connectedness." But he muddies the waters by describing this as a *logical* objectivity grasped via conceptual synthesis. The requisite objective connectedness cannot be simply *logical* objectivity. Predicative availability does not suffice to make assertoric correctness possible.

To be correct, an accomplished assertion must discover the asserted entity not only in its predicative availability but also in a manner that accords with other relevant ways in which the asserted entity is available. When, for example, a carpenter correctly asserts to her helper "That hammer is too heavy," she discovers its relative heaviness in a way that accords with the hammer's (un)suitability for the task at hand. I call the capacity of asserted entities to let our assertions be correct "predicative self-disclosure": "The predicative self-disclosure of an asserted entity lies in its offering itself for predicative practice reliably and in accordance with other ways in which the entity is available ... When the hammer discloses itself as something about which one can accurately claim 'The hammer is too heavy,' it offers itself just as that hammer is available for a particular task of carpentry, say, for setting nails."[46]

To be of use to a theory of truth, then, one's account of logical objectivity must consider how logical object functions relate to nonlogical object functions. This, I submit, Dooyeweerd does not provide, and its absence may help explain his inattention to questions of objectivity when he discusses theoretical truth, for which intermodal synthesis is crucial.[47]

Obviously more needs to be said on the topic of assertoric correctness or propositional truth. Other important factors, in addition to the asserted entity's predicative availability and self-disclosure, contribute to such correctness, and there are other ways in which our asserting can be off the mark: misspeaking, for example, or giving inappropriate responses to questions, or deliberately lying. Moreover, a speech community can be so mired in ideology and miscommunication that incorrect assertions are not exceptions but the rule. Yet I hope to have sketched in enough to show how to repair the lack of objectivity in Dooyeweerd's conception of theoretical truth.

## 5. AUTHENTICATION

Dooyeweerd's inattention to objectivity occurs in tandem with his not addressing questions of intersubjective validity when he accounts for theoretical truth. The closest he comes to such questions is when he says theoretical insights must be justified before "the forum of the [d]ivine world-order" (NC 2: 577, WW 2: 511). But this peculiar notion of justification begs questions of by whom, to whom, and in which respects the justification is to be offered. Moreover, Dooyeweerd does not distinguish between truth and justification, a topic that has become increasingly important in philosophical truth theory.[48] If he had taken up this topic, he might have recognized the need to account for epistemic intersubjectivity when one proposes a general conception of truth. He might also have noticed that a theory of theoretical truth should account for two different forms of intersubjective validity: intersubjective validity as it pertains to theoretical truth, and intersubjective validity as it pertains to the justification of theoretical truth claims. Because, arguably, an assertion can be justified but incorrect, and it can be correct but not justified, one needs to account for intersubjective validity in both regards.[49]

This Dooyeweerd does not do. Instead he substitutes for such questions an appeal to what I call "authentication." Dooyeweerd's phrase for authentication is "standing in the Truth." By making this substitution, he winds up in the same problems that afflict Heidegger and Adorno,[50] neither of whom stands where Dooyeweerd stands with respect to the fullness of truth. Yet all three of them also share a crucial insight that has gone missing in much of contemporary truth theory. All three understand that authentication is more comprehensive than a discursive justification of assertions and the like, just as truth is more comprehensive than assertoric correctness or propositional truth. Their challenge, which none successfully addresses, is to account for authentication in such a way that it neither replaces nor ignores discursive justification.

My own conception of truth responds to this challenge in three ways. First, I argue that assertoric correctness is an important mode of truth but not the decisive one. Second, I portray the justification of assertions as a mode of authentication, but again not the decisive one. Third, I give an account of the connection between truth and authentication – and, by implication, between assertoric correctness and discursive justification – that neither collapses the one into the other nor lets authentication trump truth.

## *5.1 Bearing Witness*

By "authentication" I mean all of the ways in which people bear witness to truth. By "truth," in its comprehensive sense, I mean the dynamic correlation already discussed. Given this correlation's historical character, one can easily imagine its occurring without anyone bearing witness to it: it can occur behind our backs. Still, it is behind *our* backs that truth then occurs, and we cannot but have a stake in it, whether or not we acknowledge this. If we acknowledge our stake in truth's unfolding, then we can also bear witness to it. Our bearing witness becomes an avenue along which truth itself unfolds. In this respect, authentication is an extension of truth. Yet our bearing witness to truth is not necessarily true. It is possible, indeed likely, that we sometimes bear false witness, even those of us who, in Dooyeweerd's account, claim to be "standing in the Truth." So authentication is not automatically an extension of truth. Intrinsic to authentication, however, also when it takes the form of discursive justification, is that it claims to be true. In other words, truth and authentication are distinct, even though they have an intimate connection.

What does it mean to bear witness to truth? In its fullest sense, to bear witness, to authenticate truth, is to offer testimony concerning specific correlations between societal disclosure and our fidelity to societal principles. We do so as we engage in cultural practices and as we participate in social institutions, and we do so to the extent that these practices and institutions enable us to attest to such correlations. This means, in turn, that authentication is intrinsically intersubjective. It occurs in the company of others and within the societal formation we inhabit. Further, bearing witness to truth is not simply a matter of raising and defending validity claims in a discursive manner, although it does include our engaging in discursive practices. It is practical and multidimensional, and it has an invitational quality.

To bear witness to specific correlations between fidelity and disclosure is to take part in them and, by participating, to invite others to do the same. My book *Social Philosophy after Adorno* gives the following example: "If ... the correlation of contemporary justice and human flourishing requires the elimination of systemic racism, one bears witness to this correlation by doing what one can, with others, to transform the racist practices and institutions to which one belongs, whether through gestures, policies, or public protests. To bear witness to the truth means to do what truth requires in a social context and with respect to others who co-inhabit that context. Bearing witness involves the full range of human activities, not only linguistic and discursive but also aesthetic, ethical, political, economic, and the like."[51]

This example suggests that no confessional community, including Christian organizations and the Church universal, automatically "stands in the Truth" or, as I prefer, walks and abides in truth and has truth abide in it. Conversely, no confessional community automatically stands outside the truth or, as I prefer, fails to walk and abide in truth or does not have truth abide in it. The struggle to eliminate slavery in Western countries gives ample evidence in both regards: the complicity of Christians in systemic racism, the courageous struggle against it by devout believers such as William Wilberforce and Sojourner Truth, and both complicity and resistance on the part of non-Christians. As Dooyeweerd and Vollenhoven recognize, the antitheses between truth and falsehood and between good and evil do not line up neatly with existing confessional, political, economic, or cultural divisions in society. They run through every community and through each of our hearts: "The antithesis runs right through Christian life itself."[52]

## *5.2 Discursive Justification*

My account of authentication sheds new light, I believe, on practices of discursive justification. For they, too, are ways in which we bear witness to truth. That means they are ways in which people enact specific correlations between fidelity and disclosure, invitationally, and in specific contexts. Although that fact by itself does not explain how discursive justifications can be intersubjectively valid, it does indicate that justificatory validity is important for more than simply logical or academic reasons. Such importance stems from the unique structure of justification. A discursive justification tries to bear out the purported universality of the validity claims raised in other linguistic practices by appealing to its own purported validity. The validity of discursive justifications is not a matter of other societal principles such as solidarity and justice, however. It is matter of logic and rhetoric.

Such an account does not remove justification from the field of authentication, nor does it detach assertoric correctness from comprehensive truth, as if the latter in each case has nothing to do with the former. Instead, the role of discursive practices within a multidimensional process of authentication both gives them impetus and makes them important.[53] Occurring within a more comprehensive authentication, discursive practices receive their context from other modes of authentication and make their own contributions. Like assertions, discursive justifications never have the final word, nor do they transcend truth and authentication.[54]

### *5.3 Correctness and Truth*

Neither is truth simply a theoretical concern, although it does occur as assertoric correctness and also as theoretical truth. As Dooyeweerd recognizes, truth is a matter of life and death, and it must be borne out in our lives. Unlike philosophers who consider propositions and assertions to be the "locus" of truth, I, like Heidegger and Dooyeweerd, regard them as only one way in which truth can occur. Making and discussing and debating assertions are only one way in which the correlation between human fidelity and life-giving disclosure is carried out. Yet the assertoric path is ubiquitous in the practices and institutions of contemporary society. It is not restricted to the arena of science or academic work. Whether in politics or faith, in art or education, we regularly engage in assertoric practices.

Assertoric practices are linked to comprehensive truth in three ways: by virtue of their internal structure, their societal role, and their dependence on other modes of truth. In the first place, assertoric practices involve a definite correlation between fidelity and disclosure: namely, fidelity to the principle of logical validity, and predicative self-disclosure of that about which we make assertions. The second link lies in the role assertoric correctness plays in the pursuit of other societal principles. If we were unable to make correct assertions about what justice requires, and if we did not care about the principle of logical validity, we would have difficulty recognizing the extent of injustice and the possibilities for removing it in a complex society. The third link consists of the context and support that other modes of truth provide for the pursuit of assertoric correctness. Assertoric practices primarily occur in nonassertoric contexts, and they presuppose that we are living the truth in nonassertoric ways. To pursue assertoric correctness while continually violating the principle of justice, for example, would eventually undermine the point of making correct assertions. So truth is to be lived, and not simply claimed. Yet making assertions and testing them are vital to the pursuit of truth.

With those hints of a larger research project, I come to the close of my discussion. One question remains. Does my own theoretical stance toward the idea of truth bear witness to truth? More pointedly, given the concerns of reformational philosophy to be attuned to the witness scripture bears to the truth, is my stance toward this idea biblically directed? Like Dooyeweerd and Vollenhoven, I *hope* to bear witness to truth in my thinking about it. Indeed, I hope, as they did, to give testimony to what scripture tells us about truth. Offering my proposals in such hope, I would *invite* others to judge whether my stance toward the idea of truth is biblically directed. Accordingly I cannot simply *declare* it to be biblically directed. Yet I do *propose* that it is not unbiblical to regard other philosophers, for whom the Hebrew and Christian scriptures are not authoritative, as being in the truth philosophically. God's grace is not confined to self-identified Christians, and the antithesis between truth and falsehood does not stop outside the walls of Zion. To pursue both of these biblical insights simultaneously and without compromise is, I suggest, the genius of reformational philosophy.[55]

# 15

# Science, Society, and Culture: Against Deflationism

## (2007)

Philosophy and science have a troubled relationship. What philosophers find most important about science often strikes scientists as irrelevant to their work. Reciprocally, the projects to which scientists devote their lives, philosophers can find conceptually uninteresting. Such mutual misrecognition is especially evident when philosophers talk about empirical research. The nineteenth-century philosopher John Stuart Mill was well-known for spelling out several methods of inductive inference. One he called the "Method of Agreement" and formulated as follows: "If two or more instances of the phenomenon under investigation have only one circumstance in common, the circumstance in which alone all the instances agree, is the cause (or effect) of the given phenomenon."[1] Initially this sounds like a plausible rule. But it could prove disastrous if misunderstood as a guideline for empirical research. Consider, for example, the story of the "Scientific Drinker" told in Irving Copi's *Introduction to Logic*. This chap was committed to inductive inference. He was also fond of alcohol. In fact, he got drunk every evening. Convinced by his friends that he needed to change his alcoholic ways, "he resolved to conduct a careful experiment to discover the exact cause of his frequent inebriations. For five nights in a row he collected instances of the given phenomenon, the antecedent circumstances being respectively scotch and soda, bourbon and soda, brandy and soda, rum and soda, and gin and soda. Then using [Mill's] Method of Agreement, he swore a solemn oath never to touch soda again!"[2]

In writing about a troubled relationship, I hope to fare better than this drunken scientist. To avoid his fate, I shall stick to philosophy and not pretend to do well what scientists do better. If my philosophical discussion is worthwhile, however, it will shed light not only on what scientists do but also on why the sciences are socially significant. I hope to show that this has to do with the importance of truth. I also hope to indicate why contemporary devaluations of scientific truth are misplaced.

## 1. REVALUING TRUTH

In a path-breaking book titled *Knowledge and Power*, Joseph Rouse deploys Martin Heidegger's philosophy to portray the sciences as discourses of power. Rouse's portrayal denies truth its traditional prominence as an aim of scientific inquiry. Nor does he think this is too great a sacrifice if one wants, as he does, to provide philosophical grounds for a social critique of science. He writes: "[W]e cannot isolate the scientific enterprise from the myriad other practices through which we define ourselves as human beings. The sciences have shaped the world we live in and the possibilities in terms of which we might come to understand ourselves. There is nothing politically neutral about these effects ... [H]ow we come to terms with them must ultimately merge with our most basic understanding and criticism of what is at stake in our lives ... These ... are the kinds of issues with which a philosophy of science must ultimately concern itself if we are to take seriously the importance of the sciences in the modern world."[3] For Rouse, traditional conceptions of truth, and traditional emphases on truth as the goal of science, obscure the social significance of scientific work.

I find much to endorse in Rouse's turn toward a "political philosophy of science." Yet I think his reading of Heidegger undermines the very basis on which science can contribute to human flourishing. Part of this basis is an appropriate conception of truth. So I should like to propose a different reading of Heidegger, one that reclaims the importance of truth for science. In reclaiming this, I shall also challenge truncated notions of truth that lead social epistemologists such as Rouse to deflate its importance. First I discuss Heidegger's hermeneutical conception of truth and Rouse's appropriation of Heidegger's conception (section 2). Next I propose a way to link propositional truth with a more comprehensive conception of what truth involves (section 3). Then I use this proposal to reflect on the vocation of science in contemporary society (section 4).

Before turning to Heidegger, however, I should say why the idea of truth is important. There are three sorts of reasons: historical, conceptual, and societal. Historically, the idea of truth has helped organize Western intellectual culture since ancient times. It also is a central theme in Judaism, Christianity, and Islam, the three monotheistic religions that have shaped Western society and continue to have a formative cultural influence around the world. Conceptually, the idea of truth sets a stage for fundamental debates about the point and worth of academic work: debates between realists and anti-realists in philosophy and the natural sciences, for example, or between relativists and anti-relativists in the humanities and social sciences. Societally, the idea of truth provides a normative background for ethics, law, and public discourse. Despite widespread cynicism about social institutions, we continue to expect our friends and colleagues to be truthful; we ask witnesses in courts of law to "tell the truth, the whole truth, and nothing but the truth"; and we object when journalists deliberately fabricate their reports or misrepresent what has happened. In an extended sense, we even expect artists and artworks to be true, and we accord them lesser worth when they do not live up to this expectation.

If these reasons are compelling, then it becomes surprising that many contemporary philosophers do not think the idea of truth is all that important. On both sides of "the continental divide" – in both analytic and continental philosophy – prominent philosophers now consider traditional emphases on "truth" to be vastly overstated. For example, a number of analytic philosophers have developed what they call a "deflationary" account of truth. On this account, traditional attempts to provide a theory of truth, including correspondence, coherence, and pragmatic theories, have no explanatory value. They have no explanatory value because there is nothing to explain. According to the deflationists, truth has no nature, and when we say something "is true," this is not a genuine predicate.[4] Joseph Rouse accepts a deflationary account.[5] As a result, he misses the larger potential of Heidegger's philosophy for thinking about truth in science and about science in society.

## 2. MARTIN HEIDEGGER AND JOSEPH ROUSE

Heidegger's conception of truth is a hermeneutical deepening and transformation of propositionally inflected correspondence theories. As the previous chapter indicated, Heidegger transforms such theories in three respects. First, he says that assertions or propositions derive from a more fundamental interpretation and acquire their truth via interpretation. Second, he claims that the "truth-making" capacities of facts or states of affairs stem from their being embedded in contexts of relevance. Third, he regards the "correspondence" between propositions and facts not as a fixed congruence or correlation but as deriving from the dynamic "disclosedness of Dasein."

The following quotations from Heidegger's *Being and Time* summarize his three transformations:[6]

(1) "[A]ssertion is derived from interpretation, and is an extreme case of it."[7]

(2) "That an assertion *is true* means that it discovers an entity [as it is] in itself. The [true] assertion asserts, points out, 'lets be seen' (*apophansis*) the entity in its discoveredness [*Entdecktheit*]."[8]

(3) "[O]nly with the disclosedness of Dasein is the *most primordial* phenomenon of truth attained ... In that Dasein essentially *is* its disclosedness, and, as disclosed, discloses and discovers, it is essentially 'true.' Dasein *is 'in the truth.'*"[9]

I do not intend to give a detailed exposition of Heidegger's hermeneutical conception of truth as summarized in these quotations. But let me comment sufficiently to show why I take issue with Joseph Rouse's interpretation of Heidegger.

### 2.1 *Assertoric Interpretation*

Consider first the thesis that assertions are a derivative mode of interpretation. Rouse understands this to mean that assertions derive from how we make sense of the possibilities that emerge from the world we inhabit and from the particular situations in which we find ourselves. Like all interpretation, Rouse says, assertions work out an understanding of possibilities that is "bound to concrete situations, embodied in an actual tradition of interpretive practices carried on from generation to generation, and located in persons shaped by specific situations and traditions. Understanding is thus not a conceptualization of the world but a performative grasp of how to cope with it."[10] Consequently Rouse also asserts that all knowledge, including scientific knowledge, is local.[11] But this cannot be right, for two reasons. First, it lands Rouse in the self-referential incoherence of making the universal and context-transcending assertion that no such assertion is possible. Second, it conflicts with Heidegger's description of his own universalizing and context-transcending ontology as a phenomenological *interpretation*.[12]

Contrary to Rouse's account, I do not think that Heidegger restricts interpretation to working out an understanding that is practical and tied to a local context. Now, it is the case that, when *Being and Time* first discusses understanding and interpretation in sections 31–3, Heidegger focuses on how we make sense of our context-bound, practical involvements with tools and equipment – what Heidegger calls circumspective interpretation. But he clearly indicates that there is more to understanding and interpretation than this. Indeed, what matters most to his inquiry is the "authentic understanding" that occurs when we face up to the limits of our own existence and thereby relativize all the possibilities that come with our particular situations. Even science, he suggests, can be carried out in this authentic manner.[13]

For Heidegger, assertions are a derivative mode of interpretation in three ways: they are only one of the many ways in which we interpret, they tend to universalize and decontextualize in ways that divert our attention from other practical involvements, and they seem as if they were completely context-transcending claims. In these ways, assertoric practices involve a transition from "handiness" to "objective presence." Despite my reservations about Heidegger's overemphasis on the decontextualizing tendency of assertoric practices, I think he is essentially correct about the derivative character of assertions. But I do not believe he is committed to Rousean localism in this regard.

### 2.2 "*Discoveredness*"

Heidegger also claims that the truth-making capacity of asserted entities stems from how they are embedded in contexts of relevance, from their "discoveredness" (*Entdecktheit*), which itself depends on the more comprehensive "disclosedness" (*Erschlossenheit*) of the world to which they belong. Similarly, an assertion's "discovering-ness" (*Entdeckend-sein*) – its capacity to discover an entity – depends on Dasein's more comprehensive "disclosedness." He gives the example of someone who is facing away from a wall and asserts the following about something behind her: "The picture on the wall is hanging crookedly."[14] Let's call this person Martina. When Martina turns around and perceives the picture hanging crookedly, the truth of her assertion is confirmed. In this situation, what does it mean to say that Martina's assertion is true? Heidegger replies that this means two things. First, that the asserting and assertion do indeed discover the asserted entity just as this entity is in itself: they do indeed discover the picture in its hanging crookedly. Second, that the asserted entity does indeed show itself to be in itself just as it was asserted to be: the picture does indeed show itself to be hanging crookedly, just as Martina asserted. But the truth of the assertion and the truth of the asserted entity are not fixed properties of isolated things that somehow "correspond." Rather, they are dynamic tendencies embedded in larger contexts of relevance without which neither the assertion nor the asserted entity would make sense.

Joseph Rouse has little to say about Heidegger's insistence on the "discoveredness" of asserted entities and the "disclosedness" of the world to which they belong. There are three reasons for this. First, Rouse focuses on scientific research as "circumspective activity" involving "skills, practices, and equipment,"[15] not on the domains that scientists investigate.[16] Second, he insists that "objects of scientific research" exist "only within … local, intensely pragmatic contexts."[17] Third, Rouse construes arguments about scientific claims as attempts to persuade one's peers rather than as attempts to confirm one's discoveries.[18] When combined with a deflationary account of assertoric truth and a contextualist account of linguistic meaning,[19] these three tendencies prevent Rouse from assigning truth-making capacities to entities. Although he does not want to make the *existence* of entities entirely dependent upon our interpretation of them, he also does not allow their existence to have any purchase upon whether our assertions about them are *true*.

Rouse's pragmatic non-realism,[20] if I may call it that, is fundamentally at odds with Heidegger's conception, it seems to me. Admittedly, Heidegger scholars disagree about whether and to what extent Heidegger holds a realist position with regard to what the natural sciences investigate. Whereas Taylor Carman portrays Heidegger as an *ontic* realist but not an *ontological* realist,[21] Hubert Dreyfus enlists Heidegger to defend a "robust realism" that is both pluralist and ontological.[22] Despite their disagreements about the shape of Heidegger's "realism," however, both of these astute Heidegger scholars reject Rouse's deflationary moves, and rightly so. For if the independent existence of what Heidegger calls "occurrent" or "objectively present" (*vorhanden*) entities has no purchase upon the truth of our assertions, then his entire account of "discoveredness" and "disclosedness" loses its point.

Heidegger says more than that human beings interpret things in various ways and in this process raise truth claims about them. He also says that the things we interpret accommodate or resist our interpretations, and in this either "show themselves" or do not. Some of these entities can escape our interpretive reach or send our interpretations in directions we neither expect nor control. As Carman puts it in opposition to Rouse: "The fact that our mundane practices condition our interpretations of entities, including our interpretations of occurrent entities as occurrent, in no way implies that those entities are not after all occurrent independently of our practices and interpretations … [T]he internal dependence of knowledge on practice and interpretation gives us no reason to deny that our knowledge uncovers things as they are in themselves."[23] What makes discovering and discoveredness possible, in Heidegger's account, is the fact that all understanding and interpretation are interlaced with "attunements" in which we can experience the "occurrentness" of entities in pre-hermeneutical, pre-linguistic, and pre-predicative ways.[24] This "affective" or "intuitive" dimension of human existence is completely absent in Rouse's philosophy of science, despite its prominence in Heidegger's ontology.[25]

Accordingly, when Heidegger insists that the truth-making capacity of asserted entities stems from their embeddedness in contexts of relevance, I do *not* take him to be claiming that the truth of assertions is simply a matter of interpretation. Rather, his claim is that asserted entities must show themselves to us in the right way,[26] in connection with other of their aspects, and together with other entities. Heidegger's point, in my own terminology, is that the correctness of our assertions depends to a significant extent on an entity's predicative availability and predicative self-disclosure.

### 2.3 *"Disclosedness"*

Heidegger's third thesis is that the "disclosedness of Dasein" underlies and makes possible the so-called correspondence between assertions and asserted entities, between propositions and facts. It is only because human existence is fundamentally open to other creatures and oriented toward its own future possibilities that assertions can be "true" (i.e., correct) and the entities they assert can "make them true" (i.e., be predicatively self-disclosive). Our openness and futurity are inescapable, he says, but they can also be ignored or forgotten. Hence he distinguishes between "authentic" and "inauthentic" modes of disclosedness. And he takes the key to truth to be *authentic* disclosedness as the "*truth of existence*."[27] Propositionally inflected correspondence theories of truth not only ignore questions of authenticity, but also elaborate and ratify inauthentic manners of existence in which Dasein's disclosedness is either ignored or forgotten.

I shall not rehearse Heidegger's attempt to demonstrate that correspondence theories both express and distort truth as disclosedness.[28] What is crucial is that Heidegger tries to show how the purported correspondence between assertion and object derives from the openness and future-orientation of human existence. Joseph Rouse pursues nearly the opposite tack. Rather than ground assertoric correctness in existential truth, Rouse divorces assertoric correctness from anything that is not linguistic. For Rouse, claiming that an assertion is true simply reiterates that assertion: "'Truth' adds nothing to the assertions to which it is applied … The predicate 'true' can be applied only to sentences in a language. So to this extent what is true (i.e., what *can* be true or false) depends upon what can be said in that language. But this constraint does not mean that the language has some determining interactions with the states of affairs to be spoken of."[29] Like other deflationists, then, Rouse avoids the problems inherent to correspondence theories by radically isolating the practice of asserting from other human practices and by severing connections between the assertions we make and the objects about which we make assertions.

Nothing could be farther removed from Heidegger's conception of truth. Indeed, I find Heidegger's robust ontology more instructive for a philosophy of science than the stripped-down version given us by Rouse. Heidegger is fundamentally right, it seems to me, when he refuses to reduce truth to the correctness of assertions and when he refuses to limit truth-making capacities to the discoveredness of entities. He is correct when he refuses to exclude the ontological stance of those beings for whom truth itself is always already a question. Heidegger has successfully returned this question from the realms of Platonic perfection and Cartesian certainty to the world of lived experience and ongoing struggles for proper orientation.

Yet I also find Heidegger's conception problematic in several respects. He underestimates the role of predication in assertion. He misrepresents what I call predicative availability as a distorting of nonpredicative availability. His account of the asserted entity's discoveredness relies on a static notion of "selfsameness" (*Selbigkeit*),[30] and his notion of disclosedness privileges a direct encounter that belies the mediated character of human experience. In fact, Heidegger ends up making truth dependent upon human authenticity. Rather than work out these criticisms, which I have elaborated elsewhere,[31] however, let me now show how, by appropriating Heidegger's insights, a nondeflationary and reformational conception of truth can shed light on science and its role in society.

## 3. ASSERTORIC CORRECTNESS AND COMPREHENSIVE TRUTH

To this point I have written primarily about the truth of assertions and propositions, for which I use the term "correctness." As Heidegger saw, a severe shortcoming of propositionally inflected correspondence theories is that they reduce truth to assertoric or propositional correctness. This reduction misses many ordinary senses of the words "true" and "truly" – for example, when we say, "That was a truly unique experience" or "She is true to her word" or "This is a tried and true approach." The notion of assertoric correctness does not capture the connotations of "real," "dependable," and "reliable" in such usages. Heidegger challenges us to resist this reduction without severing the link between assertoric correctness and truth in a more comprehensive sense. The challenge is to explicate the link without reducing comprehensive truth to correctness, but also without letting correctness disappear into comprehensive truth.

### *3.1 Historical Process*

In my view, truth in its most comprehensive sense is a process rather than a property or a state of being. It is a historical process in which questions of social ethics and creaturely flourishing are always at stake. Moreover, this historical process receives its direction from a future that can break open the past and the present in dramatically unexpected ways. Consequently a philosophical conception of truth needs to retain a speculative dimension that exceeds the boundaries of modern science.[32]

Let me make this first approximation more precise. As I suggested in the previous chapter, the historical process of truth is a dynamic correlation between human fidelity and societal disclosure. By human fidelity I mean faithfulness to societal principles that both commonly hold for people and hold people in common. Solidarity and justice are two such principles. Societal principles are not Platonic forms, nor Augustinian ideas in the mind of God. Nor are they regulative ideas, on a Kantian model. Rather they are inescapable horizons that have emerged during the course of human history and that take shape in cultural practices and social institutions. Although they have emerged historically, however, they are not closed horizons. Rather they are open to a currently inexpressible future. This means that human fidelity to societal principles is itself a matter of societal struggle. No person or community has a monopoly on the truth, even as all of us are caught up in the challenge to be and to do what societal principles such as solidarity and justice require. To be caught up in this challenge implies that truth, in the sense of fidelity to principles, must be lived and not simply claimed.

Fidelity to societal principles is only one side of a dynamic correlation. The other side is a life-giving disclosure of society. By this I mean a process in which human beings and other creatures come to flourish in their interconnections. This process is not simply a future telos to societal endeavours. It is always already underway. What counts as "flourishing" can only be derived from actual circumstances and experiences. One could try to envision, for example, a society without poverty where the environment is not polluted. To envision this would draw on an experience of contemporary society, where poverty and pollution persist, and would thereby allow the idea of life-giving disclosure to acquire content through a critical social stance. This content would point toward different cultural practices and social institutions, ones that promote greater equity in the ownership and distribution of economic resources, for example. It would also point toward societal arrangements that do not allow creaturely habitats to become nothing more than captive resources for myopic exploitation.

In its most comprehensive sense, then, truth is a historical process that dynamically correlates two poles: human fidelity to societal principles, and a life-giving disclosure of society. These are *indissoluble* correlates, such that to promote interconnected flourishing is the point of human fidelity, and human fidelity to societal principles is a prerequisite for societal disclosure. The unfolding of a true society occurs in part by way of people being true. Correlatively, whether we are true to societal principles is partly confirmed by the extent to which creatures flourish in their interconnections.

### *3.2 Assertoric Correctness*

But what does all of this have to do with assertoric correctness? As the previous chapter indicated, assertoric practices are linked to comprehensive truth by virtue of their internal structure, their societal role, and their dependence on other modes of truth. Internally, assertoric practices involve a correlation between fidelity to the societal principle of logical validity and the predicative self-disclosure of asserted entities. To engage in assertoric interactions, people must have a certain level of faithfulness to the principle of logical validity. They cannot proceed as if the correctness or incorrectness of assertions does not matter. Further, the object about which they make assertions must disclose itself when it is asserted and is predicatively available.

A second link lies in how assertoric correctness supports the pursuit of other societal principles. To enact correlations of fidelity and disclosure includes the challenge to test the reach of the principles at stake and to establish the extent of the circumstances in which correlations are enacted. Typically we do this by making and considering assertions. When, for example, social justice is the principle at stake, it makes a difference to the enactment itself whose justice is at issue, and whether the flourishing of some comes at the expense of others. Consequently it matters that we have assertoric practices and discursively attuned institutions where deliberation about such differences can occur.

The third link consists of how other modes of truth provide context and support for the pursuit of assertoric correctness. Heidegger calls attention to this when he emphasizes the "derivative" character of assertoric interpretation and the "primordiality" of Dasein's disclosedness. If, for example, we continually violated the principle of justice as we pursued assertoric correctness, we would eventually lose the point of making correct assertions. At the same time, of course, discrepancies of this sort do occur more often than we like to admit. What is logically true can be contextually false: a "good argument" can support unjust and destructive arrangements. Conversely, what is "true in practice" may receive articulations and defences that are logically invalid. In this sense, our achieving mutual support between assertoric correctness and other modes of truth is vital to truth in its entirety.

## 4. THE VOCATION OF SCIENCE

The links I have just sketched are crucial for understanding the character and importance of scientific truth. Of all the differentiated institutions in modern society, science and, more broadly, the academic enterprise are the institutionalized settings in which questions of assertoric correctness play a leading role. We could call them dedicated sites for the pursuit of logical validity. Here, too, fidelity to societal principles must correlate dynamically with a life-giving disclosure of society. If the sciences are dedicated sites for pursuing logical validity where truth as a dynamic correlation is to unfold, then that has implications for the nature of science, its vocation in society, and its relationships with other practices and institutions. I want to explore each of these topics.

## 4.1 *Theoretical Inquiry*

Let me begin with the "nature" of science. When I taught an undergraduate philosophy of science course in the 1980s, I used a textbook that has the title *What Is This Thing Called Science?* Although it was an excellent introduction to the field, I found its title odd. For science is not a thing, no more than, in my view, truth in its most comprehensive sense is a property. It is even debatable whether science has "a nature."[33] Nevertheless, it is not out of place to make high-level claims about what science is like and how it tends to be distinct from other institutionalized sites in society such as art or religion. One tendency that characterizes the natural sciences, and, more broadly, all academic fields, is to engage in theoretical inquiry. This is by no means the only dominant tendency of science, as Rouse rightly points out, but it is a crucial one for understanding the distinctive character of scientific truth. For theoretical inquiry involves a discursive reflexivity that doubles the universalizing and decontextualizing impetus of assertoric activities. In tandem with this doubling goes the virtualization of predicative self-disclosure.

These concepts of discursive reflexivity and virtualization need some unpacking. Following Jürgen Habermas, I use the term "discursive" to refer to ways in which we probe, debate, and legitimate validity claims that arise in ordinary conversation. Within the natural sciences, the validity claims that receive the most discursive attention are claims to logical validity. Scientists regularly ask whether their findings are accurate, whether their explanations are illuminating, and whether their arguments stand up to logical scrutiny. Attention to such matters continually informs how scientists set up laboratories, conduct experiments, and report their findings. In that sense scientific discourse is *reflexive*: a continual feedback loop connects the making of logical validity claims and our testing them; scientific assertions get made with a direct view to their being disputed; and scientific discourse occurs with a singular devotion to the assertoric side of ordinary conversation. Science provides a hothouse environment for assertions and discourse.

If that is right, then one can see why the universalizing and decontextualizing impetus of assertoric activities would proliferate in the sciences. An environment has been created for removing assertions from their usual connections with other modes of interpretation, to treat them not as abstractions *within* a context of relevance but as abstractions *from* a context of relevance. In this setting, assertions that would make sense in everyday life often seem suspect or inadequate. For example, no self-respecting scientist, when explaining to his or her peers what happens at the end of each day, would simply assert, "The sun sets in the western sky."

At the same time, the entities about which assertions get made no longer "show themselves" in a straightforward way. At stake is no longer the accord between their predicative availability and nonpredicative aspects of their availability. Experimentally removed from the multiple connections they have with other entities, and from the contexts of relevance in which they are embedded, they show themselves under a single aspect or within a scientifically interpreted domain. Scientific inquiry allows entities to function as virtual realities, if you will, to engage in what one could label "self-dis/closure." This implies a different approach to the long-running debate between realists and instrumentalists in the philosophy of science. I would say that the entities about which scientists make assertions are real entities, but what gets asserted is not the real entity as such but a virtualized entity in its predicative self-dis/closure.

Hence scientific truth should be understood primarily as a dynamic correlation between discursively reflexive fidelity to logical validity and the virtualized predicative self-dis/closure of that about which scientific assertions get made. To engage in scientific inquiry, scientists must have a heightened devotion to the principle of logical validity, as manifested in their pursuit of empirical accuracy, explanatory insight, and argumentative consistency. And that about which they make their scientific claims must predicatively disclose itself in the right way under virtualizing conditions.

## 4.2 *Science and Society*

Discursive reflexivity and virtualized predicative self-dis/closure give science an important role to play in the pursuit of other societal principles and in a life-giving disclosure of society. I have already suggested that assertoric correctness allows us to test the reach of other societal principles and to establish the extent of the circumstances in which correlations between fidelity and disclosure are to unfold. In discourse within nonscientific contexts such as law and government, this testing and establishing must remain partially universal and partially context-bound. In scientific discourse, by contrast, we can push assertoric interpretation's universalizing and decontextualizing to an outer limit. This allows a society to problematize current correlations and to discuss new visions of what truth may require. Although that may be more readily apparent in the humanities and social sciences, I think it helps constitute the vocation of the natural sciences too. It also makes worrisome the technologizing of science, according to which "knowledge is power." If scientific inquiry no longer asks whether its "applications" and their "effects" serve a life-giving disclosure, it tends to sever the link with truth that makes science societally important. Deflationary accounts of truth simply ratify this tendency.

To resist such severance, and to maintain the link, science must include a double translation project. On the one hand, the contextual implications of scientific inquiry need to enter scientists' discourse about their findings, explanations, and arguments. On the other hand, nonscientific concerns about societal principles and life-giving disclosure must inform the ways in which scientific inquiry is constituted. Although this double translation project includes what has become known as the "ethics of science," it goes far beyond the set topics of this field. It takes us into what Joseph Rouse, under different assumptions, calls the "politics of science." It even touches upon those questions of orientation and direction that scientific purists have relegated to the realms of culture and religion.

Here questions arise about relationships between science and other societal sites. To the extent that scientific inquiry intensifies the pursuit of logical validity, support for this pursuit from other modes of truth becomes both more urgent and more difficult to sustain. Integration across societal domains is very difficult in highly differentiated societies that put a premium on specialization and divisions of labour. Often integration comes via economic and administrative systems that seem impervious to questions of social ethics and creaturely flourishing.[34] Insofar as integration is left to such systems, science itself becomes increasingly isolated from nonscientific concerns about justice and solidarity. It also becomes ever more enmeshed in the flywheels of turbocapitalism, where truth, in either its comprehensive or its scientific sense, does not seem to matter. Resisting this requires new transparency between science and other societal sites, as the call to "democratize" science suggests. To benefit the sciences, however, and thereby to benefit society, the push to open science for public discussion must aim at *normative* rather than systemic integration. For this, a proper conception of scientific truth is crucial. Conversely, the deflation of truth, both scientific and otherwise, inevitably, although perhaps inadvertently, strengthens the *systemic* integration that is already far advanced in an increasingly globalized society.

### *4.3 Science, Culture, and Religion*

That introduces some brief concluding remarks on culture and religion. Although not thematized as such, relationships among science, culture, and religion have been an undercurrent in this essay. The modern understanding of science's vocation presupposes both the autonomy of science from religion and fundamental differences between natural science and the arts and humanities. Although a purportedly "postmodern" setting has exposed these frameworks to greater scrutiny, in practice the operative framework has changed very little in the past half-century.

In certain respects that is a good thing: an improper "postmodern" reintegration of science, culture, and religion could be more destructive to all three, and thereby to society, than a problematic modern differentiation. Yet I hope my proposals about truth and science help us envision these relationships in a different way. I hope they help us not only respect legitimate diversity but also recognize a deeper continuity that calls for transparent intersections. If assertoric correctness is linked to comprehensive truth, and if science is a differentiated but societally interdependent site for pursuing assertoric correctness, then the lines connecting science with culture and religion can be just as strong as the boundaries distinguishing them. At least this is so if, as Heidegger affirms, and as I reaffirm, assertions are modes of interpretation. For interpretation is inherent to both culture and religion as well. As a site where directions for life and society are explored, proclaimed, and celebrated, organized religion is thoroughly interpretive. So is culture as a whole, where traditions take shape and die out, where social practices arise and get contested, where personal identities are nurtured and embraced.

When science lives up to its vocation in society, it will not avoid questions about direction, although it also will not receive its own direction from organized religion as such. Nor will a vocationally informed science avoid its being situated amid traditions and social practices, even though it also will not deny the universalizing and context-transcending impetus to its pursuit of scientific truth. How could it avoid asking about direction or situating itself in culture, if scientists understand their professional calling to pursue scientific truth *in order to serve* human fidelity and societal disclosure? Here the depth hermeneutics of science occurs, in the interpretation of what such service means, which scientists themselves must undertake.

Both as an assertoric field, then, and as a self-critical enterprise, science is hermeneutical through and through. So is scientific truth. Yet the interpretive character of scientific truth does not make it any less true. Rather, by negating the denial of a deep continuity among science, culture, and religion, assertoric interpretation and critical self-interpretation keep science connected. They keep science connected with the ongoing and dynamic process of truth.

# Epilogue

# Earth's Lament: Suffering, Hope, and Wisdom

## ICS Inaugural Address, 21 November 2003

Colleagues, Junior Members, Distinguished Guests, Family, and Friends:

"It is astonishing how few traces of human suffering one notices in the history of philosophy."[1] That was Theodor Adorno's comment in the mid-1960s, around the time ICS appointed Hendrik Hart, my predecessor in systematic philosophy, as its first faculty member. I should like to reflect on Adorno's perceptive comment. I want to ask why Western philosophy carries so few traces of human suffering. I also want to consider what a different philosophy would be like.

I shall be brief: about twenty-five minutes. I shall also be informal: no numbered propositions, and no technical commentaries on texts by other philosophers. My aim is to share some questions and passions that I bring to my position at ICS, and to do this at a high altitude in full view. Like a trapeze artist who performs without a net, I shall be doing philosophy without footnotes.[2] I trust you to rescue me if I should fall!

### 1. SUFFERING, HOPE, AND WISDOM

Adorno's comment points to the strongest motivations of his philosophy.[3] Elsewhere in the same book he says, "The need to let suffering speak is a condition of all truth."[4] If Adorno is right – if the need to express suffering is indeed a condition of all truth – then an inability or unwillingness to address and articulate human suffering would cast doubt on the legitimacy of philosophy itself.

Such doubt goes even deeper, for human suffering does not occur in a vacuum. The earliest chapters in the Hebrew scriptures tell of a global catastrophe in which the afflictions borne by human beings arrive with a curse upon other creatures. After the first humans eat fruit from the tree of the knowledge of good and evil, all that had been created good is disrupted, not only human life but also the Earth humans inhabit. Similarly, Saint Paul's letter to the Romans says, "The whole creation has been groaning in labor pains until now" (Rom. 8:22).[5] The groans of creation redouble in the inward moans of enslaved people.[6]

Human beings participate in Earth's lament. Human suffering and the destruction of creation go hand in hand. So do steps toward their removal. This is why, in the apocalyptic vision of Saint John, the new Earth sustains a fruit-bearing tree whose leaves "are for the healing of the nations" (Rev. 22:2).

The close connection between human suffering and Earth's lament poses an additional challenge for contemporary philosophy. Western philosophy has a long history of looking down on the nonhuman world. Not only is it astonishing how few traces of *human* suffering show up in Western philosophy; it is equally remarkable how strongly this tradition has suppressed the groans of *all creation*. Yet human suffering and Earth's lament continue, challenging contemporary philosophers to lend them a voice right within the sanitized halls of academia.

To meet this challenge, philosophers need both patient hope and comprehensive wisdom: patient hope for a new Earth, and comprehensive wisdom about the shape of the old. In the Hebrew and Christian scriptures, suffering never has the last word, even though suffering can last longer and go deeper than words can tell. Suffering and hope occur together. In Genesis, the woman's labour pains give way to the birth of a child (Gen. 4:1–2). In Revelation, the apocalyptic destruction of evil ushers in a "new Earth" where God will live with human beings and "will wipe every tear from their eyes" (Rev. 21:1–4). So too, in Romans, the groans of God's children, as they await bodily liberation, arise from hope for an inexpressible future. Paul writes: "Hope that is seen is not hope. For who hopes for what is seen? But if we hope for what we do not see, we wait with patience" (Rom. 8:24–5).[7] Creation's deepest lamentations emerge from hope that things can be better, better in ways human beings can scarcely imagine. If the promise of God's future were not received in hope, the need to express human suffering might disappear.

Comprehensive wisdom about the contemporary world is also required. Here we touch a sore spot in philosophy today. Western philosophy has long described itself, in the words of Plato's *Republic*, as a friend of wisdom and in love with truth. To be a true friend of wisdom, philosophy has tried to be comprehensive, gathering all of reality into one theoretical system. But contemporary philosophy in the West has given up on that project. At most it seeks specialized insight into the world right now, not comprehensive wisdom about the world's past and future.[8] Hence Western philosophy has largely lost its speculative moment. It does not think out of hope, nor does it let intimations of a better future shape its comprehension of the present and past. Having lost touch with hope, and having abandoned the project of comprehensive wisdom, contemporary philosophy is not able to let suffering speak. And that inability casts doubt on philosophy's purported love for truth.

Currently, then, the philosophy invited by Earth's lament is in short supply. Yet Adorno's work shows how a philosophy that is committed to truth can address the need to express suffering. And the reformational philosophy of Herman Dooyeweerd, Dirk Vollenhoven, and their successors shows how a passion for comprehensive wisdom can arise out of hope for God's future. So let me explore with you the shape of a contemporary philosophy in which neither side is lacking: a philosophy committed to truth and passionate for comprehensive wisdom, a philosophy driven to express suffering out of hope for God's future. More specifically, let me discuss three topics: societal evil, spiritual struggle, and social critique.

## 2. SOCIETAL EVIL

Saint Augustine's dialogue *On Free Choice of the Will* gives a classic statement of what philosophers label "the problem of evil": If God is both all-powerful and entirely good, how can there be evil in the world? This question often arises as an argument against monotheistic faith such as one finds in Judaism, Christianity, and Islam. In response, Augustine distinguishes between evil that people do and evil that they undergo, between so-called moral evil and natural evil – for example, between my murdering someone and my being severely burned in a forest fire caused by lightning. Augustine's dialogue concentrates on moral evil, and it makes individual human beings fully responsible for what they do.

Here Augustine, like many philosophers after him, simply overlooks the most difficult type of evil. The most difficult type is not moral evil, not the evil *individuals* do. Nor is it natural evil, the evil that happens to individuals because of circumstances entirely outside human control. Rather, the most difficult evil, difficult both to understand and to resist, is evil that seeps into cultural practices and social institutions, gathers strength over the years, and comes to dominate an entire societal formation. I call this type of evil "societal evil." Societal evil cannot be explained away as a natural occurrence outside human control. Yet it also cannot be ascribed to specific individuals or groups, as if it were solely their responsibility. Societal evil is distinct from natural evil and moral evil, although not unrelated to them. If contemporary philosophy does not address the topic of societal evil, it cannot do justice to either suffering or hope.

That is why Adorno's work is crucial for philosophers today. Without flinching, Adorno asks how philosophy is possible "after Auschwitz." He recognizes that the destruction viciously inflicted upon millions during the Nazi era both defies and requires philosophical reflection. In my own terms, what happened in mid-twentieth-century Europe, and what continues to happen in equally brutal ways around the world today, are manifestations of societal evil. They are signs of evil that has seeped into our practices and institutions and gathered strength and come to dominate society.

Herman Dooyeweerd had some inkling of this when, writing about social reconstruction after World War II, he said the future of Dutch society depended upon the outcome of an antithesis between two ground motives or spiritual forces.[9] In my judgment, however, Dooyeweerd neglected a societal evil that does not neatly stem from, say, Calvinists or Catholics or socialists or liberals. He was unable to plumb the depths of an evil in which every community is implicated and to which the very structure of society contributes. The reasons for this inability were both religious and philosophical.[10]

Religiously, the Kuyperian experience of antithesis had become so firmly tied to maintaining the community's own practices and institutions that even a great thinker like Dooyeweerd tended to equate the conflict between good and evil with a power struggle between concrete communities of commitment. Yet this tendency violates Dooyeweerd's own better insight when, for example, he says the spiritual antithesis "runs right through the Christian life itself."[11]

Philosophically, Dooyeweerd was unable to plumb the depths of societal evil in the West because he gave normative priority to structural differentiation in society. He turned the idea of sphere sovereignty – Abraham Kuyper's crucial contribution to modern social policy – into a creational principle that lies beyond critique. Hence Dooyeweerd could not seriously ask whether the Western differentiation of social institutions, such as government, corporations, and universities, might not itself embody and foster societal evil. When the historical process of differentiation becomes a structural hypernorm for evaluating social change, it becomes difficult to assess the environmental, cultural, and interpersonal costs of this process. They come to seem like mere "side effects" of a process considered intrinsically good, rather than potential signs of societal evil.

What are contemporary philosophers in the tradition of Kuyper and Dooyeweerd to do? Should we reject "the antithesis" and embrace a global dialogue in which all religions become one? Should we give up the idea of sphere sovereignty as a once-useful social policy whose time has passed? I do not see how either response would make us better able to recognize and address societal evil. Instead, reformational philosophers need to reexamine the connection between spiritual struggle and normative social critique. Let me make a few proposals in that regard.

## 3. SPIRITUAL STRUGGLE

By "spiritual struggle" I do not mean something otherworldly and disembodied. Rather I mean an ongoing struggle within cultural practices and social institutions for the direction in which a societal formation will head. It is as ordinary as the clothes we wear and the housing we inhabit. Yet it is all-embracing and therefore extremely difficult to pin down. Augustine noted this struggle in his famous history of the conflict between the secular city and the city of God. So did Horkheimer and Adorno, in their formulation of a "dialectic of enlightenment," as did Karl Marx before them, in his accounts of social alienation and economic exploitation.

Faith-oriented thinkers are often tempted to place their own account of spiritual struggle on the right side of this battle. Yet it is precisely the character of spiritual struggle that such self-legitimation can never be fully justified. For the struggle always exceeds anyone's contribution to it, and any contribution can go in a different direction from the one envisioned. Perhaps this helps explain why Hegel said ultimate judgment in the struggle among nations belongs to a universal world spirit: *Die Weltgeschichte ist das Weltgericht* ("World history is the world's court of justice").[12] Unfortunately Hegel's dialectical forest obscures the tree whose leaves are "for the healing of the nations." Yet the grandeur of his narrative corrects the blindness of right-wing Christians who identify specific countries as an "evil empire" or an "axis of evil." I dare say such parochial and politically motivated identifications are themselves signs of societal evil.

Precisely because there is societal evil, philosophers must come to grips with spiritual struggle. We must ask in which direction our society is headed. Is it headed toward a new Earth in which justice and peace embrace?[13] Or does its direction simply prolong and intensify Earth's lament? Further, in the context of such global questions, we must ask about specific practices and institutions in their current constellations. To what extent does the art we promote or the schooling we provide or the government we support bear the promise of God's future? If we conclude that the contemporary societal formation is fundamentally misdirected, then reform measures will never be enough. Society as a whole will need to be transformed. This can occur only through a prolonged spiritual struggle to which our own contributions will be modest and inherently flawed.

## 4. SOCIAL CRITIQUE

If we left matters at this comprehensive level, however, the shape of societal evil would still be vague. Philosophical wisdom must be more precise. Otherwise reflections on society's direction evaporate into either abstract utopias or debilitating despair. They become abstractly utopian when we project the vision of a new Earth beyond contemporary society without any idea of how this vision could be pursued. Alternatively, our reflections turn into dirges of despair when we overlook what is already good in contemporary society. Indeed, utopianism and despair are reverse images of each other. Both are comprehensive critiques lacking concrete wisdom.[14]

Concrete wisdom is an embodied understanding of societal principles and their practical operation. By "societal principles" I mean fundamental expectations that commonly hold for people and that people hold in common. These expectations hold and are held in the context of historically developed cultural practices and social institutions. Economic resourcefulness, political justice, and social solidarity are examples of such principles at work in contemporary Western society. This does not imply, however, that societal principles are unchanging absolutes. I see them rather as "shared reference points that have emerged historically through clashes between societies and within them."[15] They are what Vollenhoven and Dooyeweerd call "norms."[16] Societal principles such as political justice are historically constituted and future-oriented callings in which the voice of God can be heard and traces of a new Earth can appear. But they are not available to us without spiritual struggle amid suffering and evil.

That fact prompts two additional comments about the task of social critique. First, no easy distinction can be made out between the structure of human societies and their direction, or between legitimately pursuing valid societal principles and inadvertently fostering societal evil. Yet, second, the notion of societal evil makes little sense apart from an idea of what is societally good.[17] And an idea of societal good must appeal to societal principles that are currently in effect, principles that the philosopher finds valid and worth pursuing.

If contemporary philosophers wish to let human suffering speak – if we wish to lend a voice to Earth's lament – then we must offer a comprehensive and normative critique of societal evil. We must offer this critique out of hope for a future that comprehends *us* much more than we comprehend *it*. We may not pretend that our own claims about justice or peace do not themselves participate in societal evil. But we also may not act as if societal evil is so powerful and pervasive that the tree of the knowledge of good and evil is not always already becoming the tree of global healing.

## 5. EARTH'S LAMENT

Perhaps an image will help. What I have said about philosophy's task resonates with a sculpture that stood for several years in the Board Room at the Institute for Christian Studies in Toronto.[18] When the artwork appears in optimal lighting, one sees a brilliantly illuminated sculpture standing on nine blocks of wood. A young corkscrew willow has been cut off before it could flourish. Its dead leaves have been removed, its bare branches disassembled. Now it stands forcibly reconstructed, twisting through a skeletal cage of whittled sumac. The willow's branches, carved into spears, are rejoined with sharp wooden rivets into the simulacrum of a tree. Snakelike, they writhe through each other as their trunk rests rootless in a nest of interlaced twigs. Cemented sand fills the nest – blasted soil where something once grew. Greying rocks, circling the tree trunk like petrified eggs, are all that remain. The gnarled but youthful branches of this caged and nested tree spiral upward toward an elevation they will never reach.

This sculpture, by Joyce Recker, is titled "Earth's Lament." In its stark complexity, it offers an open-ended metaphor for longing amid loss, for renewal amid destruction. The philosophy I have sketched here attempts a more prosaic articulation of a similar vision. Like this sculpture, it would glimpse the tree of healing within the cage of societal evil. It would lend a voice to human suffering. It would provide echoes of Earth's lament.

## APPENDIX ON SOCIETAL PRINCIPLES

Let me briefly show how my emphases on the historical embeddedness, the eschatological openness, and the vocational character of societal principles revise the notion of "norm" in Vollenhoven and Dooyeweerd. First, although I agree with them that societal principles require human formation, I do not think that societal principles are in effect prior to their formation. A societal principle such as political justice is itself a continually contested and historically unfolded outworking of the flourishing to which human beings are called within the fabric of their cultural practices and social institutions.

My second revision is to suggest that societal principles were not simply given or fixed when human beings were created. Not only do these principles emerge during the course of human history, but also they could change dramatically, in ways we cannot foresee, in God's inexpressible future. We do not know now what political justice might require in the new Earth. So we must always hold this principle open for what we do not know.

My third revision is to claim that the human ability to make logical distinctions is not definitive for the nature of societal principles. Rather the ability to distinguish, say, between justice and injustice itself manifests something deeper. It manifests an instruction and invitation and guidance that comes to societally constituted human beings from outside themselves and continually calls for their response.[19] In this sense, none of the patterns and conditions that hold for other creatures is a straightforward law for human life. They are callings that always require societally constituted responses. Where our responses foster illness and poverty or destroy habitats, we are collectively responsible, not simply for the consequences of our practices and institutions but also for the societal principles according to which these are organized and maintained.

# Publication Information

Note: This list provides information about the sources for all chapters within this volume, in their order of appearance.

1 "The Great Turning Point: Religion and Rationality in Dooyeweerd's Transcendental Critique." *Faith and Philosophy* 21 (January 2004): 65–89.

2 "Reformational Philosophy after Dooyeweerd and Vollenhoven." Panel presentation for a symposium on *Dooyeweerd or Vollenhoven: Does It Make a Difference?* at Redeemer University College, Ancaster, Ontario, 7 April 2006. Partially revised and previously unpublished.

3 "Dooyeweerd's Conception of Truth: Exposition and Critique." *Philosophia Reformata* 73 (2008): 170–89.

4 "Dooyeweerd's Modal Theory: Questions in the Ontology of Science." Originally titled "The Hermeneutic Problem of Modal Theory in *A New Critique of Theoretical Thought*." Research paper for a seminar in systematic philosophy, Institute for Christian Studies, Toronto, 1973. Stylistically revised and previously unpublished; preface and postscript added in 2015.

5 "Fantastic Things: Critical Notes Toward a Social Ontology of the Arts." *Philosophia Reformata* 60 (1995): 37–54.

6 "God, Law, and Cosmos: Issues in Hendrik Hart's Ontology." Originally published as "Existence, Nomic Conditions, and God: Issues in Hendrik Hart's Ontology." *Philosophia Reformata* 50, no. 1 (1985): 47–65.

7 "Artistic Truth, Linguistically Turned: Variations on a Theme from Adorno, Habermas, and Hart." In *Philosophy as Responsibility: A*

*Celebration of Hendrik Hart's Contribution to the Discipline*, edited by Ronald A. Kuipers and Janet Catherina Wesselius, 129–49. Lanham, MD: University Press of America, 2002.

8 "The Inner Reformation of Reason: Issues in Hendrik Hart's Epistemology." Panel presentation for a symposium on *Reason and Responsibility in Reformational Philosophy*, Institute for Christian Studies, Toronto, 27 February 2004. Previously unpublished.

9 "Metacritique: Adorno, Vollenhoven, and the Problem-Historical Method." Originally titled "Metacritique in the Historiography of Philosophy" and presented as an invited lecture at the Institute for Christian Studies, Toronto, 25 March 1985. Significantly revised and previously unpublished.

10 "Defining Humankind: Scheler, Cassirer, and Hart." Originally titled "Scheler, Cassirer, and Transfunctional Definitions of Humankind" and presented in a shorter version at the XVIII World Congress of Philosophy, Brighton, England, 21–27 August 1988. Expanded with a postscript and previously unpublished.

11 "Good Cities or Cities of the Good? Radical Augustinian Social Criticism." Originally published as "Good Cities or Cities of the Good? Radical Augustinians, Societal Structures, and Normative Critique." In *Radical Orthodoxy and the Reformed Tradition: Creation, Covenant, and Participation*, edited by James K.A. Smith and James H. Olthuis, 135–49. Grand Rapids, MI: Baker Academic Press, 2005.

12 "Religion in Public: Passages from Hegel's *Philosophy of Right*." *University of Toronto Journal for Jewish Thought* 1 (April 2010). http://tjjt.cjs.utoronto.ca/.

13 "Macrostructures and Societal Principles: An Architectonic Critique." Originally presented as an invited keynote lecture, *The Future of Creation Order* conference, VU University Amsterdam, 18 August 2011, and revised for publication in *The Future of Creation Order*, edited by Gerrit Glas, Jeroen de Ridder, Govert Buijs, and Annette Mosher (Dordrecht, Netherlands: Springer, forthcoming).

14 "Unfinished Business: Toward a Reformational Conception of Truth." *Philosophia Reformata* 74 (2009): 1–20.

15 "Science, Society, and Culture: Against Deflationism." Revised version of a paper originally titled "Truth and Interpretation: Science, Religion, and Culture" and presented as the Kenneth Konyndyk Memorial Lecture, sponsored by the Society of Christian

Philosophers, in conjunction with the Central Division Meeting of the American Philosophical Association, Chicago, 19 April 2007; first presented at Calvin College, 15 April 2004, as an invited lecture in the series *Interpreting Science and Religion: Contributions from Continental Philosophy*, and repeated at Redeemer University College in Ancaster, Ontario, 29 September 2005, and Trinity Christian College in Palos Heights, Illinois, 20 October 2005. Previously unpublished.

Epilogue. "Earth's Lament: Suffering, Hope, and Wisdom." Lightly revised inaugural lecture, Institute for Christian Studies, Toronto, 21 November 2003; original version posted online at the ICS Institutional Repository, http://hdl.handle.net/10756/294559. A revised version was published online in *The Other Journal*, issue no. 14 on *Death and Dying*, 27 January 2009. http://theotherjournal.com/2009/01/27/earths-lament-suffering-hope-and-wisdom/.

# Notes

## INTRODUCTION

1 Adorno, *Minima Moralia*, 247.
2 For a state-of-the art study of Kuyper's life and work, see Bratt, *Abraham Kuyper*.
3 Zuidervaart, "A Tradition Transfigured," 382.
4 See ch. 1 in this volume for citations and discussion of secondary literature on Dooyeweerd and Vollenhoven through approximately 2002. Van der Walt, *At the Cradle of a Christian Philosophy*, situates their thought in the broader Calvinist tradition. For a critical reconstruction of their systematic philosophies with reference to Kuyper, see Ive, *The Roots of Reformational Philosophy*. This work is available via the website *All of Life Redeemed*, which aims to give people access to information, articles, and books from a reformational perspective: http://www.allofliferedeemed.co.uk/Ive/Ive_Vollenhoven_%20%20Dooyeweerd_index2014.pdf.
5 I do not mean to suggest that Dooyeweerd and Vollenhoven simply embraced these traditions. See, for example, Tol, *Philosophy in the Making*. Tol's study of how reformational philosophy emerged in the 1920s shows that Vollenhoven developed a crucial framework for criticizing influential neo-Kantian themes within his intellectual milieu. See also Kok, *Vollenhoven*. For comparable studies on Dooyeweerd's early formative years, see the doctoral dissertation by Roger Henderson, "Illuminating Law," and Henderson's more recent essay "Gum and Wire, A Time for Everything under the Sun."
6 Reformational philosophy's troubled relationships to Western antiquity are explored in a collection of essays edited by Sweetman, *In the Phrygian Mode*. Tentative signs of greater rapprochement between Reformed epistemology and reformational philosophy have appeared in recent years. For

example, a recent issue of *Philosophia Reformata* features five essays on the work of Alvin Plantinga, with a response by Plantinga – see *Philosophia Reformata* 79 (2014): 1–96. Now the journal also carries a subtitle – *International Philosophical Journal of Christianity, Science, and Society* – to indicate that, according to its new mission statement, it welcomes contributions that contain philosophical reflection in relation to the Christian tradition without restriction to the reformational tradition.

7 See in this connection Bartholomew and Goheen, *Christian Philosophy*. In this introductory textbook, ICS alumni Bartholomew and Goheen devote most of Part 3 ("Christian Philosophy Today") to Reformed epistemology and reformational philosophy.

8 Robert VanderVennen tells ICS's story in *A University for the People*.

9 Herman Dooyeweerd, NC 1: 4, WW 1: 6; translation modified.

10 Vollenhoven, *Isagôgè Philosophiae*, 14.

11 I put "categories" in scare quotes because Dooyeweerd and Vollenhoven, like Martin Heidegger, reject both the substance metaphysics of the Aristotelian tradition and the transcendental idealism of Immanuel Kant, where "categories" play contrasting but prominent roles. Dooyeweerd prefers to speak of ontological "horizons," while Vollenhoven uses the term "determinants" (*bepaaldheden*) to indicate his fundamental ontological frameworks.

12 Vollenhoven explicitly distinguishes a third "determinant" as well – namely, the antithesis between good and evil – and he discusses this in terms of "direction" as distinct from and related to "structure." See Vollenhoven, *Isagôgè Philosophiae*, 56–62.

13 Later writings also distinguish the kinetic or kinematic modality among the pre-physical modalities. For more details on reformational philosophy's modal framework, see "Dooyeweerd's Modal Theory," ch. 4 in this volume.

14 Vollenhoven, "Divergences: Report I," 136–7.

15 Kuyper, *Lectures on Calvinism*, 70–1. As Kuyper is reported to have said in 1897, the ruling passion of his life was that "God's holy ordinances shall be established again in the home, in the school and in the State for the good of the people; to carve as it were into the conscience of the nation the ordinances of the Lord, to which Bible and Creation bear witness, until the nation pays homage again to God." Quoted by de Vries, "Biographical Note," in Kuyper, *Lectures on Calvinism*, iii.

16 According to Kuyper, the Calvinist's "faith in the ordinances of God" is "the firmly rooted conviction that all life has first been in the *thoughts* of

God, before it came to be realized in *Creation*." Moreover the "moral world-order" remains "just what it was from the beginning. It lays full claim, not only to the believer … but to every human being and to all human relationships … Calvinism … places us under the impress of the majesty of God, and subjects us to [God's] eternal ordinances and unchangeable commandments." Kuyper, *Lectures on Calvinism*, 70–2.

17 Solidarity, resourcefulness, and justice are my terms. Dooyeweerd's concepts for the modally distinguishable economic and juridical "laws" (societal principles, in my own terms) are frugality and retribution, respectively. He does not seem to have a worked-out concept of the "law-side" for the social modality, which he discusses in terms of social "intercourse" (*omgang*) and relates to "the norms of courtesy, good manners, tact, sociableness, fashion and so on" (NC 2: 141n2).

18 Dooyeweerd, *Roots of Western Culture*, 71.

19 Vollenhoven, "Norm and Law of Nature," 105.

20 In line with his emphasis on the God/law/cosmos triad, Vollenhoven says we need to replace the duality between divine law and human law with a three-part distinction among (1) "the law of God that stands as norm above the cosmos" and touches humans directly but other creaturely beings only indirectly, via human beings (this is the "double love command"); (2) the cosmos, including humankind; and (3) "positive" laws (i.e., what he calls principles elsewhere) whereby "office bearers" in various social institutions "positivize God's law, correctly or not, primarily for human life." Vollenhoven, "Divergences: Report I," 137.

21 Ibid. The crucial phrase, of course, is "in the cosmos." Law in Vollenhoven's preferred sense is not in the cosmos, not even as a Dooyeweerdian "law-side."

22 "A 'norm' is always a *rational* standard, founded in the logical manner of distinction. Therefore it is confusing to call the central commandment of love a *norm*." Dooyeweerd, NC 2: 156n2.

23 Dooyeweerd, *Roots of Western Culture*, 71; Vollenhoven, "Divergences: Report I," 138. Vollenhoven's notion of office bearer probably stems from his appropriation of Reformed theology and polity, where the ecclesiastical office bearers are the appointed or elected ministers, elders, and deacons, in cooperation with all communicant members in their general office as believers. Dooyeweerd explicitly endorses Reformed polity as the best way to understand ecclesiastical authority in light of the "structural principle" of the church as an institution, and he rejects any attempt to construe such authority along the lines of a political democracy. See Dooyeweerd, NC 3: 509–61, WW 3: 451–509.

24 Vollenhoven, *Isagôgè Philosophiae*, 72, with "institution" substituted for Vollenhoven's term "connection" (*levensverband*), itself an abbreviation for "societal connection" (*samenlevingsverband*).
25 Ibid., 71.
26 Vollenhoven, "Divergences: Report I," 138.
27 Dooyeweerd, NC 3: 180, 274–8, 324–9; WW 3: 219–21, 271–7.
28 See the essays "The Great Turning Point," "Dooyeweerd's Conception of Truth," "God, Law, and Cosmos," "Defining Humankind," and "Religion in Public," ch. 1, 3, 6, 10, and 12, respectively, in this volume.
29 See Vollenhoven, "Divergences: Report I," 139. In this report Vollenhoven also says that, unlike Dooyeweerd, he does not think the arithmetic and spatial functions belong to the temporal order (138). This clearly is a different position from the one Vollenhoven takes in *Isagôgè Philosophiae*, 33, where, like Dooyeweerd, he says we find time "in all the modalities of the subject units: in the arithmetic as succession, in the spatial as simultaneity," etc.
30 Vollenhoven, "Divergences: Report I," 140.
31 Dooyeweerd, *Roots of Western Culture*, 91, 93.
32 Vollenhoven, "Faith: Its Nature, Structure, and Significance for Science," 72–3.
33 Dooyeweerd, NC 1: 3–4, WW 1: 5; translation modified.
34 Vollenhoven, *Isagôgè Philosophiae*, 9–10.
35 For details about this intermodal revision and its implications, see esp. ch. 4, 7, 8, and 15 in this volume.
36 For some implications to these changes in social ontology, see esp. ch. 5, 12, and 13 in this volume.
37 Chaplin, *Herman Dooyeweerd*, 311.
38 See, for example, the conference volume edited by Griffioen and Verhoogt, *Norm and Context in the Social Sciences*.
39 Griffioen,"Is a Pluralist Ethos Possible?" and Mouw and Griffioen, *Pluralisms and Horizons*. In Griffioen's terminology, contextual plurality has to do with cultural differences; structural plurality, with the diversity of social institutions; and directional plurality, with religious differences in Dooyeweerd and Vollenhoven's sense (i.e., "spiritual," in my own vocabulary). The book by Mouw and Griffioen uses the term "associational" rather than "structural" to refer to institutional diversity.
40 See the two conference publications *An Ethos of Compassion and the Integrity of Creation*, ed. Walsh, Hart, and VanderVennen, and *The Future of Creation Order*, ed. Glas et al.
41 Chaplin, *Herman Dooyeweerd*, 106.

42 See esp. ch. 13 and 14 in this volume, as well as the epilogue.
43 See ch. 12 and 13 in this volume.
44 See the chapter titled "Ethical Turns" in Zuidervaart, *Social Philosophy after Adorno*, especially the section titled "Social Ethics and Global Politics," 162–75.
45 See ch. 3 and 14 in this volume.
46 I discuss Hegel's conception of art, religion, and philosophy as complementary realms of comprehensive truth in Zuidervaart, "Art, Religion, and the Sublime: After Hegel."
47 That art, religion, and science are among these differentiated social institutions of knowledge is a subtextual thread running through this volume – see esp. ch. 7, 12, and 15.
48 See, for example, Alcoff, *Real Knowing*, and Rouse, *Knowledge and Power*. I discuss Rouse's social epistemology in ch. 15 in this volume.
49 See, for example, Lynch, *Truth in Context*.
50 As I show in ch. 3, Dooyeweerd describes truth as an accordance (*overeenstemming*) between human knowledge and divine laws for creation and human life – minimally, the central religious law of love, the law-side to various modal spheres or aspects, and the structural principles of individuality. Vollenhoven, in an early essay whose "logos" theory he later abandoned, distinguishes "communicated truth" from "sought after truth," and he distinguishes "propositional truth" from "truth" as such (or truth in general), in order to make the following argument: Truth "binds the one who makes a judgment" and, in that respect, it "'holds' and has a normative authority." Yet truth as such should never be equated with the "validity (*gelden*)" of a proposition or judgment. For truth in essence is the created logos whose connection with the rest of creation is "a *cosmic* ordering," and this ordering is God's work. See Vollenhoven, "Fundamentals of a Theory of Knowledge," manuscript, 3, 6, 8. This is a translation of Vollenhoven's "Enkele grondlijnen der kentheorie."
51 This is what, following Hendrik Hart, I mean when I call truth a "totality concept" in the postscript to "Defining Humankind," ch. 10 in this volume.

## CHAPTER ONE

1 Dooyeweerd, "Foreword (Abbreviated) to the First Edition," NC 1: v, WW 1: v; translation modified.
2 Traces of neo-Kantian and Husserlian thought abound in Dooyeweerd's ontology, epistemology, and social philosophy, as others have pointed out. See Wolters, "The Intellectual Milieu of Herman Dooyeweerd," 1–19. In

the same volume, which marks the fiftieth anniversary of Dooyeweerd's first publishing *De Wijsbegeerte der Wetsidee*, Calvin Seerveld discusses the links between Dooyeweerd's and Nicolai Hartmann's ontologies; see Seerveld, "Dooyeweerd's Legacy for Aesthetics: Modal Law Theory," esp. 55–64.

3 Meynell, "The Philosophy of Dooyeweerd," 265–87, briefly mentions H. Steen, one of these early Calvinist critics, but fails to point out that Steen's book *Philosophia Deformata* is a diatribe against *Vollenhoven*, not Dooyeweerd. Steen barely discusses Dooyeweerd's writings and shows little comprehension of Vollenhoven's. The polemical character of Steen's book is apparent from the title, which mocks *Philosophia Reformata*, the scholarly journal begun in 1936, with Dooyeweerd as editor-in-chief until 1976, and with Vollenhoven as president of the Association for Calvinist Philosophy that sponsored the journal. Nor was Steen's book title very original. Like some of the book's contents, it derives from a more substantial critique of Dooyeweerd by the theologian Valentine Hepp in four brochures titled *Dreigende Deformatie*. Despite such preemptive strikes by fellow Dutch Calvinists, the journal and the association continue to thrive today.

4 Dooyeweerd began to write and speak in English after World War II, and he played an active role in the translation of NC. The following of his English-language publications are especially important for assessing how he viewed the significance of his own project: "Introduction to a Transcendental Criticism of Philosophic Thought" and *In the Twilight of Western Thought*. Similarly important is his 1956 essay "Calvinistische Wijsbegeerte" ("Calvinist Philosophy"), which has been translated by John Vriend as "Christian Philosophy: An Exploration" in Dooyeweerd, *Christian Philosophy and the Meaning of History*, 1–37.

5 The intellectual centre for fundamentalist Presbyterians was Westminster Theological Seminary in Philadelphia. Dooyeweerd's most important critic at Westminster was Cornelius Van Til, and his most important expositor there was Robert Knudsen. Van Til had an intellectualist Kuyperian background. He left a pastorate in the Christian Reformed Church to become a leading figure in Reformed apologetics. Highly instructive exchanges between Dooyeweerd and Van Til and between Knudsen and Van Til can be found in Geehan, ed., *Jerusalem and Athens*, 74–127 and 275–305. For details about Van Til's earlier criticisms of Dooyeweerd, as well as about Dooyeweerd's Dutch Calvinist precursors and early critics, see Young, *Towards a Reformed Philosophy*.

6 The postwar centre for intellectualist Kuyperians was Calvin College and Calvin Theological Seminary in Grand Rapids, Michigan. William Harry

Jellema, the leader of the opposition to Dooyeweerd, taught philosophy at the college 1920–35 and 1946–63. When H. Evan Runner joined the college's philosophy department in 1951, legendary battles began between the "Jellemanians" and the "Dooyeweerdians." Runner was a graduate of both Westminster Theological Seminary and the Vrije Universiteit in Amsterdam who wrote his dissertation under Vollenhoven's supervision. He soon became the leading North American proponent of Dooyeweerd and Vollenhoven's philosophy and a founder of the Institute for Christian Studies (ICS) in Toronto, a graduate school for interdisciplinary philosophy and theology established in 1967. Most of the original faculty at ICS had studied with Runner at Calvin College and received their graduate training at the Vrije Universiteit. By contrast, several founders of the Society of Christian Philosophers were students of Jellema or of Jellema's own students, including Alvin Plantinga, Nicholas Wolterstorff, and Kenneth Konyndyk. Although I never studied at Calvin College, I taught there in 1985–2002 and enjoyed excellent collegial relations with the "Jellemanians." My own graduate training came at the Vrije Universiteit and the Institute for Christian Studies, where I took up a position as Professor of Philosophy in 2002.

7 Published in the journal *Studiën: Tijdschrift voor godsdienst, wetenschap en letteren* 67 (1935): 85–99; 68 (1936): 152–3; and 69 (1937): 324–31. For summaries of Dutch Thomist criticisms of Dooyeweerd and his responses to them, see Choi, "Dialogue and Antithesis," 50–1, 86–97. Readers of Dutch should also consult Geertsema, "Dooyeweerd in discussie met de rooms-katholieke filosofie," 228–54.

8 Marlet, *Grundlinien der kalvinistischen "Philosophie der Gesetzesidee" als christlicher Transzendentalphilosophie*. Dooyeweerd's "Zum Geleit" appears on pages v–vii.

9 Choi, *Dialogue and Antithesis*, 91–2. See also the objections reported therein of the Dutch Calvinist Aquinas scholar J.A. Aertsen, who argues "that Dooyeweerd interprets Aquinas too exclusively from the perspective of Aristotle and too little as a Christian thinker" (93).

10 Like Calvin Seerveld, who coined the term from the Dutch "*reformatorisch*," I use "reformational" to include Dooyeweerd and Vollenhoven and those scholars who both build on their work and identify themselves as participants in the Kuyperian tradition of Calvinist Christianity. See Bartholomew and Strauss, "*Bread* and Not Stones: An Introduction to the Thought of Calvin Seerveld," esp. 3n1. Reformational scholars have produced a large body of secondary literature on Dooyeweerd, in both Dutch and English. In chronological order, representative anthologies include

*Philosophy and Christianity*, ed. W.F. De Gaay Fortman et al.; *The Legacy of Herman Dooyeweerd*, ed. C.T. McIntire; *Herman Dooyeweerd 1894–1977*, ed. Geertsema et al.; *Christian Philosophy at the Close of the Twentieth Century*, ed. Griffioen and Balk; and *Contemporary Reflections on the Philosophy of Herman Dooyeweerd*, ed. Strauss and Botting. The journal *Philosophia Reformata* is the single most important source for "in-house" debates on these issues. Since the 1980s the journal has published an increasing number of articles in English.

11 By "theoretical thought" Dooyeweerd means the sort of abstractive thinking that characterizes philosophy and the sciences. He uses the term "science" in the broad sense that attaches to "*wetenschap*" in Dutch and "*Wissenschaft*" in German. It encompasses all the academic disciplines, including mathematics, the natural sciences, the social sciences, and the humanities.

12 See Freeman, "A Comparative Study of the Relationship between Philosophy and Theology as Exemplified by Representatives of Neo-Augustinianism, Neo-Thomism, and Neo-Existentialism"; Conradie, *The Neo-Calvinistic Concept of Philosophy*; and Brümmer, *Transcendental Criticism and Christian Philosophy*. Both Conradie and Brümmer hailed from South Africa. Their interest probably stemmed from Dooyeweerd's substantial debates, dating from the 1930s, with the South African Calvinist philosopher Hendrik Stoker, himself a former student of the German phenomenologist Max Scheler.

13 The fact that the authors of the first general English-language introductions to Dooyeweerd's thought were not scholars, and certainly not professional philosophers, has not helped the academic reception of Dooyeweerd's thought in North America. (J.M. Spier was a pastor, and L. Kalsbeek was a school teacher – see the next two notes for details about their books.) Nor has it helped that these introductions are translations of Dutch popularizations. Of the two options, Kalsbeek's book is the more nuanced and has the more adequate scholarly apparatus, thanks largely to the work of the editors and the "Glossary of Terms" provided by Albert M. Wolters (an adapted version, titled "Glossary," appears in C.T. McIntire, ed., *The Legacy of Herman Dooyeweerd*, 167–71).

14 Spier, *An Introduction to Christian Philosophy*. A second English edition appeared from Craig Press in 1966 but did little to update the text in light of Dooyeweerd's later writings. Spier tells us in his "Author's Preface" (vii) that his first English edition, which appeared one year after NC I, is a translation of his "fourth revised Dutch edition published in 1950" (a few years before the publication of NC I). The Dutch original was titled *Een*

*inleiding tot de wijsbegeerte der wetsidee* [An Introduction to the Philosophy of the Law-Idea]. Like the fourth edition, the second and third editions were published by J.H. Kok (Kampen), in 1940 and 1946, respectively.

15 Kalsbeek, *Contours of a Christian Philosophy*. The Dutch original was *De wijsbegeerte der wetsidee: Proeve van een christelijke filosofie* [The Philosophy of the Cosmonomic Idea: Sample of a Christian Philosophy].

16 Kraay, "Successive Conceptions in the Development of the Christian Philosophy of Herman Dooyeweerd." Kraay labels these (1) the organon conception, (2) the Archimedean point conception, and (3) the ground motive conception.

17 The Archimedean point is distinct from the "Archè." The Archè is what a philosophy takes as the origin of everything. For Dooyeweerd's philosophy, God is the Archè on whom all creatures, including "reborn humanity," depend, and to whom they all refer. Religion is the fundamental relation, via humanity, between creation and either its divine origin or some creaturely substitute. He succinctly summarizes this ontology as follows: "*Meaning* [*zin*] is the *being* [*zijn*] of all *creaturely beings* [*creatuurlijk zijnde*], the mode-of-being [*zijnswijze*] of our selfhood too – religious in root, and divine in origin" (NC 1: 4, WW 1: 6).

18 Kraay, "Successive Conceptions," *Philosophia Reformata* 55 (1980): 35.

19 This is not transparent from the headings, however. The Introduction to the "Prolegomena" carries the subtitle "The First Way *of* a Transcendental *Critique* of Philosophic *Thought*" (NC 1: 3, emphases added). Only in the subtitle to section 2 of chapter 1 does one find mention of a "second way," and then it is called "The Second Way *to* a Transcendental *Criticism* of *Philosophy* (NC 1: 34, emphases added). Nothing of substance depends on the shift from "of" to "to" or from "critique" to "criticism" or from "philosophic thought" to "philosophy." One does hope, however, that such terminological slippage would disappear in a critical edition of NC, whenever one is published.

20 This is the only way presented in the Dutch text (WW 1: 5–33), where the heading does not label it a "transcendental critique."

21 See in this connection Knudsen, "The Religious Foundation of Dooyeweerd's Transcendental Method." Knudsen explains that religion in Dooyeweerd's sense "cannot be fixed directly in one's gaze" but "can be discerned only in depth, by ... reflecting on what is already present and is exerting influence on what one is doing. It is what Dooyeweerd calls 'the hidden player' behind all thought" (274). In a footnote Knudsen explains that the "hidden player" metaphor comes from the practice in some Dutch churches of hiding the organ console behind a screen; one hears the organ

music but does not see the organist at work. I am reminded here of Walter Benjamin's allegory for the preferred relation between "theology" and "historical materialism" in "Theses on the Philosophy of History," 253. I should add, however, that Knudsen's account of "transcendental method" is too broad to capture Dooyeweerd's mature conception of transcendental critique.

22 Dooyeweerd scholars disagree about whether to distinguish two ways of transcendental critique. H. van Eikema Hommes, Dooyeweerd's student and successor in legal philosophy at the Vrije Universiteit, argues that only the so-called "second way" can count. Henk Geertsema replies that Dooyeweerd's application of the term "transcendental critique" to his earlier and so-called first way is in keeping with the deepest motivations of Dooyeweerd's life work. See Geertsema, "Dooyeweerd's Transcendental Critique." I think Hommes's argument verges on the pedantic, but Geertsema's reply lets Dooyeweerd off too easily. *Addendum*: We now have access in English to the published doctoral dissertation of Pierre-Charles Marcel (1910–92), a prominent French Protestant scholar and pastor who studied with Dooyeweerd in the 1950s. See Marcel, *The Christian Philosophy of Herman Dooyeweerd*. The first volume of this work discusses Dooyeweerd's transcendental critique, and the second discusses his modal theory.

23 For similar formulations by Dooyeweerd, see "Christian Philosophy," 4, and *In the Twilight*, 4. The continuity of his transcendental critique with Kant's *Critique of Pure Reason* is most apparent from Dooyeweerd's formulation in *Transcendental Problems*, 19: "*How is philosophy in the theoretical sense ... possible*, that is to say, under what universal and necessary conditions? This problem is of a *radical*-critical character. It implies the question in respect to the possibility of scientific thought in all its forms ... It touches the necessary pre-*supposita* of all theoretical thought whatsoever."

24 In Dooyeweerd's own technical vocabulary, this question reads: "*What do we abstract in the antithetic attitude of theoretic thought from the structures of empirical reality as these structures are given in naïve experience? And how is this abstraction possible?*" (NC 1: 41) Or, more simply, "*what do we abstract in the intentional antithetic thought-relation from the integral structure of the horizon of our experience*," and how is this abstraction possible? ("Christian Philosophy," 11).

25 Except when I quote Dooyeweerd directly, I do not hyphenate the term "Gegenstand relation." Following his usage, I do not put "Gegenstand" in italics either, even though it is a German word traditionally translated as "object" – which in turn indicates a different concept in Dooyeweerd's

philosophy. Perhaps no other topic has drawn such sophisticated criticism from reformational philosophers as Dooyeweerd's account of the "Gegenstand relation." See especially Strauss, "An Analysis of the Structure of Analysis," and Hart, "Dooyeweerd's Gegenstand Theory of Theory." As Geertsema suggests in his summary and response to Strauss's criticisms, so much in Dooyeweerd's mature conception depends on his account of the "Gegenstand relation" that eliminating it would knock out the scaffolding for his transcendental critique. See Geertsema, "Dooyeweerd's Transcendental Critique," 86–91.

26 Although I cannot elaborate the point here, Dooyeweerd's account of theoretical thought successfully sidestepped the debate between epistemological realists and epistemological anti-realists long before that became a preoccupation of Protestant Christian philosophers in North America.

27 "*From what standpoint can we reunite synthetically the logical and the non-logical aspects of experience which were set apart in opposition to each other in the theoretical antithesis?*" (NC 1: 45) Or, "*from what standpoint can the aspects of our horizon of experience, which were set apart and in opposition to each other in the theoretical antithesis, be reunited in a theoretical synthesis?*" Dooyeweerd, "Christian Philosophy," 14.

28 English translations of Dooyeweerd often hyphenate the terms "intermodal" and "ground-motive," but not always. I have dropped the hyphens, also in quoted passages where they occur.

29 Cf. Dooyeweerd, "Christian Philosophy," 17.

30 "*How is this critical self-reflection, this concentric direction of theoretical thought to the I-ness, possible, and what is its true character?*" (NC 1: 52) Or, "*how is this critical self-reflection, this concentric direction of theoretical thought toward the self, possible, and what is its origin?*" Dooyeweerd, "Christian Philosophy," 18.

31 "The *heart* is the fullness of our selfhood, the genuinely transcendent focal point [*concentratiepunt*] of our existence. In the heart all temporal meaning-functions [*zin-functies*] come together. As such the heart is also the necessary point of departure for philosophical thought. This point of departure truly *can*not be eliminated, since our selfhood is intellectually at work [*denkende werkzaam*] in every theoretical abstraction. And the fullness of our selfhood consists solely in the *religious center* of our creaturely existence, where the *direction* for all of life is set [*bepaald wordt*] with respect to the completely true and absolute origin of everything. As Christ has said: Where your treasure is, there will your heart be also" (WW 1: 30–1, my translation; this passage does not seem to have an equivalent in NC).

32 For an explicit and nuanced account of the difference and relationship between faith and religion, see NC 2: 298–330, WW 2: 227–59. For the relevance of this to Dooyeweerd's understanding of the relation between theology and philosophy, see his *In the Twilight*, 113–72.

33 There is, to be sure, a special role for faith and a special connection between faith and religion, as James H. Olthuis indicates in "Dooyeweerd on Religion and Faith." He summarizes Dooyeweerd's view as follows: "First, spirituality – being religious – is as broad as life itself ... [R]eligion is a way of life that people engage in with their full existence and at all times ... Second, faith is *one* of the fundamental modes of being religious: a *sui generis* mode of human experience, belonging to the order of creation, in which the intrinsic spirituality of all of life receives explicit and concentrated focus" (21).

34 For an exceptionally clear and succinct statement of the transition from Dooyeweerd's three transcendental questions to his account of religious ground motives and the three transcendental ideas, see his "Christian Philosophy," 22–3, 35–7.

35 "Now a religious community is maintained by a common spirit, which as a *dynamis*, as a central motive-power, is active in the concentration-point of human existence. This spirit ... works through a *religious ground motive*, which gives contents to the central mainspring of the entire attitude of life and thought" (NC 1: 61).

36 Kuyper distinguishes five "life systems": Paganism, Islamism, Romanism, Modernism, and Calvinism. See Kuyper, *Lectures on Calvinism*, 19–40.

37 Dooyeweerd, "Christian Philosophy," 29.

38 Geertsema, "The Inner Reformation of Philosophy and Science," 15.

39 The Dutch passage from 1935 is more poignant than the English rendering from 1953, so let me attempt my own translation: "Indeed, a smug scientific stance toward immanence-philosophy hardly meshes with a Christian view of science and a Christian epistemic posture [*kennishouding*]. One has not grasped the intentions of the philosophy of the cosmonomic idea if one does not understand that [my] detailed critique of humanist immanence-philosophy ... is essentially meant as *self*-critique, as a case the Christian thinker pursues *with himself*. I would not judge so pointedly about immanence-philosophy had I not been there myself, had I not jointly and personally experienced its problematic [*haar problematiek mede persoonlijk heb ervaren*]. And I would not pass such a trenchant judgment about attempts at synthesis between this philosophy and Christian truths of faith, had I not undergone the inner tension between both myself and [had I not] personally struggled through these attempts" (WW 1: x).

40 Meynell, "The Philosophy of Dooyeweerd," 266–7.

41 Ibid., 268.
42 Ibid., 271.
43 I should note, however, that the later Dooyeweerd's worries about "historicism" complicate the question of rationality's cultural variability.
44 Plantinga, "Christian Philosophy at the End of the 20th Century," 45. Plantinga's essay originated as an address to the 1994 international symposium organized by the Association for Calvinist Philosophy in the Netherlands to mark the centennial of Dooyeweerd's birth. The essay distinguishes four divisions or tasks of Christian philosophy: "negative and positive apologetics," "philosophical theology," "Christian philosophical criticism," and "constructive Christian philosophy."
45 Meynell, "The Philosophy of Dooyeweerd," 270.
46 The vocabulary of "control beliefs" in Wolterstorff's *Religion within the Bounds of Reason* does not do justice to the complexity of relationships between religion, philosophy, and science, it seems to me. Nor does the model proposed by Brian J. Walsh and J. Richard Middleton, increasingly popular among evangelical scholars, according to which "religious world views" shape "philosophical paradigms" that shape various academic disciplines in turn. See their book *The Transforming Vision*, 163–86.
47 Geertsema, "The Inner Reformation of Philosophy and Science," 17–18.
48 Meynell, "The Philosophy of Dooyeweerd," 270–2.
49 Ibid., 272.
50 Perhaps we can say that the transcendental *function* of the "ego" or "heart" in Dooyeweerd's account resembles that of the Kantian subject, even though its *content* differs dramatically.
51 Dooyeweerd, "Christian Philosophy," 36–7.
52 Meynell, "The Philosophy of Dooyeweerd," 278.
53 See esp. NC 3: 3–29, WW 3: 1–10, where Dooyeweerd describes the metaphysical concept of substance as "a speculative exaggeration of a datum of naïve experience."
54 Jonathan Chaplin sorts out the strengths and weaknesses of Dooyeweerd's social theory in "Dooyeweerd's Notion of Societal Structural Principles," *Philosophia Reformata* 60 (1995): 16–36. I assess Dooyeweerd's cultural theory in the same journal issue, under the title "Fantastic Things," 37–54 – ch. 5 in this volume.
55 More carefully, perhaps one should say "no philosophy and (by extension) no science insofar as its boundary questions are philosophical."
56 Dooyeweerd, "Christian Philosophy," 23.
57 Here I have in mind several instructive essays by Klapwijk: "The Struggle for a Christian Philosophy," "Dooyeweerd's Christian Philosophy: Antithesis and Critique," "Antithesis, Synthesis, and the Idea of

Transformational Philosophy," and "Reformational Philosophy on the Boundary between the Past and the Future."

58 In addition to the two essays by Geertsema cited earlier, see Geertsema, "Christian Philosophy: Transformation or Inner Reformation."

59 Although I restrict my criticisms to the role Dooyeweerd's conception of religion plays in his transcendental critique, I agree with other critics that additional problems are even more pressing, such as a lack of messianic perspective, a muteness with respect to suffering and oppression, and an inability to recognize how religion, even in its most fundamental and central sense, is mediated by the practices, institutions, and structures of finite and fallible human beings. See, for example, Klapwijk, "Reformational Philosophy on the Boundary between the Past and the Future." For the main lines of my own alternative, see "Earth's Lament" (2003) and "Religion in Public" (2010), the epilogue and ch. 12 in this volume.

60 Hart, *Understanding Our World*, 325–70.

61 Zuidervaart, "Existence, Nomic Conditions, and God," ch. 6 in this volume. I address later developments in Hart's account of religion and rationality in "Artistic Truth, Linguistically Turned," ch. 7 in this volume.

62 Clouser, *The Myth of Religious Neutrality*, 16–24.

63 Ibid., 72–3, 191–4.

64 Dooyeweerd, "Christian Philosophy," 4; cf. NC 1: 37–8. Both passages give a harsh assessment of the value and pitfalls of transcendent critique. Not surprisingly, Clouser says his book "is addressed to those who believe in God" and does not try to win "unbelievers" to his point of view (Clouser, *Myth*, 5).

65 *Addendum*: What makes Clouser's approach a version of *transcendent* rather than *transcendental* critique, in my view, is its forthright reliance on a specific twofold "divinity belief," namely, that "*the divine is whatever does not depend on anything else for its existence*" and that "the fundamental teaching" in "the Scriptures accepted by Jews, Christians, and Muslims" is that God is the creator "on whom all else depends for existence while [God] does not depend on anything for [God's] existence" (Clouser, *Myth*, 17–19). In a subsequent essay Clouser argues that his approach is indeed a type of transcendental critique indebted to Dooyeweerd. Moreover, he claims to have identified and avoided the primary problems besetting Dooyeweerd's transcendental critique, which, according to Clouser, stem from Dooyeweerd's account of theoretical abstraction. See Clouser, "The Transcendental Critique Revisited and Revised." This essay has drawn an impassioned response from Glenn Friesen, who claims that Clouser seriously misreads Dooyeweerd through Aristotelian lenses and

thereby misses the central insights in Dooyeweerd's transcendental critique: "Clouser is of course entitled to maintain his belief in Aristotle's view of theory. But Dooyeweerd's philosophy provides a real alternative to Clouser's modified Aristotelianism" (Friesen, "A Response to Roy Clouser's Aristotelian Interpretation of Dooyeweerd," 114). Clouser, however, denies that he is an Aristotelian and argues that Friesen's "panentheism" is "the hidden motive driving … Friesen's misreadings of Dooyeweerd and of myself" (Clouser, "Reply to J. Glenn Friesen," 228). Neither Clouser nor Friesen takes up the problems of logical slippage and conceptual confusion identified in the current essay.

66 Perhaps this difference also helps explain why neither book discusses the other author's work, despite a personal acquaintance over many years. A cursory examination uncovers only one mention of the other author in each book, and that in an endnote, not in the main text (see Hart, 377n17, and Clouser, *Myth*, 313n6). The fact that Hart's book appeared seven years earlier might help explain his not discussing Clouser's work, but the same cannot be said the other way around.

67 I received word of H. Evan Runner's death (14 March 2002) when I was completing the revisions to this essay. I dedicate it to his memory. I also wish to thank Lee Hardy, Henk Hart, Bill Hasker, Hugo Meynell, Cal Seerveld, and Bob Sweetman for their instructive and encouraging comments on a draft of this essay.

## CHAPTER TWO

1 Friesen, "Dooyeweerd versus Vollenhoven: The Religious Dialectic within Reformational Philosophy," 132. See also Friesen, "95 Theses on Herman Dooyeweerd," and the responses in the same issue of *Philosophia Reformata* by Theodore Plantinga, Henk Geertsema, and Gerrit Glas.

2 Habermas, "Struggles for Recognition in the Democratic Constitutional State," 132.

3 In *Calvinism and the Reformation of Philosophy*, Vollenhoven emphasizes four principles that are central to Calvin's thought and a key to doing scriptural philosophy. I refer here to the excerpts in the *Dirk H.T. Vollenhoven Reader*, 21–65. The first principle is a formal one: namely, that the Bible is the word of God and has authority for our philosophical work (28). The other three principles are substantial points derived from Calvin's understanding of what scripture says (29): (1) God is directly sovereign over all that God has created. (2) Religion is a covenant that God's word revelation makes known to humankind. (3) After the fall, humans

are totally depraved, are subject to death, and are recipients of God's grace revealed in Jesus Christ. Although not identical with Dooyeweerd's "biblical ground motive" of creation, fall, and redemption, these substantial points clearly overlap Dooyeweerd's formulation.

4 Dooyeweerd, "Christian Philosophy: An Exploration," 4.

5 Ibid.

6 Dooyeweerd, *In the Twilight of Western Thought*, 1–6.

7 Zuidervaart, "The Great Turning Point," ch. 1 in this volume.

8 Nevertheless, Vollenhoven does emphasize immanent criticism in his historiography of philosophy – see ch. 9 in this volume.

9 Zuidervaart, *Adorno's Aesthetic Theory*, xx. I discuss this type of criticism as a "critical hermeneutics" in the essay "Unfinished Business," ch. 14 in this volume. See also my books *Artistic Truth*, 11–14, and *Social Philosophy after Adorno*, 6–7.

## CHAPTER THREE

1 Dooyeweerd, NC 2: 565, WW 2: 498; translation modified.

2 Vollenhoven, *De noodzakelijkheid eener christelijke logica.*

3 See especially Hart, *Draft for Proposed ICS Syllabus for Systematic Philosophy*, which addresses both ontological and epistemological issues pertaining to "truth."

4 Zuidervaart, *Artistic Truth.*

5 See Zuidervaart, "Unfinished Business," ch. 14 in this volume. I provide a more extensive exposition and critique of Dooyeweerd's conception in the longer paper from which the two essays derive. See Zuidervaart, "After Dooyeweerd: Truth in Reformational Philosophy."

6 My summary follows Dooyeweerd's use of the term "truth," capitalizing it when it refers to "absolute" or "transcendent" Truth, and not capitalizing in other uses, even when the text of NC does not consistently follow this pattern. When I present my own account of truth, however, I do not capitalize "truth" in any usages.

7 NC often hyphenates the terms "inter-modal" and "transcendental-theoretical," but not always. I have dropped the hyphens, also in quoted passages where they occur. I have also changed "fulness" to "fullness" in all quotations, to conform with current North American English.

8 Although Dooyeweerd does not specify the religious law's content in this context, other passages indicate that he has the call to love in mind. See especially NC 2: 140–63.

9 NC renders "*overeenstemming*" either as "accordance" or as "correspondence." Dooyeweerd is not discussing the relation between proposition and

fact that correspondence theories of truth emphasize but an alignment between subject-side and law-side. Hence I use "accordance" and not "correspondence" where WW uses the term "*overeenstemming*."

10 The entire definition of transcendental truth occurs in italics in Dooyeweerd's text.

11 Again, Dooyeweerd's definition of transcendental theoretical truth occurs in italics.

12 Strictly speaking, and contrary to Dooyeweerd's own formulation, these are not criteria of transcendental theoretical *truth*. They are criteria of transcendental theoretical *justification*.

13 For a lengthier discussion of this principle, see NC 2: 36–49, WW 2: 34–47.

14 For an elaboration of this principle, see NC 3: 3–52, WW 3: 1–32.

15 John 14:6, NRSV.

16 Here I discuss in greater detail the reasons for a previously published judgment that "Dooyeweerd leaves us with a perplexing, internally conflicted notion of religion that nevertheless serves as the pivot to his transcendental critique." Zuidervaart, "The Great Turning Point," 81 (ch. 1 in this volume).

17 This formulation follows Vollenhoven's Trinitarian distinction among three relationships that God sustains with creation. See Vollenhoven, "The Unity of Life."

18 For insightful comments on the metaphor of hearing and responding, see Geertsema, *Het menselijk karakter van ons kennen*. For a characterization of religion and human existence in terms of call and response, see Olthuis, "Be(com)ing: Humankind as Gift and Call" and "Crossing the Threshold."

19 Concerning the issues surrounding Dooyeweerd's conceptions of religion and transcendence, see Steen, *The Structure of Herman Dooyeweerd's Thought*.

20 Zuidervaart, "The Great Turning Point," 78.

21 Vollenhoven, *Isagôgè Philosophiae*, 108–38.

22 Ibid., 110.

23 Ibid., 111.

24 See, for example, John 8:12–59 and the Second Letter of John.

25 Kuipers, *Critical Faith*.

26 See Zuidervaart, "Unfinished Business," ch. 14 in this volume.

## CHAPTER FOUR

1 I render Dooyeweerd's terms in English as I do because *A New Critique of Theoretical Thought* (NC) is inconsistent and unreliable in its translation of the more precise terminology in *De Wijsbegeerte der Wetsidee*

(WW). Where WW uses the single term "*wetskring*" (literally, "law-sphere"), NC uses a variety of terms – "law-sphere," "modal sphere," and "modal law-sphere" – and where WW uses the single term "*zin-modaliteiten*" (literally, "meaning-modalities"), NC uses variously "modalities," "modalities of meaning," and "modal structures of meaning." WW also uses the Dutch terms "*zijden*" (literally, "sides") and "*zin-zijden*" (literally, "meaning-sides"), which NC translates as "aspects" and "modal aspects" respectively.

2 Vollenhoven, *Isagôgè Philosophiae*, 25–34. "Subject functions" are the modally distinct ways in which a "subject unit" (individual entity) functions or can function in response to modally distinct laws.

3 van Woudenberg, "'Aspects' and 'Functions' of Individual Things," and Geertsema, "Analytical and Reformational Philosophy."

4 Hart, *Understanding Our World*, 445, 449.

5 Clouser, *The Myth of Religious Neutrality*, 57 and passim. For a discussion of the origins of this formulation in Clouser's doctoral dissertation on Dooyeweerd and in his consultations with Dooyeweerd, see Clouser, "Reply to J. Glenn Friesen," esp. 221–2.

6 The mild-mannered Vollenhoven could be surprisingly caustic on this score: "A farmer distinguishes stones, plants, animals, and humans more clearly than many who are stuck with an impoverished theory of knowledge that in quasi simplicity only knows a subject-object relationship and understands this to be the relationship of thinking and what sense perceives." *Isagôgè Philosophiae*, 135.

7 See Cassirer, *"Substance and Function" and "Einstein's Theory of Relativity."* The two books published together in this translation appeared in German in 1910 and 1921, respectively. See also Cassirer, *The Philosophy of Symbolic Forms, Volume Three*, first published in German in 1929. I take up the emphasis on functional concepts in Cassirer's philosophical anthropology in "Defining Humankind," ch. 10 in this volume.

8 Here "science" needs to be understood in the broad sense that "*wetenschap*" and "*Wissenschaft*" had in Dutch and German when Dooyeweerd and Vollenhoven wrote: it includes all academic disciplines and ranges from mathematics through the natural sciences on to the humanities and social sciences.

9 Kitcher, "The Hegemony of Molecular Biology."

10 Brigandt and Love, "Reductionism in Biology."

11 Abbreviated by the initials "NC" throughout. All references to this work are cited internally by volume and page number; thus, NC 2: 7 corresponds to volume 2, page 7.

12 Seerveld proposes the following intermodal order: numerical, spatial, kinetic, physical, bio-organic, psychical, technical, aesthetical, lingual, analytical, social, economical, juridical, ethical, confessional. Dooyeweerd proposes this intermodal order: numerical, spatial, kinematic, physical, biotic, psychical, analytical, historical, lingual, social, economic, aesthetic, juridical, moral or ethical, pistic.

13 Dooyeweerd's discussion of the epistemological problem clarifies the relation between his general theory of the modes and his conception of cosmic time: the cosmic temporal horizon of human experience encompasses and determines the modal horizon as well as the plastic horizon. The temporal horizon is itself encompassed by the religious horizon (cf. NC 2: 552ff).

14 Apparently Dooyeweerd maintains not only that cosmic time is a coherent diversity referring beyond itself to a central unity-totality but also that cosmic time is the medium that breaks unity-totality into a coherent diversity: "It is the very signification of cosmic time in its correlation of order and duration to be successive refraction of meaning into coherent modal aspects" (NC 1: 106; cf. NC 1: 16, 102; NC 2: 3).

15 "The absolute limit of '*gegenständliche*' abstraction is found in the functional basic structure of the modal aspects" (NC 2: 469). It should be noted that in itself the idea of order need not be an idea of successive order. The modes could refer to each other in an orderly fashion without being successively related to each other.

16 Dooyeweerd's contention that philosophy must account for these facts without mutilating their real meaning must be taken seriously. I do not believe this contention plays a prominent enough role in Dooyeweerd's modal theorizing to be termed a criterion of modal theory.

17 Dooyeweerd defines the nucleus of the spatial way of functional coherence as continuous extension. This definition does not agree with how many modern mathematicians approach spatiality. And yet it is on the basis of this definition that Dooyeweerd builds his argument for the place of the spatial mode in the order of succession. How does Dooyeweerd derive his definition? I will consider this question later.

18 *Addendum*: Now one can compare these passages in NC with the discussion in Dooyeweerd, *Encyclopedia of the Science of Law*, vol. 1. The *Encyclopedia* is projected to contain five volumes in English translation. Of those, vol. 3 would also be worth comparing with the modal discussions of law and justice in NC. Despite his intentions, Dooyeweerd never published these volumes in Dutch; they stem from the printed notes (*dictaten*) for his lectures on jurisprudence in the Law Faculty at the VU University Amsterdam.

19 *Addendum*: Alan Cameron's "Editor's Introduction," to Dooyeweerd's *Encyclopedia*, vol. 1, 1–10, correctly notes that the concept of "retribution" may seem unsuitable in light of contemporary moves towards the idea of restorative justice in the criminal justice system, although he also tries to place Dooyeweerd's conception in a wider context. Like Chaplin in *Herman Dooyeweerd*, 187–93, I think Dooyeweerd's emphasis on retribution is inherently problematic. I discuss the concept of justice in chapters 12 and 13 of this volume.

20 I alluded to this factor in a previous footnote on Dooyeweerd's description of the spatial nucleus as continuous extension.

21 Cf. Dooyeweerd's description of his change of thinking relative to the physical and kinematic modes, NC 2: 98ff.

22 "Objectified" simply means that there are objective analogies within a mode that refer to the subject functions or to the subject/object relations belonging to a substratum mode. It does not mean that these subject functions and subject/object relations actually occur within the mode in which they are "objectified." Cf. NC 2: 373–4n4, 411–12.

23 It is difficult to understand how a point can belong to the spatial mode of continuous dimensional extension and at the same time lack extensiveness. How exactly does the continuous extension nucleus qualify the concept "point"? The problem involved here is the problem of whether object functioning should be understood anticipatorily or retrocipatorily. If the concept "point" is indeed an example of object functioning, should points be understood as belonging to the numerical mode and reaching toward the spatial mode under the guidance of the spatial mode, or should points be understood as belonging to the spatial mode and referring back to the numerical mode which it objectifies? The second alternative is Dooyeweerd's position. Abandoning this position in favour of the first alternative would alter the verificational use of the subject/object relation, which could then help verify the anticipatory structures of the modes rather than the retrocipatory structures.

24 Although I have not succeeded in completely penetrating Dooyeweerd's analysis of the juridical mode, I have noticed what seems to be an inconsistency between his analysis of the retrocipatory structure of the juridical mode and his analysis of the juridical subject/object relation. In his analysis of the juridical mode, Dooyeweerd maintains that the economic retrocipation precedes the aesthetic retrocipation; the aesthetic mode follows the economic mode and immediately precedes the juridical mode in the order of succession. In his analysis of the juridical subject/object relation, Dooyeweerd emphasizes that "the juridical object-function is strictly bound to an economical analogy" (NC 2: 406). However, Dooyeweerd's

treatment of the spatial, psychical, and logical subject/object relations seems to argue that these modes are strictly bound to a retrocipation to the substratum mode *immediately* preceding the mode under consideration (the numerical, biotic, and psychic retrocipations, respectively). In the case of the juridical mode, this retrocipation should be the aesthetic analogy, not the economic analogy. If the juridical mode exhibits an exception to the general functional structure of the subject/object relation, then Dooyeweerd should account for this exception. So far as I can tell, however, not only does he not account for the exception, but also he does not even recognize it as an exception. It would seem that the inconsistency between his analysis of the retrocipatory structure of the juridical mode and his analysis of the juridical subject/object relation calls for a reconsideration of one or both of these analyses.

25 See, for example, "Dooyeweerd's Conception of Truth," ch. 3 in this volume.

26 This is a reworking of Seerveld's modal aesthetic theory as articulated, for example, in Seerveld, "Imaginativity" and *Rainbows for the Fallen World*. For those who know about technical debates in reformational modal theory, I should mention that, like Henk Hart, I do not distinguish a "nuclear moment" as a moment "alongside" or "in addition to" "retrocipations and anticipations." A nuclear moment is simply the pervasive meaning of a dimension or mode in all its moments.

27 For details, see the chapter titled "Kant Revisited" in Zuidervaart, *Artistic Truth*, 55–73, as well as section 3.2 on artistic truth in my lengthy 2008 paper "After Dooyeweerd."

28 For details, see Zuidervaart, *Art in Public*, and the essay "Macrostructures and Societal Principles," ch. 13 in this volume.

29 Stafleu, *Time and Again* and *Theories at Work*.

30 Botha, *Metaphor and Its Moorings*, and Strauss, *Philosophy: Discipline of the Disciplines*.

31 Klapwijk, *Purpose in the Living World?*

32 Basden, *Philosophical Frameworks for Understanding Information Systems*.

33 Weideman, *Beyond Expression*.

34 Blomberg, *Wisdom and Curriculum*.

35 Hommes, *Major Trends in the History of Legal Philosophy*.

## CHAPTER FIVE

1 An earlier version of this essay was presented as a workshop paper at the Fifth International Symposium of the Association for Calvinist Philosophy, held in the Netherlands, 22–26 August 1994, on the theme of "Christian

Philosophy at the Close of the Twentieth Century." The symposium marked the hundredth anniversary of the birth of Herman Dooyeweerd (1894–1977). I want to thank the workshop participants for their helpful comments as well as Johan van der Hoeven for his careful reading of a subsequent draft. I also wish to acknowledge grants from Calvin College and the Calvin College Alumni Association in support of my writing and presenting the workshop paper.

2 Citations from Heidegger will refer to "The Origin of the Work of Art," in *Poetry, Language, Thought*, 17–87 (cited as "Origin"), and "Der Ursprung des Kunstwerkes," in *Holzwege*, 7–68 (cited as "Ursprung").

3 Citations of Dooyeweerd will come mostly from volume 3 of *A New Critique of Theoretical Thought*, titled *The Structures of Individuality of Temporal Reality*, and volume 3 of *De Wijsbegeerte der Wetsidee*, titled *De Individualiteits-Structuren der Tijdelijke Werkelijkheid*. Dooyeweerd's discussion of art (NC 3: 104–53, WW 3: 71–128) occurs during his examination of "the structures of individuality of temporal things" in the first part of volume 3 (NC 3: 1–153, WW 3: 1–128).

4 The other half of the dialogue takes place in a chapter titled "Imaginative Disclosure" in Zuidervaart, *Artistic Truth*, 101–17.

5 Heidegger, "Origin," 39, and "Ursprung," 28.

6 Among the many books on Heidegger's cultural politics and its historical setting, the following are particularly incisive: Zimmerman, *Heidegger's Confrontation with Modernity*, and Wolin, *The Politics of Being*. For an analysis of Dooyeweerd's social theory that complements my assessment of his account of art, see Chaplin, "Pluralism, Society and the State," a doctoral dissertation completed at the University of London, 1993, and Chaplin, *Herman Dooyeweerd*.

7 *Addendum*: As is explained in chapter 3 above, Dooyeweerd uses the term "plastic horizon" (as distinct from the religious, cosmic-temporal, and modal horizons of experience) to refer to the entire latticework of structural principles that govern different types of entities, events, and societal relationships. He coined the term "enkapsis" to refer to how physical things, plants, animals, and social institutions can be structurally interlaced even though the two entities interlaced have different individuality structures – for example, the symbiotic interlacement between a parasite and its host.

8 *Addendum*: Dooyeweerd uses the term "radical types" to identify the most general classes of individuality structures – see NC 3: 76–98, WW 3: 53–64. All individuality structures that belong to the same radical type have their qualifying functions at the same modal level, and the entities, etc. that have such individuality structures belong to the same kingdom or realm of

creatures. (For more about modal levels and functions, see ch. 4 above.) The three primary kingdoms or realms, governed by distinct (primary) radical types, are physical things and events (qualified physically), plants (qualified organically), and animals (qualified psychically). Humankind also makes up a primary kingdom but, being religious at heart, is not modally qualified. The various structurally distinct institutions and practices that make up human society belong to "secondary radical types" characterized by both qualifying and founding functions. Within one secondary radical type, such as the radical type that pertains to art (as distinct from, say, language or science), all the individuality structures of the entities and events in the same social sphere will have qualifying functions and founding functions at the same modal level – at the aesthetic level (qualifying) and the technical or historical level (founding), in the case of artistic entities (e.g., artworks) and events (e.g., musical performances).

9 Zigterman, "Dooyeweerd's Theory of Individuality Structure as an Alternative to a Substance Position, Especially That of Aristotle," 134.

10 During his presentation at the Fifth International Symposium of the Association for Calvinist Philosophy, Marinus Dirk Stafleu remarked that Dooyeweerd could not complete his long-projected and long-awaited philosophical anthropology because he could not come to terms with evolution. A similar problem has plagued many of Dooyeweerd's students and successors. *Addendum*: Stafleu had already noted this problem in his essay "Being Human in the Cosmos," where he says that reformational philosophy really needs to study "the evolution of [humankind] in the universe, and the position of humanity with respect to the kingdoms of plants and animals" (101) and then makes some proposals along these lines. Klapwijk's *Purpose in the Living World?* takes up this challenge, both providing a detailed study of these topics and proposing an evolutionary understanding of human life. In that context, Klapwijk singles out "essentialism" as the primary obstacle to a reformational understanding of evolution. He notes this problem not only in Dooyeweerd's work but also in Stafleu's approach, as articulated in Stafleu, *Een wereld vol relaties*, 198–210. The core to Dooyeweerd's "essentialist error," according to Klapwijk, lies in his treating biological species as immutable laws of creation: "In short, [for Dooyeweerd] the species are a type structure, the type structure is a law, and the law is immutable" (*Purpose in the Living World?* 251). What Klapwijk identifies here as "essentialism" is a version of the first reduction I criticize in the current essay: namely, Dooyeweerd's reducing structure to law. Needless to say, Klapwijk's book has stirred up considerable discussion among fellow reformational thinkers. See, for example, the entire issue devoted to this discussion in *Philosophia Reformata* 76 (2011).

11 This passage appears to have been added in the English version. In general, the worry about geneticism seems more pronounced in *New Critique* than in *Wijsbegeerte der Wetsidee*. Correlatively, the attack on the metaphysical concept of substance stands out more starkly in the Dutch version, although the English version does go on at greater length about H.G. Stoker's concept of substance – compare NC 3: 61–76 with WW 3: 42–53.

12 The sentence quoted after the colon has no equivalent in the Dutch version. This is one of the many passages significantly modified from the Dutch edition, probably by both the author and the translator. In general, the English version of the passage tones down Dooyeweerd's deterministic and religious language and emphasizes the stance of epistemological modesty, but does not substantively change the main claims he is making. Compare NC 3: 106 with WW 3: 73–4.

13 Zigterman, "Dooyeweerd's Theory of Individuality Structure," 75.

14 Ibid., 45.

15 Two examples may suffice to establish this tendency. First, although Dooyeweerd speaks frequently of the "internal structural principle" of individual entities (such as the famous linden tree in his garden), structural principles cannot be *internal* to the actual entities, since, as Dooyeweerd clearly insists, structural principles belong to the law-side of cosmic time and hence have neither genesis nor duration – see Zigterman, "Dooyeweerd's Theory of Individuality Structure," 94–5n16. Second, although Dooyeweerd claims repeatedly that law and subject exist only in correlation, he is so concerned to uphold the law-character of structures that all radical types, geno-types, and their sub-types (NC 3: 97) are said to belong to the creation order (NC 3: 95). This raises the unsettling prospect of types for which there are no tokens – unsettling because it violates Dooyeweerd's own principle of law/subject correlation: "The rigorous consistency of Dooyeweerd's position notwithstanding, allowing laws in the creation order for which there may be no subjects, seems to violate the principle … that law and subject exist only *in correlation*; there are no subjects without laws to which they are subject, but also and equally, there are no laws without subjects for which they are laws." Zigterman, "Dooyeweerd's Theory of Individuality Structure," 98n24.

16 Interestingly, the caption in Dutch speaks of the sculpture's "internal structural functions" (*interne structuurfuncties* – WW 3: 79) rather than its "internal typical structure" (NC 3: 111).

17 My summary of the fifth feature follows the Dutch text (WW 3: 80), which is more detailed and precise than the English (NC 3: 112). The English version reads here like a loose paraphrase of the Dutch.

18 See specifically NC 3: 113–28, 149–50, 637–41; WW 3: 80–97, 123–5, 561–6.

19 This reading receives confirmation from Dooyeweerd's subsequent treatment of "radical types of other normatively qualified objective thing-structures" (NC 3: 128ff, WW 3: 97ff). The analysis of utensils, for example, aims to establish their historical foundation and social qualification, to highlight the need for inner unity between their technical construction and social destination, and to understand the enkaptic relation between, say, a chair, and the "semi-manufactured materials" from which it is made.

20 The Dutch edition uses the term "*kunstwerk*" without qualification. The English edition tries to clarify this by translating "*kunstwerk*" as "work of fine art," as in the sentence introducing the analysis of *Hermes*: "As a first example of a normatively qualified objective thing we shall examine a work of fine art of the primary-type sculpture: Hermes with the boy Dionysus, the masterpiece of the Greek sculptor Praxiteles" (NC 3: 110, WW 3: 77). It should be noted that the term "masterpiece" has been inserted in the English edition; it does not occur in the Dutch version.

21 The English edition adds that the internal structural principle of pure artworks itself "binds things of an other qualification" (NC 3: 139).

22 Dooyeweerd seldom identifies the persons and positions his account of art challenges, but the paragraphs on free and bound art identify two desiderata for a Christian aesthetics. On the one hand, Christian aesthetics cannot absolutize the aesthetic modality in the fashion of "*l'art pour l'art*," which restricts the artwork to its leading structural function and ignores post-aesthetic functions. On the other hand, Christian aesthetics must defend the right of free artistic expression over tendency art (*tendenzkunst*), which makes art subservient to specific utilitarian or moral purposes (NC 3: 139, WW 3: 110).

23 NC 3: 121 inserts a passage here that specifies the types exemplified by the Praxiteles sculpture. In the order of increasing specificity, the types are: artwork (secondary radical type), plastic artwork (geno-type), sculpture (type), sculptured figures of deities (sub-type), and marble sculpture (variability type). The sub-type can also be described as a "narrower geno-type."

24 This is another of those passages whose significant modifications could have come from the translator, the author, or both. A strict translation of the Dutch would read as follows: "*Technical form* and *aesthetic import* [or content – *gehalte*] are the two aspects that, in the experience of every artwork, characterize the artwork as such" (WW 3: 91, Dooyeweerd's emphasis, my translation). Contrast that with the English edition, especially the phrases I have italicized: "Technical form and *the leading aesthetic*

*expression of the artist's conception* are the two aspects characterizing *our experience* of every *sculptural* work of art." Although the first phrase underlined is a plausible elaboration of what Dooyeweerd means by "*aesthetisch gehalte*," the other two underlined phrases are misleading, since the two aspects in question are aspects of the work, not of our experience, and since Dooyeweerd intends this characterization to hold for all artworks, not simply for sculpture.

25 New material has been added on NC 3: 122 concerning the importance of "typical modal foundational functions" for distinguishing the various radical types of human products and societal spheres. Compare in this connection the expansion and revision of WW 3: 53–64 in NC 3: 76–98, esp. NC 3: 89–92, pages that have no equivalent in the Dutch edition.

26 Calvin Seerveld's essay on "Modal Aesthetic Theory" indicates the problems attached to simply assuming that the modern notions of "art" and "artwork" can be applied to pre-modern cultures, but Seerveld follows Dooyeweerd in claiming that "a cosmogonic structuring ... prompts within ordained bounds the gradual unfolding of creation's profuse, variegated richness" and occasions "developments proper to the kind of creatureliness involved" (110). For Seerveld, such developments include the emergence of fine art in modern Europe. See *Rainbows for the Fallen World*, 104–37, esp. 109–14. More recently, Seerveld has modified this conception of historical development. See, for example, his workshop paper "Insights and Problems with Dooyeweerd's Conception of (Historical) Unfolding Process and Differentiation" for the Fifth Annual Symposium (August 1994), published as "Dooyeweerd's Idea of 'Historical Development.'" My own initial attempt to break with modernist emphases on "artwork" and "autonomy" can be found in chapter 9 of *Adorno's Aesthetic Theory*, 217–47.

27 Lydia Goehr analyzes the philosophical implications of this development for conceptions of music in *The Imaginary Museum of Musical Works*.

28 Later it becomes apparent that this criticism aims to oppose totalitarian, imperialist, and especially fascist views of the state's role in a national economy, without thereby simply rejecting the expansion of state economic planning as advocated by Keynesian economics and public policy. See NC 3: 482–5, WW 3: 420–3.

29 Dooyeweerd adds that some people might want to restrict the term "thing" to "dead objects," but he sees no serious objection against applying it to plants and animals as well, although he has systematic reasons not to apply it to the human body (NC 3: 197–8).

30 The English version adds in a footnote: "A thing in its proper sense implies a relatively constant realization of its individuality-structure. A poem, a

musical composition or a drama are imaginative totalities of an aesthetic qualification which can be reproduced only in a coherent series of mental acts and acts of performance, with the aid of their symbolical objectification in books and scores" (NC 3: 111n).

31 I leave aside here the additional problems raised by Dooyeweerd's account of books as "historically founded and symbolically qualified things," an account that would also apply to scores, scripts, and other conventions for writing in the performing arts – see NC 3: 150–3, WW 3: 125–8. Many of these problems parallel the ones in his analysis of artworks as historically founded and aesthetically qualified "things." My main argument against Dooyeweerd's account would be that books and scores are not things in the strict sense (i.e., in Dooyeweerd's own strict sense) any more than are works in the performing arts (or any other artworks, for that matter). To that extent, Dooyeweerd's contention that poems and musical compositions are "constantly objectified" in books and scores is a bogus claim.

32 The chapter in Part I where artworks are discussed is titled "The Subject-Object Relation in the Thing-Structure of Reality" (ch. III).

33 Dooyeweerd comes closer to acknowledging this in his discussion of utensils. At one point he says that chairs, being designed to give rest and support to the human body, fulfill a human "biotic-*cultural* need" and thus have a "biotic object-function" (NC 3: 134, which goes into greater detail than the parallel passage in WW 3: 104). Later he says that furniture styles should express the internal structural principle of furniture in its specific social setting (*in hun verband*) and cultural context (NC 3: 140–2, WW 3: 112–15). Moreover, furniture and all other utensils belong to a typical structural collectivity (*verbandsstructuur*) that should be expressed objectively "in their own thing-structure" (NC 3: 143, WW 3: 115). But even here Dooyeweerd insists, as he has before (NC 3: 137, 138; WW 3: 108), that "the objectively realized leading function of these everyday utensils is not to be confused with the subjective ends for which they can be used" (NC 3: 143, WW 3: 115).

34 See especially the section titled "Thing and Work" ("Origin," 20–39, "Ursprung," 10–28).

35 Part III distinguishes three types of enkapsis between thing-structures: foundational, correlative, and symbiotic. See NC 3: 640–52, WW 3: 564–79.

36 In places the English edition suggests that the later Dooyeweerd shifted his emphasis from the aesthetic conception to the objective presentation. For example, the passage I translate as "the aesthetic conception … objectified in the presentation" reads in NC 3: 640 as "The qualifying function could only be found in the objectified depiction of the aesthetic conception."

Other passages actually strengthen the subjective emphasis, however. The only conclusions I draw from such passages are that Dooyeweerd probably did not change his emphasis and that the translation is not always accurate or reliable in matters of nuance and detail.

37 Dooyeweerd actually speaks of the perceptual image *in* the marble statue and *in* the model.

38 Dooyeweerd explains that a sensory fantasy-image is the objective sensory side of the product of (psychic) imagination (*inbeelding*). As the artist's aesthetically qualified conception takes shape, the imagination projects or designs (*ontwerpt*) an objective configuration (*objectieve gestalte*) that is merely intentional and that has no more than an intentional relation to the concrete object-side of temporal reality (NC 3: 115–16, WW 3: 84). Hence the perceptible statue does not copy the sensory image of the artist's model but rather depicts or presents or expresses the merely intentional sensory fantasy-image generated by the artist's imagination and incorporated into the artist's aesthetically qualified conception. Dooyeweerd lays the groundwork for this account in volume 2, where he devotes several paragraphs to the "depictive relation" (my translation for "*afbeeldings-relatie*" – see NC 2: 375, WW 2: 312–13). See also the paragraphs on "the subject-object relation in the modal types of individuality" (NC 2: 425–6, WW 2: 355–6) in which Dooyeweerd cites sensory fantasy (*gevoelsfantasie*) as an original type of individuality in the psychic modality.

39 Part of this sculpture's reality is the objective depiction (*afbeelding*) or presentation (*uit-beelding*) of the vital function intended in the artist's aesthetic conception (NC 3: 116–17, WW 3: 85), not a copying of the living model's appearance.

40 Here the Dutch version has more bite than the English version. Whereas the English edition says the person who views the artwork "as a copy of a beautiful natural object … lacks a real experience of this sculpture" (NC 3: 115), the Dutch edition says: "De bedoelde beschouwer ziet eenvoudig het werkelijk kunstwerk voor de copie van een mooi natuurding aan en heeft dus een *onware*, een *valsche* ervaring van zijn werkelijkheid" (WW 3: 83). As is indicated already by the caustic use of "*mooi*" ("nice," "pretty"), Dooyeweerd's charge is not that the complacent naturalist "lacks a real experience" but that the experience is *false*, given the reality of the work as a work.

41 Heidegger, "Origin," 17, "Ursprung," 7.

42 I leave aside here the controversies surrounding Dooyeweerd's notion of a historical modality, which seems to me, as to critics such as Seerveld and McIntire, to dehistoricize history and historiography.

43 One exception is particularly relevant for understanding the origins of Dooyeweerd's account. Hans van Seventer has pointed out that for many years Dooyeweerd was close to the Dutch landscape painter Piet van Loo, whom Dooyeweerd once asked to write an aesthetic theory. Apparently van Loo's modus operandi matched Dooyeweerd's own account of artistry: he would sit in his studio for days forming his aesthetic conception for a piece, and then quickly paint in a stylized realist manner. With regard to philosophical kinships, both Calvin Seerveld and Nicholas Wolterstorff have observed the similarity between Dooyeweerd's emphasis on the artist's aesthetic conception and Benedetto Croce's aesthetics, although no reference to Croce actually occurs in Dooyeweerd's discussion of art.

44 For a discussion of additional functions and norms, see the final chapter of the co-authored *Dancing in the Dark*, ed. Anker, 278–309.

45 *Addendum*: Nine years after the current essay first appeared, I elaborated and revised this ontological sketch in the book *Artistic Truth*. The book distinguishes between artworks and art products; it identifies exploration, creative interpretation, and presentation as three intersubjective processes within the aesthetic dimension of life, culture, and society; and it relates these aesthetic processes to the normative expectations of authenticity, significance, and integrity that make up artistic truth. A preliminary summary of this approach to artistic truth occurs in the 2001 essay "Artistic Truth, Linguistically Turned," ch. 7 in this volume. I discuss the political, economic, and broadly cultural dimensions of art in the book *Art in Public*.

## PART TWO: INTRODUCTION

1 A more elaborate account of religion and its role in society occurs in ch. 12 ("Religion in Public") in Part III of this volume.

2 See Zuidervaart, "Refractions," 1–7.

3 The paper did, however, provide a partial basis for the discussion of transcendent, immanent, and transcendental modes of critique in the Introduction to my subsequent book on Adorno. See Zuidervaart, *Adorno's Aesthetic Theory*, xvii–xx.

## CHAPTER SIX

1 Hart, *Understanding Our World*. The book is part of the "Christian Studies Today" series co-published by University Press of America and the Institute for Christian Studies.

2 Ibid., xvii.

3 Ibid., xix.
4 Ibid., 1.
5 Ibid., xxi.
6 The theme of rationality and commitment was already explored in Hart's doctoral dissertation, *Communal Certainty and Authorized Truth*. Among his numerous more recent writings on the topic are "Critical Reflections on Wolterstorff's *Reason within the Bounds of Religion*," "The Impasse of Rationality Today: Revised Edition," and "The Articulation of Belief."
7 Hart, *Understanding Our World*, 5.
8 Ibid., 83.
9 Ibid., "Glossary," 450.
10 Ibid., 70.
11 Ibid., 72.
12 Ibid., 73.
13 Ibid., 53.
14 Ibid., 252.
15 Ibid., "Glossary," 444.
16 Ibid., 39.
17 Ibid., "Glossary," 452.
18 Hart's distinction between conditions-1 and conditions-2 may be seen as a refinement of the distinction between "structures-for" and "structures-of" creation, a distinction presented in two mimeographed papers by James H. Olthius at Toronto's Institute for Christian Studies in 1970. The papers are titled "The Reality of Societal Structures" – subsequently published in *Tydskrif vir Christelijke Wetenskap* 13 (1977): 198–207 – and "The Word of God and Science."
19 For clues to a plausible reply to this objection, see Hart, *Understanding Our World*, 365.
20 Ibid., 53.
21 Ibid., 55.
22 Ibid., 67.
23 Ibid.
24 Ibid., 56.
25 Ibid., 57.
26 Ibid., 71.
27 Ibid.
28 See ibid., 388n58–9.
29 Ibid., 164–8.
30 Ibid., 276–80.

31 Ibid., 312–18.
32 Ibid., 318–24.
33 Ibid., 318–19.
34 Ibid., 319–20.
35 In 422n53, Hart seems to suggest that even nomic conditions are "beyond the grasp of rationality." If this is indeed his suggestion, it would seem inconsistent with his analysis of nomic conditions in ch. 2.
36 Compare the comments on Hegel's critique of Kant in Adorno, *Negative Dialektik*, 374–7; *Negative Dialectics*, 381–4.
37 Hart, *Understanding Our World*, 323.
38 The exchange between Hart and Wolterstorff about Creator and creature is instructive in this connection. See Hart, "On the Distinction between Creator and Creature," and Wolterstorff, "Once Again, Creator/Creature."
39 Hart, *Understanding Our World*, 320–2.
40 Ibid., 322.
41 Ibid., 321.
42 Hart, "On the Distinction between Creator and Creature," 183.
43 Hart, *Understanding Our World*, 319.
44 Ibid., 325–34.
45 Ibid., 333, 360.
46 Ibid., 329.
47 Ibid., xix–xxi, 328, 331–2.
48 Ibid., 334.
49 Cf. ibid., xvii–xviii.
50 Ibid., "Glossary," 455.
51 An illuminating analysis of the function of "transcendental ideas" in Dooyeweerd's transcendental critique can be found in Kim, "Wissen und Glauben bei I. Kant und H. Dooyeweerd."
52 Wolterstorff, *Reason within the Bounds of Religion*, 63–84.
53 Hart, *Understanding Our World*, 331–2.
54 Ibid., 182–3.
55 In 429n29 we read that someone could "initiate a philosophical theory with a central belief in the love of God" rather than God's sovereignty. The interesting question not discussed here is why someone *would* "choose" such a significantly different ultimate assumption.
56 Hart, *Understanding Our World*, 335–8.
57 Ibid., 360–3.
58 Ibid., 336.
59 Ibid., 336.

60 Ibid., 338.

61 An example is Wolterstorff's claim in "Once Again, Creator/Creature," 62, that Hart's notion of sovereignty equates it with an unacceptable "Plotinian idea of God as condition of everything not identical with himself."

62 Hart, *Understanding Our World*, 360–3.

63 Ibid., 360.

64 Ibid., "Glossary," 452.

65 Ibid., 361.

## CHAPTER SEVEN

1 Hart, "Conceptual Understanding and Knowing *Other*-wise," 38.

2 Adorno, *Ästhetische Theorie*, 498; *Aesthetic Theory*, 335.

3 Habermas, "Questions and Counterquestions," 203.

4 See my essay "Transforming Aesthetics: Reflections on the Work of Calvin G. Seerveld," 1–22.

5 See Zuidervaart, "Kant's Critique of Beauty and Taste," 325–466.

6 Ibid., 454–6.

7 This paper was particularly helpful for sorting out Adorno's "dialectic of enlightenment"; see the chapters titled "Art as Knowledge and Praxis" and "Ambiguities of Authentic Culture" in my doctoral dissertation "Refractions," 93–126 and 127–54, respectively. Significant portions of these chapters are revised and incorporated into Zuidervaart, *Adorno's Aesthetic Theory*, 122–77.

8 "If nomic conditions are real in the [Hartian] sense that they obtain for whatever they make possible, then why would there be no other ways of knowing nomic conditions? Why, for example, could we not imagine nomic conditions, and in this imagining come to know them? Is not such imagining of nomic conditions an essential feature of artistic activity as well as of the hypothetical element in scholarship?" Zuidervaart, "Existence, Nomic Conditions, and God," 53–4, now ch. 6 in this volume. The term "nomic conditions" points to what Dooyeweerd calls "the law-side" of creation.

9 Ibid., 54.

10 Hart, "Conceptual Understanding and Knowing *Other*-wise," 39, 34–5.

11 Some of this new worry emerged in the January interim course on "Creator and Creatures" that Henk and I co-taught at ICS in 1988.

12 Here I use "linguistic turn" in an expansive sense to include the later Heidegger, the later Wittgenstein, Gadamer, and Adorno (whom I consider

half-turned) as well as structuralism, poststructuralism, analytic philosophy after World War II, postanalytical philosophy, and most versions of feminist philosophy. I do not mean to suggest that topics such as mimesis or expression have fallen out of fashion – see, for example, Walton, *Mimesis as Make-Believe*, and Davies, *Musical Meaning and Expression*. Rather, these chestnuts of philosophical aesthetics now get roasted over a fire that feeds upon the unavoidable linguistic mediation of art and aesthetic experience.

13 Posing the question in this second way allows one to connect Anglo-American philosophers such as Susanne K. Langer and Nelson Goodman with the German philosophers Gadamer and Adorno, despite many discontinuities between their intellectual traditions and, on either side of the Atlantic, strong contrasts in how each figure relates art and language. Adrienne Chaplin-Dengerink makes some astute comparisons between Langer and Goodman on this topic in her doctoral dissertation "Mind, Body and Art: The Problem of Meaning in the Cognitive Aesthetics of Susanne K. Langer."

14 Perhaps the best introduction to theories of truth in Anglo-American philosophy is by Kirkham, *Theories of Truth*, who claims that "a failure to grasp the big picture about truth is the root cause of many philosophical mistakes" (ix). Other surveys of the same tradition include Schmitt, *Truth: A Primer*, and Lynch, *Truth in Context*. For an introductory treatment that gives greater attention to continental philosophy, see Allen, *Truth in Philosophy*.

15 See Kirkham, *Theories of Truth*, 54–72; the quotes are from 54 and 59. Kirkham does explore possible worlds in which teddy bears and flowers can be bearers of truth, but the teddy bears in his thought experiment function as linguistic objects, and the flowers seem to function as propositions. See 61–3.

16 I owe this version of the approach to suggestions from my colleague in philosophy at Calvin College Del Ratzsch.

17 Kirkham, *Theories of Truth*, 70, describing a thesis that he rejects on 69–72 and 329–39.

18 I say "roughly" because truth theorists disagree about what they are trying to accomplish and have differing views concerning what can count as a theory of truth.

19 Adorno, *Ästhetische Theorie*, 194–5; *Aesthetic Theory*, 128–9.

20 Adorno, *Ästhetische Theorie*, 195; *Aesthetic Theory*, 129.

21 Here I simply summarize parts of the detailed account in *Adorno's Aesthetic Theory*. As one would expect from a critical follower of Hegel

and Marx, Adorno's characterizations are neither merely descriptive nor purely normative. They are simultaneously descriptive and normative.

22 Adorno, *Ästhetische Theorie*, 199; *Aesthetic Theory*, 132.

23 Adorno's conception of the artwork's autonomy is dialectical, complex, and not easily summarized. Autonomy has to do with the work's relative independence in society and its lack of obvious social functions, such that in enacting self-criticism it can expose hidden "contradictions" in society. For a reexamination of this conception, see Zuidervaart, "Autonomy, Negativity, and Illusory Transgression."

24 I elaborate these observations and criticisms in *Adorno's Aesthetic Theory*. See esp. ch. 8 and 9.

25 See esp. Wellmer, "Truth, Semblance, Reconciliation: Adorno's Aesthetic Redemption of Modernity." I discuss Wellmer's "stereoscopic" reading of Adorno in ch. 11 of *Adorno's Aesthetic Theory* and will not rehash that discussion here.

26 My drastically abbreviated account of Habermas's theory derives from many of his writings. His most important social-theoretical presentation is in *The Theory of Communicative Action*. He gives a lucid summary in "Actions, Speech Acts, Linguistically Mediated Interactions and the Lifeworld." The earliest comprehensive statement of his discursive theory of truth is "Wahrheitstheorien," in Fahrenbach, ed., *Wirklichkeit und Reflexion*, 211–65; republished in Habermas, *Vorstudien und Ergänzungen zur Theorie des kommunikativen Handelns*, 127–83.

27 Among monographs that elaborate and criticize Habermas's approach, I recommend three that focus on truth theory, ethics, and philosophy of language, respectively: Swindal, *Reflection Revisited*; Rehg, *Insight and Solidarity*; and Cooke, *Language and Reason*.

28 "Primarily," because Habermas holds that every speech act implicitly raises all three types of validity claim. A specific speech act in a certain context will, however, raise one claim more directly and the other two claims more indirectly. A meteorologist's statement about weather conditions to a colleague, for example, would more likely be challenged for lack of truth than for lack of appropriateness or lack of sincerity. Nevertheless, the colleague could always problematize the statement along regulative or expressive lines, if it were uttered loudly during a funeral, say, or simply dropped in the middle of a heart-to-heart sharing of their feelings toward one another.

29 Habermas, "Questions and Counterquestions," 203. Habermas's revision of his earlier account of art comes in response to Martin Jay's essay "Habermas and Modernism" in the same volume.

30 See Taylor, "Language and Society," 23–35.

31 Habermas, "A Reply." Note, for example, how little Habermas actually concedes to Taylor in "A Reply," 221–2.

32 Habermas, "Actions, Speech Acts, Linguistically Mediated Interactions and the Lifeworld," 73–4.

33 Cooke, 62–3, 74–84. In his response to Seel's "The Two Meanings of 'Communicative' Rationality," Habermas mentions "aesthetic harmony (or evaluative cogency)" as a *fourth* validity claim. He contrasts this, however, with the other three validity claims as follows: "Value standards and the corresponding evaluative utterances can be validated only indirectly, namely by means of authentically world-disclosing productions. Things are different in the case of factual, normative or experiential utterances. Here, their justification aims at proving the existence of factual matters, the acceptability of modes of action or norms, and the transparency of subjective experiences" ("A Reply," 227).

34 I indicate the need to historicize the concept of "artwork" in my essay "Fantastic Things," ch. 5 in this volume. My suggestions about artistic truth take up where the last page of that essay left off.

35 I borrow the word "disclosure" from Heidegger's account of truth in art, even though I disagree with the direction and details of his account. I go into this in much greater detail in *Artistic Truth*.

36 Perhaps these levels can also be mapped onto a Seerveldian or Hartian ontology as lingual, social, and analytic analogues, respectively, within an aesthetic domain.

37 "Talk" is intended to include reading, writing, and listening. It is difficult to find one term for all of these, especially since, like Habermas, I reserve "discourse" as a more technical term, but I find "communicative action" problematic, for reasons similar to those given by Cooke in *Language and Reason*, 76–8.

38 I use the terms "art conversation" and "art discourse" rather than "aesthetic" conversation and discourse for two reasons: to avoid a common tendency among philosophers to reduce art to its aesthetic dimension, and to avoid the equally common tendency to reduce the aesthetic dimension to art. I explain the importance of this Seerveldian anti-reductionism in my essay "Autonomy, Negativity, and Illusory Transgression."

39 *Addendum*: My book *Artistic Truth* modifies this claim about dyadic links, saying they "are neither necessary nor exclusive. Being highly fluid, art talk rarely follows the linear path I have mapped" (139).

40 Hart, "Conceptual Understanding and Knowing *Other*-wise," 21.

41 In his unpublished 1990 paper "Reason and Religion Revisited," for example, Hart writes that "Christianity is rooted in the storied and ritualized

wisdom of a people in the face of the mysteries of our ultimate origin and destiny, developed over time, giving context to human life *vis à vis* questions that none of us can avoid ... [T]his wisdom is accepted in a trust which allows us to be in the world in a certain way ... Revelation of truth is not supernatural dictation of divine propositions, but a laying bare of wisdom through trust, a disclosure of ultimate directives that give us hope in journeying to our destiny, whose truth lies in their reliability in use" (6–7).

42 Hart, "Conceptual Understanding and Knowing *Other*-wise," 34–5.

43 Ibid., 35. One peculiarity of passages like these is that Hart seems to assign truth (pragmatically defined) to concepts rather than to propositions, assertions, or judgments. A discussion of this, however, would take me too far afield.

44 Ibid., 36.

45 Ibid., 44–5.

46 Ibid., 39.

47 This Romantic inflection is puzzling, since Hart has paid careful attention to the work on metaphor done by George Lakoff and Mark Johnson. Their book *Philosophy in the Flesh* describes conceptual metaphors as "mappings across conceptual domains that structure our reasoning, our experience, and our everyday language" (47). Perhaps I have misread Hart's discussion of faith talk as metaphorical, or perhaps he employs two different concepts of metaphor.

48 I wish to thank Cal Seerveld, Clarence Joldersma, and my colleagues in the Philosophy Department at Calvin College for their helpful comments on an earlier draft of this essay.

## CHAPTER EIGHT

1 Hart, "ICS Symposium February 27" (24 February 2004 draft), 1.

2 In keeping with some of Henk Hart's own usage, here I use "faith" to refer to certain practices and institutions that are irreducible to other types of practices and institutions. I use "spirituality" as a term for the comprehensive direction of all practices and institutions, and as an equivalent for Vollenhoven and Dooyeweerd's usage of the term "religion."

3 Hart, "ICS Symposium February 27," 5.

4 Ibid., 6. I find the argument for this opaque. Hart seems to claim that animals lack access to the world's order. Because he immediately introduces the role of science in giving us *explicit* access to order, however, it is not clear whether he is saying that animals simply lack access to the world's

order altogether or that they are not capable of pursuing science and therefore have little *explicit* access to the world's order. Since hardly anyone would assert that animals are capable of science, I take his claim to be the stronger one that they simply lack access to the world's order. And this suggests that creatures capable of pre-analytic functioning are order-ignorant *by virtue of* lacking analytic functioning, rather than, for example, by virtue of not being human, spirit-directed creatures. Whether animals lack access to order is itself a contentious issue, in my view.

5 Ibid.

6 I refer here to the discussion surrounding Hart, "Creation Order in Our Philosophical Tradition: Critique and Refinement," 67–96.

7 This is a representative list, not an exhaustive one.

8 Hart, "ICS Symposium February 27," 4.

9 Ibid., 2.

10 Ibid., 3.

11 Ibid., 3.

12 *Addendum*: The discussion that follows concerning whether rationality is prelinguistic or postlinguistic is tied to questions of intermodal order discussed in ch. 4 of this volume. Both Dooyeweerd and Vollenhoven propose an intermodal order in which the logical or analytic mode (i.e., rationality) directly follows the psychic mode (the aspect of sensation and feeling) and directly precedes the historical mode, which becomes the "technoformative" mode in Seerveld's ontology and the "technical or formative" mode in Hart's ontology. Like Seerveld, Hart proposes an intermodal order in which the technical mode – not the logical or analytic mode – directly follows the psychic mode. Further the analytic mode is not only post-technical but also postlingual or, more precisely, postsymbolic in Hart's terminology, since Hart combines the aesthetic and lingual modes (which are distinct modes in Dooyeweerd, Vollenhoven, and Seerveld) into one "symbolic" mode. The different intermodal orders, then, look like this (see also the listing in the essay "Dooyeweerd's Modal Theory," ch. 4 in this volume). Dooyeweerd and Vollenhoven: numerical or arithmetic, spatial, kinematic, physical, biotic or organic, psychic, analytic or logical, historical, lingual, social, economic, aesthetic, juridical, ethical, pistic. Hart: numeric, spatial, kinematic, energetic, biotic, psychic, technical or formative, symbolic, analytic, social, economic, juridical, ethical or moral, pistic or certitudinal (see Hart, *Understanding Our World*, 190–8). Seerveld: numerical, spatial, kinetic, physical, bio-organic, psychical, technical, aesthetical, lingual, analytical, social, economical, juridical, ethical, confessional. My own work assumes the order proposed by Seerveld, although not always the

same terminology. See in this connection subsection 4.2 on "predicative availability" in the essay "Unfinished Business," ch. 14 in this volume.
13 Hart, "Whither Reason and Religion?" 190–1.
14 Olthuis, "Introduction: Philosophy as Spiritual Exercise," xxiii.
15 Hart, "Whither Reason and Religion?" 199.
16 House, "For the Birds: Science and Religion in Critical Perspective," 163. I suggest an alternative conception of scientific truth in the essay "Science, Society, and Culture," ch. 15 in this volume.
17 Hart, "Whither Reason and Religion?" 198.
18 House, "For the Birds," 168.
19 In the context I cite, "religion" appears to mean the practices of faith rather than spirituality. I provide alternative accounts of religion and religious truth in the essay "Religion in Public," ch. 12 in this volume.
20 Hart, "Whither Reason and Religion?" 195–6.
21 Ibid., 197.

## CHAPTER NINE

1 Throughout this chapter I use "historiography" to refer to the practice of historical inquiry and "history" to refer to that which historians study. Occasionally I also use "history" to refer to historical inquiry – as is common in ordinary language – but the context should make clear in those cases that I have historiography in mind.
2 Jay, *Adorno*, 11–12. Here Jay cites a passage in Adorno, *The Jargon of Authenticity*, 93.
3 Dickie, *Aesthetics*, 44.
4 The emphasis on metacriticism is not entirely peculiar to analytic philosophy. Coming from a different tradition, Adorno's *Aesthetic Theory* gives considerable attention to the concepts and criteria used in the language of art criticism. The main difference is that Adorno's treatment is dialectical rather than analytic.
5 One of the most instructive accounts of this method is by Vollenhoven, "De consequent probleemhistorische methode." A translation by Robert Sweetman, with translations of additions from 1966 by John de Kievet, appears as "The Consequential Problem-Historical Method," in Vollenhoven, *The Problem-Historical Method and the History of Philosophy*, 89–135. All citations below are from the Dutch version.
6 Vollenhoven, "De consequent probleemhistorische methode," 15.
7 Wolters, "On Vollenhoven's Problem-Historical Method." Wolters mentions the neo-Kantian philosophers Nicolai Hartmann (1882–1950) and

Richard Hönigswald (1875–1947). It is an open question whether Wolters' suggestion is accurate. Vollenhoven's own reflections on the development of his historiographic method indicate that it arose gradually as he tried to make sense of Greek philosophy. He suggests that, to a large extent, he had simply been "following his nose," so to speak, and fashioning historiographic categories to solve problems of historical interpretation. In other words, his own historiographic position emerged as this position says every philosophical position emerges: through the attempt to pose and solve fundamental philosophical problems. See Vollenhoven, "De consequent probleemhistorische methode," 1–8.

8 Wolters, "On Vollenhoven's Problem-Historical Method," 246.

9 Ibid., 246–57.

10 Vollenhoven, "De consequent probleemhistorische methode," 9; translated in Wolters, "On Vollenhoven's Problem-Historical Method," 241–2.

11 Wolters, "On Vollenhoven's Problem-Historical Method," 241–5.

12 Ibid., 234–6.

13 For an introduction to the problem of induction, see Chalmers, *What Is This Thing Called Science?* 1–21.

14 There are, of course, many levels at which a historian of philosophy can work: for example, the development of a problem or solution within one philosopher's writings, or the development of a problem or solution in an entire generation of philosophers.

15 Seerveld, "Biblical Wisdom underneath Vollenhoven's Categories for Philosophical Historiography," 134–5.

16 Seerveld's language is actually much stronger. He speaks of distortion and idolizing, and he calls monism and dualism "vivid, compassionate and damning categories pinpointing … philosophical positions that are frustrated and distracted from the way of shalom." Ibid., 137.

17 A few helpful clues to criteria for philosophical problems can be found in Bubner, *Modern German Philosophy*, 19.

18 Wolters, "On Vollenhoven's Problem-Historical Method," 234–6, 240–6, 260n9.

19 Seerveld, "Biblical Wisdom," 135.

20 Ibid., 136.

21 Vollenhoven, "De consequent probleemhistorische methode," 1–2.

22 Ibid., 2–8.

23 The manner of this movement is the most crucial challenge in metacritique. Two of the best discussions and demonstrations of this challenge occur in Hegel's *Phenomenology of Spirit* (1807) and Adorno's *Negative Dialectics* (1966).

24 McIntire, "Historical Study and the Historical Dimension of Our World," 20.
25 Ibid., 35.
26 It should be noted, however, that McIntire would probably consider a problem-historical method overly restricted and restrictive.
27 McIntire, "Historical Study," 25.
28 Ibid., 26.
29 An important study of the relationship between history and critique in recent philosophy has been provided by Echeverria, *Criticism and Commitment*. Echeverria's work has helped shape some of my own reflections on metacritique.
30 "Was im Innern des Begriffs sich vollzieht, darin erscheint stets auch etwas von der realen Bewegung" (Adorno, "Wozu noch Philosophie," 465). "Whatever takes place in the interior of the concept always reflects something of the movement of reality" (Adorno, "Why Still Philosophy," 10).
31 See, for example, Adorno's *Kierkegaard: Konstruktion des Ästhetischen*, *Zur Metakritik der Erkenntnistheorie*, and *Drei Studien zu Hegel*. *Zur Metakritik der Erkenntnistheorie* has been translated as *Against Epistemology*. My review of this translation appears in *Canadian Philosophical Reviews* 4 (April 1984), no. 2: 49–52. The English translations of the Kierkegaard and Hegel books are *Kierkegaard: Construction of the Aesthetic* and *Hegel: Three Studies*.
32 Adorno sees philosophical critique as the unifying force of philosophy's history: "Sie [die Kritik] allein, als Einheit des Problems und der Argumente, nicht die Übernahme von Thesen, hat gestiftet, was als produktive Einheit der Geschichte der Philosophie gelten mag." ("Critique alone, as the unity of the problem and its arguments, not the adoption of received theses, has laid the foundation for what may be considered the productive unity of the history of philosophy.") Adorno, "Wozu noch Philosophie," 462; "Why Still Philosophy," 8.
33 See Mekkes, "Methodology and Practice." See also the discussion of hermeneutical experience and the history of effect (*Wirkungsgeschichte*) in Gadamer, *Wahrheit und Methode*, 229–360; *Truth and Method*, 242–379.

## CHAPTER TEN

1 Scheler, *Man's Place in Nature*, 4. Further references will be to this translation. Sexist language will be avoided wherever this is possible, but not when it occurs in direct quotations. The title of the German original published in 1928, the last year of Scheler's life, is *Die Stellung des Menschen im Kosmos*.

2 Cassirer, *An Essay on Man*, 21–2.
3 Scheler, 7.
4 Ibid., 8.
5 Ibid., 78.
6 Ibid., 36.
7 Ibid., 47.
8 Scheler's notion of "objectification" implies, among other things, that one can treat phenomena as substances and define them in terms of essences. Animals cannot objectify phenomena, he says, but human beings can. Yet we cannot objectify *ourselves* as spiritual beings. This, in turn, implies that human self-consciousness and human consciousness of other persons (which he says animals lack) cannot objectify persons and their spiritual acts. Instead these involve a "centering" or "collecting" of our own persons, an "identification with" other persons, and a "participation in" their acts (Scheler, 40, 47–8).
9 Ibid., 62.
10 Ibid., 55.
11 Ibid., 70–1.
12 Ibid., 93.
13 Ibid., 70–1.
14 Cassirer, "'Geist' und 'Leben' in der Philosophie der Gegenwart"; translated as "'Spirit' and 'Life' in Contemporary Philosophy." Cassirer's critique of Scheler appeared two years after Scheler's death and one year after Cassirer completed his own three-volume *Philosophie der symbolischen Formen*.
15 Cassirer, "'Geist' und 'Leben' in der Philosophie der Gegenwart," 864.
16 Ibid., 868–71.
17 Ibid., 874–5.
18 Ibid., 875.
19 Ibid., 869.
20 Cassirer, *An Essay on Man*, 67–8.
21 Ibid., 68.
22 Ibid., 70.
23 Ibid., 228.
24 Ibid., 222.
25 Ibid., 23–6.
26 Ibid., 41.
27 Ibid., 25.
28 Ibid., 30.
29 Ibid., 223–4.

30 Cassirer, *The Philosophy of Symbolic Forms*, vol. 1, 78.

31 For the term "transfunctional," as well as some reasons to adopt it, I am indebted to Hart, *Understanding Our World*, 267–318.

32 Stafleu, "Being Human in the Cosmos."

33 Geertsema, "*Homo Respondens*." This essay summarizes ideas and arguments that the author develops in greater detail in two Dutch publications: *Het menselijk karakter van ons kennen* and *Om de humaniteit*.

34 Olthuis, "Be(com)ing: Humankind as Gift and Call" and "Of Webs and Whirlwinds: Me, Myself, and I." The first essay, like Geertsema's "*Homo Respondens*," appears in a special issue of *Philosophia Reformata* containing papers from the 1986 International Symposium "On Being Human" in the Netherlands sponsored by the Association for Calvinist Philosophy. Calvin Seerveld's daily meditations at this symposium are collected, together with appropriate music and art reproductions, in Seerveld, *On Being Human*.

35 Klapwijk, *Purpose in the Living World?* See also the review of this book by Roy Clouser in *Philosophia Reformata* 75 (2010): 82–5, the special issue of essays discussing this book in *Philosophia Reformata* 76 (2011): 1–152, and the author's response to all of these writings in Klapwijk, "Nothing in Evolutionary Theory Makes Sense Except in the Light of Creation."

36 Glas, "Christian Philosophical Anthropology." This is a translation and revision of the chapter titled "Filosofische antropologie" in van Woudenberg, ed., *Kennis en werkelijkheid*, 86–142. See also Glas, "Hierarchy and Dualism in Aristotelian Psychology," and Glas, "Ego, Self, and the Body: An Assessment of Dooyeweerd's Philosophical Anthropology," in Griffioen and Balk, ed., *Christian Philosophy at the Close of the Twentieth Century*, 67–78. The latter volume also contains Hendrik Hart's "Self as Question: A Response to Gerrit Glas" (79–84) and Elaine Storkey's "Dooyeweerd's Anthropology – The Male-Female Dimension" (85–92). Those who read Dutch will also want to consult the special issue on philosophical anthropology in *Philosophia Reformata* 54, no. 1 (1989). This issue contains two essays by Gerrit Glas, one of which develops an alternative theory of the emotions with reference to Dooyeweerd's view of the human body as an enkaptic structural whole. It also contains a series of articles in which recent Dooyeweerdian and post-Dooyeweerdian proposals by Willem J. Ouweneel and Jan D. Dengerink are elaborated, criticized, and defended by these two authors and by Andree Troost. The two books at the centre of this discussion are Ouweneel's *De Leer van de mens* and Dengerink's *De zin van de*

*werkelijkheid*. A short and accessible version of Ouweneel's philosophical anthropology appears in Ouweneel, *Heart and Soul*.

37 Chapter VII in Hart, *Understanding Our World*, 267–318.

38 Here, in addition to Hart and Olthuis, I would include De Graaff and Seerveld. See, for example, De Graaff, "Towards a New Anthropological Model," and Seerveld, "A Christian Tin-Can Theory of Man" – republished as "A Christian Tin-Can Theory of the Human Creature" in *In the Fields of the Lord*, ed. Bartholomew, 102–16.

39 See especially Dooyeweerd, "De leer van de mens in de wijsbegeerte de wetsidee," anonymously translated as "The Theory of Man: Thirty-Two Propositions on Anthropology" and distributed as a mimeograph (Toronto: Institute for Christian Studies, n.d.). An updated and revised version of this translation is available online via the home page of Dr J. Glenn Friesen at http://www.members.shaw.ca/aevum/32Propositions.html. See also Dooyeweerd's NC 3: 694–8, 765–84, and his "What Is Man?" – the last chapter in Dooyeweerd, *In the Twilight of Western Thought*, 173–95. Careful critical expositions of Dooyeweerd's anthropology in English can be found in the essays by Geertsema and Glas cited in previous notes and in Blosser, "Reconnoitering Dooyeweerd's Theory of Man."

40 Dooyeweerd applies the same notion of an "enkaptic structural whole" to human corporeality, albeit more complexly elaborated, as he applies to a sculptural artwork. I spell out my reservations about this notion with respect to art in the essay "Fantastic Things,"ch. 5 in this volume. Like Stafleu and Dengerink, I also find the notion problematic when applied to human corporeality, and I do not use it, following Vollenhoven in this regard (cf. Glas, "Christian Philosophical Anthropology," 168).

41 Vollenhoven, *Isagôgè Philosophiae*, 62. Glas, "Christian Philosophical Anthropology," 166–8, gives an illuminating summary of Vollenhoven's approach in distinction from Dooyeweerd's and suggests that the notion of the body as a "functional cloak" derives from Paul's metaphor in 2 Cor. 5:1–4 of the "earthly tent we live in."

42 Hart, *Understanding Our World*, 279.

43 Ibid.

44 Olthuis, "Be(com)ing: Humankind as Gift and Call," 170–2.

45 Although, as Klapwijk, *Purpose in the Living World?* 254–6, correctly notes, Vollenhoven rejected the constancy of species in Dooyeweerd's work and embraced evolution within realms or kingdoms, nevertheless Vollenhoven opposed the idea that evolution could occur across the boundaries of plant, animal, and human life.

46 At the same time, an evolutionary account of hominization requires a different understanding of so-called creational ordinances, as I indicate in "Macrostructures and Societal Principles," ch. 13 in this volume.

## CHAPTER ELEVEN

1 This essay incorporates parts of a talk given on the occasion of the 2000 Winifred E. Weter Faculty Award Lecture at Seattle Pacific University, 13 April 2000, in response to Professor Janet Blumberg's lecture "*Scientia et Sapientia*: Enigmas of Science and Wisdom from Plato to Derrida." I wish to thank Al Wolters for his comments on an earlier draft of this essay.

2 I use "Radical Orthodoxy" as a convenient term to indicate thinkers who have sufficiently similar projects and enough of a shared history to form what could loosely be called a school of thought. I do not wish to deny or slight the individual character of each project, nor the significant differences among the thinkers to whom the term applies.

3 Groen van Prinsterer, *Unbelief and Revolution*. This is a translation of *Ongeloof en revolutie*.

4 See especially the first lecture, titled "Calvinism a Life-System," in Kuyper, *Lectures on Calvinism*, 9–40. For an extensive commentary on this book, see Heslam, *Creating a Christian Worldview*. I comment briefly on the ambivalence in Kuyper's stances toward democracy and religious pluralism in my essay "Art Is No Fringe," 1–12.

5 See especially Runner, *The Relation of the Bible to Learning*.

6 In this respect there is a deep continuity in Hendrik Hart's work between an early publication such as *The Challenge of Our Age* and more recent essays such as "Conceptual Understanding and Knowing *Other*-wise." I comment on this essay in "Artistic Truth, Linguistically Turned," ch. 7 in this volume.

7 Seerveld, "The Cross of Scholarly Cultural Power," 201, 197.

8 Westphal, *Suspicion and Faith*, 16.

9 The Dutch version of this book appeared in 1959, and the first English translation appeared in 1979.

10 Dooyeweerd, *Roots of Western Culture*, 4.

11 Ibid., 3.

12 Ibid., 8–9.

13 Ibid., 44.

14 Nevertheless, I consider Dooyeweerd's account of societal integration to be relatively weak, and I regard it as insufficiently critical of the ways in which modern economic and technological forces of integration destroy

habitats and human life. This is tied to the fact that he relies on an unconvincing theory of "enkapsis" to compensate for inattention to the problems of societal integration in his account of modern societal differentiation. See especially Dooyeweerd, NC 3: 588–624, 653–70.

15 For the main lines of my own alternative, which wishes to address societal evil and the suffering it causes, see "Earth's Lament: Suffering, Hope, and Wisdom," the epilogue to this volume. *Addendum*: The two contrasting paths for reformational social critique are, of course, not the only options. The most fruitful social critiques by reformational thinkers after Dooyeweerd acknowledge and think through both modern differentiation and spiritual malaise, most notably in the work of Bob Goudzwaard.

16 Ward, *Cities of God*, 226. Not being sufficiently expert in the study of Augustine, I leave the accuracy and fruitfulness of Ward's interpretation for others to sort out.

17 Ibid.

18 Ibid., 227.

19 Ibid., 228.

20 Ibid., 229.

21 Ibid., 230.

22 Ibid.

23 Goudzwaard, *Capitalism and Progress*, 243. I have more to say about norms as "societal principles" in "Earth's Lament," where I describe societal principles as "historically constituted and future-oriented callings in which the voice of God can be heard and traces of a new Earth can appear."

24 See Ward, *Cities of God*, 232–3.

25 Ibid., 236.

26 Milbank, *Theology and Social Theory*, 380.

27 Obviously this last question would offend theologians who think that, as a whole, the development of modern social sciences is, like Tom Hanks, on the road to perdition. But such theologians would not, or should not, rechristen theology as a (regal) social science. I am not sure whether Milbank wants to eat his secular social scientific cake (perhaps after the rechristenation ceremony?) and have it postsecularly too.

28 Milbank slides between "social theory" and "social science" without seeming to note the difference. In my own usage, a "social theory" is a theory of society as this theory operates within one or more of the social sciences. The social sciences have theoretical components, and often these theoretical components intersect a social theory. But contemporary social sciences also have empirical components so vast that these resemble the submerged part of an iceberg. Given its almost exclusively theoretical orientation,

Radical Orthodoxy (like some of reformational philosophy before it) threatens to crash against that part of social science which the theological queen does not deign to investigate.

29 Milbank, *Theology and Social Theory*, 380–1.

30 Ibid., 381.

31 Ibid., 433.

32 At the conference where I first presented this paper, Graham Ward suggested that his approach in *Cities of God* is genealogical (à la Foucault) rather than normative (à la Habermas). I do not think this affects the point I wish to make. Here I use the terms "normative" and "normativity" to indicate a concern to ask what makes for (relative) goodness in human life, culture, and society. This concern is shared by Dooyeweerd, Ward, and Milbank, and it derives in part from Augustine. All three are radical Augustinians to whom God's creating everything good remains crucial for understanding and evaluating the contemporary world.

33 Milbank, *Theology and Social Theory*, 391.

34 Ward, *Cities of God*, 228.

35 Zuidervaart, "Response to Johan van der Hoeven's 'Development in the Light of Encounter,'" 40.

36 Wolterstorff, *Until Justice and Peace Embrace*, 33.

## CHAPTER TWELVE

1 Rorty, "Religion as Conversation-Stopper," 171.

2 My account of this relationship is indebted to two papers by Andrew Buchwalter: "The Relationship of Religion and Politics under Conditions of Modernity and Globality" and "Religion, Secularity, and the Politics of Modernity."

3 Hegel, *Elements of the Philosophy of Right*, 292.

4 Ibid., 293.

5 Ibid., 295.

6 Ibid., 301.

7 Ibid., 292.

8 Ibid., 295.

9 Ibid., 295–302.

10 Ibid., 303.

11 This distinction derives in part from the work of D.H.Th. Vollenhoven and Herman Dooyeweerd, who differentiate between "religion" (what I call "spirituality") and "faith" (what I call "religion"). For a summary and evaluation of Dooyeweerd's conception, see Olthuis, "Dooyeweerd on Religion and Faith," 21–40.

12 I do not have space to take up Hegel's account of "revealed religion" (*die offenbare Religion*) in his *Phenomenology of Spirit*. Suffice it to say that I do not think "spirit" must rise from the level of representational thinking to pure thought in order to come fully into its own. See Hegel, *Phenomenology of Spirit*, 410–93. Habermas observes that Hegel's "sublation of the world of religious representation in the philosophical concept enabled the saving of its essential contents only by casting off the substance of its piety. Certainly, the atheistic core, enveloped in esoteric insight, was reserved for the philosophers." Habermas, "Transcendence from Within, Transcendence in This World," 227.

13 Hegel, *Philosophy of Right*, 380.

14 Habermas, *Between Facts and Norms*, 505.

15 Habermas proposes that "we view law as the medium through which communicative power is translated into administrative power. For the transformation of communicative power into administrative [power] has the character of an *empowerment* within the framework of statutory authorization. We can then interpret the idea of the constitutional state in general as the requirement that the administrative system, which is steered through the power code, be tied to the lawmaking communicative power and kept free of illegitimate interventions of social power (i.e., of the factual strength of privileged interests to assert themselves)." Habermas, *Between Facts and Norms*, 150.

16 The most important sources for this all-too-brief account of civil society are Cohen and Arato, *Civil Society and Political Theory*, and Habermas's *Between Facts and Norms*, 329–87.

17 Hegel, *Philosophy of Right*, 295–6.

18 I use the term "religious economy" in quite a different sense from the way it is used in rational choice theory, for reasons similar to my objections to "market failure" accounts of the civic sector in Zuidervaart, *Art in Public*, 129–69.

19 Ibid., 143–51.

20 This difference gives rise to some of the concerns that surround government funding for "faith-based initiatives." Such funding involves a tricky balancing between the community-oriented concerns of religious organizations and the civil-society orientation of civic-sector organizations.

21 See "Models of Public Space" in Benhabib, *Situating the Self*, 89–120.

22 For a more substantial account of authentication, see Zuidervaart, *Social Philosophy after Adorno*, 101–6.

23 In addition to the account of authentication in *Social Philosophy after Adorno*, see the account of propositional truth in Zuidervaart, *Artistic Truth*, 77–100, and the discussion of both truth and authentication in

Zuidervaart, "Unfinished Business," ch. 14 in this volume. I plan to work out the details in a book manuscript on the general idea of truth.

## CHAPTER THIRTEEN

1 This essay began as a keynote lecture given at the conference on "The Future of Creation Order" at the VU University Amsterdam in August 2011. I wish to thank the conference organizers for their invitation, Govert Buijs for his informative and probing response to the lecture, the conference participants for a lively discussion, and two anonymous referees for their instructive comments on an earlier version of the essay. Much of this essay appears within the journal article "Critical Transformations: Macrostructures, Religion, and Critique," *Critical Research on Religion* 1 (2013): 243–69, published by SAGE Publications Ltd. I thank the journal editors and publisher for permission to republish these materials.

2 Kuyper, *Christianity and the Class Struggle*, 39–40, translation modified. The Dutch title of Kuyper's speech is "Het sociale vraagstuk en de Christelijke religie." A more recent translation by James W. Skillen has the title *The Problem of Poverty*.

3 "[I]mprovement undoubtedly lies – I do not shrink from the word – along the *socialistic* path, provided only you do not mean by socialistic the program of Social Democracy; but merely express this idea, in itself so beautiful, that our national society is ... a God-willed *community*, a living, human organism." Kuyper, *Christianity and the Class Struggle*, 41.

4 Ibid., 57.

5 Chaplin, *Herman Dooyeweerd*, 106–7.

6 Vollenhoven, "The Unity of Life."

7 See, for example, Olthuis, "Be(com)ing: Humankind as Gift and Call" and "Crossing the Threshold."

8 Many passages in the remainder of this essay derive from two books that contain more extensive explanations and arguments: see Zuidervaart, *Social Philosophy after Adorno* and *Art in Public*.

9 For succinct and illuminating accounts of these categories and distinctions, see Chaplin, *Herman Dooyeweerd*, 62–70, 86–155.

10 Hegel, *Elements of the Philosophy of Right*.

11 See my chapter on "Relational Autonomy" in *Art in Public*, 207–40.

12 "[W]e reject in principle every speculative metaphysics and demand an *integral empirical* method in philosophic investigations." Dooyeweerd, NC 1: 548. Jonathan Chaplin provides an excellent summary of Dooyeweerd's conception of social philosophy in an Appendix to his book *Herman Dooyeweerd*, 311–17.

13 In prepared comments on the conference paper from which this essay derives, Govert Buijs suggests that I portray two of these macrostructures – economy and state – in a negative light and that my adjectives "proprietary" and "administrative" have negative connotations. Although my descriptions of these macrostructures are not "neutral" – no architectonic critique could be neutral – my criticisms are directed toward *all three macrostructures and their interrelations*, and I do not intend my adjectives to be pejorative. "Proprietary" points to the fact that organizations and transactions in the economic macrostructure follow principles of private ownership and private profit. "Administrative" indicates that the primary political power within the states and suprastates of contemporary Europe and North America (elsewhere too) resides in the agencies of administration and not in the legislature or judiciary. There are both advantages and disadvantages to the proprietary and administrative character of these two macrostructures. I am especially interested in normative deficiencies that affect all three macrostructures.

14 In thinking about the proprietary economy, administrative state, and civil society, I have drawn most heavily on the work of Bob Goudzwaard and Jürgen Habermas. From Goudzwaard I have gained a better understanding of the spiritual underpinnings to these macrostructures and their normative distortions. See especially Goudzwaard, *Capitalism and Progress*. From Habermas I have learned to reflect more systematically about the pressures that economic and political systems exert upon civil society – what Habermas describes as "the colonization of the life world." See especially Habermas, *The Theory of Communicative Action*.

15 As will become apparent, however, I do not share Habermas's view of these systems as congelations of "norm-free sociality" that we can access only in the objectivating attitude of the social sciences. See Habermas, *The Theory of Communicative Action*, vol. 2, 171–9.

16 For a slightly more detailed version of this very brief account of civil society, see my essay "Religion in Public" (ch. 12 in this volume) where I mention as my primary sources Cohen and Arato, *Civil Society and Political Theory*, and Habermas, *Between Facts and Norms*.

17 As important or perhaps more important is the intersection between proprietary economy and administrative state, as Bob Goudzwaard rightly pointed out in comments from the floor after I presented this paper in August 2011. Habermas recognizes this as well, as can be seen from his work on "crisis tendencies" during the years leading up to *The Theory of Communicative Action*. See especially Habermas, *Legitimation Crisis*. Although I acknowledge this point, it would require a separate treatment beyond the scope of this essay.

18 For prescient analyses of how crises in economic and administrative systems reinforce each other, see Habermas, *Legitimation Crisis*, and Offe, *Contradictions of the Welfare State*.
19 Zuidervaart, *Art in Public*, 161.
20 Zuidervaart, *Social Philosophy after Adorno*, 129.
21 This description resembles the concept of justice as "tribution" that Jonathan Chaplin, drawing from a proposal by Paul Tillich, offers as a refinement to Dooyeweerd's understanding of justice as "retribution." See in particular Chaplin, *Herman Dooyeweerd*, 192–3.
22 See in this connection Brunkhorst, *Solidarity*. It would be interesting to compare Brunkhorst's historical-philosophical genealogy of "solidarity" with the genealogy of "justice" as involving inherent rights in Wolterstorff's *Justice: Rights and Wrongs*.
23 Zuidervaart, "Unfinished Business," 6–7. (The quoted passage has been deleted from the version of this essay that appears as chapter 14 in this volume.)
24 Zuidervaart, *Social Philosophy after Adorno*, 126.
25 Ibid., 129.
26 This is not intended as an exhaustive characterization of normative deficiencies in civil society. Because civil society is not a system, its normative deficiencies tend to be more varied and diffuse than those one can identify in the proprietary economy and the administrative state. In *Art in Public*, 176–90, I describe three sets of pressures – external, internal, and technological – that create or reinforce normative problems in civil society, and I discuss these pressures, respectively, as economic hypercommercialization and administrative performance fetishism, cultural balkanization and exclusion, and technologically induced pastiche and neomania. Tendencies toward balkanization and exclusion, in particular, hinder solidarity in civil society by pointing its institutions and organizations away from intercultural dialogue and social inclusion.
27 These concerns add complexity to the debate between Nancy Fraser and Axel Honneth about whether socio-economic justice requires redistribution, recognition, or both, and in which order of priority. See Fraser and Honneth, *Redistribution or Recognition?*
28 Goudzwaard, *Capitalism and Progress*, 65–8. Goudzwaard derives the idea of a simultaneous realization of norms from Dooyeweerd and the work of economist T.P. van der Kooy.
29 Zuidervaart, *Artistic Truth*, 97.
30 Van Til, *Growing Civil Society*, 153–8.
31 Rifkin, *The End of Work*, 256–67.

32 If our focus were the public sphere, we could also point toward what I have called "hidden elements of a social polity – a tendency toward genuine democracy – in both of these macrostructural systems" (Zuidervaart, *Art in Public*, 236).

33 Here I disagree with Hauke Brunkhorst, who claims that differentiated social systems "use human substance without replacing it" and that "functional systems like the market economy or sovereign state power, taken in themselves, represent new forms of social integration without solidarity" (*Solidarity*, 82–3).

34 For a more extensive account of the state's task, see my essay "Religion in Public," ch. 12 in this volume.

35 James Skillen, former President of the Center for Public Justice in Washington, DC, asked from the floor at the conference, "Who is responsible for bringing about the change you envision?" and my response was "All of us." Clearly there is more to the issue than that. Structural transformation occurs both via and despite intentional human effort, and human effort occurs in many different contexts and ways. My main point is that all the inhabitants of a social order are in some sense responsible for that order and in some sense capable of contributing to the change of that order, not simply as individuals but as members of organizations and institutions and as participants in traditions and communities. Moreover, these organizations, institutions, traditions, and communities also should and can contribute. Both an individualist "You can make a difference" and a collectivist expectation of a vanguard class or sector are insufficiently nuanced on the topic of large-scale social change – as are privatist resignation and structuralist determinism. See in this connection the chapter on "Widening Ways of Economy, Justice, and Peace" in Goudzwaard, Vander Vennen, and Van Heemst, *Hope in Troubled Times*, 169–205.

36 According to Adorno, the telos of the social order both required and prevented by the capitalist economy lies in "the negation of the physical suffering of even the least of its members, and of the internal articulations [*Reflexionsformen*] of such suffering. This negation is the interest of everyone, [and] ultimately to be achieved only by a solidarity that is transparent to itself and to every living creature." Adorno, *Negative Dialektik*, 203–4, my translation.

## CHAPTER FOURTEEN

1 Dooyeweerd, NC 2: 556, WW 2: 487, my translation.

2 Griffioen, "Review of *Artistic Truth* by Lambert Zuidervaart."

3 Zuidervaart, "Dooyeweerd's Conception of Truth," ch. 3 in this volume.
4 Zuidervaart, *Artistic Truth*, ix–xii, 1–14.
5 Zuidervaart, *Adorno's Aesthetic Theory*, xx.
6 Vollenhoven, *Calvinism and the Reformation of Philosophy*.
7 Vollenhoven, "De consequent probleemhistorische methode."
8 Klapwijk, "Antithesis, Synthesis, and the Idea of Transformational Philosophy," and Klapwijk, "Reformational Philosophy on the Boundary between the Past and the Future."
9 Zuidervaart, "Dooyeweerd's Conception of Truth."
10 Seerveld, "The Relation of the Arts to the Presentation of Truth."
11 Hart, *Understanding Our World*.
12 For a detailed account, see section 3.2 in the longer paper from which this essay derives: Zuidervaart, "After Dooyeweerd: Truth in Reformational Philosophy."
13 Zuidervaart, *Artistic Truth*, 55–77.
14 Ibid., 118–39.
15 Zuidervaart, *Art in Public*.
16 Hart, 146–7.
17 Seerveld, "Imaginativity."
18 Cf. Zuidervaart, *Social Philosophy after Adorno*, 1–15, 48–76.
19 Heidegger, *Sein und Zeit*, 152–3, 314–16.
20 Hart, *Understanding Our World*.
21 Zuidervaart, *Artistic Truth*, 97.
22 "Resourcefulness" is my term for what Bob Goudzwaard calls "stewardship." For a more detailed account of these three societal principles and their interconnection, see the chapter on globalization in Zuidervaart, *Social Philosophy after Adorno*, 107–31, which glosses "resourcefulness" as "the principle of carefully stewarding human and nonhuman potentials for the sake of interconnected flourishing" (129). *Addendum*: I have changed "ethical" to "social" in this version of the essay, having decided after 2009 that, as a societal principle, solidarity is primarily a social matter and not primarily "ethical" in Dooyeweerd and Vollenhoven's modal sense of the term.
23 Zuidervaart, "Earth's Lament" (see the epilogue to this volume).
24 Dooyeweerd, *Roots of Western Culture*, 63.
25 Ibid., 63–110.
26 The notion of interconnected flourishing as a telos has affinities with the idea of "shalom" in Wolterstorff, *Until Justice and Peace Embrace*, with the proviso that we regard it as already underway and not endlessly deferred. Wolterstorff criticizes the "Amsterdam School" for neglecting this idea and

for making societal structures seem more important than the creatures that fashion and inhabit them.

27 Zuidervaart, "Earth's Lament."

28 Griffioen, "De betekenis van Dooyeweerds ontwikkelingsidee," and Seerveld, "Dooyeweerd's Idea of 'Historical Development.'"

29 Jürgen Moltmann provides an important theological reason why philosophers should not posit an ultimate horizon: a biblical eschatology will distinguish between the future as *futurum* and as *adventus*. *Futurum* is the future we can foresee from within our present history. But *adventus* is an unforeseeable future – see Olthuis, "Unlike Any Other Hope," 186–9. To maintain openness toward *adventus*, philosophers do well not to posit an ultimate horizon.

30 Zuidervaart, "Dooyeweerd's Conception of Truth."

31 *Addendum*: Subsequent to the publication of this essay in 2009, I developed a more detailed account that distinguishes and relates propositional truth, assertoric correctness, and the practical reliability of ordinary beliefs. See Zuidervaart, "How Not to Be an Anti-Realist: Habermas, Truth, and Justification." A slightly revised version appears in Zuidervaart et al., eds., *Truth Matters*, 23–45.

32 What follows is a drastic abbreviation of chapter 4 ("Truth as Disclosure") in Zuidervaart, *Artistic Truth*.

33 Zuidervaart, *Artistic Truth*, 6.

34 Dreyfus, *Being-in-the-World*, 272.

35 Heidegger, *Sein und Zeit*, 153–60.

36 Ibid., 214–19.

37 Zuidervaart, *Artistic Truth*, 92.

38 Heidegger, *Sein und Zeit*, 219–26.

39 In line with Dooyeweerd and Vollenhoven, I distinguish questions of *objectivity* from questions of intersubjective *validity*. I take up the first of these here.

40 Vollenhoven, *Isagôgè Philosophiae*, 111–20.

41 Ibid., 122, with "analytic" replaced by "logical."

42 Ibid., 124–5.

43 Vollenhoven is very clear about this – see ibid., 124. Dooyeweerd's notion of the concept's intentional content may compromise his critique of what Rorty, *Philosophy and the Mirror of Nature*, calls representationalism.

44 Vollenhoven, *Isagôgè Philosophiae*, 124.

45 Heidegger, *Sein und Zeit*, 218.

46 Zuidervaart, *Artistic Truth*, 93.

47 Cf. Geertsema, "Dooyeweerd on Knowledge and Truth," 97–8.

48 Habermas, *Truth and Justification*, and van Woudenberg, "Wat mogen we van een theorie over waarheid verwachten?"

49 One can distinguish between truth and justification without subscribing to what René van Woudenberg calls the "standard analysis" of knowledge (as justified true belief) and of truth ("a proposition is true, if what it says to be the case actually is the case"). I disagree with van Woudenberg's claims that Dooyeweerd's conception is "a form of correspondence theory" (van Woudenberg, "Two Very Different Analyses of Knowledge," 106, 117) and that Jesus's "I am the truth" is an inappropriate point of departure when we address questions of truth theory (van Woudenberg, "Wat mogen we van een theorie over waarheid verwachten?" 66–7).

50 Zuidervaart, *Social Philosophy After Adorno*, 77–106.

51 Ibid., 103.

52 Dooyeweerd, *Roots of Western Culture*, 3. Vollenhoven's ontology is illuminating in this regard. He distinguishes the antithesis between good and evil as a "third determinant" in addition to modality and individuality. See Vollenhoven, *Isagôgè Philosophiae*, 56–62.

53 Zuidervaart, *Social Philosophy After Adorno*, 104.

54 Cf. Mekkes, "Knowing," 318.

55 Arnold DeGraaff, Peter Enneson, Henk Hart, Jim Olthuis, Cal Seerveld, and my colleagues at ICS offered illuminating comments on drafts of both this essay and "Dooyeweerd's Conception of Truth," and Matt Klaassen gave helpful research assistance. Some passages come from the Kenneth Konyndyk Memorial Lecture I presented to the Society of Christian Philosophers in April 2007 (ch. 15 in this volume). I thank Bruce Benson for graciously inviting me to give that lecture, and Lee Hardy for providing astute comments. This essay is dedicated to the memory of my former colleague Ken Konyndyk.

## CHAPTER FIFTEEN

1 As formulated in Copi, *Introduction to Logic*, 329.

2 Ibid., 354.

3 Rouse, *Knowledge and Power*, 265.

4 Deflationary accounts include Frank Ramsey's "redundancy theory," P.F. Strawson's performative theory, Willard Quine's disquotationalism, the prosentential theory put forward by Dorothy Grover, and Paul Horwich's minimalist theory. For a brief introduction to these varieties of deflationism, and representative statements of them, see Lynch, ed., *The Nature of Truth*, 419–611.

5 Rouse, *Knowledge and Power*, 147.
6 Citations are from Heidegger, *Sein und Zeit*. I use two of the existing translations: *Being and Time*, trans. Joan Stambaugh, and *Being and Time*, trans. Macquarrie and Robinson. Like Macquarrie and Robinson, I render "*Sein*" as "Being" (capital "B") and do not hyphenate "Dasein." I silently change quotations from Stambaugh's translation accordingly.
7 "Mit der Aussage wurde ein extremes Derivat der Auslegung sichtbar gemacht." Heidegger, *Sein und Zeit*, 160; Macquarrie and Robinson translation, 203.
8 Heidegger, *Sein und Zeit*, 218; my translation.
9 Heidegger, *Sein und Zeit*, 220–1; Stambaugh translation, 203.
10 Rouse, *Knowledge and Power*, 63. Rouse seems to equate the notion of "world" with one of four meanings Heidegger distinguishes in *Sein und Zeit*, 64–5: namely, "world" in the *ontical* sense of the cultural context in which "a factical Dasein 'lives.'" But this is not the *ontological* meaning that is most important in Heidegger's analytic of Dasein. For clear discussions of all four meanings, see Dreyfus, *Being-in-the-World*, 88–107, and Carman, *Heidegger's Analytic*, 128–36. Carman, 177–8, uses the distinction among "worlds" to challenge Rouse's interpretation of Heidegger.
11 Rouse, *Knowledge and Power*, 69–126. Here Rouse proposes "an analysis of scientific practice that reveals the local, existential character of the understanding it produces. Scientific knowledge is first and foremost knowing one's way about in the laboratory (or clinic, field site, etc.)." Although such knowledge is transferable into other situations, the transfer "must be understood in terms of the adaptation of one local knowledge to create another … Even our knowledge of theories … has to be accounted for in terms of such a practical, local grasp" (72).
12 Cf. *Sein und Zeit*, 34–9, where Heidegger makes the even stronger claim that philosophy as such is "universal phenomenological ontology" (38). The question guiding Heidegger's inquiry into Dasein's existence could hardly be more universal and context-transcending: What is the meaning of Being? Rouse does not comment on this question. But he does take issue with a related aspect to Heidegger's account of assertions – namely, that they are intrinsically decontextualizing. See Rouse, *Knowledge and Power*, 73–80.
13 Heidegger, *Sein und Zeit*, 356–64.
14 Ibid., 217–18.
15 Rouse, *Knowledge and Power*, 95.
16 There is a systematic reason for Rouse's focus on practices rather than on domains. As he explains in a later book, he regards practices as

"meaningful configurations of the world within which actions take place intelligibly, and thus practices incorporate the objects that they are enacted with and on and the settings in which they are enacted." Rouse, *Engaging Science*, 135.

17 Rouse, *Knowledge and Power*, 111.

18 "Scientific claims are formulated and defended with respect to the concerns and possible objections of an indefinitely extended group of scientists to whom they are addressed. There is little concern to argue for them outside this specific social context. Scientific claims are thus established within a rhetorical space rather than a logical space; scientific arguments settle for rational persuasion of peers instead of context-independent truth. Or rather, what it means for scientists to argue for the truth of their claims is to attempt rational persuasion of their peers." Ibid., 120.

19 Ibid., 141–2, 149–51. "The conditions according to which a scientific statement is understood to be true are just the conditions under which it is appropriate to assert it" (151).

20 As contrasted with, say, Hilary Putnam's "internal" or "pragmatic realism." See Putnam, *Reason, Truth and History* and *The Many Faces of Realism*.

21 By "ontic realism" Carman means "the claim that occurrent entities exist and have a determinate spatiotemporal structure independently of us and our understanding of them." *Heidegger's Analytic*, 157.

22 Dreyfus and Spinosa, "Coping with Things-in-Themselves: A Practice-Based Phenomenological Argument for Realism," 177–94. Earlier, in *Being-in-the-World*, Dreyfus had interpreted Heidegger as "a minimal hermeneutic realist about nature and the objects of natural science" (253).

23 Carman, *Heidegger's Analytic*, 178. Although Carman is on the right track, he overlooks a fundamental ambiguity in Heidegger's notion of occurrentness or objective presence (*Vorhandenheit*). It can mean either (1) the way in which entities show themselves when we have abstracted from their practical "handiness," as occurs in theoretical enterprises and, more broadly, in assertoric interpretation, or (2) the way in which they show themselves prior to their becoming either "handy" or abstracted from their handiness. *Being and Time* does not draw this distinction very clearly, and it has little to say about the second sense of the objective presence of "natural" entities. That gives some initial plausibility to Rouse's pragmatic nonrealist interpretation of Heidegger.

24 Ibid., 190–9.

25 It is common for pragmatic interpretations of Heidegger to ignore his insistence on the "equiprimordiality" of "attunement" (*Befindlichkeit*) in the structure of Dasein. See in this connection the critical commentary on

the pragmatic interpretations of Gethmann, Rorty, and Okrent in Dahlstrom, *Heidegger's Concept of Truth*, 423–33.

26 Dreyfus, *Being-in-the-World*, 278–9, summarizes this point as follows: "[T]ruth as the revealing that results from using assertions to point things out depends on Dasein, while what an assertion is true of can be independent of Dasein."

27 Heidegger, *Sein und Zeit*, 221.

28 Ibid., 219–26.

29 Rouse, *Knowledge and Power*, 160. Earlier Rouse writes: "The semantics of truth do not, then, say anything about the material conditions under which the assertion of p is justified, or about the truth conditions of p ... They say only that '"p" is true' and 'p' are materially equivalent" (150).

30 Heidegger, *Sein und Zeit*, 218.

31 See especially Zuidervaart, *Artistic Truth*, 77–100; *Social Philosophy after Adorno*, 77–106; and "Truth Matters: Heidegger and Horkheimer in Dialectical Disclosure."

32 This is why something like the "paradox of thematization" in Heidegger's ontology is unavoidable in any comprehensive philosophy of truth. On Heidegger's paradox of thematization, see Dahlstrom, *Heidegger's Concept of Truth*, 433–56. Both Dahlstrom and I would take issue with Dreyfus's interpretation of Heidegger as claiming that "one does not need and cannot have a *theory* of truth," and that "once the background practices are in place agreement is unproblematic, but one cannot give a detached, objective, theoretical account of our dwelling in the background practices" (*Being-in-the-World*, 273).

33 The textbook's author acknowledges as much when the concluding chapter suggests that"the question that constitutes the title of this book is a misleading and presumptuous one. It presumes that there is a single category 'science', and implies that various areas of knowledge ... either come under that category or do not. I do not know how such a general characterization of science can be established or defended." Chalmers, *What Is This Thing Called Science?* 166.

34 See Habermas, *The Theory of Communicative Action*.

## EPILOGUE

1 Paraphrased from Adorno, *Negative Dialectics*, 153; *Negative Dialektik*, 156.

2 The footnotes and the appendix are not part of the spoken text. They provide additional information or ideas that exceed the limits of a brief public lecture.

3 I develop this interpretation in the chapter titled "Metaphysics after Auschwitz," in Zuidervaart, *Social Philosophy after Adorno*, 48–76.

4 Adorno, *Negative Dialectics*, 17–18; *Negative Dialektik*, 29; translation modified.

5 All scripture references are from the New Revised Standard Version.

6 This is a corollary to the "cultural amplification of creation" that Seerveld correctly identifies as article 1, so to speak, in what he calls "The Biblical Charter for Artistic Activity in a Christian Community." See Seerveld, *Rainbows for the Fallen World*, 20–41.

7 According to the next verse, the Spirit intercedes on behalf of those who groan in hope and does so "with sighs too deep for words" (Rom. 8:26).

8 Arguably Hegel was the last major Western philosopher to pursue such comprehensive wisdom. He called philosophy "*its own time comprehended in thoughts*," although he cautioned against trying to transcend the contemporary world toward a future world "*as it ought to be*." See Hegel, *Elements of the Philosophy of Right*, 21–2.

9 Dooyeweerd, *Roots of Western Culture*.

10 For a longer discussion that puts Dooyeweerd into conversation with Radical Orthodoxy, see my essay "Good Cities or Cities of the Good?" – ch. 11 in this volume.

11 Dooyeweerd, *Roots of Western Culture*, 3.

12 Hegel, *Elements of the Philosophy of Right*, 371.

13 See Wolterstorff, *Until Justice and Peace Embrace*.

14 This might help explain why many intellectuals of my generation, having come of age during the 1960s when hopes for a better future ran high, turned to nihilism when those hopes shattered.

15 Zuidervaart, *Artistic Truth*, 98. The quote comes from a chapter that critically discusses Heidegger and portrays truth as a process of life-giving disclosure marked by fidelity to societal principles.

16 Unlike Vollenhoven and Dooyeweerd, however, I emphasize the historical embeddedness, the eschatological openness, and the vocational character of societal principles. See the appendix for a brief account of these emphases. Dooyeweerd distinguishes between "laws" and "norms," defining the latter as "rules of what ought to be" (*Roots of Western Culture*, 69, 75). Vollenhoven distinguishes among "laws," "norms," and "principles." By "principles" he means the results of human attempts to formulate diverse "functional laws," laws that have norming character by virtue of their holding for logical or post-logical functions in which human beings can always distinguish between their own activities and the laws that hold for

those activities. See Vollenhoven, "Norm and Law of Nature." My term "societal principles" is closer to Vollenhoven's usage than to Dooyeweerd's.

17 As Vollenhoven says, good and evil stand in an antithetical relation such that one side fundamentally and inescapably opposes the other. See his discussion of good and evil in Vollenhoven, *Isagôgè Philosophiae*, 56–62.

18 My description of the sculpture "Earth's Lament" borrows freely from the conclusion to chapter 10 ("Aesthetic Transformations") in Zuidervaart, *Artistic Truth*, 217–18.

19 Here I develop clues from Vollenhoven's distinction between the "summation" of God's law – love God above all and our neighbours as ourselves – and the "differentiation" of this law into diverse laws for different functions in human life. I combine this with his Trinitarian distinction among three relationships that God sustains with creation: (1) creating and structuring, (2) speaking and word-revealing, and (3) leading or guiding. See the essays "Norm and Law of Nature" (1951) and "The Unity of Life" (1955). Nevertheless, I take issue with Vollenhoven's emphasis, shared with Dooyeweerd, on logical functioning as the level of human activity that explains why certain laws have "norming character," such that they require formulation as "principles." Hendrik Hart lays some groundwork for the position I am advocating when he discusses humankind as that community which, in relation to other realms of creatures, "is called to be an agent for the direction of the world." But I find his accounts of responsibility and evil too focused on the agency of "persons." See the chapter "The Special Place of Humanity" in Hart, *Understanding Our World*, 267–324; quotation from p. 279.

# Works Cited

Note: Previously published essays by the author that appear as chapters in this volume are listed separately under "Publication Information."


Adorno, Theodor W. *Zur Metakritik der Erkenntnistheorie: Studien über Husserl und die phänomenologischen Antinomien* (1956). In *Gesammelte Schriften* 5, 7–245. Frankfurt am Main: Suhrkamp, 1970.

– *Drei Studien zu Hegel* (1963). In *Gesammelte Schriften* 5, 247–381. Frankfurt am Main: Suhrkamp, 1970.

– *Ästhetische Theorie*. In *Gesammelte Schriften* 7. Frankfurt am Main: Suhrkamp, 1970.

– *Negative Dialektik* (1966, 1967). In *Gesammelte Schriften* 6, 7–412. Frankfurt am Main: Suhrkamp, 1973.

– *The Jargon of Authenticity*. Translated by Knut Tarnowski and Frederic Will. London: Routledge & Kegan Paul, 1973.

– *Negative Dialectics*. Translated by E.B. Ashton. New York: Seabury Press, 1973.

– *Minima Moralia: Reflections from Damaged Life* (1951). Translated by E.F.N. Jephcott. London: NLB, 1974.

– Wozu noch Philosophie." In *Eingriffe: Neun kritische Modelle* (1963), *Gesammelte Schriften* 10.2, 459–73. Frankfurt am Main: Suhrkamp, 1977.

– *Kierkegaard: Konstruktion des Ästhetischen* (1933). *Gesammelte Schriften* 2. Frankfurt am Main: Suhrkamp, 1979.

– *Against Epistemology: A Metacritique: Studies in Husserl and the Phenomenological Antinomies*. Translated by Willis Domingo. Cambridge, MA: MIT Press, 1982.

– *Kierkegaard: Construction of the Aesthetic*. Translated by Robert Hullot-Kentor. Minneapolis: University of Minnesota Press, 1989.

– *Hegel: Three Studies*. Translated by Shierry Weber Nicholsen. Cambridge, MA: MIT Press, 1993.

– *Aesthetic Theory*. Translated by Robert Hullot-Kentor. Minneapolis: University of Minnesota Press, 1997.

– "Why Still Philosophy." In *Critical Models: Interventions and Catchwords*, translated by Henry W. Pickford, 1–17. New York: Columbia University Press, 1998.

Alcoff, Linda Martín. *Real Knowing: New Versions of the Coherence Theory*. Ithaca, NY: Cornell University Press, 1996.

Allen, Barry. *Truth in Philosophy*. Cambridge, MA: Harvard University Press, 1993.

Anker, Roy M., ed. *Dancing in the Dark: Youth, Popular Culture, and the Electronic Media*. Co-authored by Quentin J. Schultze, Roy M. Anker, James D. Bratt, William D. Romanowski, John William Worst, and Lambert Zuidervaart. Grand Rapids, MI: Eerdmans, 1991.

Bartholomew, Craig G., and Michael W. Goheen.*Christian Philosophy: A Systematic and Narrative Introduction*. Grand Rapids, MI: Baker Academic, 2013.

Bartholomew, Craig, and Gideon Strauss. "*Bread* and Not Stones: An Introduction to the Thought of Calvin Seerveld." In *In The Fields of the Lord: A Seerveld Reader*, edited by Craig Bartholomew, 3–22. Carlisle, UK: Piquant; Toronto: Toronto Tuppence Press, 2000.

Basden, Andrew. *Philosophical Frameworks for Understanding Information Systems*. Hershey, PA: IGI Publishing, 2008.

Benhabib, Seyla. *Situating the Self: Gender, Community and Postmodernism in Contemporary Ethics*. New York: Routledge, 1992.

Benjamin, Walter. "Theses on the Philosophy of History." In *Illuminations*, edited by Hannah Arendt and translated by Harry Zohn, 253–64. New York: Schocken Books, 1969.

Blomberg, Doug. *Wisdom and Curriculum: Christian Schooling after Postmodernity*. Sioux Center, IA: Dordt College Press, 2007.

Blosser, Philip. "Reconnoitering Dooyeweerd's Theory of Man." *Philosophia Reformata* 58 (1993): 192–209.

Botha, Elaine. *Metaphor and Its Moorings: Studies in the Grounding of Metaphorical Meaning*. New York: Peter Lang, 2007.

Bratt, James D. *Abraham Kuyper: Modern Calvinist, Christian Democrat*. Grand Rapids, MI: Eerdmans, 2013.

Brigandt, Ingo, and Alan Love. "Reductionism in Biology." In *The Stanford Encyclopedia of Philosophy* (Winter 2014 edition), edited by Edward N. Zalta. http://plato.stanford.edu/archives/win2014/entries/reduction-biology/.

Brümmer, Vincent. *Transcendental Criticism and Christian Philosophy: A Presentation and Evaluation of Herman Dooyeweerd's "Philosophy of the Cosmonomic Idea."* Franeker, Netherlands: Wever, 1961.

Brunkhorst, Hauke. *Solidarity: From Civic Friendship to a Global Legal Community*. Translated by Jeffrey Flynn. Cambridge, MA: MIT Press, 2005.

Bubner, Rüdiger. *Modern German Philosophy*. Translated by Eric Matthews. Cambridge: Cambridge University Press, 1981.

Buchwalter, Andrew. "The Relationship of Religion and Politics under Conditions of Modernity and Globality." *Existenz* 1.1–2 (Fall 2006). http://www.bu.edu/paideia/existenz/volumes/Vol.1Buchwalter.html.

– "Religion, Secularity, and the Politics of Modernity." Unpublished manuscript, 2009.

Carman, Taylor. *Heidegger's Analytic: Interpretation, Discourse, and Authenticity in "Being and Time."* Cambridge: Cambridge University Press, 2003.

Cassirer, Ernst. "'Geist' und 'Leben' in der Philosophie der Gegenwart." *Die Neue Rundschau* 41.1 (1930): 244–64.

– *An Essay on Man: An Introduction to a Philosophy of Human Culture*. New Haven, CT: Yale University Press, 1944.

– "'Spirit' and 'Life' in Contemporary Philosophy." In *The Philosophy of Ernst Cassirer*, edited by P.A. Schilpp, 855–80. Evanston, IL: The Library of Living Philosophers, 1949.

– *"Substance and Function" and "Einstein's Theory of Relativity."* Translated by William Curtis Swabey and Marie Collins Swabey. New York: Dover Publications, 1953.

– *The Philosophy of Symbolic Forms*. 3 vols. Translated by Ralph Manheim. New Haven, CT: Yale University Press, 1955.

Chalmers, A.F. *What Is This Thing Called Science?* 2nd ed. St. Lucia, QLD: University of Queensland Press, 1982.

Chaplin, Jonathan P. "Pluralism, Society and the State: The Neo-Calvinist Political Theory of Herman Dooyeweerd (1894–1977)." London: PhD diss., University of London, 1993.

– "Dooyeweerd's Notion of Societal Structural Principles." *Philosophia Reformata* 60 (1995): 16–36.

– *Herman Dooyeweerd: Christian Philosopher of State and Civil Society*. Notre Dame, IN: Notre Dame University Press, 2011.

Chaplin-Dengerink, Adrienne. "Mind, Body and Art: The Problem of Meaning in the Cognitive Aesthetics of Susanne K. Langer." Amsterdam: PhD diss., Vrije Universiteit, 1999.

Choi, Yong-Joon. "Dialogue and Antithesis: A Philosophical Study on the Significance of Herman Dooyeweerd's *Transcendental Critique*." Potchefstroom, South Africa: PhD diss., Potchefstroom University, 2000.

Clouser, Roy. *The Myth of Religious Neutrality: An Essay on the Hidden Role of Religious Belief in Theories*. Notre Dame, IN: University of Notre Dame Press, 1991.

– "The Transcendental Critique Revisited and Revised." *Philosophia Reformata* 74 (2009): 21–47.

– "Review of *Purpose in the Living World?* by Jacob Klapwijk." *Philosophia Reformata* 75 (2010): 82–5.

– "Reply to J. Glenn Friesen." *Philosophia Reformata* 76 (2011): 216–30.

Cohen, Jean L., and Andrew Arato. *Civil Society and Political Theory*. Cambridge, MA: MIT Press, 1992.

Conradie, Anna Louize. *The Neo-Calvinistic Concept of Philosophy: A Study in the Problem of Philosophic Communication*. Natal, South Africa: Natal University Press, 1960.

Cooke, Maeve. *Language and Reason: A Study of Habermas's Pragmatics*. Cambridge, MA: MIT Press, 1994.

Copi, Irving. *Introduction to Logic*, 3rd ed. London: Macmillan, 1968.

Dahlstrom, Daniel. *Heidegger's Concept of Truth*. Cambridge: Cambridge University Press, 2001.

Davies, Stephen. *Musical Meaning and Expression*. Ithaca, NY: Cornell University Press, 1994.

De Gaay Fortman, W.F., et al., eds. *Philosophy and Christianity: Philosophical Essays Dedicated to Professor Dr. Herman Dooyeweerd*. Kampen, Netherlands: Kok; Amsterdam: North-Holland Publishing, 1965.

De Graaff, Arnold H. "Towards a New Anthropological Model." In *Hearing and Doing: Philosophical Essays Dedicated to H. Evan Runner*, edited by John Kraay and Anthony Tol, 97–118. Toronto: Wedge Publishing Foundation, 1979.

Dengerink, Jan D. *De zin van de werkelijkheid: Een wijsgeerige benadering*. Amsterdam: VU Uitgeverij, 1986.

Dickie, George. *Aesthetics: An Introduction*. Indianapolis: Bobbs-Merrill, Pegasus, 1971.

Dooyeweerd, Herman. *De Wijsbegeerte der Wetsidee*. 3 vols. Amsterdam: H.J. Paris, 1935–36. Cited herein as WW.

– "De leer van de mens in de wijsbegeerte de wetsidee." *Correspondentiebladen van the Vereniging voor Calvinistische Wijsbegeerte* 7 (1942): 134–44.

– "Introduction to a Transcendental Criticism of Philosophic Thought." *Evangelical Quarterly* 19 (1947): 42–51.

– *Transcendental Problems of Philosophic Thought: An Inquiry into the Transcendental Conditions of Philosophy*. Grand Rapids, MI: Eerdmans, 1948.
– *A New Critique of Theoretical Thought*. 4 vols. Translated by David H. Freeman et al. Philadelphia: Presbyterian and Reformed Publishing, 1953–58. Cited herein as NC.
– *In the Twilight of Western Thought: Studies in the Pretended Autonomy of Philosophical Thought*. Philadelphia: Presbyterian and Reformed Publishing, 1960.
– "Christian Philosophy: An Exploration." Translated by John Vriend. In *Christian Philosophy and the Meaning of History*, 1–37. Lewiston, NY: Edwin Mellen Press, 1996.
– *Encyclopedia of the Science of Law*, vol. 1. Translated by Robert N. Knudsen. Edited by Alan M. Cameron. Lewiston, NY: Edwin Mellen Press, 2002.
– *Roots of Western Culture: Pagan, Secular, and Christian Options*. Translated by John Kraay. Edited by Mark Vander Vennen and Bernard Zylstra. Newly edited by D.F.M. Strauss. Lewiston, NY: Edwin Mellen Press, 2003.
– "The Theory of Man: Thirty-Two Propositions on Anthropology." Mimeograph. Toronto: Institute for Christian Studies, n.d.
Dreyfus, Hubert. *Being-in-the-World: A Commentary on Heidegger's* Being and Time, *Division I*. Cambridge, MA: MIT Press, 1991.
Dreyfus, Hubert L., and Charles Spinosa. "Coping with Things-in-Themselves: A Practice-Based Phenomenological Argument for Realism." *Inquiry* 42 (1999): 177–94.
Echeverria, Edward J. *Criticism and Commitment: Major Themes in Contemporary 'Post-Critical' Philosophy*. Amsterdam: Rodopi, 1981.
Fraser, Nancy, and Alex Honneth. *Redistribution or Recognition? A Political-Philosophical Exchange*. London: Verso, 2003.
Freeman, David H. "A Comparative Study of the Relationship between Philosophy and Theology as Exemplified by Representatives of Neo-Augustinianism, Neo-Thomism, and Neo-Existentialism." Philadelphia, PA: PhD diss., University of Pennsylvania, 1958.
Friesen, J. Glenn. "Dooyeweerd versus Vollenhoven: The Religious Dialectic within Reformational Philosophy." *Philosophia Reformata* 70 (2005): 102–32.
– "95 Theses on Herman Dooyeweerd." *Philosophia Reformata* 74 (2009): 78–104.
– "A Response to Roy Clouser's Aristotelian Interpretation of Dooyeweerd." *Philosophia Reformata* 75 (2010): 97–116.
Gadamer, Hans-Georg. *Wahrheit und Methode: Grundzüge einer philosophischen Hermeneutik* (1960). 3rd, expanded ed. Tübingen, Germany: J.C.B. Mohr (Paul Siebeck), 1975.

– *Truth and Method*. 2nd, rev. ed. Translation revised by Joel Weinsheimer and Donald G. Marshall. New York: Crossroad,1989.

Geehan, E.R., ed. *Jerusalem and Athens: Critical Discussions on the Philosophy and Apologetics of Cornelius Van Til*. Philadelphia: Reformed and Presbyterian Publishing, 1971.

Geertsema, Hendrik (Henk). *Van boven naar voren: wijsgerige achtergronden en problemen van het theologische denken over geschiedenis bij Jürgen Moltmann*. Kampen, Netherlands: Kok, 1980.

– "Christian Philosophy: Transformation or Inner Reformation." *Philosophia Reformata* 52 (1987): 139–65.

– *Het menselijk karakter van ons kennen*. Amsterdam: Buijten & Schipperheijn, 1992.

– "*Homo Respondens*: On the Historical Nature of Human Reason." *Philosophia Reformata* 58 (1993): 120–52.

– "Dooyeweerd in discussie met de rooms-katholieke filosofie." In *Herman Dooyeweerd 1894–1977: Breedte en actualiteit van zijn filosofie*, edited by H.G. Geertsema et al., 228–54. Kampen, Netherlands: Kok, 1994.

– "The Inner Reformation of Philosophy and Science." In *Christian Philosophy at the Close of the Twentieth Century*, edited by Sander Griffioen and Bert M. Balk, 11–28. Kampen, Netherlands: Kok, 1995.

– *Om de humaniteit: Christelijk geloof in gesprek met de moderne cultuur over wetenschap en filosofie*. Kampen, Netherlands: Kok, 1995.

– "Dooyeweerd's Transcendental Critique: Transforming It Hermeneutically." In *Contemporary Reflections on the Philosophy of Herman Dooyeweerd*, edited by D.F.M. Strauss and Michelle Botting, 83–108. Lewiston, NY: Edwin Mellen Press, 2000.

– "Analytical and Reformational Philosophy: Critical Reflections Regarding R. van Woudenberg's Meditation on 'Aspects' and 'Functions.'" *Philosophia Reformata* 69 (2004): 53–76.

– "Dooyeweerd on Knowledge and Truth." In *Ways of Knowing in Concert*, edited by John H. Kok, 85–100. Sioux Center, IA: Dordt College Press, 2005.

Geertsema, H.G., et al., eds. *Herman Dooyeweerd 1894–1977: breedte en actualiteit van zijn filosofie*. Kampen, Netherlands: Kok, 1994.

Glas, Gerrit. "Hierarchy and Dualism in Aristotelian Psychology." *Philosophia Reformata* 57 (1992): 95–116.

– "Ego, Self, and the Body: An Assessment of Dooyeweerd's Philosophical Anthropology." In *Christian Philosophy at the Close of the Twentieth Century*, edited by Sander Griffioen and Bert M. Balk, 67–78. Kampen, Netherlands: Kok, 1995.

– "Christian Philosophical Anthropology: A Reformation Perspective." *Philosophia Reformata* 75 (2010): 141–89.
Glas, Gerrit, Jeroen de Ridder, Govert Buijs, and Annette Mosher, eds. *The Future of Creation Order*. Dordrecht, Netherlands: Springer, forthcoming.
Goehr, Lydia. *The Imaginary Museum of Musical Works: An Essay in the Philosophy of Music*. Oxford, UK: Clarendon Press, 1992.
Goudzwaard, Bob. *Capitalism and Progress: A Diagnosis of Western Society*. Translated and edited by Josina Van Nuis Zylstra. Grand Rapids, MI: Eerdmans, 1979.
Goudzwaard, Bob, Mark Vander Vennen, and David Van Heemst. *Hope in Troubled Times: A New Vision for Confronting Global Crises*. Grand Rapids, MI: Baker Academic, 2007.
Griffioen, Sander. "De betekenis van Dooyeweerds ontwikkelingsidee." *Philosophia Reformata* 51 (1986): 83–109.
– "Is a Pluralist Ethos Possible?" *Philosophia Reformata* 59 (1994): 11–25.
– "Review of *Artistic Truth* by Lambert Zuidervaart." *Philosophia Reformata* 71 (2006): 202–5.
Griffioen, Sander, and Bert M. Balk, eds. *Christian Philosophy at the Close of the Twentieth Century: Assessment and Perspective*. Kampen, Netherlands: Kok, 1995.
Griffioen, Sander, and Jan Verhoogt, eds. *Norm and Context in the Social Sciences*. Lanham, MD: University Press of America, 1990.
Groen van Prinsterer, Guillaume. *Ongeloof en revolutie: eene reeks van historische voorlezingen*. Leiden, Netherlands: S. and J. Luchtmans, 1847.
– *Unbelief and Revolution: A Series of Lectures in History*. Amsterdam: The Groen van Prinsterer Fund, 1975.
Habermas, Jürgen. *Legitimationsprobleme im Spätkapitalismus*. Frankfurt am Main: Suhrkamp, 1973.
– "Wahrheitstheorien." In *Wirklichkeit und Reflexion. Walter Schulz zum 60. Geburststag*, edited by Helmut Fahrenbach, 211–65. Pfullingen, Germany: Neske, 1973.
– *Legitimation Crisis*. Translated by Thomas McCarthy. Boston: Beacon Press, 1975.
– *The Theory of Communicative Action*. Translated by Thomas McCarthy. 2 vols. Boston: Beacon Press, 1984, 1987.
– "Questions and Counterquestions." In *Habermas and Modernity*, edited by Richard Bernstein, 192–216. Cambridge, MA: MIT Press, 1985.
– *Vorstudien und Ergänzungen zur Theorie des kommunikativen Handelns*, 2nd ed. Frankfurt am Main: Suhrkamp, 1986.

– "A Reply." In *Communicative Action: Essays on Jürgen Habermas's* The Theory of Communicative Action, edited by Axel Honneth and Hans Joas, 214–64. Cambridge, MA: MIT Press, 1991.
– "Transcendence from Within, Transcendence in This World." In *Habermas, Modernity, and Public Theology*, edited by Don S. Browning and Francis Schüssler Fiorenza, 226–50. New York: Crossroad, 1992.
– "Actions, Speech Acts, Linguistically Mediated Interactions and the Lifeworld." In *Philosophical Problems Today, vol. I*, edited by G. Fløistad, 45–74. Dordrecht, Netherlands: Kluwer, 1994.
– "Struggles for Recognition in the Democratic Constitutional State." In *Multiculturalism: Examining the Politics of Recognition*, by Charles Taylor et al., edited by Amy Gutmann, 107–48. Princeton, NJ: Princeton University Press, 1994.
– *Between Facts and Norms: Contributions to a Discourse Theory of Law and Democracy*. Translated by William Rehg. Cambridge, MA: MIT Press, 1996.
– *Truth and Justification*. Edited and translated by Barbara Fultner. Cambridge, MA: MIT Press, 2003.

Hart, Hendrik. *Communal Certainty and Authorized Truth: An Examination of John Dewey's Philosophy of Verification*. Amsterdam: Swets & Zeitlinger, 1966.
– *The Challenge of Our Age*. Toronto: Wedge Publishing Foundation, 1968, 1974.
– *Draft for Proposed ICS Syllabus for Systematic Philosophy*. 2 vols. Toronto: Institute for Christian Studies, 1979.
– "On the Distinction between Creator and Creature." *Philosophia Reformata* 44 (1979): 183–93.
– "Critical Reflections on Wolterstorff's *Reason within the Bounds of Religion*." Mimeograph. Toronto: Institute for Christian Scholarship, 1980.
– "The Impasse of Rationality Today: Revised Edition." In *Wetenschap, Wijsheid, Filosoferen*, edited by P. Blokhuis, 174–200. Assen, Netherlands: Van Gorkum, 1981.
– "The Articulation of Belief: A Link between Rationality and Commitment." In *Rationality in the Calvinian Tradition*, edited by Hendrik Hart, Johan van der Hoeven, and Nicholas Wolterstorff, 209–48. Lanham, MD: University Press of America, 1983.
– *Understanding Our World: An Integral Ontology*. Lanham, MD: University Press of America, 1984.
– "Dooyeweerd's Gegenstand Theory of Theory." In *The Legacy of Herman Dooyeweerd*, edited by C.T. McIntire, 143–66. Lanham, MD: University Press of America, 1985.

– "Reason and Religion Revisited." Manuscript, 1990.
– "Whither Reason and Religion?" In Kai Nielsen and Hendrik Hart, *Search for Community in a Withering Tradition: Conversations between a Marxian Atheist and a Calvinian Christian*, 148–235. Lanham, MD: University Press of America, 1990.
– "Creation Order in Our Philosophical Tradition: Critique and Refinement." In *An Ethos of Compassion and the Integrity of Creation*, edited by Brian J. Walsh, Hendrik Hart, and Robert E. Vander Vennen, 67–96. Lanham, MD: University Press of America, 1995.
– "Self as Question: A Response to Gerrit Glas." In *Christian Philosophy at the Close of the Twentieth Century*, edited by Sander Griffioen and Bert M. Balk, 79–84. Kampen, Netherlands: Kok, 1995.
– "Conceptual Understanding and Knowing *Other*-wise: Reflections on Rationality and Spirituality in Philosophy." In *Knowing* Other-*wise*: *Philosophy at the Threshold of Spirituality*, edited by James H. Olthuis, 19–53. New York: Fordham University Press, 1997.
– "ICS Symposium February 27" (24 February 2004 draft). Manuscript, 2004.
Hegel, G.W.F. *Phenomenology of Spirit*. Translated by A.V. Miller. Oxford, UK: Oxford University Press, 1977.
– *Elements of the Philosophy of Right*. Edited by Allen W. Wood. Translated by H.B. Nisbet. Cambridge: Cambridge University Press, 1991.
Heidegger, Martin. "Der Ursprung des Kunstwerkes." In *Holzwege*, 7–68. Frankfurt am Main: Vittorio Klostermann, 1950.
– *Being and Time*. Translated by John Macquarrie and Edward Robinson. New York: Harper & Row, 1962.
– "The Origin of the Work of Art." In *Poetry, Language, Thought*, translated by Albert Hofstadter, 17–87. New York: Harper Colophon Books, 1971.
– *Sein und Zeit*, 15th edition. Tübingen, Germany: Max Niemeyer, 1979.
– *Being and Time*. Translated by Joan Stambaugh. Albany: State University of New York Press, 1996.
Henderson, Roger D. "Illuminating Law: The Construction of Herman Dooyeweerd's Philosophy 1918–1928." Amsterdam: PhD diss., Vrije Universiteit, 1994.
– "Gum and Wire, A Time for Everything under the Sun: From Kuyperian Root to Dooyeweerdian Fruit and Back." *Philosophia Reformata* 78 (2013): 1–17.
Hepp, Valentine. *Dreigende deformatie*. Kampen, Netherlands: J.H. Kok, 1936–37.
Heslam, Peter S. *Creating a Christian Worldview: Abraham Kuyper's Lectures on Calvinism*. Grand Rapids, MI: Eerdmans; Carlisle, UK: Paternoster Press, 1998.

Hommes, Hendrik Jan van Eikema. *Major Trends in the History of Legal Philosophy*. Amsterdam and New York: North-Holland, 1979.

House, D. Vaden. "For the Birds: Science and Religion in Critical Perspective." In *Philosophy as Responsibility: A Celebration of Hendrik Hart's Contribution to the Discipline*, edited by Ronald A. Kuipers and Janet Catherina Wesselius, 151–69. Lanham, MD: University Press of America, 2002.

Ive, Jeremy George Augustus. *The Roots of Reformational Philosophy: The Thought of Dirk H.Th. Vollenhoven and Herman Dooyeweerd in the Light of the Trinitarian Vision of Abraham Kuyper*. Author, 2014. http://www.allofliferedeemed.co.uk/Ive/Ive_Vollenhoven_Dooyeweerd.pdf.

Jay, Martin. *Adorno*. London: Fontana Paperbacks, 1984.

– "Habermas and Modernism." In *Habermas and Modernity*, edited by Richard Bernstein, 125–39. Cambridge, MA: MIT Press, 1985.

Kalsbeek, L. *De wijsbegeerte der wetsidee: Proeve van een christelijke filosofie*. Amsterdam: Buijten & Schipperheijn, 1970.

– *Contours of a Christian Philosophy: An Introduction to Herman Dooyeweerd's Thought*. Edited by Bernard and Josina Zylstra. Toronto: Wedge Publishing Foundation, 1975.

Kim, Jong Doo. "Wissen und Glauben bei I. Kant und H. Dooyeweerd." *Philosophia Reformata* 48, no. 2 (1983): 3–145.

Kirkham, Richard L. *Theories of Truth: A Critical Introduction*. Cambridge, MA: MIT Press, 1992.

Kitcher, Philip. "The Hegemony of Molecular Biology." *Biology and Philosophy* 14 (1999): 195–210.

Klapwijk, Jacob. "The Struggle for a Christian Philosophy: Another Look at Dooyeweerd." *The Reformed Journal* 30, no. 2 (February 1980): 2–15.

– "Dooyeweerd's Christian Philosophy: Antithesis and Critique." *The Reformed Journal* 30, no. 3 (March 1980): 20–4.

– "Antithesis, Synthesis, and the Idea of Transformational Philosophy." *Philosophia Reformata* 51 (1986): 138–52.

– "Reformational Philosophy on the Boundary between the Past and the Future." *Philosophia Reformata* 52 (1987): 101–34.

– *Purpose in the Living World? Creation and Emergent Evolution*. Translated and edited by Harry Cook. Cambridge: Cambridge University Press, 2008.

– "Nothing in Evolutionary Theory Makes Sense Except in the Light of Creation." *Philosophia Reformata* 77 (2012): 57–77.

Knudsen, Robert D. "The Religious Foundation of Dooyeweerd's Transcendental Method." In *Contemporary Reflections on the Philosophy of*

*Herman Dooyeweerd*, edited by D.F.M. Strauss and Michelle Botting, 271–85. Lewiston, NY: Edwin Mellen Press, 2000.

Kok, John H. *Vollenhoven: His Early Development*. Sioux Center, IA: Dordt College Press, 1992.

Kraay, John N. "Successive Conceptions in the Development of the Christian Philosophy of Herman Dooyeweerd." *Philosophia Reformata* 44 (1979): 137–49; 45 (1980): 1–40.

Kuipers, Ronald A. *Critical Faith: Toward a Renewed Understanding of Religious Life and Its Public Accountability*. Amsterdam: Rodopi, 2002.

Kuyper, Abraham. "Het sociale vraagstuk en de Christelijke religie." Amsterdam: J.A. Wormser, 1891.

– *Lectures on Calvinism*. Grand Rapids, MI: Eerdmans, 1931.

– *Christianity and the Class Struggle* (1891). Translated by Dirk Jellema. Grand Rapids, MI: Piet Hein Publishers, 1950.

– *The Problem of Poverty*. Translated by James W. Skillen. Washington, DC: Center for Public Justice; Grand Rapids, MI: Eerdmans, 1991.

Lakoff, George, and Mark Johnson. *Philosophy in the Flesh: The Embodied Mind and Its Challenge to Western Thought*. New York: Basic Books, 1999.

Lynch, Michael P. *Truth in Context: An Essay on Pluralism and Objectivity*. Cambridge, MA: MIT Press, 1998.

– ed. *The Nature of Truth: Classic and Contemporary Perspectives*. Cambridge, MA: MIT Press, 2001.

Marcel, Pierre. *The Christian Philosophy of Herman Dooyeweerd*. 2 vols. Translated and edited by Colin Wright. N.p.: WordBridge Publishing, 2013.

Marlet, Michael Fr. J. *Grundlinien der kalvinistischen "Philosophie der Gesetzesidee" als christlicher Transzendentalphilosophie*. Munich, Germany: Karl Zink, 1954.

McIntire, C.T. "Historical Study and the Historical Dimension of Our World." In *History and Historical Understanding*, edited by C.T. McIntire and Ronald A. Wells, 17–40. Grand Rapids, MI: Eerdmans, 1984.

– ed. *The Legacy of Herman Dooyeweerd: Reflections on Critical Philosophy in the Christian Tradition*. Lanham, MD: University Press of America, 1985.

Mekkes, J.P.A. "Knowing." In *Jerusalem and Athens: Critical Discussions on the Philosophy and Apologetics of Cornelius Van Til*, edited by E.R. Geehan, 306–19. Nutley, NJ: Presbyterian and Reformed Publishing, 1971.

– "Methodology and Practice." In *The Idea of a Christian Philosophy: Essays in Honour of D.H.Th. Vollenhoven*, edited by K.A. Bril, Hendrik Hart, and Jacob Klapwijk, with an introduction by Herman Dooyeweerd, 77–83. Toronto: Wedge, 1973.

Meynell, Hugo A. "The Philosophy of Dooyeweerd: A Transcendental Thomist Appraisal." *Faith and Philosophy* 20 (July 2003): 265–87.

Milbank, John. *Theology and Social Theory: Beyond Secular Reason*. Oxford, UK: Blackwell, 1990.

Mouw, Richard, and Sander Griffioen. *Pluralisms and Horizons: An Essay in Christian Public Philosophy*. Grand Rapids, MI: Eerdmans, 1993.

Offe, Claus. *Contradictions of the Welfare State*. Edited by John Keane. Cambridge, MA: MIT Press, 1984.

Olthuis, James H. "The Reality of Societal Structures." *Tydskrif vir Christelijke Wetenskap* 13 (1977): 198–207.

– "Dooyeweerd on Religion and Faith." In *The Legacy of Herman Dooyeweerd: Reflections on Critical Philosophy in the Christian Tradition*, edited by C.T. McIntire, 21–40. Lanham, MD: University Press of America, 1985.

– "Be(com)ing: Humankind as Gift and Call." *Philosophia Reformata* 58 (1993): 153–72.

– "Crossing the Threshold: Sojourning Together in the Wild Spaces of Love." In *Knowing* Other-*wise: Philosophy at the Threshold of Spirituality*, edited by James H. Olthuis, 235–57. New York: Fordham University Press, 1997.

– "Of Webs and Whirlwinds: Me, Myself, and I: Reformational Anthropology at the Dawn of the Second Millennium." In *Contemporary Reflections on the Philosophy of Herman Dooyeweerd*, edited by D.F.M. Strauss and Michelle Botting, 31–48. Lewiston, NY: Edwin Mellen Press, 2000.

– "Introduction: Philosophy as Spiritual Exercise." In *Philosophy as Responsibility: A Celebration of Hendrik Hart's Contribution to the Discipline*, edited by Ronald A. Kuipers and Janet Catherina Wesselius, xi–xxiii. Lanham, MD: University Press of America, 2002.

– "Unlike Any Other Hope: The Eschatological Structure of Hope." In *The Logic of Incarnation: James K.A. Smith's Critique of Postmodern Religion*, edited by Neal DeRoo and Brian Lightfoot, 182–92. Eugene, OR: Pickwick Publications, 2009.

– "The Word of God and Science." Toronto: Association for the Advancement of Christian Scholarship, n.d.

Ouweneel, Willem J. *De Leer van de mens: Proeve van een christelijk-wijsgerige antropologie*. Amsterdam: Buijten & Schipperheijn, 1986.

– *Heart and Soul: A Christian View of Psychology*. Translated by Theodore Plantinga. Grand Rapids, MI: Paideia Press, 2008.

Plantinga, Alvin. "Christian Philosophy at the End of the 20th Century." In *Christian Philosophy at the Close of the Twentieth Century*, edited by Sander Griffioen and Bert M. Balk, 29–53. Kampen, Netherlands: Kok, 1995.

Putnam, Hilary. *Reason, Truth and History*. Cambridge: Cambridge University Press, 1981.

– *The Many Faces of Realism*. La Salle, IL: Open Court, 1987.

Rehg, William. *Insight and Solidarity: A Study in the Discourse Ethics of Jürgen Habermas*. Berkeley, CA: University of California Press, 1994.

Rifkin, Jeremy. *The End of Work: The Decline of the Global Labor Force and the Dawn of the Post-Market Era*. New York: G.P. Putnam's Sons, 1995.

Robbers, Joannes Henricus. "Review of *De Wijsbegeerte der Wetsidee* by Herman Dooyeweerd." *Studiën: Tijdschrift voor godsdienst, wetenschap en letteren* 67 (1935): 85–99; 68 (1936): 152–3; and 69 (1937): 324–31.

Rorty, Richard. *Philosophy and the Mirror of Nature*. Princeton, NJ: Princeton University Press, 1979.

– "Religion as Conversation-Stopper." In *Philosophy and Social Hope*, 168–74. London: Penguin Books, 1999.

Rouse, Joseph. *Knowledge and Power: Toward a Political Philosophy of Science*. Ithaca, NY: Cornell University Press, 1987.

– *Engaging Science: How to Understand Its Practices Philosophically*. Ithaca, NY: Cornell University Press, 1996.

Runner, H. Evan. *The Relation of the Bible to Learning*. The Unionville Lectures for 1959 and 1960. Toronto: Wedge Publishing Foundation, 1974.

Scheler, Max. *Man's Place in Nature*. Translated by Hans Meyerhoff. New York: Farrar, Straus and Giroux, 1962.

Schmitt, Frederick F. *Truth: A Primer*. Boulder, CO: Westview Press, 1995.

Seel, Martin. "The Two Meanings of 'Communicative' Rationality: Remarks on Habermas's Critique of a Plural Concept of Reason." In *Communicative Action: Essays on Jürgen Habermas's* The Theory of Communicative Action, edited by Axel Honneth and Hans Joas, 36–48. Cambridge, MA: MIT Press, 1991.

Seerveld, Calvin G. "The Relation of the Arts to the Presentation of Truth." In *Truth and Reality: Philosophical Perspectives on Reality*, 161–75. Braamfontein, South Africa: De Jong's Bookshop, 1971.

– "Biblical Wisdom underneath Vollenhoven's Categories for Philosophical Historiography." In *The Idea of a Christian Philosophy: Essays in Honour of D.H.Th. Vollenhoven*, edited by K.A. Bril, Hendrik Hart, and Jacob Klapwijk, with an introduction by Herman Dooyeweerd, 127–43. Toronto: Wedge, 1973.

– *Rainbows for the Fallen World: Aesthetic Life and Artistic Task*. Toronto: Toronto Tuppence Press, 1980.

– "A Christian Tin-Can Theory of Man." *Journal of the American Scientific Affiliation* 33 (June 1981): 74–81.

– "Dooyeweerd's Legacy for Aesthetics: Modal Law Theory." In *The Legacy of Herman Dooyeweerd: Reflections on Critical Philosophy in the Christian Tradition*, edited by C.T. McIntire, 41–79. Lanham, MD: University Press of America, 1985.
– "Imaginativity." *Faith and Philosophy* 4 (1987): 43–58.
– *On Being Human: Imaging God in the Modern World*. Burlington, ON: Welch Publishing, 1988.
– "Dooyeweerd's Idea of 'Historical Development': Christian Respect for Cultural Diversity." *Westminster Theological Journal* 58 (1996): 41–61.
– "The Cross of Scholarly Cultural Power." In *In the Fields of the Lord: A Seerveld Reader*, edited by Craig Bartholomew, 197–204. Carlisle, UK: Piquant; Toronto: Toronto Tuppence Press, 2000.
Spier, J.M. *Een inleiding tot de wijsbegeerte der wetsidee*. Zutphen, Netherlands: G.J.A. Ruys, 1938.
– *An Introduction to Christian Philosophy*. Translated by David Freeman. Philadelphia, PA: Presbyterian and Reformed Publishing, 1954.
Stafleu, Marinus Dirk. *Time and Again: A Systematic Analysis of the Foundation of Physics*. Toronto: Wedge Publishing Foundation,1980.
– *Theories at Work: On the Structure and Functioning of Theories in Science, in Particular during the Copernican Revolution*. Lanham, MD: University Press of America, 1987.
– "Being Human in the Cosmos." *Philosophia Reformata* 56 (1991): 101–31.
– *Een wereld vol relaties: Karakter en zin van natuurlijke dingen en processen*. Amsterdam: Buijten & Schipperheijn, 2002.
Steen, Hendrik. *Philosophia Deformata*. Kampen, Netherlands: J.H. Kok, 1937.
Steen, Peter. *The Structure of Herman Dooyeweerd's Thought*. Toronto: Wedge, 1983.
Storkey, Elaine. "Dooyeweerd's Anthropology – The Male-Female Dimension." In *Christian Philosophy at the Close of the Twentieth Century*, edited by Sander Griffioen and Bert M. Balk, 85–92. Kampen, Netherlands: Kok, 1995.
Strauss, D.F.M. "An Analysis of the Structure of Analysis." *Philosophia Reformata* 49 (1984): 35–56.
– *Philosophy: Discipline of the Disciplines*. Grand Rapids, MI: Paideia Press, 2009.
Strauss, D.F.M., and Michelle Botting, eds. *Contemporary Reflections on the Philosophy of Herman Dooyeweerd*. Lewiston, NY: Edwin Mellen Press, 2000.
Sweetman, Robert, ed. *In the Phrygian Mode: Neo-Calvinism, Antiquity and the Lamentations of Reformational Philosophy*. Lanham, MD: University Press America, 2007.

Swindal, James. *Reflection Revisited: Jürgen Habermas's Discursive Theory of Truth*. New York: Fordham University Press, 1999.

Taylor, Charles. "Language and Society." In *Communicative Action: Essays on Jürgen Habermas's* The Theory of Communicative Action, edited by Axel Honneth and Hans Joas, 23–35. Cambridge, MA: MIT Press, 1991.

Tol, Anthony. *Philosophy in the Making: D.H.Th. Vollenhoven and the Emergence of Reformed Philosophy*. Sioux Center, IA: Dordt College Press, 2010.

VanderVennen, Robert E. *A University for the People: A History of the Institute for Christian Studies*. Sioux Center, IA: Dordt College Press, 2008.

van der Walt, B.J. *At the Cradle of a Christian Philosophy: In Calvin, Vollenhoven, Stoker, Dooyeweerd*. Potchefstroom, South Africa: Institute for Contemporary Christianity in Africa, 2014.

Van Til, John. *Growing Civil Society: From Nonprofit Sector to Third Space*. Bloomington, IN: Indiana University Press, 2000.

van Woudenberg, René. "'Aspects' and 'Functions' of Individual Things." *Philosophia Reformata* 68 (2003): 1–13.

– "Two Very Different Analyses of Knowledge." In *Ways of Knowing in Concert*, edited by John H. Kok, 100–22. Sioux Center, IA: Dordt College Press, 2005.

– "Wat mogen we van een theorie over waarheid verwachten?" *Philosophia Reformata* 72 (2007): 53–68.

van Woudenberg, René, ed. *Kennis en werkelijkheid: Tweede inleiding tot een christelijke filosofie*. Amsterdam: Buijten & Schipperheijn; Kampen, Netherlands: Kok, 1996.

Vollenhoven, Dirk H.T. "Enkele grondlijnen der kentheorie." *Stemmen des Tijds* 15 (April 1926): 380–401.

– "Fundamentals of a Theory of Knowledge" (1926). Translated by John H. Kok. Manuscript, n.d.

– *De noodzakelijkheid eener christelijke logica*. Amsterdam: H.J. Paris, 1932.

– "De consequent probleemhistorische methode." *Philosophia Reformata* 26 (1961): 1–34.

– *Dirk H.T. Vollenhoven Reader*. Edited and translated by John H. Kok. Manuscript, 1998.

– "Excerpt from *Calvinism and the Reformation of Philosophy*" (1933). In *Dirk H.T. Vollenhoven Reader*, edited and translated by John H. Kok, 21–65. Manuscript, 1998.

– "Faith: Its Nature, Structure, and Significance for Science" (1950). In *Dirk H.T. Vollenhoven Reader*, edited and translated by John H. Kok, 72–7. Manuscript, 1998.

– "Norm and Law of Nature" (1951). In *Dirk H.T. Vollenhoven Reader*, edited and translated by John H. Kok, 103–11. Manuscript, 1998.
– "Divergences: Report I" (1953). In *Dirk H.T. Vollenhoven Reader*, edited and translated by John H. Kok, 135–40. Manuscript, 1998.
– "The Unity of Life" (1955). In *Dirk H.T. Vollenhoven Reader*, edited and translated by John H. Kok, 146–56. Manuscript, 1998.
– "The Consequential Problem-Historical Method." Translated by Robert Sweetman. In D.H.Th. Vollenhoven, *The Problem-Historical Method and the History of Philosophy*, edited by Kornelis A. Bril, 89–135. Amstelveen, Netherlands: De Zaak Haes, 2005.
– *Isagôgè Philosophiae: Introduction to Philosophy*. Translated by John H. Kok. Edited by John H. Kok and Anthony Tol. Sioux Center, IA: Dordt College Press, 2005.
Walsh, Brian J., and J. Richard Middleton. *The Transforming Vision: Shaping a Christian World View*. Downers Grove, IL: InterVarsity Press, 1984.
Walsh, Brian J., Hendrik Hart, and Robert E. VanderVennen, eds. *An Ethos of Compassion and the Integrity of Creation*. Lanham, MD: University Press of America, 1995.
Walton, Kendall L. *Mimesis as Make-Believe: On the Foundations of the Representational Arts*. Cambridge, MA: Harvard University Press, 1990.
Ward, Graham. *Cities of God*. London and New York: Routledge, 2000.
Weideman, Albert. *Beyond Expression: A Systematic Study of the Foundations of Linguistics*. Grand Rapids, MI: Paideia Press, 2009.
Wellmer, Albrecht. "Truth, Semblance, Reconciliation: Adorno's Aesthetic Redemption of Modernity." In *The Persistence of Modernity: Essays on Aesthetics, Ethics, and Postmodernism*, translated by David Midgley, 1–35. Cambridge, MA: MIT Press, 1991.
Westphal, Merold. *Suspicion and Faith: The Religious Uses of Modern Atheism*. Grand Rapids, MI: Eerdmans, 1993.
Wolin, Richard. *The Politics of Being: The Political Thought of Martin Heidegger*. New York: Columbia University Press, 1990.
Wolters, Albert M. "On Vollenhoven's Problem-Historical Method." In *Hearing and Doing: Philosophical Essays Dedicated to H. Evan Runner*, edited by John Kraay and Anthony Tol, 231–62. Toronto: Wedge, 1979.
– "The Intellectual Milieu of Herman Dooyeweerd." In *The Legacy of Herman Dooyeweerd: Reflections on Critical Philosophy in the Christian Tradition*, edited by C.T. McIntire, 1–19. Lanham, MD: University Press of America, 1985.
Wolterstorff, Nicholas. "Once Again, Creator/Creature." *Philosophia Reformata* 46 (1981): 60–7.

– *Until Justice and Peace Embrace*. Grand Rapids, MI: Eerdmans, 1983.
– *Reason within the Bounds of Religion*. 2nd ed. Grand Rapids, MI: Eerdmans, 1984.
– *Justice: Rights and Wrongs*. Princeton, NJ: Princeton University Press, 2008.
Young, William. *Towards a Reformed Philosophy: The Development of a Protestant Philosophy in Dutch Calvinist Thought Since the Time of Abraham Kuyper*. Franeker, Netherlands: Wever, 1952.
Zigterman, Kent. "Dooyeweerd's Theory of Individuality Structure as an Alternative to a Substance Position, Especially That of Aristotle." Toronto: Master's thesis, Institute for Christian Studies, 1977.
Zimmerman, Michael E. *Heidegger's Confrontation with Modernity: Technology, Politics, and Art*. Bloomington, IN: Indiana University Press, 1990.
Zuidervaart, Lambert. "Kant's Critique of Beauty and Taste: Explorations into a Philosophical Aesthetics." Toronto: Master's thesis, Institute for Christian Studies, 1977.
– "Refractions: Truth in Adorno's Aesthetic Theory." Amsterdam: PhD diss., Vrije Universiteit, 1981.
– "Review of *Against Epistemology: A Metacritique; Studies in Husserl and the Phenomenological Antinomies* by Theodor W. Adorno." *Canadian Philosophical Reviews* 4, no. 2 (April 1984): 49–52.
– "Response to Johan van der Hoeven's 'Development in the Light of Encounter.'" In *Norm and Context in the Social Sciences*, edited by Sander Griffioen and Jan Verhoogt, 37–42. Lanham, MD: University Press of America, 1990.
– *Adorno's Aesthetic Theory: The Redemption of Illusion*. Cambridge, MA: MIT Press, 1991.
– "Transforming Aesthetics: Reflections on the Work of Calvin G. Seerveld." In *Pledges of Jubilee: Essays on the Arts and Culture*, edited by Lambert Zuidervaart and Henry Luttikhuizen, 1–22. Grand Rapids, MI: Eerdmans, 1995.
– "Autonomy, Negativity, and Illusory Transgression: Menke's Deconstruction of Adorno's Aesthetics." In *Philosophy Today*, SPEP Supplement 1999: 154–68.
– "Art Is No Fringe: An Introduction." In *The Arts, Community and Cultural Democracy*, edited by Lambert Zuidervaart and Henry Luttikhuizen, 1–12. London: Macmillan; New York: St. Martin's Press, 2000.
– *Artistic Truth: Aesthetics, Discourse, and Imaginative Disclosure*. Cambridge: Cambridge University Press, 2004.
– "A Tradition Transfigured: Art and Culture in Reformational Aesthetics." *Faith and Philosophy* 21 (2004): 381–92.

– *Social Philosophy after Adorno*. Cambridge: Cambridge University Press, 2007.
– "Truth Matters: Heidegger and Horkheimer in Dialectical Disclosure." *Telos*, no. 145 (Winter 2008): 131–60.
– "After Dooyeweerd: Truth in Reformational Philosophy." Manuscript, 2008. ICS Institutional Repository: http://ir.icscanada.edu/icsir/handle/10756/305241.
– *Art in Public: Politics, Economics, and a Democratic Culture*. Cambridge: Cambridge University Press, 2011.
– "How Not to Be an Anti-Realist: Habermas, Truth, and Justification." *Philosophia Reformata* 77 (2012): 1–18.
– "Art, Religion, and the Sublime: After Hegel." *The Owl of Minerva* 44, nos. 1–2 (2012–13): 119–42.
– "Critical Transformations: Macrostructures, Religion, and Critique." *Critical Research on Religion* 1 (2013): 243–69.

Zuidervaart, Lambert, Allyson Carr, Matthew Klaassen, and Ronnie Shuker, eds. *Truth Matters: Knowledge, Politics, Ethics, Religion*. Montreal: McGill-Queen's University Press, 2013.

# Index